Pro IBM® WebSphere® Application Server 7 Internals

■ ■ ■

Colin Renouf

Pro IBM® WebSphere® Application Server 7 Internals

Copyright © 2009 by Colin Renouf

ISBN-13 (pbk): 978-1-4302-1958-3

ISBN-13 (electronic): 978-1-4302-1959-0

Printed and bound in the United States of America 9 8 7 6 5 4 3 2 1

Trademarked names may appear in this book. Rather than use a trademark symbol with every occurrence of a trademarked name, we use the names only in an editorial fashion and to the benefit of the trademark owner, with no intention of infringement of the trademark.

Lead Editors: Matt Moodie and Steve Anglin
Technical Reviewer: Kunal Mittal
Editorial Board: Clay Andres, Steve Anglin, Mark Beckner, Ewan Buckingham, Tony Campbell,
    Gary Cornell, Jonathan Gennick, Michelle Lowman, Matthew Moodie, Jeffrey Pepper, Frank Pohlmann,
    Ben Renow-Clarke, Dominic Shakeshaft, Matt Wade, Tom Welsh
Project Manager: Molly Sharp
Copy Editors: Bill McManus, Jennifer Whipple
Associate Production Director: Kari Brooks-Copony
Production Editor: Katie Stence
Compositor: ContentWorks, Inc.
Proofreader: Nancy Sixsmith
Indexer: Julie Grady
Artist: April Milne
Cover Designer: Kurt Krames
Manufacturing Director: Tom Debolski

Distributed to the book trade worldwide by Springer-Verlag New York, Inc., 233 Spring Street, 6th Floor, New York, NY 10013. Phone 1-800-SPRINGER, fax 201-348-4505, e-mail orders-ny@springer-sbm.com, or visit http://www.springeronline.com.

For information on translations, please contact Apress directly at 233 Spring Street, 6th Floor, New York, NY 10013. Phone 1-800-SPRINGER, fax 201-348-4505, e-mail info@apress.com, or visit http://www.apress.com.

Apress and friends of ED books may be purchased in bulk for academic, corporate, or promotional use. eBook versions and licenses are also available for most titles. For more information, reference our Special Bulk Sales–eBook Licensing web page at http://www.apress.com/info/bulksales.

The information in this book is distributed on an "as is" basis, without warranty. Although every precaution has been taken in the preparation of this work, neither the author(s) nor Apress shall have any liability to any person or entity with respect to any loss or damage caused or alleged to be caused directly or indirectly by the information contained in this work.

Nothing in this book is based on any information covered in nondisclosure agreements or any discussions between the author and any IBM staff member. All information in this book is publicly derivable by examining the WebSphere Application Server environment, traces, and log file output. This book in not sponsored by IBM. The normal IBM disclaimer for use of non-public APIs applies:

No user, developer or implementer should in any way rely on information that has been publicly deduced but does not form part of the published specifications and documentation of the product. Such internals information is liable to change without notice and IBM may not be able to restore previous behaviors, so any reliance on information that has been deduced is made entirely at the reader's own risk.

The source code for this book is available to readers at http://www.apress.com.

I would like to dedicate this book to my family, as God has blessed me with a wonderful one. So, to my wife, Kathryn, and my children, Michael and Olivia—this book is for you even if you never read it. Also, I must thank my parents, Trevor and Maureen, for instilling within me a desire to learn.

Contents at a Glance

Contents

Foreword

My role providing technical advice to clients on the delivery of complex, challenging solutions requires that I ask, and get answers to, hard questions about how technical components behave, under all conditions. Most documentation either does not contain this information at all, or more likely does not contain it in one concise, comprehensive guide, and you can end up trawling the Internet and user groups.

This sort of book, written by an expert in the field, is invaluable as it brings an understanding of internal structures and algorithms, and not only provides the answer to the question you asked, but most likely gives you a new one to consider—one an expert would ask.

If you don't have access to Colin—or to an SME like him—this book will help you and your project save time and money, possibly a great deal. I've already recently had the benefit of the information in this book when WebSphere load balancing needed to be understood at a detailed level.

Paul Fletcher
Principal Advisor, Financial Services Advisory, KPMG LLP (UK)

About the Author

COLIN RENOUF has been in the computer industry for 30 years—well, sort of. At the end of the 1970s, his forward-thinking school taught computer science on early DECs and arranged a holiday job working on Honeywell mainframes as an operator. After learning at a good university to be an aeronautical engineer, but discovering he and the aircraft trade were not a match made in heaven, Colin became a salesman while learning to become an IT professional. This included another part-time stint at university, where he obtained a First-Class Honours degree in Social Sciences and Computer Science.

Since 1987 Colin has been working at a UK bank, where he has been a C/Windows systems programmer, systems analyst, Java coder, DBA, technical architect, infrastructure architect, Unix guru, and domain architect. During this time he has worked closely with vendors such as IBM, Oracle, and Microsoft and has made friends and formed good contacts on the frontiers of the industry. As a result, he has spoken at conferences on Windows prototyping, AIX, Unix and Linux, Java, J2EE/JavaEE, and WebSphere. Now Colin is the Chairman of the POWERAIX User Group in the UK, Vice Chairman of the UK WebSphere User Group (which is one of the world's largest), and is just starting out in the UK zLinux User Group.

Colin has a particular interest in teaching and speaking on how things work under the covers, particularly with Unix and WebSphere, where he has shared the stage with some of the top names at IBM. IBM approached him to write on the internals and architecture subjects for its magazines and some documentation.

Colin is married to Kathryn and has two smart and energetic children, Michael and Olivia. His hobbies include computing (everything techie), church, reading, and being beaten at everything by his children.

About the Technical Reviewer

KUNAL MITTAL serves as an Executive Director of Technology at Sony Pictures Entertainment, where he is responsible for the SOA and Identity Management programs. He provides a centralized engineering service to different lines of business and consults on the content management, collaboration, and mobile strategies.

Kunal is an entrepreneur who helps startup companies to define their technology strategy, product roadmap, and development plans. With strong relations with several development partners worldwide, he is able to help startups, and even large companies, build appropriate development partnerships. He generally works in an Advisor or Consulting CTO capacity, and serves actively in the Project Management and Technical Architect functions.

Kunal has authored and edited several books and articles on J2EE, WebLogic, and SOA. He holds a master's degree in Software Engineering and is an instrument-rated private pilot.

Acknowledgments

I must thank the Apress team for all their help and backing in producing from my Word documents the physical book you hold in your hands, despite much wrestling with the Word technology. Particular thanks go to Molly Sharp, who cajoled me into meeting every date despite difficult circumstances some of the time.

My friends who helped me learn about WebSphere deserve praise because much of the information in this book comes from our working together. My good friend Rick Smith and my former boss William Soo have always encouraged me to learn about the WebSphere environment, but have also helped me with boundaries and direction. I must also thank my friends Hugh Byrne, Richard Bettison, Dan Morgan, Simon Johnson, and Yogesh Patel, who made me learn about JavaEE and all things WebSphere through friendly arguments about how things work. And who could leave out Peter Kovari, the author of many WebSphere books himself while at IBM! I have been fortunate to work with all of you. It has been fun and a privilege.

Over the last few years, as a result of user groups, I have also been privileged to work with many people from WebSphere teams past and present who have helped with my understanding without giving too much away. So, thanks to Jerry Cuomo, Tim Vanderham, Mark Cathcart, Mark Thomas, Andrew Ferrier, David Currie, Phil Coxhead, Trent Gray-Donald, Alan Chambers, and Graham Wallis. I couldn't leave out Tim Francis, who is the only human ever to have successfully hosted a large presentation with a description of slides after a failed motherboard. Finally, thanks to the web services dynamic duo of Greg Truty and Henry Chung—you guys are so helpful!

Introduction

This book is about WebSphere Application Server version 7 (WAS 7). It is not about JavaEE application servers in general, although there is obviously some commonality with similar products from other vendors because the functionality is essentially the same. This is particularly true of Oracle WebLogic Server 10 and 11 and JBoss, both of which have followed a similar component model based on OSGi for new functionality and base key subsystems on the same open source reference engines, but this is not a book about them.

WebSphere is an IBM brand, its most popular software brand ever, and is increasingly a name used to sell other products, most of which are based on WebSphere Application Server (e.g., WebSphere Process Server, WebSphere ESB, and WebSphere Portal Server) or are often coupled with it in some way (e.g., WebSphere MQ and WebSphere Message Broker).

The original product to carry the name was WebSphere Application Server, and this book is about the seventh version of that product. Actually, that designation is a misnomer, as the name started with version 3, which was derived from IBM Component Broker, and then became 3.5, 4, 5, 5.1, 6, and 6.1 before 7, and the product went through a number of rewrites on the way. J2EE, the enterprise services standard specification for Java, became standardized along the way at different versions until it became Java EE 5, which is the version that WAS 7 is targeted at. WAS 7 is an incremental development of the stable, J2EE 1.4–compliant version 6.1 product, which had a number of Feature Packs that brought its functionality closer to that of version 7 than the original release and added compliance with some parts of the JavaEE 5 specification. Version 6.1 of WAS introduced the Eclipse plugin/Equinox OSGi model that you will see throughout the book.

So, the book is about WAS 7, but because this product is split into multiple editions, with different types of functionality aimed at different markets, we will focus on one edition in particular: WebSphere Application Server 7 Network Deployment (WAS-ND) Edition. This is the edition that targets the enterprise, with support for high availability, clustering, failover, load balancing, and distributed management. This is also the most interesting edition as its extra functionality helps highlight some of the relationships between key components. It is also the edition on which many of the other important WebSphere-branded products are based. So, expect to hear about how many subsystems and components relate to clustering and high availability throughout the book.

The key part of the title of the book is *Internals*. This book is about how WAS-ND is structured internally. Sometimes the discussion will be at the architectural level, sometimes (actually most of the time) it will be at the component level, describing how important components and subsystems work, and sometimes it will involve a detailed description of the code that you would see in a debugger if you traced through that important component or subsystem. I use the word "important" here to describe what is covered because WAS is far too big a product to cover everything in a single book.

Who decides what is important? Well, based on years of experience with the product in various versions; writing and listening to presentations at conferences; conversations with friends developing the product at IBM; and many long hours being called in on high-pressure, problem-determination conference calls; I did. This book covers the internals that the rest of the product is built on, that are important for the most general cases, and that provide a basis for further investigation by the reader, either to help solve problems or to develop new components that bolt into WAS (or even just for the sheer fun of understanding how it works). However, the perspective as to what is important is essentially mine and there are many other equally valid perspectives.

Why Write This Book?

For a few years I have helped run one of the largest WebSphere User Groups in the world, based in the United Kingdom, with a few hundred attendees at every event we run. These events get a lot of attention inside IBM, so many developers, chief architects, vice presidents, and even CTOs of IBM attend and present. What became apparent very early on is that most attendees wanted to know more about how everything in WAS worked. Many of the presentations aimed to address that topic to some extent, but IBM itself would not support a comprehensive, detailed description of its most important software product, produced by its own staff. So, the task to work out what happens under the covers of WAS and explain it to others was left to outsiders.

I also work closely with the System p/AIX team, and in 2007 I was approached to help produce an IBM Redbook that would cover best practices for using WAS 6.1 on AIX and also explain how it all fits together, which required some explanation of the internals. This Redbook, and the explanations of how things worked, was based on various presentations given at the user groups, but, even though it was sponsored at the highest levels within IBM, any internals detailed had to be publicly derivable and not covered by a nondisclosure agreement. From this Redbook, a detailed presentation of how things worked was written for the UK user group. This presentation was as heavily attended as the keynote presented by the IBM WebSphere CTO, Jerry Cuomo. From this experience, I learned that there is an audience for information on how WAS works.

What motivated me to take up this task? Well, I have to solve problems, come up with ideas, and explain how things work and fit together on a daily basis. I was a Java J2EE developer and helped produce some of the certification test questions that are available on the Web for people who want to assess their skill level before they take the test for real. However, I am no longer a developer and am now an enterprise architect in a large bank, with responsibility for how things fit together using—you guessed it—WebSphere-branded middleware. I do still get called upon most days to answer development questions, and far too regularly to answer questions for support personnel as to why an application deployed to the WAS environment doesn't work in the manner the developer intended (although on many occasions I do have doubts as to whether the developer ever had any intention of the code working).

Also, I am just interested. The WebSphere CTO, Jerry Cuomo, has described me at conferences as the WebSphere PhD and as the "sort of person who would buy a top-end BMW and strip it down to its constituent parts to find out how it works." So, in addition to the work-related reasons, I simply like to know how things work. I write utilities that use reflection to poke around inside the WAS environment and often trace functionality through dumps, stack dumps, and debuggers just to improve my understanding. This book is a result of such research over the last few WAS versions.

Who This Book Is Aimed At

I am an architect who needs to know how things work so that I can efficiently bolt them together. I often consider myself to be a systems plumber who connects systems together so that information can flow through them freely. If you are a middleware architect, infrastructure architect, solutions architect, or some variation of architect, this book is aimed at you, even though it may be considerably more low level than the level you work at on a daily basis.

This book is aimed at end-user administrators and support professionals who work with WebSphere-branded products as their daily bread-winning endeavor. I still get called into conference calls when problems occur, and have often found the IBM support professionals not as helpful as I would like on these calls in dealing with specific problems. This level of helpfulness is to be expected; the first line of support is provided by generalists who don't know everything about WAS. It is such a big product, they obviously can't understand all the details of your specific use of it, so their objective is to map your use onto a specific subsystem within WAS and either look for existing related known issues that have a fix or identify the area of expertise within IBM that will need to be consulted.

This book is for support professionals who want to be able to focus on the target subsystems themselves to provide detailed information to IBM support as to what the issue is when a problem arises, or even to be able to derive their own workarounds when the crisis occurs in the middle of the night. I feel your pain, I really do.

This book is also targeted at developers. Not just any developers but Java developers who want to exploit JavaEE by understanding how the code they produce is executed, and specifically how the code they write is executed by WAS. Again, this helps in problem determination but also can help in deciding whether some application server–specific artifacts (e.g., ibm-webservicesclient-bnd.xmi) are really worth having. Developers who want to write their own WAS extensions to either understand it more or even to produce a saleable product are also a target of this book, although be aware that support from IBM is not likely to be provided for products that work at the level described in this book.

This book is not targeted at managers or IT sales consultants; or children, animals, or even inanimate objects for that matter.

Teaching Style

As you may have already noticed, I repeat myself a lot. I repeat myself a lot. This is intentional. In the past I used to study lots of different subjects, including how to best engage the brain to learn things, and repetition in a different context is a good way of learning.

I also go into detail to explain how something works and show the step-by-step evidence that backs this up or examples that demonstrate the point I am trying to make. Some of these examples may seem unrelated to the task at hand, but please bear with them as they all have a point. In some cases I have tried to create code using tools similar to those that IBM uses to mimic the architecture, solution, or behavior of the component I am describing. The changing context should make understanding the content a lot easier.

However, at this point I need to explain that I will sometimes give an incomplete or slightly misleading description in the name of promoting understanding. Thus, if some set of patterns is repeated throughout WAS, I will concentrate on some patterns and dismiss others when they are presented, and will then detail them in other chapters. For example, the title of Chapter 4, "Underlying WAS Runtime," may suggest that a complete set of all runtime components is going to be described, but only those shipped as part of the core WAS runtime are described as a complete unit; other runtime components that are also loaded are examined in later chapters in the appropriate context. Similarly, I briefly refer to collaborators when describing some containers, but detail various aspects of their use more specifically when covering the EJB and web containers, the aim of which is to ensure that the book isn't too large and covers important points only once, thereby promoting understanding.

Many years ago, I was told that the style adopted here is pedagogical; i.e., a teaching style where one explanation builds on another in another context. More recently I have been asked what *pedagogical* means and why I use such long words...

What You Need to Know to Benefit from This Book

You need to understand a bit about Java development, preferably in an IDE such as Eclipse, but if you don't, some information is covered in the chapters themselves to get you going. You also need to understand the basic functions of a JavaEE application server and how it is an implementation of "paperware"; i.e., a specification. This is important so you know what the containers should be doing as well as how they do it. Finally, some understanding of architecture is expected, although the diagrams should give enough direction to appreciate the text.

The Structure of a WAS Installation

I will use Unix and Linux as the basis of my descriptions, although the same features and disk layout apply at the lower levels for other platforms. It's just where the highest level of the WAS installation is found that changes between platforms.

So, look under /usr/IBM for most Unix platforms (or /opt/IBM for others) to find the default installation of WAS, under WebSphere/AppServer. We will spend most of our time in the following subdirectories:

- bin: Contains executable files and scripts, including shared objects or DLLs that are part of the WAS runtime itself rather than the JVM.

- configuration: Where OSGi stores its configuration in a config.ini file. Eclipse plugin/OSGi bundle log files can also sometimes be found in here.

- java: Contains the JVM, the IBM J9 Java Virtual Machine, that ships with the WAS environment.

- plugins: This is the directory where we will spend most of our time. WAS is now composed of Eclipse plugins or OSGi bundles, effectively distinct components that are used together to create the complete runtime environment.

- profiles: Contains the configuration of the particular cell, cluster, and WAS instances. If you don't know what these terms mean, don't worry as I will explain them later.

The Important WAS Files

While there are many different perspectives on what the most important files are in WAS, the key components we will concentrate on can be found in the `/plugins` directory:

- `com.ibm.ws.runtime.jar`: Contains the core of the WAS environment itself, and the majority of the functionality for the containers. Much of this book, and the functionality in WAS itself, relates to the functionality in this plugin.

- `com.ibm.ws.wlm.jar`: Contains additional functionality for clustering, high availability, and load balancing that builds upon that in the core runtime plugin.

- `com.ibm.ws.webcontainer.jar`: Contains the functionality for the web container, a key subsystem, that builds upon the functionality within the core runtime but also provides support for other key subsystems.

- `com.ibm.wsfp.main.jar`: Contains the JAX-WS support for WAS, where the Axis2 open source web services engine is wrapped and integrated into the WAS runtime environment as if it were a native subsystem written for WAS from the ground up.

There are other files that we will look at along the way, but these are the key files and each is an Eclipse plugin or OSGi bundle (depending on how you look at it). This brings another key point to light: we will have to look in great detail at the Eclipse Equinox OSGi runtime that underpins WAS and makes all of the component integration possible.

What This Book Covers

We will start with an overview of the WAS architecture and then "deep-dive" into the internals from the ground up, starting with the IBM J9 JVM, moving up through the Eclipse/OSGi implementation into the core WAS runtime that builds on it, and then investigating the core subsystems and JavaEE containers and how they provide enterprise-level qualities of service, before finishing with a look at configuration and how IBM builds upon WAS for some of its other products.

Let's look at what each chapter contains in a little more detail.

Chapter 1: WAS Architecture Outline from 50,000 Feet

WAS 7 is based on (usually) an IBM J9 JVM for Java 6 that allows IBM to exploit some proprietary features higher up the WAS stack, an Eclipse 3.2.1/Equinox/OSGi runtime to allow dynamic extension, a core JavaEE runtime, and a number of extensions to the core that provide the JavaEE "policy" atop the core runtime services implementation. This chapter looks at how it all fits together and the different components and subsystems. The chapter is brief but sets the context for the rest of the book.

Chapter 2: The IBM J9 Java Virtual Machine for Java 6

A standard JVM has specific features that you need to be familiar with to understand what makes a process appear to be a "machine" to the core runtime. IBM modifies and extends the standard JVM features, including using its own terms to describe core JVM architectural subsystems, to support functionality such as native code sharing across JVM instances or intelligent garbage collection. We will look at how the IBM J9 JVM is structured and works, and where it exploits open source technologies.

Chapter 3: Eclipse/OSGi Runtime

The Eclipse project is best known for its IDE, but it defines an architecture for general applications, even on the server side. Eclipse runtime functionality offers many benefits to the general application, particularly in the support for dynamic extension. Eclipse has taken on the OSGi (which originally stood for Open Services Gateway initiative) architecture to support bundles and service management. An Eclipse/OSGi application must be built in a certain way, and this chapter shows what this is and how WAS conforms to it. Finally, this chapter shows how this benefits WAS 7.

Chapter 4: Underlying WAS Runtime

The WAS architecture depends on core functionality exposed from the core runtime, such as thread pool management, dynamic extension management, and connection management. This chapter explains in detail how this core runtime functionality works, how it is implemented as a series of components exposing services, and how WAS exposes the functionality to the higher layers using the Eclipse/OSGi features.

Chapter 5: The EJB Container

Enterprise JavaBeans are basically scalable business-function and data-related components, so understanding the details of what makes the components scalable while maintaining transactional integrity is valuable to a JavaEE developer. The WAS runtime provides the features that make the EJB container possible, with the core functionality implemented as a container built upon an Enterprise Java Services (EJS) container, with collaborators to support integration from other subsystems. We will cover how this all works in depth.

Chapter 6: The Web Container

To understand the behavior of a typical web application, or even some web services applications, you must understand the servlet API and how it is implemented by WAS. This extends the core WAS runtime and is implemented in a separate plugin, again through an underlying container with collaborators to support external integration from other subsystems. We will look at how this all works and how to create our own similar integration with the web container.

Chapter 7: Web Services

Web services is an area with a number of different application implementation variations that are reflected in the different subsystems involved in the application server required to support them. The web container is important for core web services support, so this chapter examines in detail both the JAX-RPC and JAX-WS implementations and how they integrate.

Chapter 8: Service Integration Bus

The Service Integration Bus has a number of components to support enterprise service bus features, and even has a Java implementation of the original WebSphere MQ/MQSeries functionality to support JMS. At the core of the functionality is the Messaging Engine (ME), also known as the WebSphere Platform Messaging (WPM) engine, which implements support for the WMQ protocol and formats. The JMS implementation uses JFAP (Java Formats and Protocols) to which extra headers are added to interoperate with WMQ native systems via MQ FAP. Web services and gateway support is built upon this. We will look at how this messaging subsystem works and some of the requirements of the underlying protocol that dictate how other subsystems work, such as for high availability.

Chapter 9: High Availability

As the Java Virtual Machine appears to the JavaEE environment to be a machine in its own right, a highly available (HA) solution for JavaEE requires access to knowledge of what is going on inside the JVM process. This means that external HA solutions, such as IBM HACMP or Linux Heartbeat/HA, can't properly manage a scalable and available JavaEE environment. For example, subsystems such as the Messaging Engine need to support the singleton pattern to ensure operational ordering; which in this case is a requirement of the default MQ FAP protocol. The WAS HAManager provides the functionality to support JavaEE high availability, and this chapter describes how this works.

Chapter 10: Load Balancing and Scalability

To scale a WAS environment, the concepts of the cell, the cluster, the HTTP plugin, and session management must be understood. The key to much of this relies on the use of the JSESSIONID JavaEE standard header for HTTP, and the Data Replication Services (DRS)/Distribution and Consistency Services (DCS) subsystems. The concepts of the Deployment Manager and the core group are explained in terms of how the administrative, scalability, and high-availability objectives are met. Underpinning this are the Admin Service for configuration and the implementations in the com.ibm.ws.wlm.jar plugin. This chapter explains how this all fits together.

Chapter 11: Configuration

The key to understanding the behavior of WAS is a knowledge of the underlying configuration XML files. In addition to explaining what these files are and how they differ between different members of a cluster, this chapter covers the key files (server.xml and serverindex.xml) that must be understood from a problem determination perspective. This chapter also provides some explanation of security management and how it relates to the core WAS runtime. The underlying Eclipse/OSGi runtime also has its own configuration, even down to the individual plugin level, so this "undocumented" functionality is explained to allow quicker focus on a WAS component when an emergency arises (typically at 2 a.m. on a Sunday morning). While this isn't strictly internals being considered, it does strongly relate to the core subject of the book.

Chapter 12: Related Products

This chapter explains WebSphere Enterprise Service Bus (WESB) Service Component Architecture (SCA) functionality and how it makes use of the WAS Service Integration Bus, and describes the BPEL Process Choreography engine that extends this to form WebSphere Process Server. Finally, the extensions to the web container to support the WebSphere Portal Server are explained. This chapter has to refer to an earlier version of WAS (6.1), with its similar architecture, because it will be some time before WAS 7–based WebSphere products are released. Rather unsurprisingly, the way these WebSphere products build upon WAS is to use the Eclipse/OSGi functionality to extend the WAS internal services and extension points.

■■■

CHAPTER 1

WAS Architecture Outline from 50,000 Feet

This chapter provides a high-level overview of the WebSphere Application Server (WAS) architecture. To help you understand why WAS is structured in the way that it is, the chapter first looks at the Java, J2EE, and WebSphere domains from a historical perspective. During that discussion I will identify the requirements of a Java Platform, Enterprise Edition 5 (Java EE 5) application server. Finally, the chapter describes the WAS architecture and explains how it implements the Java EE 5 specification while also providing the high-availability and performance "quality of service" features that we expect from IBM.

Placing WAS in Historical Context

Initially, Java was targeted at the client- and Internet-related market because it included support for TCP/IP and portable multithreading "out of the box." The simple component model called JavaBeans was based on naming of getters and setters for variables. However, dynamic production of web pages was still based on sharing environment variables between a web server and multiple processes, a model that did not scale well. The multithreading and TCP/IP facilities in Java provided the basis of a solution for the server side, and Sun created the servlet API standard. At the same time, transaction monitors such as IBM's Customer Information and Control System (CICS) and Information Management System (IMS) were being further developed, with support for objects being added, leading to the object transaction monitoring wave that delivered Microsoft Transaction Server (MTS) and the Enterprise JavaBeans (EJB) standard. IBM led the transaction monitoring market at the high end with CICS, but Tuxedo had the lead in other markets. The dynamic web page generation and object transaction monitoring solutions were combined with other Java specifications to form the J2EE standard, with significant input from IBM, which wanted to build on the knowledge gained from CICS and compete more in other nonmainframe markets.

At this time, IBM was in the Distributed Computing Environment (DCE) market with its Component Broker product; the Common Object Request Broker Architecture (CORBA) market with its Distributed System Object Model (DSOM) facilities in the IBM operating systems; and the transaction monitoring market with CICS, IMS, and Encina. From this work, with Component Broker at its core and the support for Java with the servlet API, WAS was born.

The servlet engine and little else was supported in version 1.0, with CORBA support added soon after in version 2.0. It wasn't until version 3.0, when Java 2 and J2EE were fully standardized and available, that WAS became a true J2EE 1.0–compliant application server with multiple editions to support different IBM added-value features for the enterprise. Version 3.5 followed soon after with various improvements. Version 4 added support for the J2EE 1.2 standard.

WAS 4.0 still had some dependencies on legacy C/C++ code, so IBM completely rewrote the code for WAS 5.0 to be almost entirely pure Java. It wasn't until this release that IBM finally removed the support for DCE, on which the original product was built, and the migration path for DCE developers became a complete application rewrite.

From the early versions of WAS, IBM added extra functionality that was not part of the J2EE specification, or produced versions for specific roles. Up until WAS 5.0, the Express Edition contained only a web container; the Standard Edition was a stand-alone J2EE application server; the Network Deployment (or Advanced) Edition supported high-availability clustering; and the Enterprise Edition included extra functionality, which IBM referred to as Programming Model Extensions (PME), to make development easier and to add new facilities to allow WAS to take on new roles (e.g., to provide limited workflow services).

This all led to a larger code base, so from WAS 5.1 the Enterprise Edition became WebSphere Business Integration Server Foundation (WBISF), which IBM eventually transformed into WebSphere Process Server, and IBM initiated a drive to move to a common code base across all platforms and editions, which meant supporting dynamic extensions and pushing some of the extensions into the base code.

WAS 6.0 was another major rewrite, again to improve the code performance, serviceability, architecture, and usability. It was this code base that formed the basis of the componentization work that was introduced with version 6.1. It was in version 6.1 that the Eclipse/OSGi runtime was introduced, at version 3.1.2, to underpin WAS, and the use of plug-ins and components inside containers was introduced. In many ways, WAS 6.1 should have been called WAS 7.0, which in turn should have been called WAS 7.5, because the major architectural work was introduced with the version 6.1 platform.

Versions 6.0 and 6.1 were targeted at the J2EE 1.4 platform, although the version 6.1 product was based on IBM J9 Java Virtual Machine (JVM) for Java 5 for performance improvements. J2EE 1.4 had some inherent problems with scalability in the EJB tier and serialization issues that affected performance in the web services code, so Java EE 5 introduced major changes in these areas, with EJB 3 and Java Persistence API (JPA) replacing EJB 2.1 in J2EE 1.4, and JAX-WS replacing JAX-RPC in J2EE 1.4 as the primary web services standard.

IBM responded by taking the best of the open source implementations of these standards, OpenJPA and Axis2, and wrapping them up as Feature Packs for version 6.1 to provide some Java EE 5 functionality. This code was then rolled into the WAS 7.0 implementation (see Figure 1-1), along with new features for administration, management of groups of related applications together (business-level applications), and higher-level web services stack support to provide a full Java EE 5 implementation, albeit on a Java 6 JVM.

This brief historical overview helps to explain some of the unusual features of the WAS architecture that you are about to look at. I will concentrate on the WebSphere Application Server Network Deployment (WAS-ND) Edition because it provides the high-availability features used in most enterprises, which differentiates the product from other application server products and also forms the basis for a number of other IBM products targeted at the enterprise (e.g., WebSphere ESB, WebSphere Process Server, WebSphere Portal Server, etc.). So, how do all the different pieces of WAS, particularly WAS-ND, fit together? Read on.

WebSphereApplication Server 7.0

At the end of 2008 WAS 7.0 was released

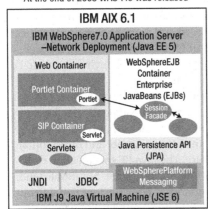

- **Java EE 5 standard support**

- **Changes from previous versions are:**

  - Java EE 5 compliant on a Java 6 Virtual Machine with improved memory management

  - EJB 3/JPA support for data access

  - JAX WS standards support for web services

  - WS Policy Support

  - Support for a group of related applications to be treated as one with business-level applications

  - Support for injection

  - Improved management facilities with the Admin Agent and Job Manager

- Network Deployment adds clustering and centralized management to the base product.

- A unit of management is a cell, which is managed by a central WAS Deployment Manager, usually on a separate box. This central box needs its own high availability, but it manages administration and clustering for a group of WAS nodes.

- Each operating system image (e.g., AIX LPAR) is a node with a WebSphere Node Agent to manage it.

- Multiple WebSphere Application Server instances can run on a node, but management is handled via the Node Agent communicating back to the Deployment Manager.

- WAS instances can be clustered on the same box for scalability and across boxes for high availability.

- A cell can contain many clusters.

Figure 1-1. *WebSphere Application Server 7.0 architectural overview*

Examining the WAS High-Level Architecture

Unlike other players in the application server domain, IBM is also a reseller of hardware. Exploiting the features of the hardware requires explicit support in the JVM and operating system, so although the JVM is not strictly part of WAS, it does have some features that WAS exploits to run better on IBM hardware. As an example platform, I will use the IBM System POWER6 AIX 6.1 environment. WAS does run on other platforms, of course, as it offers extensions for Windows, Solaris, Linux, and HP-UX, but it is on the IBM platforms that the benefits of WAS are most apparent.

Starting from the ground up, there are Unix and Windows scripts that start IBM J9 JVM for Java 6 with an Eclipse/OSGi 3.2.1 runtime environment and a launcher program that starts the WAS core runtime as a collection of components. J9 is IBM's own JVM, which also includes some features of the open source Apache Harmony JVM (after all, IBM is a contributor), and it is to this JVM that the extensions for WAS for IBM hardware were first added. The J9 JVM is also available for some other platforms, such as Windows and Linux, but the license restricts its usage to running WAS.

Most Java developers are familiar with the Eclipse IDE, and many are familiar with the plug-in model that it uses. The IBM OTI team that produced the VisualAge tools originally developed Eclipse as an IDE on which it could build tools. IBM subsequently contributed Eclipse to the open source community. With Eclipse 3.X, the tool architects wanted to extend the plug-in model (with its Extension Registry that extensions use to extend XML-declared extension points) to add dynamic behavior, so they borrowed from the mobile technology market, where a group of major vendors had started the Open Services Gateway initiative (OSGi, now called the OSGi Alliance) to provide a dynamic and efficient Java system architecture. With Eclipse Equinox, the two technologies were merged, but another change introduced at the same time is what brings the benefits to WAS: support for the server side; i.e., there is no user interface, which allows dynamic and extensible application server environments to be built from independent components that collaborate at runtime.

The WAS runtime loads as a set of containers, starting with the base server container, which starts the lowest-level components that handle tasks such as thread pooling, followed by the base application server container, which starts the components that support the functions that underlie Java EE and the higher-level containers, and then the EJB, web, and other containers, which are directly represented in the Java EE architecture. The Java EE specification does separate the base server container from the web container and EJB container, but IBM extends this model. Some components and subsystems use collaborators to hook the functionality in particular containers and listeners for the services to watch for and respond to changes in the application or environment. IBM uses its own internal service registry to manage the components, and this registry uses support from the Eclipse plug-in and OSGi facilities.

Generally, the implementation is split into interfaces, interface classes, and implementation classes with the same name as the service and component and the Impl suffix in accordance with the strategy pattern implementation. So, for example, the Web Container Service offers a WebContainer interface that is implemented by the WebContainerImpl implementation class (see Figure 1-2). Underlying some parts of the infrastructure components are shared objects or DLLs, although this tendency has lessened with more recent WAS releases. Most WAS functionality, however, is based on a core Eclipse plug-in called com.ibm.ws.runtime.jar, with numerous other plug-ins providing extensions to the services and extension points it exposes to provide the higher-level functions. Configuration of the whole environment is handled through XML files, with the server.xml file being particularly important.

With later releases of WAS, such as 6.1, IBM sought to support new Java EE features on a J2EE 1.4 base soon after availability without major rewrites. The component/service model supported this, with the new features delivered as Feature Packs. These extensions often used industry-leading open source implementations of the new features and wrapped them with components and services that tied them into the core WAS runtime. For example, the EJB 3 Feature Pack provided support for the JPA and EJB 3 by wrapping the OpenJPA engine, and the Web Services Feature Pack used the Axis2 engine to provide JAX-WS support. It is the use of plug-ins from Eclipse, the use of dynamic service-based component interfaces from OSGi, and the way in which the subsystems were re-architected in the WAS 6.0 product to be more independent that has made this possible.

With the release of WAS 7.0, the use of Feature Packs will continue, with the SCA (Service Component Architecture) Feature Pack, but the code from the earlier Feature Packs has been rolled into the base product (often leaving the fp in the package names). Thus, WAS 6.1 started the support for some Java EE 5 specification standards, and WAS 7.0 completes this support by adding incremental changes to the code provided by the Feature Packs. In other words, WAS 6.1 was a stepping stone to the full WAS 7.0 environment, and companies currently using WAS 6.1 can add the Feature Packs to begin their migration to WAS 7.0.

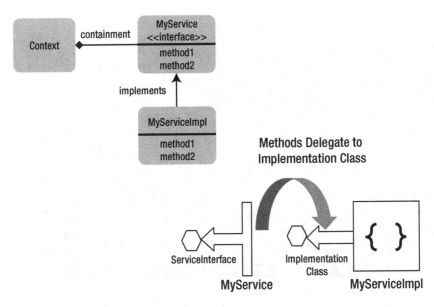

Figure 1-2. *WAS services and the strategy pattern*

Let's now look at the major features of WAS 7.0.

IBM J9 Java Virtual Machine

IBM J9 JVM for Java 6 is based on the earlier J9 versions and uses highly optimizing back ends with functionality similar to that of the back-end C/C++ compilers that IBM sells. The core optimizers are designed to exploit fully the underlying platform, and the JIT (Just In Time) compiler optimizes the Java byte code and native code based on expected and actual usage patterns. The underlying shared class cache mechanism that allows code to be shared between WAS instances has now been changed to support memory-mapped files to allow greater amounts of optimized code to be shared, which minimizes startup time and improves memory utilization across a whole set of instances.

Because the J9 JVM is OS- and hardware-aware to exploit memory optimizations—for example, it uses 32- and 64-bit pointers where each is best for performance on a 64-bit JVM, and software partitioning is available (i.e., AIX WPARs)—the shared classes and optimizations for the platform greatly enhance scalability through better use of resources. When placed on IBM hardware, such as the POWER6 platform that offers Virtual Partition Memory to map memory pages across local partitioning (LPAR) OS images (see Figure 1-3), the memory utilization for WAS is reduced even further, to such an extent that it makes sense to deploy lots of WAS-based applications on the same machine because the memory utilization does not go up significantly.

Use shared ethernet adapter failover between the two virtual I/O server
partitions to avoid the virtual I/O server being a single point of failure

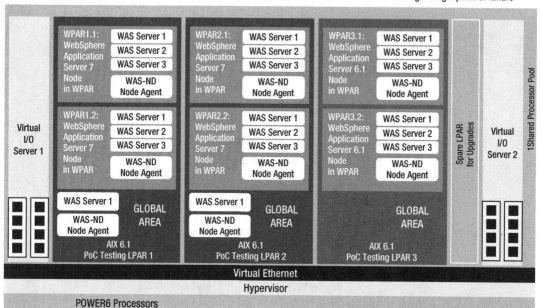

Note that the IBM Java 6 J9 JVM-based WAS maps classes from the global area into a WPAR because it uses memory-mapped
files for shared classes, but the Java 5-based version uses shared memory, so it is completely isolated. The Virtual Partition
Memory feature of the Hypervisor on POWER6 hardware even allows memory to be shared between LPARs.

Figure 1-3. *IBM System p POWER6/AIX 6.1 partitioning with WAS-ND 7.0 deployed*

Eclipse/OSGI Runtime

The Eclipse 3.2.1 runtime underlies WAS, and the WAS code exploits both the Eclipse Extension Registry, which allows code to expose extension points that other code extends, and
the OSGi Service Registry, which allows services to be exposed to other components. The
Eclipse Extension Registry is actually implemented on top of the OSGi Service Registry in this
release. The runtime allows components to have their MANIFEST.MF or plugin.xml file read at
startup dynamically, after which the code is loaded when required, which improves the use
of memory. This mechanism is examined in more detail in later chapters, but essentially it
allows components that have no direct knowledge of each other to offer a service or extension
interface that can be dynamically extended at runtime, with the code that wants to use that
extension performing a lookup in a registry for an interface.

WAS exploits this runtime to componentize its own code and to allow specific WAS configurations for particular roles. The com.ibm.cds.jar file that comes with Eclipse allows the
Eclipse runtime environment to tie into and exploit the IBM J9 JVM class-sharing facilities.
WAS also exposes for use by applications its own high-level public Eclipse Extension Registry,
which is distinct from its own internal registry. This enables Java EE application vendors to
also benefit from the Eclipse/OSGi model in building applications from components dynamically at runtime, which may be the start of a true third-party component market, because
other application server vendors are also driving in this direction.

Base Runtime

Most of the core WAS runtime is implemented in the `com.ibm.ws.runtime.jar` plug-in, which is bootstrapped by the `com.ibm.ws.bootstrap.jar` plug-in that sets up the internal WAS service registry. Components are loaded into a number of WAS containers, which are essentially phases of loading based on particular extension points declared in the `plugin.xml` file. Some core functionality is provided in other plug-ins, such as the `com.ibm.ws.wlm.jar` file, which contains much of the support for high availability, but most of what makes WAS-ND the product it is can be found in the `com.ibm.ws.runtime.jar` file.

The WAS core runtime, with the containers that normally constitute a Java EE application server, loads as a base server container, a base application server container, a scheduler container, an EJB container, and a web container, although other components and containers also load using the same component mechanism. Within these containers, the components often declare services to use elsewhere, some of which offer listeners. These components are the basis of all of the functionality within WAS. Of particular interest are the Metadata Service and Application Manager Service—each provided by its own component implementation offering registered service interfaces—that monitor the application environment for deployed object changes and notify registered listeners about any such changes so that the listeners can take appropriate action. Some components declare collaborators for the EJB container and web container so that they can watch for changes and hook the internal functionality.

WAS Implementation on Different Platforms

The implementation of WAS is the same on most platforms, although there are some differences on the IBM System i platform and a considerable number of differences on the IBM System z/zOS platform. On the IBM System zOS platform, multiple processes run to represent the single JVM view, with control regions to handle system-level functions and servant regions to handle application-level functions. The system-level architectures of these platforms, developed from the System 38/AS/400 and System 360/370/390 families of midrange and high-end systems, respectively, are sufficiently different in operation from other, more-standard Unix, Windows, and Linux platforms that a number of workarounds are needed to support Java EE; WAS accommodates this through platform-specific Java code.

Underlying Communications

Underlying communications are split into transport chains that build from basic TCP support up to higher-level protocols by chaining channels together to form a communications pipe. So, to provide HTTPS support, TCP, SSL, and HTTP functionality are chained together. This extends to support the Java Message Service (JMS) and Message Queueing (MQ) Formats and Protocols (FAP) functionality to support connectivity via JMS and WebSphere MQ, respectively. This subsystem is part of the Channel Framework Service, which is one of the fundamental services that underpin the operation of WAS, so expect to see in subsequent chapters a lot of information about how this subsystem works and is used, particularly when the EJB and web containers are discussed in Chapters 5 and 6, respectively.

WAS Enterprise Features

You have had a glimpse at some of the key architectural features of the base WAS 7.0 product, but one of the areas that differentiates WAS and some of the high-end products from other application servers is its enterprise features. These features affect the internals of WAS significantly, even the base product, particularly in the way the server configuration XML file usage is reflected throughout the product component implementations. So, it is essential that you understand some of the clustering and high-availability concepts in a typical enterprise deployment before you delve into the depth of WAS (see Figure 1-4). Remember that the base WAS 7.0 product, as found in the stand-alone and Express editions, and the high-end products, such as WAS-ND, are built from the same components, although for the base product fewer components are shipped and installed. As stated earlier, this book focuses on WAS-ND because it is the core for other products yet is also the product that fully implements the true WAS 7.0 architecture that targets the enterprise.

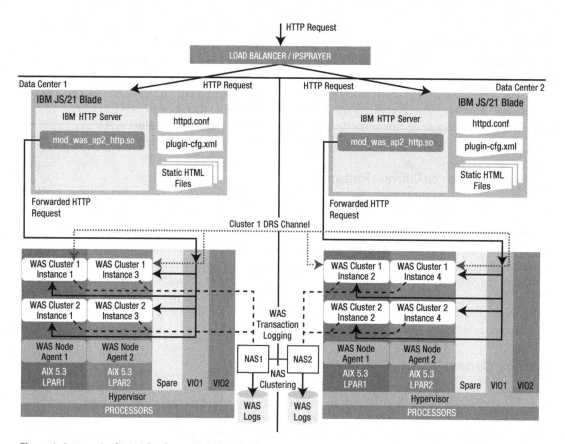

Figure 1-4. *A typical WAS high-availability deployment*

WAS Network Deployment Edition includes high-availability (HA) support via the High Availability Manager (HA Manager). This component uses the Data Replication Services (DRS), Distribution and Consistency Services (DCS), and other features to handle failover of singletons such as the Service Integration Bus Messaging Engine. WAS administration is based on the concept of a *cell* that is administered as a whole unit. A cell can contain one or more clusters that can be considered to be units of failover or high availability, with a cluster consisting of one or more WAS instances that are paired together using DRS to share data. IBM HTTP Server (or equivalent) runs the proxy plug-in (mod_was_ap2_http.so) that is configured (via plugin-cfg.xml) to understand the cluster composition and targets a single WAS instance to maintain a sticky session, but can route to other cluster members if the original instance fails. The JSESSIONID header is used to implement this routing magic.

An application is deployed to a cell and then configured to run on one or more clusters within that cell. The core group within the cell allows a further grouping of instance configuration to reduce the cell complexity of large cells and the communications between them. The Node Agent instance sits inside each OS image running WAS instances and maintains a copy of the configuration of the cell as it relates to the instances running in that environment as pushed out from the WAS Deployment Manager that manages that cell. The configuration is handled completely through XML files maintained by the Deployment Manager, which itself is a specialized WAS instance. The Deployment Manager maintains a picture of the cell contents and communicates this topology to each of the Node Agents. The Node Agents then provide to each WAS instance running inside that OS image the XML configuration required. Multiple WAS instances inside a single cluster can be run inside the OS image for scalability purposes, which is known as *vertical clustering*, and a cluster can exist across multiple OS images on different machines for traditional *horizontal clustering* for high availability.

With the introduction of the Admin Agent and Job Manager, the cell and cluster facilities can be simplified or extended, respectively. The Admin Agent reduces the need for the Node Agent for management in a simplified environment, and the Job Manager allows a single Deployment Manager to schedule from a single location deployments and administration across a number of cells.

Note Whereas the Deployment Manager, Node Agent, Admin Agent, and Job Manager are just special-case WAS 7.0 installations, the HA Manager, DRS, DCS, and Service Integration Bus Messaging Engine are all core components of the architecture, so I will cover them in more detail in later chapters.

As Figure 1-5 illustrates, within the cell, one or more clusters can be set up to act as failover partners (as previously described), a number of instances can run on a node representing (usually) an OS image, and the Node Agent usually relates to this OS image.

Configuration Files

All of these conceptual levels of administration are represented using a collection of XML configuration files. The server.xml file represents the configuration of an instance in terms of connections, chains, thread pools, etc. to support the given applications. The serverindex.xml file represents the ports and TCP/IP connectivity. The security.xml file represents the security configuration. Many other XML files are used to support the environment, and these are pushed out and controlled, usually, from the central point called the Deployment Manager. So, to understand the topology of a complete WAS cell, you look at the directory structure on the Deployment Manager containing all of the XML files, but to concentrate on the clusters and instances on a single node, you look at the Node Agent and instance XML files. On the nodes, the XML configuration for the partners involved in the cluster on other nodes is also included to allow failover.

Clustering and Availability

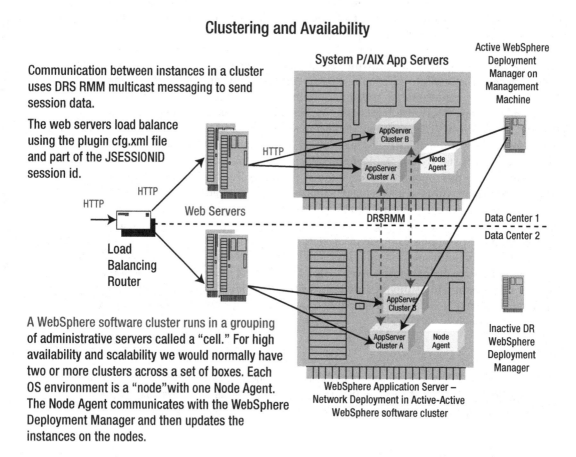

Communication between instances in a cluster uses DRS RMM multicast messaging to send session data.

The web servers load balance using the plugin cfg.xml file and part of the JSESSIONID session id.

A WebSphere software cluster runs in a grouping of administrative servers called a "cell." For high availability and scalability we would normally have two or more clusters across a set of boxes. Each OS environment is a "node"with one Node Agent. The Node Agent communicates with the WebSphere Deployment Manager and then updates the instances on the nodes.

Figure 1-5. *WebSphere Application Server Network Deployment cell and cluster topology*

Web Container

The web container consists of a service offered by a component implementation that supports the operations to be expected of a web container (such as registration of servlet lifecycle listeners), but with additional listeners and collaborator interfaces supported to allow other subsystems to register themselves with the web container to assist in its operations. The implementation delegates to a lower-level implementation (WSWebContainer) that provides the infrastructural support, and which uses helper classes to wrap web applications, their WAR files, and the actual servlet implementations (see Figure 1-6).

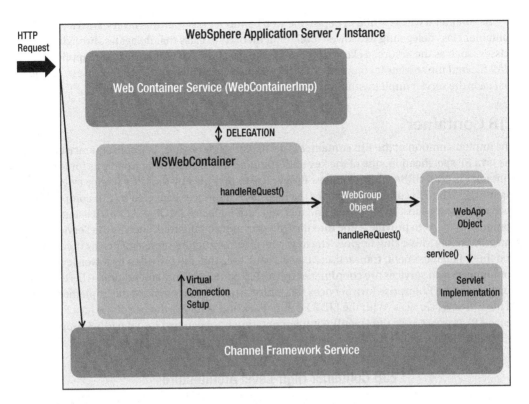

Figure 1-6. *Web container high-level architecture*

The web container was originally designed to support servlets, but the Apache Jasper JSP engine from Tomcat was customized and adapted to provide the JSP functionality within WAS. Ultimately, a servlet or servlet variant is what runs. We will cover the way this works in detail in future chapters, and the pattern is repeated for the use of open source technology elsewhere in WAS under the covers, but this customization is necessary in a high-end enterprise application server to put the failover (e.g., state) and scalability (e.g., threads and connections) under the control of the application server core runtime. Implementation is provided, mostly, in the com.ibm.ws.webcontainer.jar plug-in.

Many other components either watch for deployed object changes in the web container or install collaborators to hook functionality. I will explain more about collaborators in later chapters, but these follow a standard technology pattern used throughout the WAS runtime to allow multiple containers to cooperate on a single request without tight coupling—that is, a collaborator interface is declared and a component registers to add itself to the list of users who can use that interface.

New container features appearing in the Java Specification Requests (JSRs) as part of the Java Community Process are being released regularly, so the use of a loose coupling registration architecture for key subsystems allows IBM to respond rapidly to any changes in the JSRs. Two containers that extend the functionality in the web container in this way are the JSR 286 portlet container, which allows portlet components to be hosted inside WAS in the same way as servlets are hosted, and the SIP container, which allows VoIP and instant messaging solutions that support the Session Initiation Protocol to maintain a session context with WAS.

As Chapter 6 will describe in depth, the web container has multiple layers, with a web container class delegating to a lower-level implementation class that delegates through other classes (such as the WebGroup class) to get to the WebApp class that wraps the target application WAR file and the servlets it contains, with this wrapper implementing a handleRequest method that calls the servlet implementation.

EJB Container

The implementation of the EJB container is particularly interesting. As a consequence of the Java EE specification, one of the key underpinning infrastructure components for this container is the CORBA Object Request Broker (ORB) provided by the ORB Service (see Figure 1-7). The EJB container provides the high-level interfaces expected by EJB components such as session beans, entity beans, and message-driven beans (MDBs). An MDB listener component loads to provide a line into the JMS providers configured, such as the Service Integration Bus Messaging Engine. The lower-level infrastructure services, such as memory and thread management, transaction management, etc., that are provided by lower-level components and services are coordinated by the EJS container implementation, where the EJS container is the Enterprise Java Services (EJS) infrastructure that provides the implementation of the EJB-level services. With the EJB 3 Feature Pack and WAS 7.0, the use of the Java Persistence API as exposed by the OpenJPA implementation has been tied into the EJB 3 support within the EJB container through a service-registration mechanism.

EJB Container High-Level Architecture

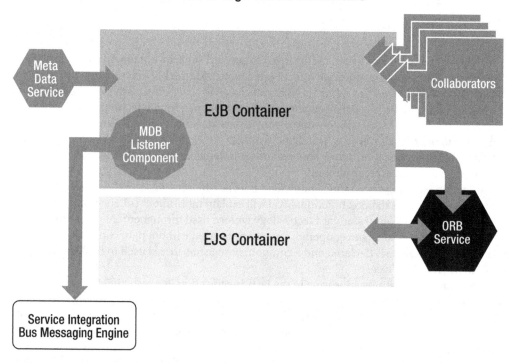

Figure 1-7. *EJB container architecture*

Service Integration Bus

The Service Integration Bus (SIB) was derived from the Web Services Gateway implementation in earlier releases, and later the JMS and MQ support in the WebSphere Platform Messaging Engine was added such that SIB can interoperate with WebSphere MQ environments via MQLinks and MQ FAP, support generic JMS via JMS FAP (JFAP), and essentially provide a Java-based drop-in replacement for much of the WebSphere MQ functionality. Most of this is implemented outside of the core runtime via a separate set of plug-ins, as discussed in future chapters.

Web Services Support

Originally, the JAX-RPC functionality in WAS 6.1 was based on an Axis1-derived implementation that provided optimized support for WS-I Basic Profile 1.0a with the related SOAP 1.1 support. The Web Services Feature Pack for WAS 6.1 and the WAS 7.0 implementation are based on an Axis2-derived JAX-WS engine with support for WSI-Basic Profile 1.1 and SOAP 1.2, but in WAS 7.0 many higher levels of the web services stack, such as WS-Policy, are also supported. This support is complex because multiple engines need to be supported, so discussion of the complex architecture will be left to a later chapter, other than to say that the component architecture of the core WAS runtime and collaborators tying into the EJB container and Web container provide the mechanism by which web services are delivered using the JAX-RPC and JAX-WS engines.

Summary

You now have had a quick overview of the route you will travel in your journey through the internals of WAS. You have looked at the history of Java, J2EE/Java EE, and WAS to get a sense of how the WAS architecture has evolved, and you have been introduced to the underlying architecture that supports Java EE and the IBM value-added components in the WAS 7.0 release. This chapter has particularly emphasized the functionality provided in WAS-ND, because this edition provides the basis of other enterprise products and fully implements the architecture designed to support enterprise-class quality of service.

For the rest of your journey through this book, you will drill down from the landscape-level view into the foundational depths of the implementation. However, at this point I should note that there are a number of views regarding the WAS internals and architecture, none of which is wrong, and the particular views that I offer in this book are those that I believe to be useful from a support and understanding perspective. WAS and its extensions is a huge subject that could not be covered in a single volume. If the view you need isn't in here, it is my hope that the discussion and the description of the tools used for investigation will enable you to embark on a little guided self-discovery, but feedback is always welcome.

CHAPTER 2

■■■

The IBM J9 Java Virtual Machine for Java 6

You may be wondering why we are examining the IBM J9 Java Virtual Machine (JVM) implementation in a book about WebSphere Application Server (WAS). The vendor that first comes
to mind for Java Virtual Machines is Sun Microsystems, the inventor of Java. By definition,
anything that calls itself Java EE must be able to run on this JVM. The Sun JVM is generic in
nature and designed to be able to exploit the most general usage cases, but it isn't optimized
for either IBM hardware or the enterprise server-side features of an application server such as
WAS. While the IBM JVM exploits the features of IBM hardware, it also provides assistance to
some features of WAS (e.g., class sharing) and allows IBM to exploit other optimizations that
might not be fully in Sun's interest to provide. When run on IBM hardware, features in the IBM
Hypervisors for virtualization can be exploited. IBM also improves performance through use
of the Open Source Apache Harmony code wherever this makes sense. So, for the best performance and features for WAS, it should be run on an IBM JVM on IBM hardware; hence the
inclusion of this chapter about the IBM J9 JVM in a book about the internals of WAS.

This chapter introduces a generic JVM implementation and its features at a high level,
and compares this with the IBM implementation. We will look at specific IBM J9 JVM features
exploited by WAS and some of the key changes to the IBM JVM to provide those features.
IBM currently has to license the source code for the JVM to target IBM-specific hardware,
and then has to target the given processor (e.g., POWER), and only then can it give the JVM
the "value-added" features to exploit particular IBM hardware. The license for producing a
JVM is very specific in that it must be provided with some other IBM product, such as WAS
for environments such as Windows or the hardware itself as is the case with the IBM POWER
processor family. The licensing is restrictive, which makes sense if Java standards are to be
adhered to, and costly in that each time the base Sun JVM source changes IBM has to apply
its own changes to the Sun code again, which can be problematic if the changes are in the
same places.

The value-added features that IBM provides can exploit particular features of the hardware, so on the POWER6 processor, the Virtual Partition Memory features that allow code
to be seen between POWER Logical Partitions (LPARs) and Workload Partitions (WPARs) is
exploited, as is the page-size handling, short pointer offset handling, asynchronous I/O features, and specific `BigInteger` acceleration on the processor. This all makes software running
on top of the IBM JVM, known as J9, faster and more efficient, which is the case with WAS.

The license restrictions set by Sun make it difficult to be responsive to Java changes and to target non-IBM hardware, so IBM has been a contributor to the Apache Harmony open source JVM and has begun rolling the code for that back into the J9 JVM. This also allows IBM to use the most optimal code, using the Sun JVM implementation where it performs best and using the Apache Harmony code where it is more efficient. This is not the first time that IBM has ventured into the open source JVM-related market; IBM contributed the Jikes JIT compiler.

IBM J9 JVM for Java 6 Features

The Java J9 JVM for Java 6 shipped with WAS 7, with other IBM software, and for use on IBM hardware is based on the third generation of the J9 JVM that was introduced with the Java 5 release. The core code is still derived from a licensed Sun JVM implementation that IBM enhances and builds upon for its own products.

For the Java 5 release, the product was rewritten to incorporate features from a traditional optimizing compiler, to support pluggable features and libraries suited to different types of platforms, to have enhanced type safe and generational garbage collection features, and to support class sharing of read-only immutable optimized class information. The Java 6 release essentially tuned the environment more in terms of improved optimization, further garbage collection enhancements, and improved class sharing.

The original features of the Java J9 JVM for Java 5 were

- Shared classes

- Type safe and generational garbage collection

- Asynchronous, queued compilation in a background thread

- Five levels of code optimization with continuous sampling and profiling

- Support for specific hardware optimizations such as large page sizes

- Support for Reliability, Availability, and Serviceability (RAS) enhancements

- Common code base for all Java platform editions with pluggable interfaces

- Class library independence

- Java 5 language features (autoboxing, generics, enumerations, annotations, for each loop, library enhancements for concurrency and management, JVM Tool Interface [JVMTI])

The Java 6 release adds the following features:

- The use of some Apache Harmony code in place of some Sun code, which greatly improves performance in some areas (e.g., TreeMap).

- Compressed references (i.e., use offsets rather than full 64-bit addresses to improve memory footprint and performance)

- Incremental improvements to garbage collection and class sharing

- Exploitation of new hardware features on POWER and z/Architecture platforms

What Does a Java Virtual Machine Do?

In its purest sense a JVM simply runs an instruction set for a machine that doesn't exist in hardware but rather in software. Essentially, it needs to do all of the things that a real machine, with its processor and operating system, does. So, it must

- Handle multitasking/multithreading
- Allocate and manage memory
- Load and free applications and classes
- Verify the classes loaded will not damage the virtual machine or other classes
- Secure the environment to ensure the code can do only what it is authorized to do
- Manage I/O
- Run the instructions of the given instruction set

The definition of what the JVM has to support in terms of instructions and behavior is provided in the Java Virtual Machine Specification available from Sun and can be ratified by an extensive test suite. The general architecture of a generic JVM is outlined in Figure 2-1.

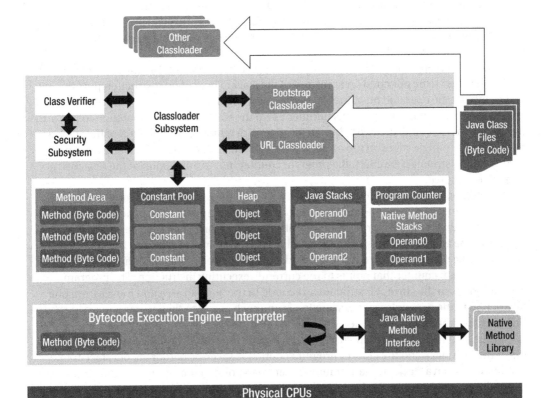

Figure 2-1. *Architecture of a generic Java Virtual Machine*

You've seen the architecture from a high level—i.e., the static picture of the JVM—but this doesn't tell you how it all works. For the dynamic picture, you have to understand the use of memory (i.e., the stack and heap, and garbage collection), operations and how they relate to the memory usage, and how the operations are loaded into the JVM (i.e., class files and class loaders). Viewing the dynamic behavior of these processing attributes will make clear to you how the static architecture is used to make the JVM do its work.

Virtual Machine Stack-Based Architecture

The JVM has a stack-based architecture rather than a register-based architecture like physical hardware, and it is this feature that allows the JVM to run the same code irrespective of the real hardware. Register-based machines differ in the size and number of registers and how they are used with respect to main memory. Operands are loaded from memory onto a software stack and operated on there. In many ways the closest real architecture to this is the Reduced Instruction Set Computing (RISC) model implemented in processors such as the POWER processors, where the load-store nature of operating only on registers that are mapped to memory contents via explicit instructions is akin to copying values to the top of the stack before operating on them.

With a stack-based architecture, the operands for an instruction or method call are pushed onto the stack like plates in a restaurant plate dispenser, and then the operation takes place and leaves the result on the top of the stack. The only artifact like a register is the program counter that works just like that on a real processor in keeping track of the current instruction being executed.

Consider a method that adds two numbers, shown in Figure 2-2. The first instruction puts the first number to be operated on at the top of the stack. The second instruction puts the second number to be operated on at the top of the stack, which has the effect of moving the stack up and seeming to push the previous number down the stack. When the operation to perform the addition is executed, the two values to be added are removed from the top of the stack and replaced with a single value on top of the stack that is the result of the addition. Throughout this, as each instruction executes, the program counter moves on to point at the next instruction to be executed.

In addition to stack operations in place of registers, the normal stack operations that take place on traditional processors and operating systems still happen when a method is invoked; i.e., a stack frame is created for the method call. The collection of stack frames is the Java Stack and the frame at the top that is currently executing is the active stack frame. The stack frame consists of the operands passed to the method, enough space to hold all of the local variables, and the program counter that points to the currently executing instruction. The program counter points to the current instruction executing in the method area and moves from one instruction to the next unless the instruction is one such as a goto that causes a jump in execution to some other point in the method.

When a method call is executed, a new stack frame is created, and this becomes the top of the Java stack and the current program counter is saved as part of the old stack frame before the new Java stack program counter is set up to point to the first instruction in the new method. When the new method completes and returns, the program counter is set to the next instruction in the original method following the method call.

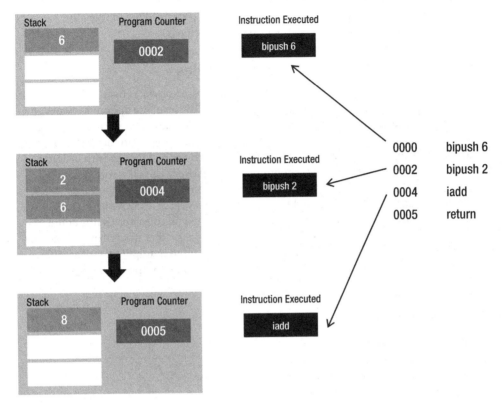

Figure 2-2. *Operation to add two numbers and the effect on the Java stack*

As native code—i.e., non-Java code that exists outside of the JVM but that is accessed via a Java Native Interface (JNI) class interface—may work differently from how the JVM works and thus cannot be guaranteed from a verification point of view, separate stacks are used for JNI managed code.

Heap

The heap is another area of memory outside of the stack. Objects are created using classes as a template and are stored on the heap. Each object contains a reserved piece of memory for each nonstatic field or variable within the object, which includes the reservations for the class template, the superclass template, and so on.

The heap often contains tens of thousands or millions of objects. The references to the objects used in methods and method calls are usually held on the stack within a stack frame.

In the past, one of the common causes of programming errors in C and C++ was poor management of memory, usually the freeing of memory (C) or deleting of objects (C++)—or more accurately, not doing these properly, which leads to heap memory leaks. To avoid this problem, Java uses garbage collection, where objects that are no longer referenced directly or indirectly are removed. This lack of references can happen when an object created with a reference on the stack is no longer accessible when the method returns and the stack frame is deleted. Garbage collection traditionally takes place on a thread using a mark-and-sweep mechanism, where objects that are believed to no longer be referenced are marked for deletion and, if not accessed by the time of the next sweep, deleted.

Java Byte Code, Instructions, and Class Files

The instructions that handle the operations on the operands are known as byte code. Byte code is essentially the machine code of the JVM. To illustrate the level the operations work at, consider the Jasmine assembler written to explain the JVM operation where a mnemonic maps to a single bytecode instruction, with the javap utility that comes with the JVM allowing the output of an existing class file in assembler form that can be edited for use with Jasmine.

The instructions of even the simplest program show that every class is a subclass of java.lang.Object and every class has an underlying <init> "method" that essentially implements the constructor. Calling a method uses the invokevirtual, invokenonvirtual, invokestatic, or invokeinterface operation. Classes are named like directory paths at the bytecode level; i.e., java/lang/Object relates to java.lang.Object. Operations exist to load different integral data types to and from positions on the stack and to manipulate those values.

Consider Listing 2-1, a typical minimal class implementation to output a message to a user.

Listing 2-1. *A Simple Java Class to Output a Message*

```
package com.myname.mypackage;
public class MyMessageOutputter {
        private final String myMessage = "Hello from the JVM!";
        private String message;

        public MyMessageOutputter() {
                message = myMessage;
        }

        public void outputMessage() throws Exception {
                System.out.println(message);
        }

        public static void main(String[] args) {
                MyMessageOutputter mmo = new MyMessageOutputter();
                try {
                        mmo.outputMessage();
                } catch (Exception e) {
                        e.printStackTrace();
                }
        }
}
```

The standard JVM environment includes a tool to turn this into byte code and mnemonics called javap. This outputs this class as the assembler-level listing shown in Listing 2-2.

Listing 2-2. *Assembler-Level Listing of the Minimal Class*

```
colin@ubuntu:~/testclass/test$ javap -c -s com.myname.mypackage.MyMessageOutputter
Compiled from "MyMessageOutputter.java"
public class com.myname.mypackage.MyMessageOutputter extends java.lang.Object{
public com.myname.mypackage.MyMessageOutputter();
  Signature: ()V
  Code:
   0:   aload_0
   1:   invokespecial  #14; //Method java/lang/Object."<init>":()V
   4:   aload_0
   5:   ldc  #8; //String Hello from the JVM!
   7:   putfield  #16; //Field myMessage:Ljava/lang/String;
   10:  aload_0
   11:  ldc  #8; //String Hello from the JVM!
   13:  putfield  #18; //Field message:Ljava/lang/String;
   16:  return

public void outputMessage()    throws java.lang.Exception;
  Signature: ()V
  Code:
   0:   getstatic  #28; //Field java/lang/System.out:Ljava/io/PrintStream;
   3:   aload_0
   4:   getfield  #18; //Field message:Ljava/lang/String;
   7:   invokevirtual  #34; //Method java/io/PrintStream.println:(Ljava/lang/String;)V
   10:  return

public static void main(java.lang.String[]);
  Signature: ([Ljava/lang/String;)V
  Code:
   0:   new  #1; //class com/myname/mypackage/MyMessageOutputter
   3:   dup
   4:   invokespecial  #42; //Method "<init>":()V
   7:   astore_1
   8:   aload_1
   9:   invokevirtual  #43; //Method outputMessage:()V
   12:  goto  20
   15:  astore_2
   16:  aload_2
   17:  invokevirtual  #45; //Method java/lang/Exception.printStackTrace:()V
   20:  return
  Exception table:
   from   to  target type
      8   12     15   Class java/lang/Exception
}
```

Statements in the byte code handle load and store operations to the stack, as shown in Listing 2-2 in the astore_2 and aload_2, astore_1 and aload_1, and aload_0 instructions that handle local reference variables 2, 1, and 0, respectively, by pushing them on to the top of the stack. The invokevirtual instructions operate on the operands pushed on to the top of the stack in reverse order, and the numbers after them refer to the method names from the method table. A hexdump of the class shows the layout of this class file and how the method names are referenced, as shown in Listing 2-3.

Listing 2-3. *Hexdump of the Byte Code in the Class File for the Minimal Class*

```
colin@ubuntu:~/testclass/test$ hd com/myname/mypackage/MyMessageOutputter.class
00000000  ca fe ba be 00 00 00 31  00 37 07 00 02 01 00 27  |.......1.7.....'|
00000010  63 6f 6d 2f 6d 79 6e 61  6d 65 2f 6d 79 70 61 63  |com/myname/mypac|
00000020  6b 61 67 65 2f 4d 79 4d  65 73 73 61 67 65 4f 75  |kage/MyMessageOu|
00000030  74 70 75 74 74 65 72 07  00 04 01 00 10 6a 61 76  |tputter......jav|
00000040  61 2f 6c 61 6e 67 2f 4f  62 6a 65 63 74 01 00 09  |a/lang/Object...|
00000050  6d 79 4d 65 73 73 61 67  65 01 00 12 4c 6a 61 76  |myMessage...Ljav|
00000060  61 2f 6c 61 6e 67 2f 53  74 72 69 6e 67 3b 01 00  |a/lang/String;..|
00000070  0d 43 6f 6e 73 74 61 6e  74 56 61 6c 75 65 08 00  |.ConstantValue..|
00000080  09 01 00 13 48 65 6c 6c  6f 20 66 72 6f 6d 20 74  |....Hello from t|
00000090  68 65 20 4a 56 4d 21 01  00 07 6d 65 73 73 61 67  |he JVM!...messag|
000000a0  65 01 00 06 3c 69 6e 69  74 3e 01 00 03 28 29 56  |e...<init>...()V|
000000b0  01 00 04 43 6f 64 65 0a  00 03 00 0f 0c 00 0b 00  |...Code.........|
000000c0  0c 09 00 01 00 11 0c 00  05 00 06 09 00 01 00 13  |................|
000000d0  0c 00 0a 00 06 01 00 0f  4c 69 6e 65 4e 75 6d 62  |........LineNumb|
000000e0  65 72 54 61 62 6c 65 01  00 12 4c 6f 63 61 6c 56  |erTable...LocalV|
000000f0  61 72 69 61 62 6c 65 54  61 62 6c 65 01 00 04 74  |ariableTable...t|
00000100  68 69 73 01 00 29 4c 63  6f 6d 2f 6d 79 6e 61 6d  |his..)Lcom/mynam|
00000110  65 2f 6d 79 70 61 63 6b  61 67 65 2f 4d 79 4d 65  |e/mypackage/MyMe|
00000120  73 73 61 67 65 4f 75 74  70 75 74 74 65 72 3b 01  |ssageOutputter;.|
00000130  00 0d 6f 75 74 70 75 74  4d 65 73 73 61 67 65 01  |..outputMessage.|
00000140  00 0a 45 78 63 65 70 74  69 6f 6e 73 07 00 1b 01  |..Exceptions....|
00000150  00 13 6a 61 76 61 2f 6c  61 6e 67 2f 45 78 63 65  |..java/lang/Exce|
00000160  70 74 69 6f 6e 09 00 1d  00 1f 07 00 1e 01 00 10  |ption..........|
00000170  6a 61 76 61 2f 6c 61 6e  67 2f 53 79 73 74 65 6d  |java/lang/System|
00000180  0c 00 20 00 21 01 00 03  6f 75 74 01 00 15 4c 6a  |.. .!...out...Lj|
00000190  61 76 61 2f 69 6f 2f 50  72 69 6e 74 53 74 72 65  |ava/io/PrintStre|
000001a0  61 6d 3b 0a 00 23 00 25  07 00 24 01 00 13 6a 61  |am;..#.%..$...ja|
000001b0  76 61 2f 69 6f 2f 50 72  69 6e 74 53 74 72 65 61  |va/io/PrintStrea|
000001c0  6d 0c 00 26 00 27 01 00  07 70 72 69 6e 74 6c 6e  |m..&.'...println|
000001d0  01 00 15 28 4c 6a 61 76  61 2f 6c 61 6e 67 2f 53  |...(Ljava/lang/S|
000001e0  74 72 69 6e 67 3b 29 56  01 00 04 6d 61 69 6e 01  |tring;)V...main.|
000001f0  00 16 28 5b 4c 6a 61 76  61 2f 6c 61 6e 67 2f 53  |..([Ljava/lang/S|
00000200  74 72 69 6e 67 3b 29 56  0a 00 01 00 0f 0a 00 01  |tring;)V........|
00000210  00 2c 0c 00 18 00 0c 0a  00 1a 00 2e 0c 00 2f 00  |.,........./.|
00000220  0c 01 00 0f 70 72 69 6e  74 53 74 61 63 6b 54 72  |....printStackTr|
00000230  61 63 65 01 00 04 61 72  67 73 01 00 13 5b 4c 6a  |ace...args...[Lj|
00000240  61 76 61 2f 6c 61 6e 67  2f 53 74 72 69 6e 67 3b  |ava/lang/String;|
00000250  01 00 03 6d 6d 6f 01 00  01 65 01 00 15 4c 6a 61  |...mmo...e...Lja|
00000260  76 61 2f 6c 61 6e 67 2f  45 78 63 65 70 74 69 6f  |va/lang/Exceptio|
```

```
00000270  6e 3b 01 00 0a 53 6f 75   72 63 65 46 69 6c 65 01   |n;...SourceFile.|
00000280  00 17 4d 79 4d 65 73 73   61 67 65 4f 75 74 70 75   |..MyMessageOutpu|
00000290  74 74 65 72 2e 6a 61 76   61 00 21 00 01 00 03 00   |tter.java.!.....|
000002a0  00 00 02 00 12 00 05 00   06 00 01 00 07 00 00 00   |................|
000002b0  02 00 08 00 02 00 0a 00   06 00 00 00 03 00 01 00   |................|
000002c0  0b 00 0c 00 01 00 0d 00   00 00 47 00 02 00 01 00   |..........G.....|
000002d0  00 00 11 2a b7 00 0e 2a   12 08 b5 00 10 2a 12 08   |...*...*.....*..|
000002e0  b5 00 12 b1 00 00 00 02   00 14 00 00 00 12 00 04   |................|
000002f0  00 00 00 08 00 04 00 05   00 0a 00 09 00 10 00 0a   |................|
00000300  00 15 00 00 00 0c 00 01   00 00 00 11 00 16 00 17   |................|
00000310  00 00 00 01 00 18 00 0c   00 02 00 19 00 00 00 04   |................|
00000320  00 01 00 1a 00 0d 00 00   00 39 00 02 00 01 00 00   |.........9......|
00000330  00 0b b2 00 1c 2a b4 00   12 b6 00 22 b1 00 00 00   |.....*....."....|
00000340  02 00 14 00 00 00 0a 00   02 00 00 00 0d 00 0a 00   |................|
00000350  0e 00 15 00 00 00 0c 00   01 00 00 00 0b 00 16 00   |................|
00000360  17 00 00 00 09 00 28 00   29 00 01 00 0d 00 00 00   |......(.).......|
00000370  6b 00 02 00 03 00 00 00   15 bb 00 01 59 b7 00 2a   |k...........Y..*|
00000380  4c 2b b6 00 2b a7 00 08   4d 2c b6 00 2d b1 00 01   |L+..+...M,..-...|
00000390  00 08 00 0c 00 0f 00 1a   00 02 00 14 00 00 00 16   |................|
000003a0  00 05 00 00 00 11 00 08   00 13 00 0f 00 14 00 10   |................|
000003b0  00 15 00 14 00 17 00 15   00 00 00 20 00 03 00 00   |........... ....|
000003c0  00 15 00 30 00 31 00 00   00 08 00 0d 00 32 00 17   |...0.1.......2..|
000003d0  00 01 00 10 00 04 00 33   00 34 00 02 00 01 00 35   |.......3.4.....5|
000003e0  00 00 00 02 00 36                                   |.....6|
000003e6
```

A class file can be identified, as you can see in the hexdump, by the signature "cafe babe" at the start (address 00000000), which is followed by minor and major versions of the Java language class file format specification this class adheres to, in this case major version 0x31 or 49. This signature in the class file is followed by the constant pool that identifies the constants used by the class, such as String values and method names. This is followed by class information such as access flags, number of interfaces, number methods, number of fields, etc.

A class file is loaded into the class area where its byte code for methods is loaded into the method area, and constants are copied into the constant pool. Classes are templates for object creation, and the objects created from them are placed on the heap. A class is loaded into the class area, which is the combination of the method area and the constant pool, by a classloader. When an object created from a class is no longer needed, it is garbage collected, and at some time after all objects based on that class have been removed, the class itself may also be garbage collected.

A class consists of a number of properties that are all immutable (i.e., cannot be changed), so to change these properties within the context of a class loader, the class itself has to be unloaded when all of its object references have been removed through garbage collection, after which a new version of the class can be loaded. The properties of the class are the inheritance hierarchy, particularly the superclass, the list of interfaces the class exposes, the list of fields and their accessibility, a list of methods and their implementations that are to be loaded into the method area, and a list of constants that are to be loaded into the constant pool. For Java 5 and higher, annotations are also stored.

Note For more information on the class file layout, consult *The Sun Java Virtual Machine Specification* or examine the Apache Harmony code.

Native Methods

To integrate with the underlying operating system environment or to perform low-level tasks that can't be done in Java, the Java specification supports the use of native code through the JNI specification, where external libraries (DLLs or shared objects) are dynamically loaded and then wrapped with Java classes. An inherent risk exists in native code where pointers are available, and there is nothing to protect code from itself, so the JVM has to protect itself as best it can. There is no direct integration between the JVM and the libraries loaded, and all interaction goes though the Java wrapper, so a separate native stack is used by the libraries when interacting with the JVM.

Garbage Collection

As mentioned earlier, the memory used by objects that are no longer accessible needs to be reclaimed, and the JVM solution for this is garbage collection.

If an object has a reference to it from the stack, in a local variable, in a static field, or in a field in another active object, then it is accessible and is not eligible for garbage collection. Some objects may be kept alive by the JVM to support its operations, such as for native methods.

In reality, there are two general types of object lifetimes, and in more complex garbage collection it makes sense to treat them differently, a technique called *generational garbage collection*. Applications tend to have some key objects, often singletons or management objects, that have long lifetimes that extend to that of the application as a whole, i.e., thread pool managers, services, etc.; but applications also have considerably more short-lived objects that exist just for the lifetime of a single method—these are young objects.

According to the Sun JVM Specification, a developer has no control as to when garbage collection is run. It may run when available memory is low, to a schedule, when the system has idle cycles free, or as a result of a developer invoking the System.gc method. As a result of this, finalize methods should not be relied upon because there is no control as to when or even whether they are going to get called.

Garbage collection may involve all threads being paused while garbage collection takes place on a foreground thread or it may run continually in a background thread. A great deal of research has been devoted to finding the most effective garbage collection techniques and there are books on the subject. The most common technique is the mark-and-sweep technique in which the garbage collector periodically marks each of the objects referenced from the Java stack collection of stack frames, operand stacks, and local variables as live, and then all objects referenced from the objects marked as live are also marked live. Any objects not referenced are not accessible and thus can be considered garbage. Periodically a sweep occurs that deletes the unreferenced objects, and the remaining objects may be moved and coalesced to remove memory fragmentation in a process known as *compaction*. This process can be slow, so having multiple memory pools that are checked separately or having generational pools based on when and how an object is created can also speed up the process.

Class Loading and Verification

One of the key features of the Java language is its security and verification mechanism and the use of classloaders to provide some levels of isolation between code. The specification covers two key classloaders and the verification rules required to check a class file when it is loaded.

Every JVM must have a bootstrap classloader that is (usually) responsible for loading the classes that are needed to get the base JVM code running. This tends to be the only classloader that is not implemented in Java but rather in the native language used to implement the JVM itself. Then, a number of other classloaders are used to build up a parent-child hierarchy of classloaders that each provides a protection domain for the classes it loads, with a system class-loader at the bottom of the chain and various user-defined classloaders that are derived from the URLClassLoader or the SecureClassLoader. Threads have a context classloader. Java EE has specific rules for how classloaders are configured to load libraries, i.e., parent first, parent last, etc.

Classloading is a two-step process—loading, and linking and verification—handled by the loadClass method of the classloader, which must always be a derivative of java.lang.ClassLoader.

The first phase, loading, gets the bytes that make up the class and loads them into memory, where they are passed to the JVM environment as the official implementation of a given class. The specification does not limit the locations from which the class can be loaded, so a database, file system, web page, or any other storage mechanism can be used; the only requirement is that the class is loaded and provided to the JVM in the class file format. To fully populate the class information, the class loader must also load the superclass, and the entire parent hierarchy of the class. This provides the class file, all fields and methods, and the class hierarchy information to the core of the JVM. From Java 5 onward, the annotations also are loaded and are made available for APIs to access, but beyond the use as deployment or developer information, or placeholders, these annotations have no effect on the running of the JVM.

The second phase, linking and verification, is more complex. Unlike other languages, all linking in Java is dynamic. In this phase the class hierarchy loaded is verified to ensure that it is well formed and complies with the Java security constraints. As a side effect of this loading additional classes may be loaded.

The verification process within the second classloading phase is multistep. First the class file is checked to make sure that it is of the correct format (i.e., the magic numbers, method counts, field counts, and interface counts match the values expected, etc.), has valid constants, has valid instructions (valid operation codes with the right number of variables, branches that point to instructions, valid stacks and arrays referenced by instructions, correct types for instructions, etc.), has valid external references, and obeys the syntax rules of Java. The class is then initialized by allocating space for variables and assigning default values. Finally, the class clinit method of the class is called by the JVM to bring the class into a ready state before execution.

The separation of loading and linking avoids loop dependencies in the classes that reference each other. The verification process also makes use of the security verifier to ensure that the class can do only what it is allowed to do before it executes.

Threads and Synchronization

The Java language is unlike most other languages in specifying threading and thread synchronization as part of the language rather than the platform, leaving it up to the JVM implementor to decide whether the threads will truly run concurrently or sequentially with some context swapping. By defining threading at the language level rather than the platform level, true portability can be obtained, but some of the synchronization semantics that are easily achieved in hardware and an OS for protection from re-entrancy (i.e., atomic test and set) are harder to achieve in software, so the JVM has specific noninterruptable instructions for this. Thus, the synchronized keyword results in an object or class being locked, and this results in the use of the monitorenter and monitorexit instructions being used in the code that prevents concurrent access to the object or class from other threads running inside the JVM.

Threads are literally just developer constructs that enable the declaration of bundles of operations that can be run concurrently and for which priorities and dependencies can be defined. The bundles of threads can also be grouped. Conversely, while a developer defines the grouping of instructions that can be run concurrently on a thread, some parts of the core runtime are *not* thread safe and therefore cannot be accessed concurrently from multiple threads. The Java 5 standard improved on the base Java thread classes and the implementation in java.lang.Object for concurrency support by adding new higher-level java.util. concurrent classes and some thread-safe utility structural classes (i.e., java.util.Queue).

Code Generation

Despite statements to the contrary, it is perfectly possible to execute languages other than Java on a JVM, with the only requirement being that the language can work on operands on the stack and be compiled down to byte code that gets loaded in classes.

Once the byte code has been produced, it can be optimized using similar techniques as have been used for many years in optimizing compilers. This may be through removal of unnecessary instructions, constant propagation (variables are replaced with constants), strength reduction (complex instructions such as multiplications are replaced by shift operations), loop unrolling (a loop that executes a known number of times is replaced by inlined copies of the loop block), or inlining itself (method calls are replaced by the code from the target method). The optimizations performed must be considered carefully so as to not change the interface contract or break the Java specification; e.g., inlining is fine for private methods but not public ones.

Importantly, the preceding paragraph does not mention anything about how the JVM instructions are executed. The specification leaves to the implementor to decide whether to interpret every instruction to map it down to the underlying hardware instructions or to perform a "just in time" (JIT) compilation to turn the class into executable code just before it executes. As the class loader can be used dynamically via the Class.forName mechanism, an option to precompile everything into a binary executable native to the hardware before execution is not a valid one.

Inside the IBM J9 JVM for Java 6

The IBM J9 JVM is derived from the Sun JVM source code, with a considerable number of IBM extensions added. It supports various sizes and implementations of JVM for different platforms (MIDP up to Java SE) with a common code base by having some components be "pluggable"—that is, they are loaded dynamically into the JVM to provide additional functionality. The JVM Profiler, JIT Compiler, Debugger, and Realtime Profiler are all pluggable subsystems, with the JVM Profiler and JIT Compiler being essential for normal WAS operation. To support different runtime environments, the JVM also supports pluggable Java class libraries.

General Architecture

The IBM J9 JVM has a number of important subsystems, as shown in Figure 2-3. When set up for use by WAS, where the library required is always Java SE 6, which uses the Apache Harmony TreeMap implementation that greatly improves performance, some of the subsystems that are pluggable can always be assumed to be present.

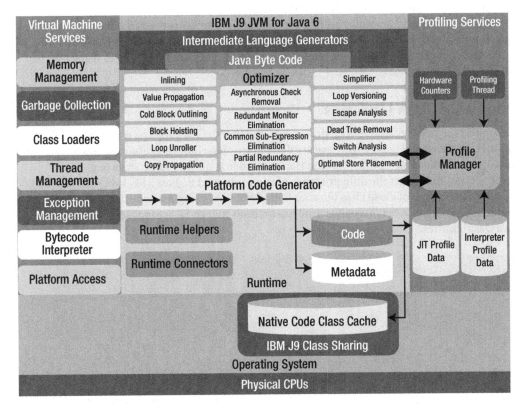

Figure 2-3. *The IBM J9 Java Virtual Machine architecture*

At the core of the J9 implementation is the Virtual Machine Services subsystem, along with the code generators and the runtime. The JIT Compiler with the optimization facilities and the Profiling Services are pluggable components that are key for WAS. The class-sharing mechanism is external, but with the help of the memory-mapped files implementation and the com.ibm.cds.jar code with the Eclipse runtime, this provides optimized class native code sharing across JVM instances and, with the help of Virtual Partition Memory on System p/AIX with the POWER6 Hypervisor, even across LPARs and OS instances.

The Virtual Machine Services include the memory-management facilities, which include the mixed pointer support for 32-bit addresses used for most operations and 64-bit only where necessary to get the extra performance of 32-bit addresses and the extra memory accessibility of 64-bit addressing. This is known as *compressed references support*.

The JVM also includes the garbage collection facilities that assist the memory management. The bootstrap and shared classes class loaders and class verification are implemented within the Virtual Machine Services subsystem, as would be expected from the generic JVM architecture.

Thread and Exception management and Platform Services access are managed to support the actual runtime facilities required by the language and the mapping of the Java implementation onto the target OS environment. Finally, the Byte Code Interpreter is part of these services.

The Optimizer is part of the JIT Compiler and provides a number of optimization techniques to improve code performance, and this requires the Profiling Services support to generate the statistics to support the cost-benefit heuristics to identify the most appropriate optimizations to apply for each piece of code.

The platform code generator is platform specific and supports the generation of the native code for the platform, and on the Java 6 release this native code is also shared between WAS instances within an OS image, if the platform supports it, and across OS images using the class-sharing mechanism.

Pluggable Class Libraries

To support the needs of different environments, the IBM J9 JVM supports pluggable class libraries, as shown in Figure 2-4. These are derivatives of the Sun class libraries, but for the Java 6 version, the more optimal Apache Harmony code is used in some areas (e.g., the TreeMap class) that target the different types of environment, i.e., Java 5 SE, Java 6 SE, CLDC, CDC, or MIDP. Each of these class libraries is implemented using JNI code using the Java Class Library (JCL) natives, a set of a native implementations that can be composed to support the Java class libraries.

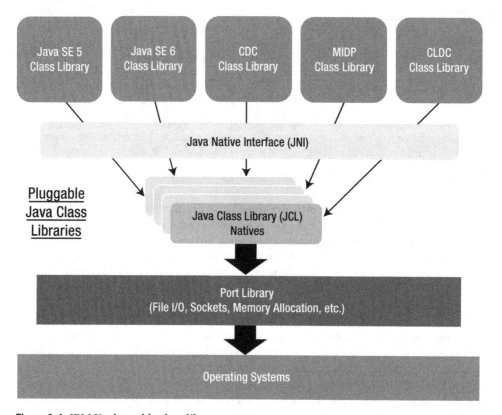

Figure 2-4. *IBM J9 pluggable class library support*

The Port library that underpins the JCL natives is a thin native layer that isolates the use of OS-specific services and resources and handles memory access, file management, threading, IP sockets, locks, I/O, and interrupts. This protects the higher layers of the class libraries from having to know the details of the underlying platform.

Multiple independent port libraries can be simultaneously supported. The shared objects and DLLs that are installed with the JVM provide this functionality. Under the WAS installation directory, there is a java subdirectory and under this a lib directory. For the given platform, in this case Linux, the DLLs or shared objects can be found in a directory that is named in relation to the platform type. For a Linux platform, this is shown in Listing 2-4.

Listing 2-4. *IBM J9 JVM Shared Objects*

```
  71198  2 Mar 05:04 libJdbcOdbc.so
  12400  2 Mar 05:04 libattach.so
 592021  2 Mar 05:04 libawt.so
 398182  2 Mar 05:04 libcmm.so
 181185  2 Mar 05:04 libdcpr.so
  89831  2 Mar 05:04 libdeploy.so
  18108  2 Mar 05:04 libdt_socket.so
 636345  2 Mar 05:04 libfontmanager.so
 231258  2 Mar 05:04 libhprof.so
  45881  2 Mar 05:04 libinstrument.so
  20138  2 Mar 05:04 libioser12.so
  83316  2 Mar 05:04 libiverel24.so
  98406  2 Mar 05:04 libj9bcv24.so
 235828  2 Mar 05:04 libj9dbg24.so
 160515  2 Mar 05:04 libj9dmp24.so
 149695  2 Mar 05:04 libj9dyn24.so
 662303  2 Mar 05:04 libj9gc24.so
  81603  2 Mar 05:04 libj9gcchk24.so
  18227  2 Mar 05:04 libj9hookable24.so
   6479  2 Mar 05:04 libj9jar24.so
1068918  2 Mar 05:04 libj9jextract.so
5363542  2 Mar 05:04 libj9jit24.so
 347232  2 Mar 05:04 libj9jitd24.so
 130975  2 Mar 05:04 libj9jnichk24.so
 255521  2 Mar 05:04 libj9jvmti24.so
 170749  2 Mar 05:04 libj9prt24.so
  20359  2 Mar 05:04 libj9rdbi24.so
 322595  2 Mar 05:04 libj9shr24.so
  58518  2 Mar 05:04 libj9thr24.so
  63188  2 Mar 05:04 libj9trc24.so
 106925  2 Mar 05:04 libj9ute24.so
 597923  2 Mar 05:04 libj9vm24.so
 185345  2 Mar 05:04 libj9vrb24.so
  60154  2 Mar 05:04 libj9zlib24.so
   6019  2 Mar 05:04 libjaas.so
```

```
   8786  2 Mar 05:04 libjaasauth.so
 161860  2 Mar 05:04 libjava.so
  25123  2 Mar 05:04 libjava_crw_demo.so
  80858  2 Mar 05:04 libjavaplugin_jni.so
 262805  2 Mar 05:04 libjavaplugin_nscp.so
   5316  2 Mar 05:04 libjawt.so
 521396  2 Mar 05:04 libjclscar_24.so
 275883  2 Mar 05:04 libjdwp.so
 209044  2 Mar 05:04 libjpeg.so
 147099  2 Mar 05:04 libjpkcs11.so
  11306  2 Mar 05:04 libjsig.so
 238170  2 Mar 05:04 libjsound.so
  75182  2 Mar 05:04 libjsoundalsa.so
   5508  2 Mar 05:04 libmanagement.so
 833884  2 Mar 05:04 libmlib_image.so
  99352  2 Mar 05:04 libnet.so
  41461  2 Mar 05:04 libnio.so
  12840  2 Mar 05:04 libnpt.so
   4835  2 Mar 05:04 librmi.so
 268767  2 Mar 05:04 libsplashscreen.so
 132819  2 Mar 05:04 libunpack.so
  77080  2 Mar 05:04 libzip.so
```

Code Optimization

With the third-generation J9 JVM, the features of an optimizing compiler are used, but at run-time in the JVM. Byte code may run interpreted on the JVM, but in most cases commonly used code is optimized by the Testarossa JIT compiler.

Traditionally, byte code is loaded by the JVM and either interpreted on an instruction-by-instruction basis or passed to a JIT compiler on a synchronous thread for compilation. The IBM J9 JVM handles things differently. Cost-based analysis is used to assess whether a class should be interpreted or compiled asynchronously on a background thread by the Testarossa JIT compiler and what level of optimization is worth performing. Optimization is expensive on CPU and memory resources, so heuristics determine the expense of each level of optimization for a particular piece of code, and this is compared with the time taken to execute the code at each level of optimization and an assessment as to how often it is likely to be run based on the previous number of executions.

There are five levels of execution, with interpreted being the lowest and slowest, and native code compilation and multilevel optimization making up the other four levels. The JVM identifies the potential benefits of optimization for a method by assigning it a temperature level from cold (poorly optimized), through hot, to scorching.

During code execution, the JVM profiles each class to gather the statistics, using a combination of methods. The interpreted code is profiled using JVM interpreter sampling of execution time. The JIT compiler also performs sampling. The JVM may even insert profiling hooks into the code itself.

The JVM, and thus WAS running on it, is self-optimizing, and the applications running on it may get faster over time as the statistics of application usage get ever more detailed. This is attributable to a process known as dynamic recompilation with runtime execution profiling where heavily used classes and methods are identified, assessed for the benefits of additional optimization, and then recompiled with further optimizations on a background thread with the resulting code transactionally replacing the code in the native compiled code pool.

Every class and method starts out as interpreted code running directly on the JVM at level 1 optimization. The heuristics are used against the statistics gathered as the code executes to assess the benefits of optimization, and this may result in commonly executed code being passed on a background thread to the Testarossa JIT compiler for optimization to cold or warm levels to replace the interpreted code execution. In the background, the sampling thread executes to identify hot methods that could benefit from further optimization. Hot methods may be considered worthy of profiling to gain statistics for a cost-benefit analysis of further scorching optimization, so for these, profiling hooks are inserted. Both the JVM interpreter and the JIT compiler perform profiling and analysis of methods to get the statistics used for optimization.

So, the five levels of optimization are interpreted, cold compiled, hot compiled, hot compiled and profiling, and scorching. This can best be understood with an example. If a method takes 0.2 second to execute and could be optimized to execute in 0.1 second if 0.2 second of effort was put into optimizing it, there is no benefit for the resource cost if the code is only executed once. However, if the code is executed more than twice, the benefits outweigh the cost because the optimization takes place only once but the benefits are realized on every execution.

The IBM J9 JIT compiler performs a large number of optimizations. Its functionality is similar to that of the IBM C/C++ optimizing compilers, and in many cases the dynamic nature of its operation and runtime environment leads to the code it produces running faster on the J9 JVM than if equivalent code was compiled and run natively.

When the Testarossa JIT compiler operates, it takes byte code and converts it to an intermediate language (IL) tree form at a level between that of machine code and byte code, and this level facilities control graph analysis and optimization. The optimizations performed are outlined in Table 2-1.

Table 2-1. *IBM J9 Testarossa JIT Compiler Optimizations*

Optimization Technique	Description
Inlining	The call to a method is replaced by the method body itself. This saves the setup of the call stack, but adds to code size in memory so is only for relatively small methods. Cache sizes affect the performance impact in that the bigger code sequence must fit in the cache.
Cold block outlining	Code that isn't used often is moved out of the normal code sequence to reduce gaps in the instruction stream to make better use of the cache and to avoid jump instructions. Often the code moved out is for error or exception handling.
Value propagation	Variables and their values are tracked and the variables are replaced by the constant values, where it makes sense, to avoid extra memory/stack references.
Block hoisting	Code that is invariant and that need not be executed repeatedly in a loop is taken outside of the loop.
Loop unroller	The number of iterations of a loop is reduced by duplicating the body of the loop sequentially within it.

Continued

Table 2-1. *Continued*

Optimization Technique	Description
Asynchronous check removal	Java insists on checks on code to maintain its integrity. Those checks that are unnecessary because they have already been performed elsewhere in the code path are removed.
Copy propagation	Replace occurrences of direct assignment targets with their values.
Loop versioning	Array index checking is expensive, particularly when repeated in a loop, so this creates unsafe code that performs array bounds checks and safe code that doesn't require the check outside the loop. The index is then checked on entry to decide which version of the code should be used.
Common subexpression elimination	Instances of identical expressions or subexpressions that equate to the same value are replaced with a variable and a single sub-expression calculation. This sort of optimization is often used in looping.
Partial redundancy elimination	Partially redundant code exists in only some paths through a program, so the aim of partial redundancy elimination is to place the expression on all paths through the program and compensate for it to make it fully redundant. It reduces access to instance variables and moves invariant code out of loops.
Optimal store placement	Heuristics are applied to determine what variables should be cached in registers from the stack and local variables and what can be left in memory.
Simplifier	Complex expressions and code are replaced by simpler and faster equivalents.
Escape analysis	The scope of references are checked (i.e., whether they get passed to other methods) and any optimizations of simplifications are performed based on the results.
Dead tree removal	Code is compiled by building expression trees that are closer to machine code representations. Some trees are unreachable or have no effect on the behavior of the code and thus are removed.
Switch analysis	Branch conditions are optimized and combined and invariant code is moved out of the conditions.
Redundant monitor elimination	The synchronized keyword puts monitors into the code to handle re-entrancy, but sometimes this is unnecessary because re-entrancy is already handled, so the monitors are removed.
Devirtualization	Virtual method calls are replaced with faster nonvirtual or static calls to avoid the overhead of late binding.
Partial inlining	Large methods are broken up into hot (frequently executed) and cold (infrequently executed) portions, which may make the hot code small enough to benefit from being inlined.
Lock coarsening	In adjacent code protected by locks (synchronized), the lock overhead can be reduced by a merged set of code with a single lock.
Register allocators	Analysis is performed to make the best use of system registers to maximize performance.
Live range reduction	Where the range of a variable is known at runtime, its value bounds can be used to perform code optimization.
Idiom recognition	Commonly used bytecode sequences are replaced by optimized code that cuts down on the overhead of stack usage.

All of these features are added to by the additional facility of supporting hot code replace (HCR), where recently modified code is loaded transactionally to replace that currently executing to assist in development, and full-speed debug (FSD).

Class Cache and Sharing

When a class is first used, it is loaded and split into ROMClass and RAMClass information, where the ROMClass information is the immutable information pertaining to the class, such as the byte code and constants, and the RAMClass information is the local data that changes with every instance of the class. The ROMClass information has a signature associated with it that is used to detect if the class has changed on disk during its lifetime and, if so, it is reloaded.

The ROMClass information is loaded in the class cache for class sharing. The com.ibm.cds.jar plug-in for Eclipse handles integrating this into the WAS component-loading mechanism.

In the previous, Java 5 version of the third-generation J9 JVM, the class-sharing mechanism was limited by using shared memory. This effectively limited its memory usage to about 50MB on a Unix system to avoid impacting other processes, but it did substantially improve startup time and reduce memory overhead because the shared class cache was shared between JVM instances running in a single OS image. It contained the ROMClass information, as this can safely be shared across JVMs, and optimized byte code/IL code to speed up all JVMs. So, in general usage, as one WAS instance on a node gets faster, the performance of all JVMs improves. Security is provided by sharing the class cache between users in the same primary group, i.e., the user IDs under which WAS runs. The semaphores protecting concurrent access to the class cache can be identified by looking in the /tmp/javasharedresources directory on a Unix platform.

The use of shared memory for the class-sharing implementation was a limiting factor in the Java 5 release, as the 50MB practical limit was brought about because shared memory gets mapped into every process address space. For the Java 6 implementation, memory-mapped files are used, the advantage of which is that the file backing up memory-mapped files can be stored in a shared location on the physical machine and mapped into multiple OS images to allow class sharing across virtualized partitions. With the Java 6 version, the optimized native code is stored in the shared cache if available. If this is coupled with IBM features like the POWER Virtual Partition Memory facility, then common code across partitions results in a single copy of the binaries being in real memory no matter how many OS images are running and no matter how many WAS instances are running.

Garbage Collection

Garbage collection is one of the key features of the JVM that a vendor can capitalize on. There are a number of algorithms implemented that vary as to how the objects are stored on the heap and how the applications running behave with respect to object creation.

The default mark-and-sweep mechanism that is suitable for most applications is given by the optthruput setting. This has some intermingling of garbage collection and application work for good raw throughput for an average application. The application is paused each time garbage collection occurs, so some GC (garbage collection) pause must be acceptable for this option to be used. As this is the default and all objects are considered in the same way, this is the starting point for tuning.

For many applications, particularly with web services–based JAX-RPC applications or those using rules engines where a large number of objects are repeatedly created and destroyed, generational collection is advised and is set by the gencon setting. In this there are some objects at the application level that are long lived, but on repeated code or code answering a request, there are large numbers of objects created in a short time that are used and then released when the request completes, the transaction commits, or the loop ends. These objects are young objects so they should be separated from the older, long-lived objects to avoid heap space memory fragmentation issues. In this the nursery, or young, objects are kept in their own space that can be managed and freed via direct copying and deallocation, and a separate garbage collection phase called a minor collection takes place on this space regularly. Older objects migrate to the old generation space, and this is managed via the traditional mark-and-sweep garbage collection that covers both the young and old objects followed by a compaction. This mechanism improves performance and reduces memory fragmentation.

Some applications (but not WAS normally unless it is operating with a heap above 4GB and is running on a 64-bit JVM) benefit from the use of the optavgpause garbage collection setting, which minimizes the GC pause time at the cost of a little overall performance reduction.

For use on large multiprocessor machines where there is an overhead on contention for the heap from multiple concurrent threads running on different processors, the subpool GC policy can be set, which effectively splits the heap into multiple pools that are managed separately.

All of the preceding mechanisms are implemented with a set of algorithms for garbage collection and a set of algorithms for memory management that are handled by the JVM according to a single policy set by the gcpolicy command-line switch that causes the appropriate algorithms to be loaded.

Java Standard Library and Apache Harmony

I have briefly mentioned the mechanism used to implement the Java standard libraries and how the native code and port mechanisms work. One of the issues IBM has had with the JVMs is the license restriction from Sun on using and deploying the IBM J9 JVM except with another IBM product. Some of the licensed code carries an additional burden in performance. IBM has found major performance enhancements for WAS in the use of the Apache Harmony TreeMap implementation instead of the Sun version. IBM is a contributor to Apache Harmony, so the integration was not problematic.

Much of the security, JavaBeans handling, JNDI handling, logging, JDBC, and the underlying JVM shared object/DLL layer implementation is implemented using Apache Harmony code. To see this, execute grep -R harmony * in the Java directory tree for the WAS installation. The use of Apache Harmony code in WAS is likely to continue to increase in the future.

Summary

This chapter examined the requirements, features, and some of the architecture of the Java language implementation and the Java Virtual Machine that supports it. The IBM J9 implementation was mapped onto this with a view of understanding the differences and the value-added features that the IBM J9 JVM brings to a WAS environment. Most notable among the features, beyond the optimizations, are the particular class library implementations that enhance performance, the optimization mechanisms in the JIT compiler, and the class-sharing mechanism.

CHAPTER 3

■ ■ ■

Eclipse/OSGi Runtime

The core of WebSphere Application Server is, as of version 6.1, an Eclipse plug-in and OSGi bundle in the truest sense; that is, it uses the necessary interfaces, is built in the appropriate way, and builds upon the expected behavior. Why has it been built this way? Well, this approach allows WAS to be componentized and extended in a safe, low-overhead, and dynamic way. Componentization is a key IBM objective for the future of WAS. Componentization supports a reduction in the WAS footprint, because only the facilities required are loaded. Componentization also provides a mechanism for extensibility because services are declared in a Service Registry, and components and subsystems can look up service interfaces in the Service Registry and build upon them.

The Eclipse project is best known for its integrated development environment (IDE), but at the detail level it defines an extensible architecture for general applications. The official description of Eclipse is "an open extensible IDE for anything and yet nothing in particular," but to support this goal, a runtime platform was required to allow easy addition of new functionality without affecting the core.

Eclipse runtime functionality offers many benefits to the general application, particularly in the support for extensibility. Eclipse has taken on the OSGi architecture to support bundles and service management to make that extensibility dynamic. An Eclipse/OSGi application must be built in a certain way. This chapter explains what this "way" is and how WAS conforms to it. It then shows how this benefits WAS. Finally, it examines how you can extend WAS yourself.

First, you must understand the Eclipse and OSGi architectures and runtimes so that you know where to look for them in WAS. This involves some basic coding and examination of the Eclipse and OSGi models. If you already understand the Eclipse and OSGi runtime models, then feel free to skip to the section "Monitoring the Internals of WAS," which puts these models into the context of WAS 7. If you are not a developer, but an advanced administrator, architect, or support technician, don't be alarmed by the prospect of coding; the examples are based on Eclipse code generators and are only simple code.

Finding the Eclipse/OSGi Runtime in WAS

One of the things that disturbs developers and administrators when they learn about the most current WAS version architectures is that the WAS runtime is an Eclipse plug-in. Most people in the Java trade associate Eclipse plug-ins with developer tools and the Eclipse IDE, and immediately their thoughts turn to rich client user interfaces, which clearly isn't something WAS is typically associated with. Eclipse has another side to it, though, that makes it so powerful on the server side for products such as WAS: its ability to dynamically support extension.

Evidence of WAS being tied into Eclipse can be found in the WAS startup command line that starts the underlying Eclipse runtime, as well as in the presence of `org.eclipse.*.jar` files in the `plugins` directory. In fact, even the existence of a `plugins` directory is a hint. Inside the `plugins` directory, you can find all of the following Eclipse JAR files, so the relationship between WAS and Eclipse is clearly a strong one:

```
org.eclipse.ant.core.jar

org.eclipse.core.runtime.compatibility.jar

org.eclipse.core.runtime_.jar

org.eclipse.emf.ecore.jar

org.eclipse.equinox.common_.jar

org.eclipse.equinox.registry.jar

org.eclipse.jdt.core.jar

org.eclipse.osgi_.jar

org.eclipse.update.configurator_.jar
```

Both Eclipse and WAS include their own Ant support to manage deployments. The `org.eclipse.core.runtime*`, `org.eclipse.equinox*`, `org.eclipse.osgi_.jar`, and `org.eclipse.update.configurator_.jar` files are all key parts of the most basic Eclipse/OSGi runtime in that they support the startup and infrastructure for Eclipse and its ability to support dynamic updates. The `org.eclipse.equinox.registry.jar` file handles the registry with which plug-in components register their extension points. The `org.eclipse.jdt.core.jar` file is used because some developer support is required to handle tasks such as debugging and compilation of deployed Java EE artifacts. The `org.eclipse.emf.ecore.jar` file, the main library for the Eclipse Modeling Framework (EMF), is key to the WAS support for some standards in that IBM creates the models in XML and then generates the supporting framework code. IBM has added an underscore (_) character to some of the names of the open source files, which normally end in the version number, to give IBM the flexibility to change versions, but they are the same files under the covers.

The underlying Eclipse/OSGi runtime for WAS 7 is from Eclipse 3.2.1. With the release of WAS 6.1, the underlying runtime of WAS moved to being Eclipse/OSGi-based, using the Eclipse Equinox features, to allow dynamic loading, dynamic extension, and dynamic service and extension registration to be added to the underlying features first shipped in WAS 6.0. The key here is that WAS could support dynamic configuration. This initial Eclipse runtime was Eclipse 3.1.2M6, using exactly the same code that can be downloaded for each of the target platforms for WAS in source form from http://www.eclipse.org. WAS 7 is evolutionary rather than revolutionary in that it uses the Eclipse 3.2.1 runtime rather than the more recent Eclipse 3.3 and 3.4 releases, primarily because version 3.2.1 supported the dynamic OSGi features yet had proven stability when IBM started developing WAS 7. For WAS 6.1, IBM used Eclipse 3.1.2, and 3.2.1 is architecturally similar to that.

To examine this further, take a look at the AppServer configuration directory and open the config.ini file, which contains a build identifier for the Eclipse runtime:

```
# The build identifier
eclipse.buildId=M20060921-0945
```

The build date here is 21 September 2006 at 09:45, exactly the time of the Eclipse 3.2.1 release. This doesn't prove adequately that this is a major version, so you need to look at the code. Copy the org.eclipse.core.runtime_.jar file to somewhere where you can examine it further, and look at the MANIFEST.MF file in the META-INF directory within it:

```
Manifest-Version: 1.0
Bundle-Name: %pluginName
Bundle-Activator: org.eclipse.core.internal.runtime.PlatformActivator
Bundle-RequiredExecutionEnvironment: CDC-1.0/Foundation-1.0,J2SE-1.3
Bundle-Vendor: %providerName
Bundle-ManifestVersion: 2
Bundle-Localization: plugin
Bundle-SymbolicName: org.eclipse.core.runtime; singleton:=true
Require-Bundle: org.eclipse.osgi;bundle-version="[3.2.0,4.0.0)";visibi
 lity:=reexport,org.eclipse.equinox.common;bundle-version="[3.2.0,4.0.
 0)";visibility:=reexport,org.eclipse.core.jobs;bundle-version="[3.2.0
 ,4.0.0)";visibility:=reexport,org.eclipse.equinox.registry;bundle-ver
 sion="[3.2.0,4.0.0)";visibility:=reexport,org.eclipse.equinox.prefere
 nces;bundle-version="[3.2.0,4.0.0)";visibility:=reexport,org.eclipse.
 core.contenttype;bundle-version="[3.2.0,4.0.0)";visibility:=reexport,
 org.eclipse.core.runtime.compatibility.auth;bundle-version="[3.2.0,4.
 0.0)";resolution:=optional
Export-Package: org.eclipse.core.internal.preferences.legacy;x-interna
 l:=true,org.eclipse.core.internal.runtime;x-friends:="org.eclipse.cor
 e.runtime.compatibility",org.eclipse.core.runtime
Bundle-Version: 3.2.0.v20060603
Eclipse-LazyStart: true
```

The Bundle-Version at the bottom of the file is 3.2.0v20060603. In the past IBM used to ship the Eclipse runtime files unchanged not only in their contents but also in their names, so you could easily determine the version of the runtime from the file name. Here you have to pay attention to the Bundle-Version and compare it to the Eclipse Plugin Version Table on the Eclipse.org site: http://wiki.eclipse.org/Eclipse_Plugin_Version_Table. The pertinent line from that table is shown in Table 3-1, indicating that this bundle ships with Eclipse 3.2.0 and Eclipse 3.2.1. Thus, more investigation is required.

Table 3-1. *Eclipse Core Runtime 3.2.x Releases*

Plug-in	3.2.0 Release	3.2.1 Release
org.eclipse.core.runtime	3.2.0.v20060603	3.2.0.v20060603

Take a look at the entry in the Eclipse Plugin Version Table for the org.eclipse.equinox. registry_.jar file, shown in Table 3-2. This file is distinct in each runtime version.

Table 3-2. *Eclipse Registry 3.2.x Releases*

Plug-in	3.2.0 Release	3.2.1 Release
org.eclipse.equinox.registry	3.2.0.v20060601	3.2.1.R32x_v20060814

So, having identified that the version of the Eclipse/OSGi runtime is most likely 3.2.1, look inside MANIFEST.MF file for the org.eclipse.equinox.registry.jar file for confirmation:

```
Manifest-Version: 1.0
Bundle-Activator: org.eclipse.core.internal.registry.osgi.Activator
Import-Package: org.eclipse.core.runtime.jobs;resolution:=optional,org
 .eclipse.osgi.storagemanager,org.eclipse.osgi.util,org.eclipse.osgi.s
 ervice.datalocation,org.eclipse.osgi.service.debug,org.eclipse.osgi.s
 ervice.environment,org.eclipse.osgi.service.resolver,org.osgi.framewo
 rk,org.osgi.service.packageadmin,org.osgi.util.tracker,org.xml.sax,or
 g.xml.sax.helpers,javax.xml.parsers
Bundle-RequiredExecutionEnvironment: J2SE-1.4,CDC-1.0/Foundation-1.0,J
 2SE-1.3
Export-Package: org.eclipse.core.internal.registry;x-friends:="org.ecl
 ipse.core.runtime",org.eclipse.core.internal.registry.osgi;x-friends:
 ="org.eclipse.core.runtime",org.eclipse.core.internal.registry.spi;x-
 internal:=true,org.eclipse.core.runtime; registry="split"; mandatory:
 ="registry",org.eclipse.core.runtime.dynamichelpers,org.eclipse.core.
 runtime.spi
Bundle-Version: 3.2.1.R32x_v20060814
Eclipse-LazyStart: true
Bundle-Name: %pluginName
Bundle-ClassPath: runtime_registry_compatibility.jar, .
Bundle-ManifestVersion: 2
Bundle-Vendor: %providerName
Bundle-SymbolicName: org.eclipse.equinox.registry; singleton:=true
Bundle-Localization: plugin
Require-Bundle: org.eclipse.equinox.common;bundle-version="[3.2.0,4.0.0)"
Eclipse-ExtensibleAPI: true
```

The Bundle-Version here clearly identifies the file as coming from the Eclipse 3.2.1 release. You can download the source for this exact same code from the Eclipse web site if you want to investigate further the internals of the Eclipse runtime.

So far, all you have been able to see is that WAS ships with files from the Eclipse 3.2.1 release. To see why this is relevant and to understand what the benefit is to WAS, you need to understand a little more about Eclipse, plug-ins, bundles, and Equinox.

Eclipse and OSGi Basics

When the IBM OTI team decided to move away from its Smalltalk-written VisualAge tools to Java-based tools, it architected an extensible runtime. This consisted of a platform runtime with an inbuilt static component *Extension Registry*, and an extensible component model that consisted of *extension points* that can be built upon by *extensions*, with relationships between the extensions and the extension points they build upon described by XML files. The components building upon the core Eclipse platform are known as *plug-ins*. This compares with the OSGi model, which declares *services* via its *Service Registry*, with implementation components declared in *bundles*. The OSGi model declares its metadata in the MANIFEST.MF file, whereas in the Eclipse model metadata is declared in the plugin.xml file. Recent Eclipse 3.0 and later releases have redefined the Eclipse plug-in and extension point model in terms of bundles and services. The OSGi model is dynamic in that bundles can be started and stopped as required, with the metadata guiding the platform as to what service interfaces are being offered.

Each component deployed to the Eclipse platform in the earlier versions, and to some extent in the current versions, had its plugin.xml manifest file read at startup and the description written to the Eclipse Extension Registry. This is static extension, because the XML files are read at startup, and once the component is loaded for use when its extension point is extended, it stays in memory. In the XML file, the plug-in component lists the extension points it extends and any extension points it offers, including those it may wish to re-extend (see Figure 3-1). Some extension points are standard for the platform, such as UI action sets in the IDE, and require additional metadata.

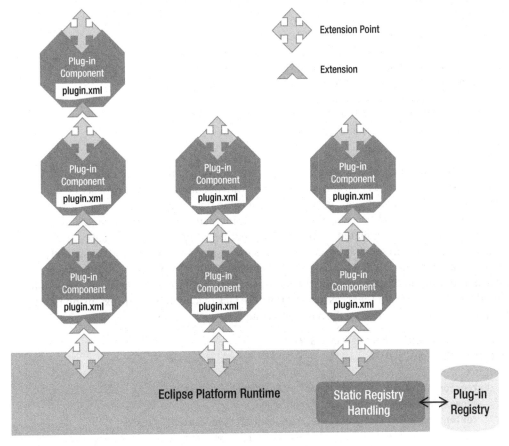

Figure 3-1. *Eclipse Platform plug-in and extension model*

When a plug-in wants to extend a component, it declares that it has an extension that extends the named extension point. Similarly, when a plug-in wants to offer an extension point, it declares it. The plugin.xml file contains these declarations. The Extension Registry allows the search for extension points to be dynamic based on the contents of the plugin.xml file for the collection of plug-ins. The plugin.xml declarations underpin the extension mechanism. However, in this model the user of an extension point needs to know its interface ahead of time even if it finds it dynamically, and once the plug-in has been loaded and extended, it remains in memory until the platform shuts down.

This can be seen best by examining the core Eclipse runtime that WAS uses, which itself is a plug-in. It can be downloaded in source form from http://www.eclipse.org for your platform, but be sure to get the Eclipse 3.2.1 version. If you open org.eclipse.core.runtime_3.2.0.v20060603.jar and look at its plugin.xml file, you can see the extension points offered by the Eclipse runtime itself to the components that run on it:

```
<?xml version="1.0" encoding="UTF-8"?>
<?eclipse version="3.0"?>
<plugin>
    <extension-point id="applications" name="%applicationsName"
        schema="schema/applications.exsd"/>
    <extension-point id="products" name="%productsName"
        schema="schema/products.exsd"/>
    <extension-point id="adapters" name="%adaptersName"
        schema="schema/adapters.exsd"/>
    <extension-point id="preferences" name="%preferencesName"
        schema="schema/preferences.exsd"/>
    <extension-point id="contentTypes" name="%contentTypesName"
        schema="schema/contentTypes.exsd"/>
</plugin>
```

The extension points offered for extension by the platform in release 3.2.1 are applications, products, adapters, preferences, and contentTypes, with a schema supplied to describe the format of the additional metadata each of these extension points requires. Extension points are declared in the plugin.xml file using the extension-point element (note the hyphen).

If you now look at the related org.eclipse.core.contenttype_3.2.0.v20060603.jar plugin.xml file, you can see that the contentTypes extension point is redeclared and, within that redeclaration, the original contentTypes extension point is extended and metadata is provided about some additional content-type elements and properties. The keyword element to extend an extension point is extension, but note the lack of a hyphen as the extension point being built upon is identified by the point attribute.

```
<?xml version="1.0" encoding="UTF-8"?>
<?eclipse version="3.0"?>
<plugin>
    <extension-point id="contentTypes" name="%contentTypesName"
        schema="schema/contentTypes.exsd"/>
    <extension point="org.eclipse.core.contenttype.contentTypes">
        <content-type id="org.eclipse.core.runtime.text"
            name="%textContentTypeName"
            priority="high"
```

```
                file-extensions="txt">
                <describer
                    class="org.eclipse.core.internal.content.TextContentDescriber"/>
                <property name="org.eclipse.core.runtime.bom"/>
                <property name="org.eclipse.core.runtime.charset"/>
            </content-type>
            <content-type id="org.eclipse.core.runtime.xml"
                name="%xmlContentTypeName"
                base-type="org.eclipse.core.runtime.text"
                priority="high"
                file-extensions="xml">
                <property name="org.eclipse.core.runtime.charset"
                    default="UTF-8"/>
                <describer
                    class="org.eclipse.core.internal.content.XMLContentDescriber"/>
            </content-type>
<!-- a placeholder for setups where JDT's official type is not available -->
            <content-type id="org.eclipse.core.runtime.properties"
                name="%propertiesContentTypeName"
                base-type="org.eclipse.core.runtime.text"
                alias-for="org.eclipse.jdt.core.javaProperties"
                file-extensions="properties">
                <property name="org.eclipse.core.runtime.charset"
                    default="ISO-8859-1"/>
            </content-type>
        </extension>
</plugin>
```

The Basics of Eclipse Plug-ins

To follow along with the text here, you may want to download the Eclipse IDE for your chosen development platform and its source code. Although it is not a current version, the most appropriate version for your investigation is that used under the covers of WAS, Eclipse 3.2.1. You'll want to use the Plug-in Development Environment (PDE) version to enable you to build a plug-in just like the WAS core itself. It may be necessary to download the SDK version and add the PDE toolkit as a separate download that is unzipped over the top of the SDK, although this is not usually necessary for release 3.2.1. Download mirrors for archive versions of Eclipse can be found by following the links at http://archive.eclipse.org.

The simplest of all Eclipse plug-ins is nothing more than a plugin.xml file. Not very useful, but it does illustrate how Eclipse works.

Writing a Simple Eclipse Plug-in

You should now have a directory called eclipse and, within it, an Eclipse executable and a startup.jar file with configuration, plugins, and features directories. In the configuration directory there should be a config.ini file and subdirectories identical to those from the WAS 7 configuration directory. While unlikely to be identical, the `config.ini` file should be very close to that from WAS 7 and have an identical build ID (M20060921-0945) from Eclipse 3.2.1. The `plugins` directory should have some of the same basic plug-in names from the WAS 7 `plugins` directory, although the WAS 7 versions have had the version numbers removed from the file name.

For your basic plug-in, create a directory under the `plugins` directory called `firstWAS7test`, and in it create a file (not using Eclipse at this point, to avoid creating a project) called `plugin.xml` with the following contents:

```
<?xml version="1.0" encoding="UTF-8"?>
<plugin
        id="org.testwas7.test1"
        name="firstWAS7test"
        version="1.0.0"
        provider-name="Inside WAS7">
</plugin>
```

If you now start Eclipse itself, open Help ➤ About Eclipse SDK, and then click the Plug-in Details button, you should see that your basic plug-in is loaded because your text has appeared toward the bottom of the list. This shows that the most basic plug-in is just XML (see Figure 3-2). Note that the Help option may differ depending on which Eclipse package was downloaded.

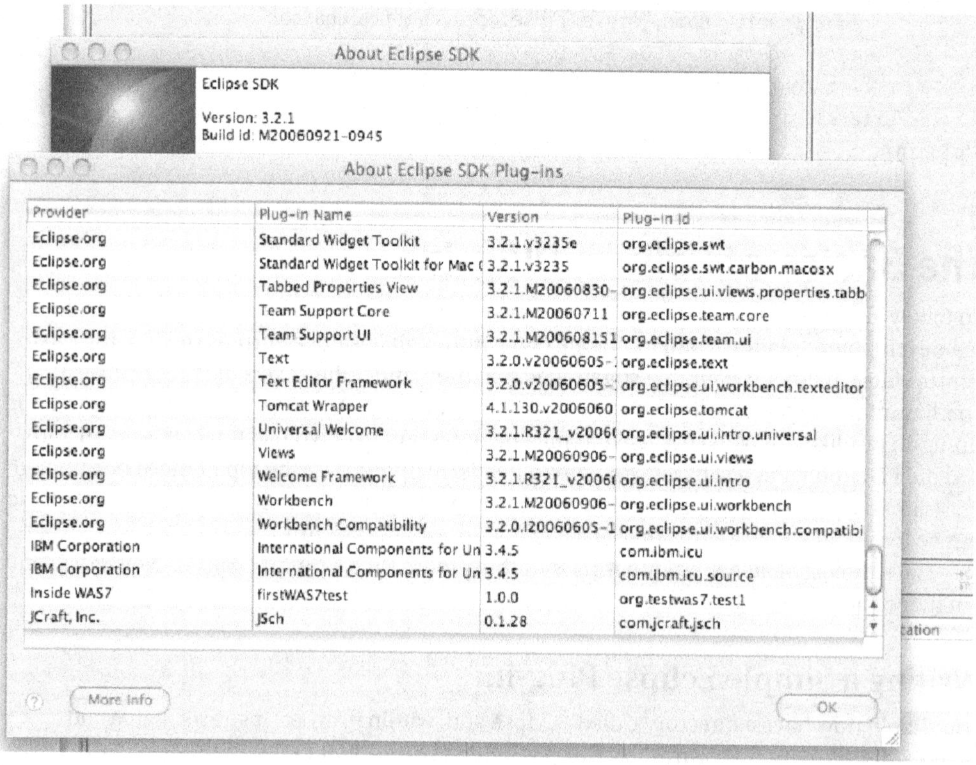

Figure 3-2. *About Eclipse SDK Plug-ins dialog box and loaded plug-ins*

This plug-in isn't very useful, but you can build on it to create an executable plug-in just like WAS 7 itself. I could just offer you a "Hello World!" example, but that wouldn't show the dependency model between plug-ins that underlies Eclipse, so for the next example you will write a simple browser based on the Eclipse Standard Widget Toolkit (SWT) windowing system.

Using Extension Points to Create a Browser Application

To start, you will use the Eclipse IDE you downloaded to generate an Eclipse plug-in, but you will use only the essential components to build what you need for the example:

1. Start the Eclipse environment from the given executable and create a workspace outside of the Eclipse directory structure.

2. Select File ➤ New ➤ Project to get a list of project types, select Plug-in Project to open the New Plug-in Project wizard, and click the Next button.

3. On the Plug-in Project screen, shown in Figure 3-3, ensure that Eclipse version 3.2 is selected and click the Next button.

Figure 3-3. *Eclipse New Plug-in Project wizard Plug-in Project screen*

4. On the Plug-in Content screen, enter the details as shown in Figure 3-4. Make sure that the "Generate an activator, a Java class that controls the plug-in's life cycle" and "This plug-in will make contributions to the UI" check boxes are cleared and that the "Would you like to create a rich client application?" option is set to No. This creates the

most basic of plug-in projects that you can then build upon without getting extraneous details that aren't relevant for a server side plug-in or for the present example. This is a pure Eclipse plug-in without the activator and related MANIFEST.MF artifacts that would start to introduce OSGi features. Click Next.

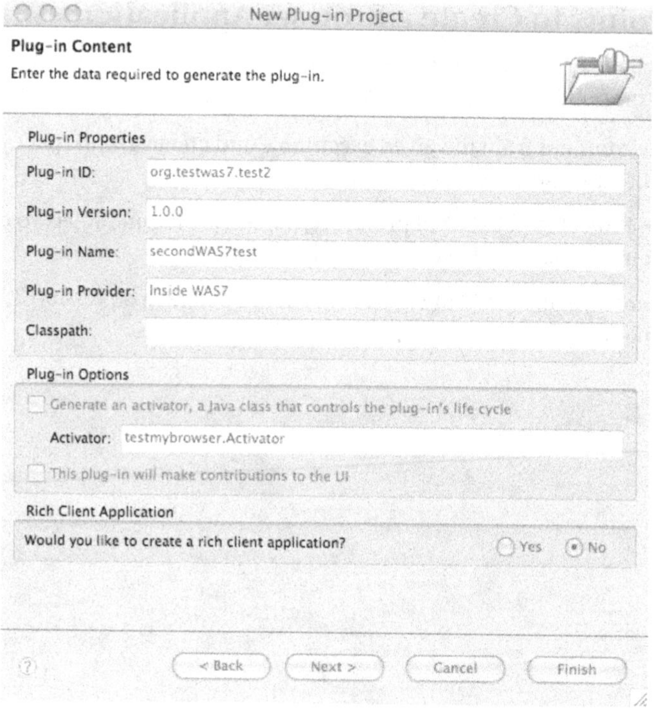

Figure 3-4. *Eclipse New Plug-in Project wizard Plug-in Content screen*

5. On the Templates screen, shown in Figure 3-5, clear the "Create a plug-in using one of the templates" check box and click Finish. A template adds extra code for demonstration purposes, but because you want to build your own example from scratch, you don't want this code.

You have now created a basic Eclipse plug-in project but still need to add the necessary dependent plug-in and library support before adding your code. You next have to update the dependencies for your plug-in so that you can compile the code. You are dependent on the Eclipse runtime with its compatibility library and SWT for your browser. The setup in the tooling is only for development at this point because it uses the OSGi model of updating the MANIFEST.MF file rather than the plugin.xml file, but a plugin.xml file will be created when you add an extension, so you can retrofit your changes to that manually before deployment to emulate the way WAS handles its metadata.

For now, click the Dependencies tab at the bottom of the main window and add support for org.eclipse.swt, org.eclipse.core.runtime, and org.eclipse.core.runtime.compatibility by clicking the Add button and entering the target plug-in for each one (see Figure 3-6).

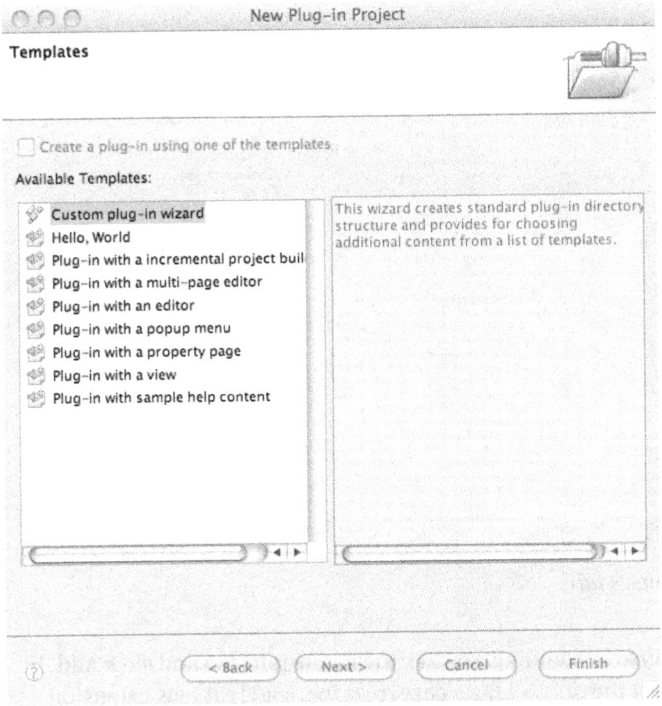

Figure 3-5. *Eclipse New Plug-in Project wizard Templates screen*

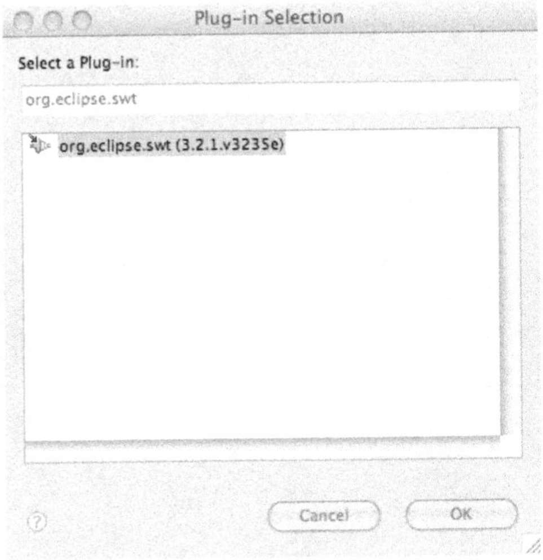

Figure 3-6. *Eclipse Plug-in Selection dialog box*

The resulting page after you have added all of the plug-in dependencies should look like
Figure 3-7.

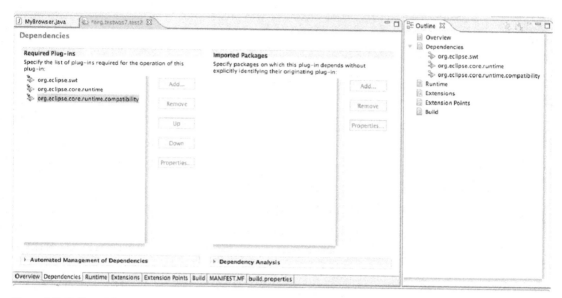

Figure 3-7. *Eclipse MANIFEST.MF Dependencies tab*

Now you must define what you are extending, so click the Extensions tab and click Add. In the New Extension dialog box, select the org.eclipse.core.runtime.applications extension point for extension, as shown in Figure 3-8, because you are going to create an application to run on top of the Eclipse runtime.

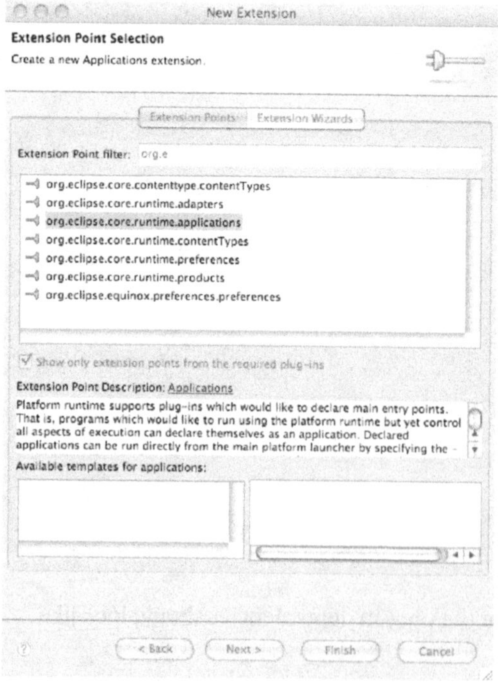

Figure 3-8. *Eclipse New Extension dialog box*

Save the current state of the project using File ➤ Save and create a new package by click-ing the project src icon and selecting File ➤ New ➤ Class. In the New Java Class dialog box (see Figure 3-9), name the package org.testwas7 and the Java class MyBrowser.

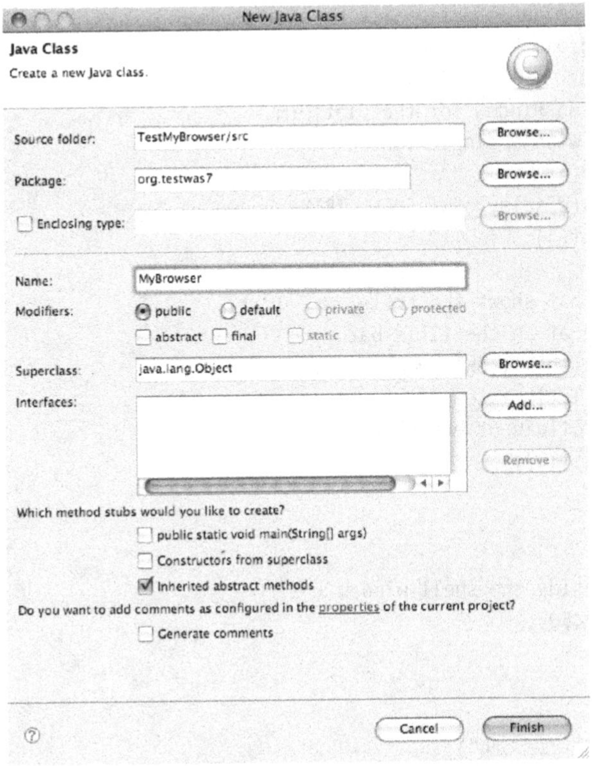

Figure 3-9. *Eclipse New Java Class dialog box*

Open the generated Java file and enter the following Eclipse SWT code to create a simple browser application:

```
package org.testwas7;

import org.eclipse.swt.*;
import org.eclipse.swt.browser.Browser;
import org.eclipse.swt.browser.TitleEvent;
import org.eclipse.swt.browser.TitleListener;
import org.eclipse.swt.layout.*;
import org.eclipse.swt.widgets.*;
import org.eclipse.core.runtime.IPlatformRunnable;

/*
 * Simple Browser
 */
```

```java
// IPlatformRunnable makes this an Eclipse application
public class MyBrowser implements IPlatformRunnable {

    // The IPlatformRunnable interface that makes this an eclipse application
    // has only a run method that takes an Object as its parameter list
    public Object run(Object args) throws Exception {

        // Create a sizable application Window for the platform
        // that we are going to fill with a single control
        Display display = new Display();
        final Shell shell = new Shell(display, SWT.SHELL_TRIM);
        shell.setLayout(new FillLayout());

        // Create a browser control that shows the title
        // of the page we are looking at in the title bar
        Browser browser = new Browser(shell, SWT.NONE);
        browser.addTitleListener(new TitleListener() {
                public void changed(TitleEvent event) {
                    shell.setText(event.title);
                }
        });

        // Open the browser window inside the shell window
        browser.setBounds(0, 0, 640, 480);
        shell.pack();
        shell.open();

        browser.setUrl("http://www.eclipse.org");

        // Process events while we have them and while they are not telling
        // us to close the window and exit
        while(!shell.isDisposed()) {
            if (!display.readAndDispatch()) {
                display.sleep();
            }
        }

        // We have finished so exit happily
        return EXIT_OK;
    }
}
```

Now open the `plugin.xml` file and make it look as follows:

```
<?xml version="1.0" encoding="UTF-8"?>
<plugin
        id="org.testwas7.test2"
        name="secondWAS7test"
        version="1.0.0"
        provider-name="Inside WAS7">

    <extension point="org.eclipse.core.runtime.applications" id="MyBrowser">
        <application>
            <run class="org.testwas7.MyBrowser"/>
        </application>
    </extension>

    <requires>
        <import plugin="org.eclipse.swt"/>
        <import plugin="org.eclipse.core.runtime"/>
        <import plugin="org.eclipse.core.runtime.compatibility"/>
    </requires>
</plugin>
```

In the preceding code, the extension ID `MyBrowser` extends the extension point `org.eclipse.core.runtime.applications` to allow the class it indicates in the `<application><run class="..."></application>` section of the XML to run as an Eclipse-hosted application. The `<requires> <imports plugin="..."> </requires>` sections, found in the `MANIFEST.MF` file in OSGi applications, indicate the plug-ins on which this plug-in depends.

To ensure that everything works, right-click the project name and select Run As ➤ Eclipse Application. Ignore the warnings that appear regarding the fact that you have duplicated information in the `MANIFEST.MF` and `plugin.xml` files (although any red crosses that appear are genuine errors that you must correct). You should see a small browser window appear that can be resized and that displays the contents of the Eclipse.org web site.

Running inside the Eclipse IDE isn't what WAS does, so you now need to replicate how WAS 7 does things and execute your application from the command line. Eclipse ships a JAR file called `startup.jar` with a main method called `org.eclipse.core.launcher.Main` to start Eclipse applications that are based on the `org.eclipse.core.runtime.applications` extension point. So, exit the Eclipse IDE and create a directory called `secondWAS7test` under the Eclipse `plugins` directory and copy the binary class file directory structure (starting with the `org` directory as the root of the structure) and the `plugin.xml` file from the directory holding the Eclipse IDE project you created in your workspace into it.

Finally, open a command line into the Eclipse IDE directory that has the `plugins` directory in it and run the following command:

```
java -cp startup.jar org.eclipse.core.launcher.Main -consoleLog -application
  org.testwas7.test2.MyBrowser
```

On a Mac OS X environment it should be

```
java -XstartOnFirstThread -cp startup.jar org.eclipse.core.launcher.Main -consoleLog
  -application org.testwas7.test2.MyBrowser
```

A browser window should now appear, as shown in Figure 3-10, but no Eclipse IDE. You have created an Eclipse-based application that does *not* use an Eclipse IDE UI.

Figure 3-10. *Your MyBrowser Window*

Starting WAS with Eclipse/OSGi

By now you might be asking how this all relates to WAS, but you will soon see that each of the features illustrated here is found in WAS. In the past, the org.eclipse.core.runtime.applications extension and the Java command line using the startup.jar file were used to start WAS, although they were hidden inside scripts and batch files. For WAS 7, IBM has ported the startup.jar main method that started the Eclipse runtime and passed it an Eclipse application to execute with the bootstrap.jar file, which can be seen at the bottom of a stack trace from an instance of WAS 7 that has failed to start.

If you can see the full command line for a WAS instance and you look carefully, you will see how what you have examined thus far relates back to WAS:

```
/usr/IBM/WebSphere7/AppServer1/java/bin/java -Declipse.security -Dwas.status.socket=
33623 -Dosgi.install.area=/usr/IBM/WebSphere7/AppServer1 -Dosgi.configuration.area=
/usr/IBM/WebSphere7/AppServer1/profiles/Dmgr01/configuration -Djava.awt.headless=
true -Dosgi.framework.extensions=com.ibm.cds,com.ibm.ws.eclipse.adaptors
-Xshareclasses:name=webspherev70_%g,groupAccess,nonFatal -Xscmx50M -Xbootclasspath
/p:/usr/IBM/WebSphere7/AppServer1/java/jre/lib/ext/ibmorb.jar:/usr/IBM/WebSphere7/
AppServer1/java/jre/lib/ext/ibmext.jar -classpath /usr/IBM/WebSphere7/AppServer1/
```

```
profiles/Dmgr01/properties:/usr/IBM/WebSphere7/AppServer1/properties:/usr/IBM/
WebSphere7/AppServer1/lib/startup.jar:/usr/IBM/WebSphere7/AppServer1/lib/bootstrap.
jar:/usr/IBM/WebSphere7/AppServer1/lib/jsf-nls.jar:/usr/IBM/WebSphere7/AppServer1/
lib/lmproxy.jar:/usr/IBM/WebSphere7/AppServer1/lib/urlprotocols.jar:/usr/IBM/
WebSphere7/AppServer1/deploytool/itp/batchboot.jar:/usr/IBM/WebSphere7/AppServer1/
deploytool/itp/batch2.jar:/usr/IBM/WebSphere7/AppServer1/java/lib/tools.jar -Dibm.
websphere.internalClassAccessMode=allow -Xms50m -Xmx256m -Dws.ext.dirs=/usr/IBM/
WebSphere7/AppServer1/java/lib:/usr/IBM/WebSphere7/AppServer1/profiles/Dmgr01/
classes:/usr/IBM/WebSphere7/AppServer1/classes:/usr/IBM/WebSphere7/AppServer1/lib:/
usr/IBM/WebSphere7/AppServer1/installedChannels:/usr/IBM/WebSphere7/AppServer1/lib/
ext:/usr/IBM/WebSphere7/AppServer1/web/help:/usr/IBM/WebSphere7/AppServer1/
deploytool/itp/plugins/com.ibm.etools.ejbdeploy/runtime -Dderby.system.home=
/usr/IBM/WebSphere7/AppServer1/derby -Dcom.ibm.itp.location=/usr/IBM/WebSphere7/
AppServer1/bin -Djava.util.logging.configureByServer=true -Duser.install.root=
/usr/IBM/WebSphere7/AppServer1/profiles/Dmgr01 -Djavax.management.builder.initial=
com.ibm.ws.management.PlatformMBeanServerBuilder -Dwas.install.root=/usr/IBM/
WebSphere7/AppServer1 -Dpython.cachedir=/usr/IBM/WebSphere7/AppServer1/
profiles/Dmgr01/temp/cachedir -Djava.util.logging.manager=com.ibm.ws.bootstrap.
WsLogManager -Dserver.root=/usr/IBM/WebSphere7/AppServer1/profiles/Dmgr01
-Dcom.ibm.security.jgss.debug=off -Dcom.ibm.security.krb5.Krb5Debug=off -Djava.
security.auth.login.config=/usr/IBM/WebSphere7/AppServer1/profiles/Dmgr01/
properties/wsjaas.conf -Djava.security.policy=/usr/IBM/WebSphere7/AppServer1/
profiles/Dmgr01/properties/server.policy com.ibm.wsspi.bootstrap.WSPreLauncher
-nosplash -application com.ibm.ws.bootstrap.WSLauncher com.ibm.ws.runtime.WsServer
/usr/IBM/WebSphere7/AppServer1/profiles/Dmgr01/config spock44pCell02
spock44pCellManager02 dmgr
```

From a Java perspective, the main method run as an entry point for this Deployment Manager is found in com.ibm.wsspi.bootstrap.WSPreLauncher from the lib/bootstrap. jar file. This loads and executes the Eclipse runtime and passes it com.ibm.ws.bootstrap. WSLauncher as an executable and its main method. The Eclipse runtime is now running and, as in the MyBrowser example, it reads the plugin.xml file to determine which Eclipse executable application to run using the named extension that extends the extension point org.eclipse. core.runtime.applications—i.e., the run method of the class com.ibm.ws.runtime.eclipse. WSStartServer, which then starts WAS as in the MyBrowser example.

The lib/startup.jar and lib/bootstrap.jar files are on the command line, but rather than org.eclipse.core.launcher.Main executing, com.ibm.ws.bootstrap.WSLauncher executes. The lib/startup.jar file is exactly the same one as provided by default with the Eclipse 3.2.1 environment.

In reality things are more complex than this. If you start the Deployment Manager and then immediately list the running processes, you will see two processes with similar startup sequences for WAS. The first starts the com.ibm.ws.management.tools.WsServerLauncher class that is added as the APP_EXT_ID by the startManager.sh, startServer.sh, and startNode.sh scripts. This is not a class that extends the Eclipse org.eclipse.core.runtime.applications extension point, but an IBM internal equivalent to it, com.ibm.ws.bootstrap.applications.

The startXXXX.sh scripts add this class to the command line:

```
# Bootstrap values ...
APP_EXT_ID=com.ibm.ws.management.tools.WsServerLauncher
```

The underlying class can be found in the plug-in com.ibm.ws.admin.service.jar file that is loaded by the Eclipse runtime as soon as it starts, as mandated by the entry in the MANIFEST. MF file inside it that has the Eclipse-AutoStart: true value set and has the com.ibm.ws.runtime plug-in as a required dependency. I will explain more of this later. However, the responsibility of this class is to set up and check the necessary environment for the server to start up, including the main server.xml file for the profile, and then to initiate the startup of the server and monitor its status. On a Windows platform this class also manages the interface to the Windows service environment.

This can be seen in the bottom of the stack dump of a WAS 7 instance that has failed to start because it can't access the server.xml file that provides its configuration:

```
************* Start Display Current Environment *************
Host Operating System is AIX, version 5.3
Java version = J2RE 1.6.0 IBM J9 2.4 AIX ppc-32 jvmap3260-20080526_19754
(JIT enabled, AOT enabled)
J9VM - 20080526_019754_bHdSMr
JIT  - r9_20080523_1338
GC   - 20080526_AA, Java Compiler = j9jit24, Java VM name = IBM J9 VM
was.install.root = /usr/IBM/WebSphere7/AppServer1
user.install.root = /usr/IBM/WebSphere7/AppServer1/profiles/AppSrv01
Java Home = /usr/IBM/WebSphere7/AppServer1/java/jre
ws.ext.dirs = /usr/IBM/WebSphere7/AppServer1/java/lib:/usr/IBM/WebSphere7/
AppServer1/classes:/usr/IBM/WebSphere7/AppServer1/lib:/usr/IBM/WebSphere7/
AppServer1/installedChannels:/usr/IBM/WebSphere7/AppServer1/lib/ext:/usr/IBM/
WebSphere7/AppServer1/web/help:/usr/IBM/WebSphere7/AppServer1/deploytool/itp/
plugins/com.ibm.etools.ejbdeploy/runtime
Classpath = /usr/IBM/WebSphere7/AppServer1/profiles/AppSrv01/properties:/usr/IBM/
WebSphere7/AppServer1/properties:/usr/IBM/WebSphere7/AppServer1/lib/startup.jar:
/usr/IBM/WebSphere7/AppServer1/lib/bootstrap.jar:/usr/IBM/WebSphere7/AppServer1/lib/
lmproxy.jar:/usr/IBM/WebSphere7/AppServer1/lib/urlprotocols.jar:/usr/IBM/WebSphere7/
AppServer1/java/lib/tools.jar
Java Library path = /usr/IBM/WebSphere7/AppServer1/java/jre/lib/ppc:/usr/IBM/Web-
Sphere7/AppServer1/java/
jre/lib/ppc/j9vm:/usr/IBM/WebSphere7/AppServer1/java/jre/lib/ppc:/usr/IBM/
WebSphere7/AppServer1/java/jre/../lib/ppc:/usr/IBM/WebSphere7/AppServer1/bin::/usr/
IBM/WebSphere7/AppServer1/java/jre/lib/ppc/j9vm:/usr/IBM/WebSphere7/AppServer1/java/
jre/lib/ppc:/usr/lib
Current trace specification = *=info
************* End Display Current Environment *************
[30/07/08 22:10:36:888 GMT] 00000000 ManagerAdmin  I   TRAS0017I: The startup trace
state is *=info.
[30/07/08 22:10:37:929 GMT] 00000000 AdminTool     A   ADMU0128I: Starting tool with
the AppSrv01 profile
[30/07/08 22:10:37:940 GMT] 00000000 AdminTool     A   ADMU3100I: Reading
configuration for server: server1
[30/07/08 22:10:38:940 GMT] 00000000 WsServerLaunc E   ADMU3002E: Exception
attempting to process server server1
[30/07/08 22:10:38:946 GMT] 00000000 WsServerLaunc E   ADMU3007E: Exception
```

```
java.io.FileNotFoundException: /usr/IBM/WebSphere7/AppServer1/profiles/AppSrv01/
config/cells/spock44pCell02/nodes/spock44pNode03/servers/server1/server.xml
(A file or directory in the path name does not exist.)
        at java.io.FileInputStream.<init>(FileInputStream.java:112)


...


        at javax.xml.parsers.SAXParser.parse(Unknown Source)
        at com.ibm.ws.runtime.config.ConfigDocumentImpl.load(ConfigDocumentImpl.
java:128)
        at com.ibm.ws.runtime.config.ConfigServiceImpl.getDocument(ConfigServiceImpl.
java:182)
        at com.ibm.ws.runtime.config.ConfigServiceImpl.getDocumentObjects(
ConfigServiceImpl.java:126)
        at com.ibm.ws.runtime.config.ConfigServiceImpl.getDocumentObjects(
ConfigServiceImpl.java:120)
        at com.ibm.ws.management.tools.WsServerLauncher.
initializeRepositoryAndLauncher(WsServerLauncher.java:407)
        at com.ibm.ws.management.tools.WsServerLauncher.runTool(
WsServerLauncher.java:277)
        at com.ibm.ws.management.tools.AdminTool.executeUtility(AdminTool.java:269)
        at com.ibm.ws.management.tools.WsServerLauncher.main(
WsServerLauncher.java:132)
        at sun.reflect.NativeMethodAccessorImpl.invoke0(Native Method)
        at sun.reflect.NativeMethodAccessorImpl.invoke(
NativeMethodAccessorImpl.java:45)
        at sun.reflect.DelegatingMethodAccessorImpl.invoke(
DelegatingMethodAccessorImpl.java:25)
        at java.lang.reflect.Method.invoke(Method.java:599)
        at com.ibm.ws.bootstrap.WSLauncher.main(WSLauncher.java:270)
```

You can see here, at the bottom of the stack trace working upward, that the bootstrap launcher com.ibm.ws.bootstrap.WSLauncher.main method is the entry point for the first thread that starts the environment. This uses reflection to execute the com.ibm.ws.management.tools. WsServerLauncher.main method. The actual launching of the Eclipse runtime is done by the com.ibm.wsspi.bootstrap.WSPreLauncher class in the lib/bootstrap.jar file. The trail requires a complex stack dump to follow, but eventually the plugin.xml file from the com.ibm.ws.runtime.jar file is read by the Eclipse runtime and started up in exactly the same way as in our example using the org.eclipse.core.runtime.applications extension point. The code invoked is WSStartServer and OSGi comes into play, but the line that leads to this from plugin.xml in the JAR file is familiar:

```
...
<extension id="startWsServer" point="org.eclipse.core.runtime.applications">
    <application>
        <run class="com.ibm.ws.runtime.eclipse.WSStartServer"/>
    </application>
  </extension>
...
```

The two processes that contributed to the startup can be seen in the output from the Unix ps utility:

```
UID    PID   PPID  C    STIME   TTY  TIME CMD
       root    1     0  0 12:44:42     -  0:01 /etc/init
       root 69694     1  0 12:45:18     -  0:00 /usr/ccs/bin/shlap64
       root 77964     1  0 12:45:17     -  0:00 /usr/sbin/syncd 60
...
       root 172210 303140 149 13:14:43  pts/0  1:07 /usr/IBM/WebSphere7/AppServer1/
java/bin/java -Declipse.security -Dwas.status.socket=34554 -Dosgi.install.area=
/usr/IBM/WebSphere7/AppServer1 -Dosgi.configuration.area=/usr/IBM/WebSphere7/
AppServer1/profiles/Dmgr01/configuration -Djava.awt.headless=true -Dosgi.
framework.extensions=com.ibm.cds,com.ibm.ws.eclipse.adaptors -Xshareclasses:name=
webspherev70_%g,groupAccess,nonFatal -Xscmx50M -.
...
Djava.security.policy=/usr/IBM/WebSphere7/AppServer1/profiles/Dmgr01/properties/
server.policy com.ibm.wsspi.bootstrap.WSPreLauncher -nosplash -application
com.ibm.ws.bootstrap.WSLauncher com.ibm.ws.runtime.WsServer
/usr/IBM/WebSphere7/AppServer1/profiles/Dmgr01/config spock44pCell02
spock44pCellManager02 dmgr
...
       root 299230 192630  1 13:01:47     -  0:00 sshd: root@pts/1
       root 303140 135216  0 13:14:18  pts/0  0:22 /usr/IBM/WebSphere7/AppServer1/
java/bin/java -Dosgi.install.area=/usr/IBM/WebSphere7/AppServer1 -Dosgi.
configuration.area=/usr/IBM/WebSphere7/AppServer1/profiles/Dmgr01/
configuration -Dws.ext.dirs=/usr/IBM/WebSphere7/AppServer1/java/lib:/usr/
IBM/WebSphere7/AppServer1/classes:/usr/IBM/WebSphere7/AppServer1/lib:/usr/IBM/
WebSphere7/AppServer1/installedChannels:/usr/IBM/WebSphere7/AppServer1/lib/ext:
/usr/IBM/WebSphere7/AppServer1/web/help:/usr/IBM/WebSphere7/AppServer1/deploytool/
itp/plugins/com.ibm.etools.ejbdeploy/runtime -Dwas.install.root=/usr/IBM/WebSphere7/
AppServer1 -Djava.util.logging.manager=com.ibm.ws.bootstrap.WsLogManager -Djava.
util.logging.configureByServer=true -Duser.install.root=/usr/IBM/WebSphere7/
AppServer1/profiles/Dmgr01 -classpath /usr/IBM/WebSphere7/AppServer1/profiles/
Dmgr01/properties:/usr/IBM/WebSphere7/AppServer1/properties:/usr/IBM/WebSphere7/
AppServer1/lib/startup.jar:/usr/IBM/WebSphere7/AppServer1/lib/bootstrap.jar:
/usr/IBM/WebSphere7/AppServer1/lib/lmproxy.jar:/usr/IBM/WebSphere7/AppServer1/lib/
urlprotocols.jar:/usr/IBM/WebSphere7/AppServer1/java/lib/tools.jar
com.ibm.ws.bootstrap.WSLauncher com.ibm.ws.management.tools.WsServerLauncher
/usr/IBM/WebSphere7/AppServer1/profiles/Dmgr01/config spock44pCell02
spock44pCellManager02 dmgr -dmgr
```

Note that the top process (172210), running the com.ibm.ws.runtime.WsServer application entry point, has been started by the bottom process (303140) that is running the com.ibm.ws.management.tools.WsServerLauncher application entry point.

So far you have created an Eclipse-based application using static extension and I have shown how some of this is used in the WAS startup. What WAS requires is dynamic extension, and for this you have to turn to the OSGi standard and its Eclipse Equinox implementation.

The Minimal Eclipse/OSGi Runtime Constituents

The Eclipse FAQs for version 3.X state that the minimum Eclipse/OSGi environment consists of the following:

- `startup.jar`: Located in the `lib` directory for WAS 7 installations, contains the bootstrap `org.eclipse.core.launcher.main` entry point that finds and loads the plug-in that starts the platform. The one provided with WAS 7 is exactly the same one supplied with Eclipse 3.2.1 for the given platform.

- A bootstrap configurator, which is `org.eclipse.update.configurator` for WAS 7: Finds and loads the plug-ins and configuration for the given application, which by default includes all of the plug-ins in the `plugins` directory. Uses the `config.ini` file that is found in the `configuration` directory.

- `org.eclipse.core.runtime`: The core of the Eclipse platform runtime, exposes the Eclipse Extension Registry. This plug-in parses the `plugin.xml` files for all plug-ins in the configuration and creates the runtime registry in memory. With the OSGi versions, any unconverted plug-ins that do not use the `MANIFEST.MF` file for plug-in information will have their `plugin.xml` files read, converted, and stored in the `org.eclipse.osgi/manifests` directory under the `configuration` directory. With WAS 7 all plug-ins mostly use the new OSGi format for configuration in the `MANIFEST.MF` file, but not all plug-ins use the latest settings. This is the plug-in that finds, loads, and executes the class identified by the `-application` parameter on the command line.

- `org.eclipse.osgi`: Replaces three earlier OSGi plug-ins and provides the underlying OSGi support for the Eclipse runtime to support dynamic plug-ins. The Eclipse Equinox project developed this runtime as `org.eclipse.osgi.util_3.1.100.v20060601.jar` for the Eclipse 3.2.1 release but IBM has bundled it differently for the WAS 7 release. The main class entry point for this is `org.eclipse.core.runtime.adapter.EclipseStarter`, as seen on many stack dumps.

This list refers to the use of the Eclipse runtime that is built on the OSGi runtime. The Eclipse project has its own OSGi implementation, called Equinox, and the preceding startup requirements are for it; for the pure OSGi runtime without the Eclipse elements, things are much simpler and only a single "bundle" is required: `org.eclipse.osgi`. So, what is OSGi and how does it relate to Eclipse and the WAS runtime that builds upon it?

OSGi Bundles and Services

When you created your application earlier in the chapter using the Eclipse New Plug-in Project wizard, you did not generate an OSGi bundle activator; you deselected that option (refer to Figure 3-4) because it would introduce OSGi artifacts. You also did not deploy the `MANIFEST.MF` file from your project, but instead hand-crafted a `plugin.xml` file. The `MANIFEST.MF` file and the bundle activator class are OSGi artifacts that are used by the OSGi runtime that is implemented in Eclipse through the OSGi Equinox components.

OSGi Bundles

Before Eclipse adopted the OSGi model, it had been successful with its model support for the addition of plug-ins, which the original developers had not envisaged. However, once loaded, these plug-ins stayed in memory, giving Eclipse applications the reputation of being memory hogs. What was needed was dynamic behavior, so the Eclipse team started to look around for an existing model and came across the OSGi model for dynamic Java extension. The model was sufficiently similar to the existing plug-in model in that OSGi had bundles to equate to Eclipse plug-ins. Also, Eclipse had an Extension Registry and OSGi had a Service Registry. The Eclipse team set about merging the two technologies and the Eclipse Equinox project was born in Eclipse 3.X.

Note OSGi originally stood for the Open Services Gateway initiative but is now called the OSGi Alliance. The model has always simply been called the OSGi model.

Why use OSGi? The Eclipse pre-OSGi model for extension was not fully dynamic. OSGi bundles can be started and stopped, and added and removed, by the runtime at any point, so an environment supporting OSGi, in theory, need never be taken down except to upgrade the OS or base OSGi runtime, because individual bundles can be upgraded in place.

The Eclipse component model is based around plug-ins that declare extension points that are extended by extensions, with the `plugin.xml` file declaring to the runtime what extension points are declared by plug-ins and what extension points are from other plug-ins. To look up the availability of particular extension points and features, the Eclipse Extension Registry is used. The OSGi equivalent of the plug-in is the bundle. A bundle has an activator class implementing the `BundleActivator` interface that has `start` and `stop` methods to allow control by the OSGi runtime (accessed through the supplied `BundleContext`). The `BundleContext` gives access to a Service Registry where OSGi bundles declare their reusable methods for use by other bundles. The most basic Java source code for an OSGi bundle follows:

```java
package basicosgi;

import org.osgi.framework.BundleActivator;
import org.osgi.framework.BundleContext;

public class Activator implements BundleActivator {

        public void start(BundleContext context) throws Exception {
                System.out.println("Hello World!!");
        }

        public void stop(BundleContext context) throws Exception {
                System.out.println("Goodbye World!!");
        }
}
```

The runtime examines the MANIFEST.MF file to determine what the activator class is (Bundle-Activator), the name the runtime will use to refer to it (Bundle-SymbolicName), and its dependencies:

```
Manifest-Version: 1.0
Bundle-ManifestVersion: 2
Bundle-Name: BasicOSGI Plug-in
Bundle-SymbolicName: BasicOSGI
Bundle-Version: 1.0.0
Bundle-Activator: basicosgi.Activator
Eclipse-LazyStart: true
Bundle-RequiredExecutionEnvironment: J2SE-1.5
Import-Package: org.osgi.framework;version="1.3.0"
```

To generate the preceding example, create a new plug-in project as before, using the New Plug-in Project wizard, but this time check the "Generate an activator, a Java class that controls the plug-in's life cycle" check box (refer to Figure 3-4). Do not check the "This plug-in will make contributions to the UI" check box, and do not use a template (i.e., clear the "Create a plug-in using one of the templates" check box on the Templates wizard screen; refer to Figure 3-5). For this exercise, call the project BasicOSGI.

Your BasicOSGI plug-in can be started and stopped dynamically by the runtime environment, but it isn't really very useful in itself. The power of OSGi bundles comes through the declaration and use of services and their access via the Service Registry. In principle, this is similar in concept to the way SOA with web services operates in a large enterprise, so you could consider OSGi to be "service oriented."

OSGi Services

To offer a service to other bundles, you declare an interface that exposes the operations you want to offer, along with an implementation class, and you register it with the OSGi runtime through the registerService method of the BundleContext. To make use of this service, you use a service tracker that uses the BundleContext and service name to "get" the service and cast the response to the given interface and call it. A ServiceTracker is a utility class provided by the OSGi runtime to make finding and using services easier. The best way to demonstrate this is with an example that splits the preceding functionality into two bundles, one a service producer and the other a service consumer.

Consider a simple Math service that offers basic mathematical operations. You will reuse your BasicOSGI plug-in project and develop the earlier example with a bundle to host your service. The operations are defined in an interface that is registered as a service, and the implementation is hidden within the OSGi bundle that supports that service. You will add these classes to your simple OSGI example.

The service interface is very simple and offers basic operations using the BigDecimal class:

```
package basicosgi;

import java.math.BigDecimal;

public interface SimpleMaths {
```

```
        public BigDecimal add(BigDecimal first, BigDecimal second);
        public BigDecimal subtract(BigDecimal first, BigDecimal second);
        public BigDecimal multiply(BigDecimal first, BigDecimal second);
        public BigDecimal divide(BigDecimal first, BigDecimal second);
}
```

The implementation class that provides the functionality for the service within the bundle is not much more complex than the interface itself:

```
package basicosgi;

import java.math.BigDecimal;

public class SimpleMathsImpl implements SimpleMaths {

        public BigDecimal add(BigDecimal first, BigDecimal second) {
                return (first.add(second));
        }

        public BigDecimal subtract(BigDecimal first, BigDecimal second) {
                return (first.subtract(second));
        }

        public BigDecimal multiply(BigDecimal first, BigDecimal second) {
                return (first.multiply(second));
        }

        public BigDecimal divide(BigDecimal first, BigDecimal second) {
                return (first.divide(second));
        }
}
```

Finally, the service registration logic is a simple change to your existing OSGi functionality to register the service with metadata to allow a consumer to examine necessary properties such as its version:

```
package basicosgi;

import java.util.Hashtable;

import org.osgi.framework.BundleActivator;
import org.osgi.framework.BundleContext;

public class Activator implements BundleActivator {

        public void start(BundleContext context) throws Exception {
```

```
        // Create the service and its metadata for the registry to use
        SimpleMaths service = new SimpleMathsImpl();
        Hashtable<String, String> metadata = new Hashtable<String, String>();
        metadata.put("Version", "1.0");
        context.registerService(SimpleMaths.class.getName(), service, metadata);
    }

    public void stop(BundleContext context) throws Exception {
    }
}
```

To use your new service, you create a new consumer bundle in the same way you created your basic OSGi bundle, but use a service tracker to find the SimpleMaths service, get access to it and open it, and then call its methods. To make compilation easier, this project should reference the previous project in the Eclipse build environment, so amend the project Properties by right-clicking and adding the BasicOSGI project on the Project References Dependencies tab (see Figure 3-11). At runtime, the OSGi platform also needs to know about the dependency, so change the MANIFEST.MF file for your new project and add the dependency there.

Figure 3-11. *Project References Dependencies tab*

For the purposes of this exercise, this code is added to the activator, but in real use it would be used to compose a new service from fine-grained services or to support an application environment:

```java
package testsimplemaths;

import java.math.BigDecimal;

import org.osgi.framework.BundleActivator;

import org.osgi.framework.BundleContext;
import org.osgi.util.tracker.ServiceTracker;

import basicosgi.SimpleMaths;

public class Activator implements BundleActivator {
    private SimpleMaths service;
    private ServiceTracker BigDecimalServiceTracker;

    public void start(BundleContext context) throws Exception {
        // Create a tracker and track the service
        ServiceTracker SimpleMathsServiceTracker = new ServiceTracker(context,
                SimpleMaths.class.getName(), null);
        SimpleMathsServiceTracker.open();

        // Grab the service and use it
        service = (SimpleMaths) SimpleMathsServiceTracker.getService();
        BigDecimal result = service.add(new BigDecimal(5.1), new BigDecimal(5.3));
        System.out.println("The result is " + result.toString());
    }

    public void stop(BundleContext context) throws Exception {
        // Close the service tracker
        BigDecimalServiceTracker.close();
        BigDecimalServiceTracker = null;
        service = null;
    }
}
```

The preceding code creates your ServiceTracker object using the context and your interface name, which under the covers will make use of the OSGi Service Registry to find your service. You must allow Java to access the methods supplied by this interface, so you cast the response after opening the service tracker object. Then you call the methods on the interface as if it was local. When you stop the bundle, you want to close the service tracker and ensure that the object is garbage collected.

Running Your Sample OSGi Service

To run your service, you must export the code you have written so that it can be run in a basic OSGi environment. For each of these separate projects, you need to right-click the name and select Export to initiate the Export wizard. When the wizard opens, expand the Plug-in Development folder and select "Deployable plug-ins and fragments" (see Figure 3-12). Click Next. On the next wizard screen, make sure the correct project, target, and archive file are selected. The archive file will be put into a zip file that contains the bundle in a JAR file under a /plugins directory.

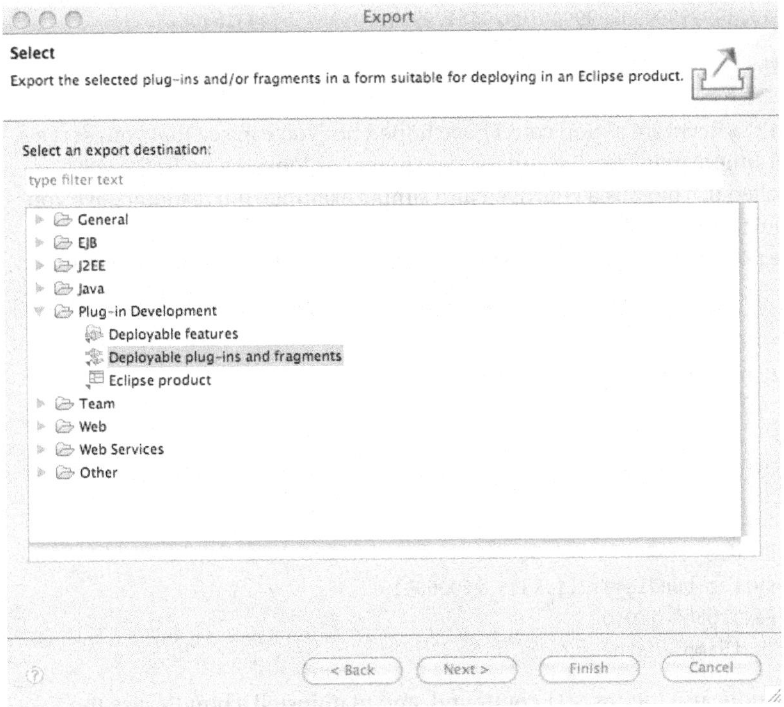

Figure 3-12. *Plug-in Export wizard Select screen*

You have your code, but you don't yet have an OSGi runtime. Surprisingly, the OSGi runtime is just a small, single library that includes an administration console environment, and you can find and use it even within WAS itself. So, create a directory and in it copy your two plug-in archive zip files. Unzip both archive files to create the /plugins subdirectory within this directory. Then, from an Eclipse environment or even a local copy of WAS, copy the file org.eclipse.osgi_3.2.1.R32x_v20060919.jar from the plugins directory to your plugins subdirectory. Next, within the /plugins subdirectory, create a /configuration directory and in it put in a config.ini file with contents like the following:

```
osgi.bundles=BasicOSGI_1.0.0.jar@start, testSimpleMaths_1.0.0.jar@start
eclipse.ignoreApp=true
```

In this configuration file, the two JAR files are what I named my service producer bundle and service consumer bundle, respectively, and the names must match the names of the files in the /plugins subdirectory.

Finally, it's time to run your code and see why you have taken this path into your understanding of WAS. OSGi has a console environment that you can use to control the environment, so use it to see your output.

From the directory above the /plugins subdirectory, run the OSGi JAR file and pass it the -console parameter:

```
java -jar plugins/org.eclipse.osgi_3.2.1.R32x_v20060919.jar -console
osgi> The result is 10.39999999999999946709294817992486059665679931640625

osgi>
```

Well, the math isn't as accurate as you could have hoped but you can see that your service producer has offered a simple math service and the consumer has looked it up in the OSGi Service Registry and called it. This was a contrived and simple example, but it should give you an idea of how powerful this technology can be. The example is not finished yet, though, as you have yet to see the power of OSGi at work. Next you are going to do a little administration.

OSGi Administration

To see the bundles that are loaded, use the ss command:

```
osgi> ss

Framework is launched.

id      State        Bundle
0       ACTIVE       system.bundle_3.2.1.R32x_v20060919
1       ACTIVE       BasicOSGI_1.0.0
2       ACTIVE       testSimpleMaths_1.0.0
```

To install a new bundle, use the install command, and to uninstall a bundle, use the uninstall command. You can start and stop bundles dynamically by using the start and stop commands, respectively, and the related methods in the activator class are called as a result. You can find the list of bundles the system knows about by using the bundles command, and you can see the details of a particular bundle by using the bundle command followed by a bundle ID or location. You can see the active bundles by using the active command as follows:

```
osgi> active
System Bundle [0]
initial@reference:file:BasicOSGI_1.0.0.jar/ [1]
initial@reference:file:testSimpleMaths_1.0.0.jar/ [2]
   3 active bundle(s).
```

Of particular interest for your investigation here is the services command that lists the registered services and their users. Even with your simple environment, the list of services is very long, but your service is at the bottom:

```
{basicosgi.SimpleMaths}={Version=1.0, service.id=20}
  Registered by bundle: initial@reference:file:BasicOSGI_1.0.0.jar/ [1]
  Bundles using service:
    initial@reference:file:testSimpleMaths_1.0.0.jar/ [2]
```

Your current setup is missing the Equinox dynamic support, so you can't add new plug-ins dynamically. For now just type exit to leave the OSGi console environment. You need to copy the dynamic bundle control support to your /plugins subdirectory and change the configuration to use them. From the same location that the org.eclipse.osgi_3.2.1*.jar file came from, copy the following two JAR files:

```
org.eclipse.equinox.common_3.2.0.v20060603.jar
org.eclipse.update.configurator_3.2.1.v20092006.jar
```

The config.ini file in the configuration subdirectory must be changed to load the dynamic bundle management subsystem, so edit it to read as follows:

```
osgi.bundles=org.eclipse.equinox.common@2:start, org.eclipse.update.configurator@3:
start, BasicOSGI_1.0.0.jar@start, testSimpleMaths_1.0.0.jar@start
eclipse.ignoreApp=true
```

When you run your OSGi environment now, the results are as before, but running ss will show a different bundle configuration:

```
osgi> ss

Framework is launched.

id      State       Bundle
0       ACTIVE      system.bundle_3.2.1.R32x_v20060919
1       ACTIVE      BasicOSGI_1.0.0
2       ACTIVE      testSimpleMaths_1.0.0
3       ACTIVE      org.eclipse.equinox.common_3.2.0.v20060603
4       ACTIVE      org.eclipse.update.configurator_3.2.1.v20092006
```

It is important at this point that you leave the OSGi console running. The final key piece behind its use in application servers such as WAS 7, is the ability to dynamically load and unload bundles. So, copy another bundle into the environment and load it dynamically. For this example, the Eclipse plug-in development wizard was used to generate a "Hello World!" sample bundle that merely outputs a message. Generate the bundle, export it as before, and unzip it into the /plugins subdirectory. Now, using the full path name to the library in which you will install the test bundle, start it running, stop it, and uninstall it to show how OSGi can dynamically control bundles. Use the bundle ID as an identifier throughout.

```
osgi> install file:///Users/colinrenouf/Documents/WAS7OSGI/plugins/
testService_1.0.0.jar
Bundle id is 8

osgi> start 8
Howdy y'all
HOWDY Y'ALL!!!
```

```
osgi> ss

Framework is launched.

id      State       Bundle
0       ACTIVE      system.bundle_3.2.1.R32x_v20060919
1       ACTIVE      BasicOSGI_1.0.0
2       ACTIVE      testSimpleMaths_1.0.0
3       ACTIVE      org.eclipse.equinox.common_3.2.0.v20060603
4       ACTIVE      org.eclipse.update.configurator_3.2.1.v20092006
8       ACTIVE      testService_1.0.0

osgi> stop 8

osgi> uninstall 8

osgi> ss

Framework is launched.

id      State       Bundle
0       ACTIVE      system.bundle_3.2.1.R32x_v20060919
1       ACTIVE      BasicOSGI_1.0.0
2       ACTIVE      testSimpleMaths_1.0.0
3       ACTIVE      org.eclipse.equinox.common_3.2.0.v20060603
4       ACTIVE      org.eclipse.update.configurator_3.2.1.v20092006
```

Why have you done all of this? Well, the Eclipse runtime that underpins WAS is now implemented using this OSGi service mechanism, but more than this, WAS itself and every major application server is now implemented using this underlying mechanism of services exposed from OSGi bundles and accessed via the Service Registry.

Monitoring the Internals of WAS

You are now going to see how the OSGi environment lets you not just make use of the Service Registry but also place listeners on it so that you can dynamically monitor and respond to events in the environment. This will be useful later when you build a simple bundle to monitor the internals of WAS and log its behavior. Listeners can be placed on the Extension Registry, the Service Registry, the collection of bundles, and runtime jobs so that the listeners are notified of any changes to these items.

By now you are almost certain to have started wondering what all of this has to do with the enterprise-class WebSphere Application Server. Surprisingly, WAS doesn't do much to hide this functionality from the administrator. Go into the /bin directory of a WAS profile directory and you will find an osgiConsole.sh or osgiConsole.bat file that gives access to the same OSGi console as above, and in this you can see and control the bundles and their related services:

```
WP61ONWAS7:/opt/IBM/WebSphere/wp_profile/bin # ./osgiConsole.sh
osgi> ss

Framework is launched.

id      State       Bundle
0       ACTIVE      system.bundle_3.2.1.R32x_v20060919
                    Fragments=1, 2
1       RESOLVED    com.ibm.cds_2.0.4.200802251155
                    Master=0
2       RESOLVED    com.ibm.ws.eclipse.adaptors_7.0.0
                    Master=0
3       ACTIVE      org.eclipse.equinox.common_3.2.0.v20060603
4       STARTING    org.eclipse.update.configurator_3.2.1.v20092006
5       RESOLVED    org.eclipse.core.runtime_3.2.0.v20060603
6       RESOLVED    com.ibm.ws.admin.core_7.0.0
7       RESOLVED    com.ibm.ws.admin.services_7.0.0
8       RESOLVED    com.ibm.ws.bootstrap_7.0.0
9       RESOLVED    com.ibm.ws.coregroupbridge_7.0.0
10      RESOLVED    com.ibm.ws.debug.osgi_7.0.0
12      RESOLVED    com.ibm.ws.ejbportable_7.0.0
                    Master=73
13      RESOLVED    com.ibm.ws.emf_2.1.0
14      RESOLVED    org.eclipse.emf.common_2.2.1.v200609210005
15      RESOLVED    org.eclipse.emf.commonj.sdo_2.1.0.v200609210005
16      RESOLVED    org.eclipse.emf.ecore.change_2.2.0.v200609210005
17      RESOLVED    org.eclipse.emf.ecore_2.2.1.v200609210005
18      RESOLVED    org.eclipse.emf.ecore.sdo_2.2.0.v200609210005
19      RESOLVED    org.eclipse.emf.ecore.xmi_2.2.1.v200609210005
20      RESOLVED    com.ibm.wsspi.extension_7.0.0
21      RESOLVED    com.ibm.ws.runtime.gateway_7.0.0


....

133     INSTALLED   com.ibm.ws.portletcontainer_6.1.0
134     INSTALLED   com.ibm.jaxb.tools_2.0.0
135     INSTALLED   com.ibm.ws.portletcontainer.internal_6.1.0
142     ACTIVE      com.ibm.ws.runtime.mqjms_7.0.0.0

osgi>
```

Thus, in a WAS 7 system you see the same behavior and many of the same underlying Eclipse and OSGI bundles as you saw previously in the chapter. All of the same OSGi features are available for use, so you can dynamically install and remove bundles, which is why this technology is of so much interest to companies such as IBM and Oracle/BEA who want to have servers that are easy to update with new features that are added dynamically via a rich component model. In a WAS environment, there are many bundles, but the breakdown between components by Java EE functionality can easily be seen. Note particularly the large number of EMF classes that provide the EMF Ecore functionality that allows IBM to use XSDs representing key Java EE and other models and generate the code to handle them, such as with JSR235 Service Data Objects (SDO).

After looking at the services in the environment, most of which are from the core Eclipse and Equinox/OSGi functionality, you will use the WAS 7 OSGi console to dynamically load a bundle that you can use to monitor the WAS functionality, but this functionality first has to be developed. For now, use the OSGi console to examine the WAS 7 OSGi Service Registry:

```
osgi> services
{org.osgi.service.packageadmin.PackageAdmin}={service.ranking=2147483647, service.
pid=0.org.eclipse.osgi.framework.internal.core.PackageAdminImpl, service.vendor=
Eclipse.org, service.id=1}
  Registered by bundle: System Bundle [0]
  Bundles using service:
    System Bundle [0]
    initial@reference:file:plugins/org.eclipse.update.configurator_.jar/ [4]
    update@plugins/org.eclipse.equinox.registry.jar [96]
    initial@reference:file:plugins/org.eclipse.core.runtime_.jar/ [5]
    update@plugins/org.eclipse.equinox.preferences.jar [95]
    update@plugins/org.eclipse.core.jobs.jar [89]
{org.osgi.service.startlevel.StartLevel}={service.ranking=2147483647, service.pid=
0.org.eclipse.osgi.framework.internal.core.StartLevelManager, service.vendor=
Eclipse.org, service.id=2}
  Registered by bundle: System Bundle [0]
  No bundles using service.
{org.eclipse.osgi.framework.log.FrameworkLog}={service.ranking=2147483647, service.
pid=0.org.eclipse.core.runtime.adaptor.EclipseLog, service.vendor=Eclipse.org,
service.id=3}
  Registered by bundle: System Bundle [0]
  Bundles using service:
    initial@reference:file:plugins/org.eclipse.update.configurator_.jar/ [4]
    initial@reference:file:plugins/org.eclipse.core.runtime_.jar/ [5]
    update@plugins/org.eclipse.equinox.preferences.jar [95]

...

{org.osgi.service.prefs.PreferencesService}={service.id=28}
  Registered by bundle: update@plugins/org.eclipse.equinox.preferences.jar [95]
  No bundles using service.
{org.eclipse.core.runtime.jobs.IJobManager}={service.id=29}
  Registered by bundle: update@plugins/org.eclipse.core.jobs.jar [89]
  No bundles using service.
{org.eclipse.osgi.service.runnable.ParameterizedRunnable}={eclipse.application=
default, service.id=30}
  Registered by bundle: initial@reference:file:plugins/org.eclipse.core.runtime_.
jar/ [5]
  Bundles using service:
```

```
     System Bundle [0]
{org.eclipse.osgi.service.runnable.ApplicationLauncher}={service.id=31}
   Registered by bundle: System Bundle [0]
   No bundles using service.


osgi>
```

Generating Your Own Monitoring Bundle

For your monitor, you are dependent on the Eclipse runtime registry, so you need the necessary support declared. In this section, you will generate your monitor and configure these dependencies. You will use the New Plug-in Project wizard to generate another plug-in project in the Eclipse IDE called WAS7Monitor that is dependent on the Eclipse 3.2 runtime, does not contribute to the UI, is not a rich client application, and has an Activator in a package called was7monitor. You will not use a template for this. The steps are as before for generating a standard Eclipse plug-in project, but this time we must also generate the OSGI activator:

1. On the Plug-in Project wizard screen (see Figure 3-13), name the project WAS7Monitor, select the Eclipse 3.2 option, and click Next.

Figure 3-13. *Plug-in Project wizard screen for your WAS7Monitor*

2. On the Plug-in Content wizard screen (see Figure 3-14), choose to generate a bundle activator class and enter a name in the Plug-in Provider field. You do *not* want this application to contribute to the UI or to be a rich client application, because this bundle is going to run on the server and not the client, so deselect those options. Click Next.

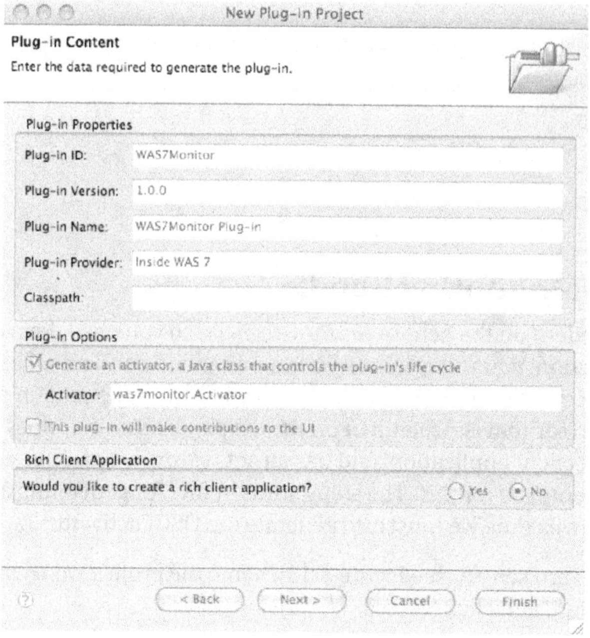

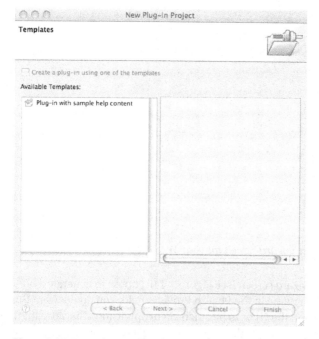

Figure 3-14. *Plug-in Content wizard screen for your WAS7Monitor*

3. On the Templates wizard screen (see Figure 3-15), because you do not want to use a template, clear the "Create a plug-in using one of the templates" check box and click Finish.

Figure 3-15. *Templates wizard screen for your WAS7Monitor*

The generated code will have an `Activator.java` source file that contains the start and stop methods that all OSGi bundles require. These methods receive a `BundleContext` class parameter that can be used to interact with the runtime environment. In this file, you are going to output the bundles loaded in the environment and set up the Eclipse registry, job, service, and bundle monitoring while making use of a set of utility functions in a separate Java source file called `Utility.java` that you also have to create. The `Utility` class will offer static methods to allow their use from anywhere. In your class, you will also see how you can set up a job to perform the output periodically to a schedule using an Eclipse job, but I will comment out the code for the purposes of the exercise here.

For your monitoring functionality, you need access to the Eclipse runtime registry as well as the OSGi features, so declare the following dependencies:

`org.eclipse.equinox.registry`: Eclipse Extension Registry access

`org.eclipse.osgi`: OSGi functionality, such as bundle support

`org.eclipse.equinox.common`: Eclipse Equinox OSGi implementation support

`org.eclipse.core.jobs`: Eclipse job scheduling support

`org.eclipse.core.runtime`: Core Eclipse support

`org.eclipse.core.runtime.compatibility`: Compatibility between OSGi/Equinox current Eclipse versions and earlier implementations

To make this declaration, open the `MANIFEST.MF` file for the project and click the Dependencies tab (see Figure 3-16). Then click the Add button to add each dependency.

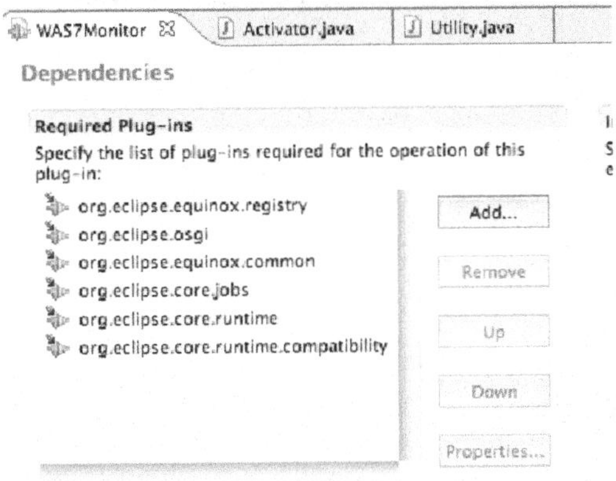

Figure 3-16. *WAS7Monitor plug-in dependencies*

You also need to ensure that your plug-in is loaded so that it can install its hooks into the environment to monitor it, so click the `MANIFEST.MF` tab and change the line at the end reading `Eclipse-LazyStart: true` to be `Eclipse-LazyStart: false`. This ensures that the plug-in is actually loaded when it is examined by the runtime, rather than just having its `MANIFEST.MF` read.

Adding the Monitoring Code to Your WAS7Monitor Bundle

Next you must add your code. First click the New button in Eclipse in the top-left corner of the IDE and add a new class in the was7monitor package called Utility. This class should not have a main method, so clear the "public static void main (String[] args)" check box and click Finish.

In your Utility class, you will first create a method called output that will get access to the Eclipse Extension Registry and for each extension point will log all of the extensions making use of it, list each service with its users, and list each bundle with its users. You then will add a method as required for each of the listener interfaces you are implementing for dynamic monitoring, although the listener interfaces will be exposed from the Activator class.

One of the useful features of both OSGi and Eclipse is the ability to dynamically extend. For the Eclipse side of things care must be taken because an Eclipse extension point is an XML description and need not have code with it, so to examine the Java method level of what can be extended in WAS, you need to look at the extensions that extend the extension point and use reflection to query the method details for any classes provided. This uses the createExecutableExtension functionality for the extension and the configuration elements.

Similarly, for the OSGi services, you can register for and access the service and then query its class and method details. This is one of the great features of standard Sun Java reflection, the underpinning of the JavaBeans component model, because it allows us to access an object we know little about and ask it its class (getClass()), get a detailed list of its methods (getMethods()), and enumerate the details. In doing this we can get enough details about the interfaces inside WAS to know how to add our own extensions, although these will not be supported by IBM.

The resulting Utility class should look as follows. The code is commented to describe what is being undertaken in each method.

```
package was7monitor;

import java.io.FileWriter;
import java.io.IOException;
import java.lang.reflect.Method;
import java.util.Date;

import org.eclipse.core.runtime.CoreException;
import org.eclipse.core.runtime.IConfigurationElement;
import org.eclipse.core.runtime.IExtension;
import org.eclipse.core.runtime.IExtensionDelta;
import org.eclipse.core.runtime.IExtensionPoint;
import org.eclipse.core.runtime.IExtensionRegistry;
import org.eclipse.core.runtime.IRegistryChangeEvent;
import org.eclipse.core.runtime.IRegistryChangeListener;
import org.eclipse.core.runtime.Platform;
import org.eclipse.core.runtime.jobs.IJobChangeEvent;
import org.eclipse.core.runtime.jobs.Job;
import org.osgi.framework.Bundle;
import org.osgi.framework.BundleContext;
import org.osgi.framework.BundleEvent;
```

```java
import org.osgi.framework.ServiceEvent;
import org.osgi.framework.ServiceReference;



/**
 * Utility class to output the Eclipse environment details to a log
 *
 * @author colinrenouf
 *
 */
public class Utility {

    /**
     * Output the extensions, extension points, and bundle details to a log
     *
     * @param context
     */
    @SuppressWarnings("unchecked")
    public static void output(BundleContext context,
        IRegistryChangeListener regListener) {
        // Get the details of the Extension Registry and enumerate it,
        // outputting to a log
        try {
            FileWriter outlog = new FileWriter("/tmp/logs/WASMonitorStartup."
                                    + new Date().toString() + ".log", true);
            outlog.write("Initial Output: Getting Platform Registry.\n");
            outlog.flush();

    // For pure Eclipse and not OSGi use Platform.getExtensionRegistry.
            // For the OSGi way of doing things, use a ServiceTracker.
            // With compatibility both should work.
            IExtensionRegistry reg = Platform.getExtensionRegistry();
            if (reg != null) {
                outlog.write("Registry is: " + reg.toString() + "\n");
                outlog.flush();
                for (IExtensionPoint point: reg.getExtensionPoints()) {
                    if ((point.getUniqueIdentifier() != null)
                    && !point.getUniqueIdentifier().toLowerCase().equals("null")) {
                        outlog.write("ID: " + point.getUniqueIdentifier() + "\n");
                    }

                    for (IExtension ext: point.getExtensions()) {
                        if ((ext.getUniqueIdentifier() != null) &&
                        !ext.getUniqueIdentifier().toLowerCase().equals("null")) {
                            outlog.write("-->Extension:"
                                + ext.getUniqueIdentifier() + "\n");
                            for (IConfigurationElement element:
```

```
ext.getConfigurationElements()) {
                            try {
                                Object obj =
                                    element.createExecutableExtension("class");
                                if (obj != null) {
                                    Class clazz = obj.getClass();
                                    if (clazz != null) {
                                        outlog.write("\t--->Class: "
                                            + clazz.getName() + "\n");
                                        for (Method method: clazz.getMethods()) {
                                            if (method != null) {
                                                outlog.write("\t----->Method: " +
method.toString() + "\n");

                                            }
                                        }
                                    }
                                }
                            } catch (CoreException e) {
                                outlog.write(
                                    "Could not dynamically create an extension
for "

                                        + point.getUniqueIdentifier() + "\n");
                        }
                    }
                }
            }
        }

        // Make sure that things get written
        outlog.flush();

        // Enumerate the bundles
        Bundle bundles[] = context.getBundles();
        for (Bundle bundle: bundles)  {
            outlog.write("Bundle Name: "
                + ((bundle.getSymbolicName() != null)
                    ? bundle.getSymbolicName() : "null") + ", ID: "
                + bundle.getBundleId()
                + ", State: " + bundle.getState() + "\n");

            // If there are fragments for this bundle then output this
            Bundle fragments[] = Platform.getFragments(bundle);
            if (null != fragments) {
                for (Bundle fragment: fragments) {
                    outlog.write("Fragment Bundle Name: " +
                        ((fragment.getSymbolicName() != null)
                        ? fragment.getSymbolicName() : "null") + ", ID: "
                        + fragment.getBundleId() + ", State: "
```

```java
                        + fragment.getState() + "\n");
            }
        }

        // Make sure everything gets written
        outlog.flush();

        // Output the Service Registry information for the bundle
        if (null != bundle.getRegisteredServices()) {
            for (ServiceReference sr: bundle.getRegisteredServices()) {
                if (sr != null) {
                    outlog.write("\t-->Service Reference:"
                        + sr.toString() + "\n");
                    if (sr.getUsingBundles() != null) {
                        for (Bundle b: sr.getUsingBundles()) {
                            outlog.write("\t---->Used By: "
                                + ((b.getSymbolicName() != null)
                                ? b.getSymbolicName() : "null") + "\n");
                        }
                    }

                    // For the service get the class for the object
                    // and use reflection to enumerate it
                    Object obj = context.getService(sr);
                    if (obj != null) {
                        Class clazz = obj.getClass();
                        if (clazz != null) {
                            outlog.write("\t--->Class: "
                                + clazz.getName() + "\n");
                            for (Method method: clazz.getMethods()) {
                                if (method != null) {
                                    outlog.write("\t----->Method: "
                                        + method.toString() + "\n");
                                }
                            }
                        }
                    }
                    context.ungetService(sr);
                    outlog.flush();
                }
            }
        }
    } else {
        outlog.write("Registry is null.\n");
    }
```

```java
                // Make sure everything gets properly written
                outlog.flush();
                outlog.close();
            } catch (IOException ioe) {
                ioe.printStackTrace();
            }
        }
    }

    /**
     * Output the registry changes to a log
     *
     * @param event
     */
    public static void outputRegistryChange(IRegistryChangeEvent event) {
        // Get the details of the Extension Registry change and output them
        try {
            FileWriter outlog = new FileWriter("/tmp/logs/WASMonitorRegistryChanges."
                    + new Date().toString() + ".log", true);
            outlog.write("Registry change at: " + new Date().toString() + "\n");
            outlog.flush();
            IExtensionDelta[] deltas = event.getExtensionDeltas();
            for (int i = 0; i < deltas.length; i++) {
                if (deltas[i].getKind() == IExtensionDelta.ADDED) {
                    outlog.write("Extension "
                            + deltas[i].getExtension().getUniqueIdentifier() +
"Added.\n");
                } else {
                    outlog.write("Extension "
                            + deltas[i].getExtension().getUniqueIdentifier()
                            + "Removed.\n");
                }
                outlog.flush();
            }

            // Make sure that things get written
            outlog.flush();
            outlog.close();
        } catch (IOException ioe) {
            ioe.printStackTrace();
        }
    }

    /**
     * Output the job changes to a log
     *
     * @param event
     */
```

```java
public static void outputJobChange(IJobChangeEvent event, String change) {
    // Get the details of the job change and output it
    try {
        FileWriter outlog = new FileWriter("/tmp/logs/WASMonitorJobChanges."
                                + new Date().toString() + ".log", true);
        outlog.write("Job change at: " + new Date().toString() + "\n");
        Job job = event.getJob();
        outlog.write("Job " + job.getName() + change + ".\n");

        // Make sure that things get written
        outlog.flush();
        outlog.close();
    } catch (IOException ioe) {
        ioe.printStackTrace();
    }
}


/**
 * Output the bundle changes to a log
 */
public static void outputBundleChange(BundleEvent event) {
    // Get the details of the bundle change and output it
    try {
        FileWriter outlog = new FileWriter("/tmp/logs/WASMonitorBundleChanges."
                                + new Date().toString() + ".log", true);
        outlog.write("Bundle change at: " + new Date().toString() + "\n");
        outlog.write("Bundle: "
            + ((event.getBundle().getSymbolicName() != null)
            ? event.getBundle().getSymbolicName() : "null")
            + ", ID: " + event.getBundle().getBundleId());
        switch (event.getType()) {
            case BundleEvent.INSTALLED:
                outlog.write(" INSTALLED.\n");
                break;

            case BundleEvent.RESOLVED:
                outlog.write(" RESOLVED.\n");
                break;

            case BundleEvent.STARTED:
                outlog.write(" STARTED.\n");
                break;

            case BundleEvent.STARTING:
                outlog.write(" STARTING.\n");
                break;
```

```
                case BundleEvent.STOPPED:
                    outlog.write(" STOPPED.\n");
                    break;

                case BundleEvent.STOPPING:
                    outlog.write(" STOPPING.\n");
                    break;
                case BundleEvent.UNINSTALLED:
                    outlog.write(" UNINSTALLED.\n");
                    break;

                case BundleEvent.UNRESOLVED:
                    outlog.write(" UNRESOLVED.\n");
                    break;

                case BundleEvent.UPDATED:
                    outlog.write(" UPDATED.\n");
                    break;
            }

            // Make sure that things get written
            outlog.flush();
            outlog.close();
        } catch (IOException ioe) {
            ioe.printStackTrace();
        }
    }


    /**
     * Output the service changes to a log
     */
    public static void outputServiceChange(ServiceEvent event) {
        // Get the details of the bundle change and output it
        try {
            FileWriter outlog = new FileWriter("/tmp/logs/WASMonitorServiceChanges."
                    + new Date().toString() + ".log", true);
            outlog.write("Service change at: " + new Date().toString() + "\n");
            ServiceReference sr = event.getServiceReference();
            if (sr != null) {
                outlog.write("Service Reference: " + sr.toString()
                    + ", Bundle: "
                    + ((sr.getBundle().getSymbolicName() != null)
                        ? sr.getBundle().getSymbolicName() : "null")
                    + ", Bundle ID: " + sr.getBundle().getBundleId());

                switch (event.getType()) {
                    case ServiceEvent.MODIFIED:
```

```
                    outlog.write(" MODIFIED.\n");
                    break;

                case ServiceEvent.REGISTERED:
                    outlog.write(" REGISTERED.\n");
                    break;

                case ServiceEvent.UNREGISTERING:
                    outlog.write(" UNREGISTERING.\n");
                    break;
            }

            if (sr.getUsingBundles() != null) {
                for (Bundle b: sr.getUsingBundles()) {
                    outlog.write("\t---->Used By: "
                        + ((b.getSymbolicName() != null)
                        ? b.getSymbolicName() : "null") + "\n");
                }
            }
        }

        // Make sure that things get written
        outlog.flush();
        outlog.close();
    } catch (IOException ioe) {
        ioe.printStackTrace();
    }
  }
}
}
```

Similarly, the activator class that maps to this utility functionality is also commented to explain what it is doing (as shown in the following listing). The setting up of an Eclipse job is deliberately commented out at this point because you want to output what is being loaded by WAS immediately, but the job can be used to schedule it separately. Note that the class implements the various listener interfaces and then maps the calls down to the implementation in the Utility class.

```
package was7monitor;

import org.eclipse.core.runtime.IExtensionRegistry;
import org.eclipse.core.runtime.IRegistryChangeEvent;
import org.eclipse.core.runtime.IRegistryChangeListener;
import org.eclipse.core.runtime.Platform;
import org.eclipse.core.runtime.Plugin;
import org.eclipse.core.runtime.jobs.IJobChangeEvent;
import org.eclipse.core.runtime.jobs.IJobChangeListener;
import org.eclipse.core.runtime.jobs.IJobManager;
import org.osgi.framework.BundleContext;
```

```java
import org.osgi.framework.BundleEvent;
import org.osgi.framework.BundleListener;
import org.osgi.framework.ServiceEvent;
import org.osgi.framework.ServiceListener;

/**
 * The activator class controls the plug-in life cycle
 */
public class Activator
extends Plugin
implements IRegistryChangeListener, IJobChangeListener, BundleListener, ServiceLis-
tener {

    // The plug-in ID
    public static final String PLUGIN_ID = "WAS7Monitor";

    // The shared instance
    private static Activator plugin;

    /**
     * The constructor
     */
    public Activator() {
        plugin = this;
    }

    /*
     * (non-Javadoc)
     * @see org.eclipse.core.runtime.Plugins#start(org.osgi.framework.BundleContext)
     */
    public void start(final BundleContext context) throws Exception {
        super.start(context);
        System.out.println(
            "WAS7Monitor:Bundle Activator start method called");

        // Add a JobManager listener
        IJobManager manager = Platform.getJobManager();
        manager.addJobChangeListener(this);

        // Now output the OSGi artifact information
        // Add a bundle listener
        context.addBundleListener(this);

        // Add a service listener
        context.addServiceListener(this);
```

```java
        // Output the Eclipse runtime artifact information
        Utility.output(context, this);

        // Add a registry change listener
        // For pure Eclipse and not OSGi use Platform.getExtensionRegistry.
        // For the OSGi way of doing things, use a ServiceTracker.
        // With compatibility both should work.
        IExtensionRegistry reg = Platform.getExtensionRegistry();
        if (reg != null) {
            reg.addRegistryChangeListener(this);
        }
    }

    /*
     * (non-Javadoc)
     * @see org.eclipse.core.runtime.Plugin#stop(org.osgi.framework.BundleContext)
     */
    public void stop(BundleContext context) throws Exception {
        plugin = null;
        super.stop(context);
        System.out.println("WAS7Monitor:Bundle Activator stop method called");

        // Remove our Extension Registry listener
        IExtensionRegistry reg = Platform.getExtensionRegistry();
        if (reg != null) {
            reg.removeRegistryChangeListener(this);
        }
    }

    /**
     * Returns the shared instance
     *
     * @return the shared instance
     */
    public static Activator getDefault() {
        return plugin;
    }

    /**
     * Call our utility method to output the registry change
     *
     * @param event
     */
    public void registryChanged(IRegistryChangeEvent event) {
        Utility.outputRegistryChange(event);
    }
```

```java
/**
 * Call our utility method to output the job changes
 *
 */
public void aboutToRun(IJobChangeEvent event) {
    Utility.outputJobChange(event, " about to run");
}

public void awake(IJobChangeEvent event) {
    Utility.outputJobChange(event, " awake");
}

public void done(IJobChangeEvent event) {
    Utility.outputJobChange(event, " done");
}

public void running(IJobChangeEvent event) {
    Utility.outputJobChange(event, " running");
}

public void scheduled(IJobChangeEvent event) {
    Utility.outputJobChange(event, " scheduled");
}

public void sleeping(IJobChangeEvent event) {
    Utility.outputJobChange(event, " sleeping");
}

/**
 * Call our utility method to output the bundle changes
 *
 * @param event
 */
public void bundleChanged(BundleEvent event) {
    Utility.outputBundleChange(event);
}

/**
 * Call our utility method to output the service changes
 *
 * @param event
 */
public void serviceChanged(ServiceEvent event) {
    Utility.outputServiceChange(event);
}
}
```

Executing Your WAS7Monitor Functionality

Now that you have created your monitor, you have to export it and configure WAS to use it. Right-click the WAS7Monitor project and select Export. In the Export dialog box, expand the Plug-in Development folder, select "Deployable plug-ins and fragments," and then enter a name for an archive file. Outside the Eclipse environment, unzip the archive file and a /plugins directory will be created that contains the WAS7Monitor_1.0.0.jar file you are going to deploy to the WAS environment. Copy this file into the /plugins directory of the WAS environment, but not on a production environment where the IBM support would be affected.

Before continuing, you need to ensure that you have a directory for your logs to be written to and that your WAS environment hosting the monitor bundle has write access to it. The directory you used previously was /tmp/logs, so you need to either create this directory on the target platform or change the previous code to log somewhere else. On a Unix platform, to make the directory writable by everybody, use sudo chmod a+w /tmp/logs. For Windows, change the properties and permissions so Everybody can write to the directory. The monitor writes files with data and a timestamp to allow the log files to be tied to changes within the environment. The logs have the following contents (XXXX refers to the date and time when the activity occurs—when the bundle is started or stopped or when a change to the environment within WAS occurs):

WASMonitorJobChanges.XXXX.log: Contains the details of any Eclipse jobs running in the environment and when they are running.

WASMonitorServiceChanges.XXXX.log: Contains details of any OSGi services declared and used within the environment and notes when any changes occur.

WASMonitorBundleChanges.XXXX.log: Contains details of any changes to the OSGi bundles running in the environment as new bundles are started and existing bundles are stopped, and notes when these changes occur.

WASMonitorStartup.XXXX.log: Contains details of the static relationships between bundles, extensions, services, and the classes that implement them. This runs when the bundle is started and when the bundle is stopped.

To see the effect of your monitoring extension and learn about how WAS works, you need to load the extension into the context of the WAS runtime environment. WAS needs to be running to be monitored, which may mean running startServer.sh or startServer.bat to get it running. If you had to cold start WAS, wait until the message about the process ID is displayed before performing the next step. To install the monitor, start the OSGi console using osgiConsole.sh or osgiConsole.bat. If the WAS environment was running when the bundle was copied to the /plugins WAS subdirectory, then you must install the bundle. In the example that follows, WAS was started after the bundle was copied, so you need to obtain the bundle ID using ss and then start to start the bundle running to enable your monitor. Remember, your aim is to obtain the relationship between the extensions, bundles, and services within WAS and use Java reflection to access their interfaces.

```
142    ACTIVE      com.ibm.ws.runtime.mqjms_7.0.0.0
161    RESOLVED    WAS7Monitor_1.0.0
236    RESOLVED    osgi_bundles.introspector.bundle_0.0.3.200804202025
```

```
osgi> start 161
```

```
osgi> WAS7Monitor:Bundle Activator start method called
```

So, what have you learned? You can see some of the internals of WAS. Your view is from the Eclipse and OSGi perspective, but in this you can see the foundation on which IBM is building the WebSphere products of the future—the Eclipse/OSGi (Equinox) component model.

Viewing Eclipse and OSGi in WAS

Before looking at the static structure of the OSGi and Eclipse components inside WAS, the dynamic behavior is worthy of examination. In your /tmp/logs directory, you should find a number of log files named in accordance with the file name patterns described earlier.

Viewing the WAS Eclipse Services

First look at the files called WASMonitorJobChanges.XXXX.log. These files show Eclipse jobs, which are pieces of work scheduled to run in the background by Eclipse in accordance with a set of job rules and priorities. Applications use the Eclipse JobManager APIs to handle the scheduling.

```
...
Job change at: Mon Dec 08 12:14:18 GMT 2008
Job Compacting memory scheduled.
Job change at: Mon Dec 08 12:19:18 GMT 2008
Job Compacting memory about to run.
Job change at: Mon Dec 08 12:19:18 GMT 2008
Job Compacting memory running.
Job change at: Mon Dec 08 12:19:18 GMT 2008
Job Compacting memory done.
Job change at: Mon Dec 08 12:19:18 GMT 2008
Job Compacting memory scheduled.
Job change at: Mon Dec 08 12:24:18 GMT 2008
Job Compacting memory about to run.
Job change at: Mon Dec 08 12:24:18 GMT 2008
Job Compacting memory running.
Job change at: Mon Dec 08 12:24:18 GMT 2008
Job Compacting memory done.
Job change at: Mon Dec 08 12:24:18 GMT 2008
Job Compacting memory scheduled.
...
```

In these files on a normal running WAS system, as is true for many other Eclipse environments, there are entries for Compacting Memory jobs with a job scheduled and run usually about every five minutes. These are the jobs that operate at the Eclipse level to perform for Eclipse itself, plug-ins, and bundles tasks that are analogous to the tasks the JVM garbage collector performs, insofar as memory and resources are "tidied up." This is important in a dynamic environment such as Eclipse/OSGi. The entries seen in this file tend to not vary between applications running on top of WAS, even from a heavily used portal server such as in the example here, and are purely from the Eclipse runtime level. However, there is nothing stopping WAS or developers for applications that run on WAS using the jobs mechanism to schedule tasks in the same way as this.

Now, look at the bundle changes that occurred in this example WebSphere Portal 6.1 application running on top of WAS 7. You can see these in the WASMonitorBundleChanges. XXXX.log files:

```
Bundle change at: Mon Dec 08 12:03:26 GMT 2008
Bundle: org.eclipse.core.contenttype, ID: 86 STARTED.
Bundle change at: Mon Dec 08 12:03:26 GMT 2008
Bundle: org.eclipse.core.resources, ID: 90 STARTED.
Bundle change at: Mon Dec 08 12:03:26 GMT 2008
Bundle: com.ibm.wsfp.main, ID: 104 STARTED.
Bundle change at: Mon Dec 08 12:03:26 GMT 2008
Bundle: com.ibm.ws.emf, ID: 13 STARTED.
Bundle change at: Mon Dec 08 12:03:26 GMT 2008
Bundle: org.eclipse.emf.common, ID: 14 STARTED.
Bundle change at: Mon Dec 08 12:03:26 GMT 2008
Bundle: org.eclipse.emf.ecore, ID: 17 STARTED.
Bundle change at: Mon Dec 08 12:03:26 GMT 2008
Bundle: com.ibm.ws.admin.services, ID: 7 STARTED.
Bundle change at: Mon Dec 08 12:03:26 GMT 2008
Bundle: com.ibm.ws.admin.core, ID: 6 STARTED.
Bundle change at: Mon Dec 08 12:03:26 GMT 2008
Bundle: com.ibm.ws.proxy, ID: 113 STARTED.
Bundle change at: Mon Dec 08 12:03:26 GMT 2008
Bundle: com.ibm.wspolicy.main, ID: 105 STARTED.

...
Bundle change at: Mon Dec 08 12:09:08 GMT 2008
Bundle: WAS7Monitor, ID: 161 STARTED.
Bundle change at: Mon Dec 08 12:09:10 GMT 2008
Bundle: com.ibm.ws.wccmbase, ID: 76 STARTED.

...
Bundle change at: Mon Dec 08 12:09:42 GMT 2008
Bundle: org.eclipse.emf.commonj.sdo, ID: 15 STARTED.
Bundle change at: Mon Dec 08 12:09:42 GMT 2008
Bundle: org.eclipse.emf.ecore.sdo, ID: 18 STARTED.
Bundle change at: Mon Dec 08 12:09:42 GMT 2008
Bundle: org.eclipse.emf.ecore.change, ID: 16 STARTED.
Bundle change at: Mon Dec 08 12:09:55 GMT 2008
Bundle: com.ibm.icu, ID: 83 STARTED.
Bundle change at: Mon Dec 08 12:10:08 GMT 2008
Bundle: com.ibm.wps.plugin.ext, ID: 132 STARTED.
```

In this output, captured during the creation of a WebSphere Portal 6.1 site, a number of bundles are activated for a period. Your WAS7Monitor bundle is activated whenever your listeners are called, so you can ignore their entries.

A number of entries are from the EMF and the IBM controller bundle for it. Within the WAS environment there is a requirement for standards compliance with various XML standards and a desire for the products to be developed to a model. To support this, IBM uses the generators from the EMF (Ecore, etc.) to generate the Java support for those other model standards (i.e., UML, XML, etc.). This can be seen particularly with the JSR235 SDO support at the end of the list that is closely linked with the EMF/Ecore code and defined in terms of it.

This SDO support is especially visible in WebSphere ESB and WebSphere Process Server environments that make heavy use of SDO and the related SCA and WS-BPEL standards, as shown in the next listing:

```
Bundle: com.ibm.ws.emf, ID: 13 STARTED.
Bundle change at: Mon Dec 08 12:03:26 GMT 2008
Bundle: org.eclipse.emf.common, ID: 14 STARTED.
Bundle change at: Mon Dec 08 12:03:26 GMT 2008
Bundle: org.eclipse.emf.ecore, ID: 17 STARTED.
...
Bundle change at: Mon Dec 08 12:09:08 GMT 2008
Bundle: com.ibm.ws.emf, ID: 13 STARTED.
Bundle change at: Mon Dec 08 12:09:08 GMT 2008
Bundle: org.eclipse.emf.common, ID: 14 STARTED.
Bundle change at: Mon Dec 08 12:09:08 GMT 2008
Bundle: org.eclipse.emf.ecore, ID: 17 STARTED.
...
Bundle change at: Mon Dec 08 12:09:10 GMT 2008
Bundle: org.eclipse.emf.ecore.xmi, ID: 19 STARTED.
...
Bundle change at: Mon Dec 08 12:09:42 GMT 2008
Bundle: org.eclipse.emf.commonj.sdo, ID: 15 STARTED.
Bundle change at: Mon Dec 08 12:09:42 GMT 2008
Bundle: org.eclipse.emf.ecore.sdo, ID: 18 STARTED.
Bundle change at: Mon Dec 08 12:09:42 GMT 2008
Bundle: org.eclipse.emf.ecore.change, ID: 16 STARTED.
```

Anything with the prefix com.ibm.ws refers to standard WAS core functionality. If the extension to this is either admin or admin with another suffix, the bundle is for administration. Some components are part of independent subsystems. For example, anything with com.ibm.ws.sib refers to the Service Integration Bus, which is the messaging and web services gateway functionality for WAS.

```
Bundle change at: Mon Dec 08 12:03:26 GMT 2008
Bundle: com.ibm.ws.sib.utils, ID: 125 STARTED.
Bundle change at: Mon Dec 08 12:03:26 GMT 2008
Bundle: com.ibm.ws.sib.server, ID: 124 STARTED.
Bundle change at: Mon Dec 08 12:03:26 GMT 2008
```

Similarly, components containing the prefix com.ibm.sip refer to the SIP container that supports the Session Initiation Protocol to handle integration with instant messaging, VoIP phones, etc.

```
Bundle change at: Mon Dec 08 12:09:18 GMT 2008
Bundle: com.ibm.ws.sip.container, ID: 115 STARTED.
...
Bundle change at: Mon Dec 08 12:09:19 GMT 2008
Bundle: com.ibm.ws.sip.quorum, ID: 117 STARTED.
...
Bundle change at: Mon Dec 08 12:09:20 GMT 2008
Bundle: com.ibm.ws.sip.interface, ID: 70 STARTED.
...
Bundle: com.ibm.ws.sip.proxy, ID: 116 STARTED.
Bundle change at: Mon Dec 08 12:09:40 GMT 2008
```

Some of the bundles refer to high availability, notably those that refer to the core group and core group bridge and the first failure data capture (FFDC):

```
Bundle change at: Mon Dec 08 12:09:15 GMT 2008
Bundle: com.ibm.ffdc, ID: 80 STARTED.
Bundle change at: Mon Dec 08 12:09:15 GMT 2008
Bundle: com.ibm.ws.coregroupbridge, ID: 9 STARTED.
```

Given that this is a portal environment that uses a portlet container for composing a portal page rendered to a client from a number of portlets, you should not be surprised to see the portlet container bundle (com.ibm.ws.portletcontainer.internal) activated, as well as the web container that it hooks. This is a key part of the WAS runtime.

Much of the web container core support is in the WAS runtime bundle itself (com.ibm.ws.runtime), but higher levels of the web container support are implemented elsewhere, such as com.ibm.ws.webcontainer, which controls much of the policy side of serving servlets. The high-level portal side of things rounds off the portal support, and it is this that provides the hooks from the WebSphere Portal 6.1 product into WAS 7 itself. WAS 7 provides the portlet container itself, and the WebSphere Portal Server 6.1 product runs as a standard Java EE/J2EE application on top of it, but with the com.ibm.wps.plugin.ext bundle providing the hooks so that the product can be (at least partially) treated as an extension to WAS rather than as a plain application. This has benefits for scalability.

```
Bundle change at: Mon Dec 08 12:09:15 GMT 2008
Bundle: com.ibm.ws.portletcontainer.internal, ID: 38 STARTED.
...
Bundle change at: Mon Dec 08 12:09:18 GMT 2008
Bundle: com.ibm.ws.webcontainer, ID: 74 STARTED.
...
Bundle change at: Mon Dec 08 12:10:08 GMT 2008
Bundle: com.ibm.wps.plugin.ext, ID: 132 STARTED.
```

The new WAS 7 Centralized Installation Manager (CIM) that allows WAS to be deployed from a central repository to supporting nodes can be seen in this environment:

```
Bundle change at: Mon Dec 08 12:09:17 GMT 2008
Bundle: com.ibm.ws.cimgr, ID: 130 STARTED.
```

A number of the bundles refer to the WebSphere Common Configuration Model (WCCM), which controls and validates the XML configuration for the various WAS subsystems. Seeing these bundles started shows that WAS is ensuring that any required configuration changes (in this case, as a result of creating a new portal site) are valid and that the dependent subsystem configurations are kept in step:

```
Bundle: com.ibm.ws.wccmbase, ID: 76 STARTED.
Bundle change at: Mon Dec 08 12:09:10 GMT 2008
...
Bundle change at: Mon Dec 08 12:09:15 GMT 2008
Bundle: com.ibm.ws.wccm.cimgr, ID: 131 STARTED.
Bundle change at: Mon Dec 08 12:09:15 GMT 2008
...
Bundle: com.ibm.ws.sib.wccm, ID: 126 STARTED.
Bundle change at: Mon Dec 08 12:09:19 GMT 2008
```

One key entry that warrants further note is that of com.ibm.wsfp.main, which refers to the core of the Web Services Feature Pack:

```
Bundle change at: Mon Dec 08 12:03:26 GMT 2008
Bundle: com.ibm.wsfp.main, ID: 104 STARTED.
```

In the original WAS 6.1 product for J2EE 1.4, the web services were based around an Axis1-derived core with hooks into the core WAS runtime to handle transport chains and threads as part of the core application server rather than as part of an application. Axis1 had some fundamental issues due to the versions of the WS-I Basic Profile 1.0a–compliant standards it implemented, such as creating large object trees for serialization and deserialization.

When the standards changed to support WS-I Basic Profile 1.1 web services, the Java community changed the supporting APIs to JAX-WS and provided them as part of Java EE 5. Because the improvements were major and WAS 7 wasn't due for some time, IBM used the Eclipse/OSGI component model support (Eclipse 3.1.2) to take the Axis2 runtime and extend it to use the same facilities from the base runtime that the Axis-based code used. This extension for WAS 6.1 was known as the Web Services Feature Pack (introduced in Chapter 1) and introduced full JAX-WS functionality by integrating the Axis2 web services engine directly into the WAS runtime.

The core classes for the Java EE 5 JAX-WS and higher levels of the stack were implemented in the com.ibm.wsfp component tree, and because WAS 7 is fully Java EE 5 compliant, it should come as no surprise that this same tried and tested support from WAS 6.1 has found its way through to the core of WAS 7, although the component name is now a little misleading. IBM built heavily on this core for the WS-Policy, WS-ReliableMessaging, and other web services standards support in WAS 7.

Viewing the WAS OSGi Services

Before you look at the static structure of WAS, this section completes your view of the dynamic structure of WAS at the Eclipse/OSGi level, particularly in the OSGi services area. To start, examine the files named WASMonitorServiceChanges.XXXX.log, where XXXX is the date and time of the service change. Because there are so many of the services changed, this section looks only at those that are related to WAS directly. By examining the order in which they load and are run, you can see the dependencies between them as one base service is built upon by another component to provide its service, so this section breaks down the output into related groups to make these dependencies more apparent. These service changes take place over a period of time and the environment is multithreaded, so the order need not express relationships, but you will see later that these examples and groupings are not contrived and relate to the structure of WAS and the container implementation.

In the following output, you can see why WAS can be described as service oriented. A number of utility infrastructure services are registered and exposed by the base WAS runtime, com.ibm.ws.runtime, and these services are available for use by higher-level parts of the WAS infrastructure. At the top of the list, you can see a number of services with the com.ibm.ws.runtime.service that relate to the base functions for a repository, configuration, tracing, a component manager (used to host lower-level components for functionality provided by the containers), the base application server itself, a thread monitor, and an endpoint manager.

```
...
Service change at: Mon Dec 08 12:09:09 GMT 2008
Service Reference: {com.ibm.ws.runtime.service.Repository}={service.id=34}, Bundle:
com.ibm.ws.runtime, Bundle ID: 73 REGISTERED.
Service change at: Mon Dec 08 12:09:09 GMT 2008
Service Reference: {com.ibm.wsspi.runtime.config.ConfigService}={service.id=35},
Bundle: com.ibm.ws.runtime, Bundle ID: 73 REGISTERED.
Service change at: Mon Dec 08 12:09:09 GMT 2008
Service Reference: {com.ibm.ws.runtime.service.VariableMap}={service.id=36}, Bundle:
com.ibm.ws.runtime, Bundle ID: 73 REGISTERED.
Service change at: Mon Dec 08 12:09:09 GMT 2008
Service Reference: {com.ibm.ws.runtime.service.TraceService}={service.id=37},
Bundle: com.ibm.ws.runtime, Bundle ID: 73 REGISTERED.
Service change at: Mon Dec 08 12:09:14 GMT 2008
Service Reference: {com.ibm.ws.runtime.service.ComponentManager}={service.id=38},
Bundle: com.ibm.ws.runtime, Bundle ID: 73 REGISTERED.
Service change at: Mon Dec 08 12:09:15 GMT 2008
Service Reference: {com.ibm.ws.runtime.service.Server}={service.id=39}, Bundle:
com.ibm.ws.runtime, Bundle ID: 73 REGISTERED.
Service change at: Mon Dec 08 12:09:15 GMT 2008
Service Reference: {com.ibm.ws.runtime.service.ThreadMonitor}={service.id=40},
Bundle: com.ibm.ws.runtime, Bundle ID: 73 REGISTERED.
Service change at: Mon Dec 08 12:09:15 GMT 2008
Service Reference: {com.ibm.ws.runtime.service.EndPointMgr}={service.id=41}, Bundle:
com.ibm.ws.runtime, Bundle ID: 73 REGISTERED.
```

The next batch of service definitions shows the dependency between the runtime facilities for threading, buffer management, and the network transport facilities. These are the core facilities offered by the WAS runtime.

```
Service change at: Mon Dec 08 12:09:15 GMT 2008
Service Reference: {com.ibm.ws.channelfw.secure.FirstChannelActionsService}=
{service.id=42}, Bundle: com.ibm.ws.runtime, Bundle ID: 73 REGISTERED.
Service change at: Mon Dec 08 12:09:15 GMT 2008
Service Reference: {com.ibm.ws.runtime.service.ThreadPoolMgr}={service.id=43},
Bundle: com.ibm.ws.runtime, Bundle ID: 73 REGISTERED.
Service change at: Mon Dec 08 12:09:15 GMT 2008
Service Reference: {com.ibm.wsspi.channel.framework.TransportChannelLoader}=
{service.id=44}, Bundle: com.ibm.ws.runtime, Bundle ID: 73 REGISTERED.
Service change at: Mon Dec 08 12:09:15 GMT 2008
Service Reference: {com.ibm.wsspi.buffermgmt.WsByteBufferPoolManager}=
{service.id=45}, Bundle: com.ibm.ws.runtime, Bundle ID: 73 REGISTERED.
Service change at: Mon Dec 08 12:09:15 GMT 2008
Service Reference: {com.ibm.ffdc.provider.FfdcProvider}={service.id=46}, Bundle:
com.ibm.ws.runtime, Bundle ID: 73 REGISTERED.
Service change at: Mon Dec 08 12:09:15 GMT 2008
Service Reference: {com.ibm.ws.management.service.Admin}={service.id=47}, Bundle:
com.ibm.ws.admin.core, Bundle ID: 6 REGISTERED.
...
Service change at: Mon Dec 08 12:09:17 GMT 2008
Service Reference: {com.ibm.ws.ssl.service.SSLService}={service.id=49}, Bundle:
com.ibm.ws.runtime, Bundle ID: 73 REGISTERED.
Service change at: Mon Dec 08 12:09:17 GMT 2008
Service Reference: {com.ibm.ws.pmi.component.PMI}={service.id=50}, Bundle:
com.ibm.ws.runtime, Bundle ID: 73 REGISTERED.
Service change at: Mon Dec 08 12:09:18 GMT 2008
Service Reference: {com.ibm.wsspi.http.channel.error.HttpErrorPageService}=
{service.id=51}, Bundle: com.ibm.ws.runtime, Bundle ID: 73 REGISTERED.
Service change at: Mon Dec 08 12:09:18 GMT 2008
Service Reference: {com.ibm.wsspi.channel.framework.ChannelFrameworkService}=
{service.id=52}, Bundle: com.ibm.ws.runtime, Bundle ID: 73 REGISTERED.
```

Next in the listing, you can see one of the fundamental components offered as a service, the CORBA Object Request Broker that underpins some of the Java EE specification:

```
Service change at: Mon Dec 08 12:09:18 GMT 2008
Service Reference: {com.ibm.ws.runtime.service.ORB}={service.id=53}, Bundle:
com.ibm.ws.runtime, Bundle ID: 73 REGISTERED.
```

One of the core facilities for production usage is Workload Management, and you can see this registered as a service:

```
Service change at: Mon Dec 08 12:09:18 GMT 2008
Service Reference: {com.ibm.ws.runtime.service.WLM}={service.id=54}, Bundle:
com.ibm.ws.bootstrap, Bundle ID: 8 REGISTERED.
```

WebSphere Application Server Network Deployment (WAS-ND) uses WAS clusters to create a group of WAS instances to act as failover cover for each other and to also provide higher scalability. High availability for some of the singleton components within that cluster, such as the SIB messaging engine, is provided by the HA Manager. This uses a bulletin board facility to notify about status between other cluster members. A core group is used to relate the JVM instances. You can see some of the relationships in the next group of services:

```
Service change at: Mon Dec 08 12:09:18 GMT 2008
Service Reference: {com.ibm.wsspi.cluster.adapter.channel.ChannelSelectionAdapter}=
{service.id=55}, Bundle: com.ibm.ws.bootstrap, Bundle ID: 8 REGISTERED.
Service change at: Mon Dec 08 12:09:18 GMT 2008
Service Reference: {com.ibm.wsspi.cluster.ClusterMemberService}={service.id=56},
Bundle: com.ibm.ws.bootstrap, Bundle ID: 8 REGISTERED.
Service change at: Mon Dec 08 12:09:18 GMT 2008
Service Reference: {com.ibm.wsspi.hamanager.bboard.BulletinBoardScopes}=
{service.id=57}, Bundle: com.ibm.ws.coregroupbridge, Bundle ID: 9 REGISTERED.
```

The next group of service relationships shows how the transport chains are formed by adding additional facilities to other more primitive transport facilities, and how the rest of the application server builds upon this. Security is also added to this environment. Much of the relationship can be seen by examining the server.xml file for a particular server and the plugin.xml file for com.ibm.ws.runtime.

```
Service change at: Mon Dec 08 12:09:18 GMT 2008
Service Reference: {com.ibm.ws.handlerfw.HandlerFrameworkService}={service.id=58},
Bundle: com.ibm.ws.runtime, Bundle ID: 73 REGISTERED.
Service change at: Mon Dec 08 12:09:18 GMT 2008
Service Reference: {com.ibm.ws.runtime.service.MultibrokerDomain}={service.id=59},
Bundle: com.ibm.ws.runtime, Bundle ID: 73 REGISTERED.
Service change at: Mon Dec 08 12:09:18 GMT 2008
Service Reference: {com.ibm.ws.webservices.admin.component.WebServicesAdminComponent
}={service.id=60}, Bundle: com.ibm.wsfp.main, Bundle ID: 104 REGISTERED.
Service change at: Mon Dec 08 12:09:18 GMT 2008
Service Reference: {com.ibm.ws.cluster.channel.WLMChainEventListener}=
{service.id=61}, Bundle: com.ibm.ws.bootstrap, Bundle ID: 8 REGISTERED.
Service change at: Mon Dec 08 12:09:18 GMT 2008
Service Reference: {com.ibm.ws.extensionhelper.ExtensionHelper}={service.id=62},
Bundle: com.ibm.ws.runtime, Bundle ID: 73 REGISTERED.
Service change at: Mon Dec 08 12:09:18 GMT 2008
Service Reference: {com.ibm.wsspi.odc.ODCManager}={service.id=63}, Bundle:
com.ibm.ws.runtime, Bundle ID: 73 REGISTERED.
Service change at: Mon Dec 08 12:09:18 GMT 2008
Service Reference: {com.ibm.ws.security.service.SecurityService}={service.id=64},
Bundle: com.ibm.ws.runtime, Bundle ID: 73 REGISTERED.
Service change at: Mon Dec 08 12:09:18 GMT 2008
Service Reference: {com.ibm.websphere.management.authorizer.service.
AdminAuthzService}={service.id=65}, Bundle: com.ibm.ws.admin.core, Bundle ID: 6
REGISTERED.
Service change at: Mon Dec 08 12:09:19 GMT 2008
```

```
Service Reference: {com.ibm.ws.runtime.service.WSSecurityService}={service.id=66},
Bundle: com.ibm.ws.runtime, Bundle ID: 73 REGISTERED.
```

Note that even the application server itself is registered as a service on which other services are built:

```
Service change at: Mon Dec 08 12:09:19 GMT 2008
Service Reference: {com.ibm.ws.runtime.service.ApplicationServer}={service.id=67},
Bundle: com.ibm.ws.runtime, Bundle ID: 73 REGISTERED.
```

After the application server service has been registered, more base functionality in terms of an object pool service and related transport facilities is registered:

```
Service change at: Mon Dec 08 12:09:19 GMT 2008
Service Reference: {com.ibm.ws.objectpool.ObjectPoolService}={service.id=68},
Bundle: com.ibm.ws.runtime, Bundle ID: 73 REGISTERED.            .
Service change at: Mon Dec 08 12:09:19 GMT 2008
Service Reference: {com.ibm.ws.runtime.service.MetaDataService}={service.id=69},
Bundle: com.ibm.ws.runtime, Bundle ID: 73 REGISTERED.
Service change at: Mon Dec 08 12:09:19 GMT 2008
Service Reference: {com.ibm.ws.runtime.service.MetaDataFactoryMgr}={service.id=70},
Bundle: com.ibm.ws.runtime, Bundle ID: 73 REGISTERED.
Service change at: Mon Dec 08 12:09:19 GMT 2008
Service Reference: {com.ibm.ws.runtime.service.VirtualHostMgr}={service.id=71},
Bundle: com.ibm.ws.runtime, Bundle ID: 73 REGISTERED.
```

One of the features of the WebSphere product family is that much of the core functionality, without the controlling policy, from the higher-level members of the family such as WebSphere Process Server is provided by the Programming Model Extensions (PME) facilities. The metadata controlling this can be seen to be registered as a service:

```
Service change at: Mon Dec 08 12:09:19 GMT 2008
Service Reference: {com.ibm.ws.wccm.services.pme.metadata.MetaDataHelperService}=
{service.id=72}, Bundle: com.ibm.ws.runtime, Bundle ID: 73 REGISTERED.
```

Facilities and the transports that underpin them are closely related in WAS:

```
Service change at: Mon Dec 08 12:09:19 GMT 2008
Service Reference: {com.ibm.wsspi.runtime.component.TransportMap}={service.id=73},
Bundle: com.ibm.ws.runtime, Bundle ID: 73 REGISTERED.
Service change at: Mon Dec 08 12:09:19 GMT 2008
Service Reference: {com.ibm.ws.asynchbeans.AsynchBeansService}={service.id=74},
Bundle: com.ibm.ws.runtime, Bundle ID: 73 REGISTERED.
Service change at: Mon Dec 08 12:09:19 GMT 2008
Service Reference: {com.ibm.ws.runtime.service.ResourceMgr}={service.id=75}, Bundle:
com.ibm.ws.runtime, Bundle ID: 73 REGISTERED.
```

The underpinning of the Web Services facilities is SOAP, so the runtime for web services registers its core facilities and a SOAP handling facility before building upon it with the Axis2 facilities implemented by the com.ibm.wsfp components:

```
Service change at: Mon Dec 08 12:09:19 GMT 2008
Service Reference: {com.ibm.ws.soap.container.SoapContainerService}={service.id=76},
Bundle: com.ibm.ws.runtime, Bundle ID: 73 REGISTERED.
Service change at: Mon Dec 08 12:09:19 GMT 2008
Service Reference: {com.ibm.ws.webservices.WebServicesSystemService}=
{service.id=77}, Bundle: com.ibm.ws.runtime, Bundle ID: 73 REGISTERED.
Service change at: Mon Dec 08 12:09:19 GMT 2008
Service Reference: {com.ibm.ws.cache.CacheService}={service.id=78}, Bundle:
com.ibm.ws.runtime, Bundle ID: 73 REGISTERED.
Service change at: Mon Dec 08 12:09:19 GMT 2008
Service Reference: {com.ibm.ws.webservices.WebServicesService}={service.id=79},
Bundle: com.ibm.ws.runtime, Bundle ID: 73 REGISTERED.
Service change at: Mon Dec 08 12:09:19 GMT 2008
Service Reference: {com.ibm.wsspi.websvcs.WASAxis2Service}={service.id=80}, Bundle:
com.ibm.wsfp.main, Bundle ID: 104 REGISTERED.
```

The SIP facilities are implemented with quorum supported via a service:

```
Service change at: Mon Dec 08 12:09:19 GMT 2008
Service Reference: {com.ibm.ws.sip.quorum.SIPQuorumComponentImpl}={service.id=81},
Bundle: com.ibm.ws.sip.quorum, Bundle ID: 117 REGISTERED.
```

WAS has facilities additional to that of Java EE. It has a base scheduler, an application handler that relates components, and an injection engine to support some of the newer facilities (such as JPA, Spring, etc.):

```
Service change at: Mon Dec 08 12:09:19 GMT 2008
Service Reference: {com.ibm.wsspi.injectionengine.InjectionEngine}={service.id=82},
Bundle: com.ibm.ws.runtime, Bundle ID: 73 REGISTERED.
Service change at: Mon Dec 08 12:09:19 GMT 2008
Service Reference: {com.ibm.ws.scheduler.SchedulerService}={service.id=83}, Bundle:
com.ibm.ws.runtime, Bundle ID: 73 REGISTERED.
Service change at: Mon Dec 08 12:09:19 GMT 2008
Service Reference: {com.ibm.ws.handlerfw.impl.ApplicationHandlerManagerService}=
{service.id=84}, Bundle: com.ibm.ws.runtime, Bundle ID: 73 REGISTERED.
```

To allow extension and usage, the EJB container itself is registered as a service:

```
Service change at: Mon Dec 08 12:09:19 GMT 2008
Service Reference: {com.ibm.ws.runtime.service.EJBContainer}={service.id=85},
Bundle: com.ibm.ws.runtime, Bundle ID: 73 REGISTERED.
```

Message listeners and transports are closely related:

```
Service change at: Mon Dec 08 12:09:19 GMT 2008
Service Reference: {com.ibm.ws.runtime.service.MessageListenerManager}=
{service.id=86}, Bundle: com.ibm.ws.runtime, Bundle ID: 73 REGISTERED.
Service change at: Mon Dec 08 12:09:19 GMT 2008
Service Reference: {com.ibm.ws.localhttp.channel.LocalInboundChainFactory}=
{service.id=87}, Bundle: com.ibm.ws.runtime, Bundle ID: 73 REGISTERED.
```

The web container itself is registered as a service for extension and use:

```
Service change at: Mon Dec 08 12:09:19 GMT 2008
Service Reference: {com.ibm.ws.webcontainer.WebContainerService}={service.id=88},
Bundle: com.ibm.ws.webcontainer, Bundle ID: 74 REGISTERED.
```

Again, various higher-level components and facilities use the lower-level components loaded earlier and provide new facilities:

```
Service change at: Mon Dec 08 12:09:20 GMT 2008
Service Reference: {com.ibm.ws.runtime.service.ApplicationMgr}={service.id=89},
Bundle: com.ibm.ws.runtime, Bundle ID: 73 REGISTERED.
Service change at: Mon Dec 08 12:09:20 GMT 2008
Service Reference: {com.ibm.ws.runtime.service.LibraryMgr}={service.id=90}, Bundle:
com.ibm.ws.runtime, Bundle ID: 73 REGISTERED.
Service change at: Mon Dec 08 12:09:20 GMT 2008
Service Reference: {com.ibm.ws.rsadapter.spi.RRAHPPropertyLoader}={service.id=91},
Bundle: com.ibm.ws.runtime, Bundle ID: 73 REGISTERED.
Service change at: Mon Dec 08 12:09:20 GMT 2008
Service Reference: {com.ibm.ws.runtime.service.CompositionUnitMgr}={service.id=92},
Bundle: com.ibm.ws.runtime, Bundle ID: 73 REGISTERED.
Service change at: Mon Dec 08 12:09:38 GMT 2008
Service Reference: {org.osgi.service.url.URLStreamHandlerService}={url.handler.
protocol=[wsjar],
service.id=93}, Bundle: com.ibm.ws.runtime, Bundle ID: 73 REGISTERED.
                 ---->Used By: system.bundle
```

Rather unsurprisingly, the workload controller and the HA Manager are related:

```
Service change at: Mon Dec 08 12:09:40 GMT 2008
Service Reference: {com.ibm.ws.runtime.service.WLC}={service.id=94}, Bundle:
com.ibm.ws.runtime, Bundle ID: 73 REGISTERED.
Service change at: Mon Dec 08 12:09:42 GMT 2008
Service Reference: {com.ibm.wsspi.hamanager.corestack.CoreStack}={service.id=95},
Bundle: com.ibm.ws.runtime, Bundle ID: 73 REGISTERED.
Service change at: Mon Dec 08 12:09:46 GMT 2008
Service Reference: {com.ibm.ws.scheduler.SchedulerConfigService}={service.id=96},
Bundle: com.ibm.ws.runtime, Bundle ID: 73 REGISTERED.
```

Finally, WS-Addressing support in the web services facilities uses the OSGi URL stream handling and the endpoint mapping makes use of this support:

```
Service change at: Mon Dec 08 12:09:54 GMT 2008
Service Reference: {org.osgi.service.url.URLStreamHandlerService}=
{url.handler.protocol=[reference], service.id=97}, Bundle: com.ibm.ws.runtime,
Bundle ID: 73 REGISTERED.
                 ---->Used By: system.bundle
Service change at: Mon Dec 08 12:10:04 GMT 2008
Service Reference: {com.ibm.ws.wsaddressing.integration.WSAddressingBaseService}=
{service.id=98}, Bundle: com.ibm.ws.runtime, Bundle ID: 73 REGISTERED.
```

Service change at: Mon Dec 08 12:10:04 GMT 2008
Service Reference: {com.ibm.ws.wsaddressing.integration.EndpointMapService}=
{service.id=99}, Bundle: com.ibm.ws.runtime, Bundle ID: 73 REGISTERED.

After a period of time in a steady state, the services and bundle changes stop unless substantial changes occur in what is running on WAS and what facilities are required from the applications. All of this service registration and management takes place through the WAS WsServiceRegistry that we will cover in Chapter 4.

Viewing the Bundles and Extensions

Now that you have seen the dynamic behavior of WAS and the order in which services are loaded, it is time to look at the bundles, what they extend and offer for extension, what services they offer, and (where it can be determined) the classes and methods used to access the extension points and services for higher-level extending. You need to understand this last area to understand how to extend WAS yourself.

There is a great deal of data in WASMonitorStartup.XXX.log, so I am leaving it to you as an exercise to run the example and generate the raw data.

First, consider the extension point to extension relationship—i.e., what the environment offers up for extension and then what makes use of that extension. For the purposes of readability, I have processed the data and placed it in the Appendix. If you review this, you can see that many extension points have nothing that extends them, and that the WCCM classes and the JAX-WS Web Services Feature Pack/Axis2 classes are the most common users of the Eclipse Extension Registry and the extension model.

So what does this tell you? There are a number of different types of behavior and usage described in this table. A large number of extension points have no extensions that use them. This may seem illogical, but there is a reason for this. If you were to open one of the larger bundle JAR files and look at the plugin.xml file, the reason soon becomes clear. These extension points are place markers and XML containers, which allows the Extension Registry to be used to look them up. The attributes and data held within them can then be queried using the registry APIs.

This is best explained through an example that you will examine for WAS 7 in more detail in Chapter 4, which shows the WAS container and component model in action. In WAS 6.1, a number of sections of the plugin.xml file contained entries with the name including an identifier for one of the WAS containers, and within it a number of component entries with IDs. The components identified the facilities the container required and the implementations for them, and the ID signified the order in which they were to be loaded within that container. Thus, these are mostly placeholders for internal configuration data. The Eclipse development guides describe the most simple Eclipse plug-in as simply XML, and this is the case here.

Some of the entries have only a single extension. This allows the implementation of a function to be developed separately from the interface and bound together at runtime.

Some extension points, however, have multiple extensions related to them and have declared Java interfaces to use for implementation. These are for extension by multiple subsystems as service providers. This is particularly the case for administration facilities, facilities for running applications on the Eclipse and the WAS runtime within the same JVM (as for the OSGi Console you used earlier), and the Web Services Feature Pack. These uses make perfect sense as each of these could be extended at some point in the future without the need to change the base implementation.

For example, many of the WebSphere product sets extend the Deployment Manager and other administrative functionality when they are deployed onto the WAS-ND environment. New facilities can be added to run on WAS, such as for performance monitoring. Pay particular attention to the startWsServer extension that extends the Eclipse runnable applications, because this is the startup of WAS itself that initiates the WsServer extension to IBM runnable applications on the base environment, where WsServer is the core runtime of WAS. Web services facilities are increasing all of the time, so providing some of the base functions in a manner that allows them to be hooked and extended later is a sensible design feature.

To see how this might be done, take a look at one of the implementation classes for an extension point that you queried earlier. Consider the extension point com.ibm.wsfp.main. ibmaxis2-thread-ctx-migrator-client that is used to allow the extensions some access to the underlying threading and context management for the container running the web services implementation with Axis2. This has the following core methods that are common across all implementations (ignoring those from java.lang.Object):

```
public void migrateContextToThread(org.apache.axis2.context.MessageContext)
        throws org.apache.axis2.AxisFault

public void cleanupThread(org.apache.axis2.context.MessageContext);

public void migrateThreadToContext(org.apache.axis2.context.MessageContext)
        throws org.apache.axis2.AxisFault

public void cleanupContext(org.apache.axis2.context.MessageContext);
```

Because the preceding method signatures are the same across all of the extensions, remembering that the extensions may have methods for other reasons too, you can be relatively sure that this is the interface you would need to extend the com.ibm.wsfp.main. ibmaxis2-thread-ctx-migrator-client to tie yourself into the base runtime facilities. The same technique can be adopted elsewhere for other extension points.

Without a desire to extend, why else would this information be of use to you? Well, sometimes when a problem occurs in WAS due to some runtime problem or due to an application problem, seeing the relationships between the different parts of WAS can be difficult because they are hidden in the Eclipse Extension and Service Registries. Understanding how each of the extensions is used can help you to identify and fix the problem.

With the services declarations, there is little that can be seen at the time of enumeration beyond the core services offered by the Eclipse/OSGi runtime:

```
Bundle Name: system.bundle, ID: 0, State: 32
Fragment Bundle Name: com.ibm.cds, ID: 1, State: 4
Fragment Bundle Name: com.ibm.ws.eclipse.adaptors, ID: 2, State: 4
        -->Service Reference:{org.osgi.service.packageadmin.PackageAdmin}={service.
ranking=2147483647, service.pid=0.org.eclipse.osgi.framework.internal.core.PackageAd-
minImpl, service.vendor=Eclipse.org, service.id=1}
            ---->Used By: system.bundle
            ---->Used By: org.eclipse.update.configurator
            ---->Used By: org.eclipse.equinox.registry
            ---->Used By: org.eclipse.core.runtime
            ---->Used By: org.eclipse.equinox.preferences
```

```
        ---->Used By: org.eclipse.core.jobs
        ---->Used By: org.eclipse.equinox.common
        -->Service Reference:{org.osgi.service.startlevel.StartLevel}={service.rank-
ing=2147483647, service.pid=0.org.eclipse.osgi.framework.internal.core.StartLevelMan-
ager, service.vendor=Eclipse.org, service.id=2}
        ---->Used By: system.bundle
...
        -->Service Reference:{java.lang.Runnable}={name=splashscreen, service.id=19}
Bundle Name: com.ibm.cds, ID: 1, State: 4
Bundle Name: com.ibm.ws.eclipse.adaptors, ID: 2, State: 4
Bundle Name: org.eclipse.equinox.common, ID: 3, State: 32
...
        -->Service Reference:{org.eclipse.osgi.service.runnable.
ParameterizedRunnable}={eclipse.application=default, service.id=30}
Bundle Name: com.ibm.ws.admin.core, ID: 6, State: 32
Bundle Name: com.ibm.ws.admin.services, ID: 7, State: 32
Bundle Name: com.ibm.ws.bootstrap, ID: 8, State: 32
Bundle Name: com.ibm.ws.coregroupbridge, ID: 9, State: 4
Bundle Name: com.ibm.ws.debug.osgi, ID: 10, State: 4
Bundle Name: com.ibm.ws.ejbportable, ID: 12, State: 4
Bundle Name: com.ibm.ws.emf, ID: 13, State: 32
Bundle Name: org.eclipse.emf.common, ID: 14, State: 32
Bundle Name: org.eclipse.emf.commonj.sdo, ID: 15, State: 4
...
Bundle Name: com.ibm.ws.jpa, ID: 34, State: 4
...
Bundle Name: org.eclipse.jdt.core, ID: 46, State: 4
Fragment Bundle Name: com.ibm.ws.jdt.core, ID: 77, State: 4
...
Bundle Name: com.ibm.ws.amm, ID: 71, State: 4
Bundle Name: org.apache.myfaces1_2, ID: 72, State: 4
Bundle Name: com.ibm.ws.runtime, ID: 73, State: 32
Fragment Bundle Name: com.ibm.ws.ejbportable, ID: 12, State: 4
Fragment Bundle Name: com.ibm.ws.security.crypto, ID: 69, State: 4
Fragment Bundle Name: com.ibm.ws.runtime.dist, ID: 100, State: 4
Fragment Bundle Name: com.tivoli.pd.amwas.tai, ID: 123, State: 4
Bundle Name: com.ibm.ws.webcontainer, ID: 74, State: 4
Bundle Name: com.ibm.ws.wccm.compatibility, ID: 75, State: 4
Bundle Name: com.ibm.ws.wccmbase, ID: 76, State: 4
Fragment Bundle Name: com.ibm.ws.amm, ID: 71, State: 4
Fragment Bundle Name: com.ibm.ws.wccm.compatibility, ID: 75, State: 4
Bundle Name: com.ibm.ws.jdt.core, ID: 77, State: 4
...
Bundle Name: com.ibm.jaxb.tools, ID: 102, State: 4
Bundle Name: org.apache.axis2, ID: 103, State: 4
Bundle Name: com.ibm.wsfp.main, ID: 104, State: 32
Bundle Name: com.ibm.wspolicy.main, ID: 105, State: 32
```

```
...
Bundle Name: com.ibm.ws.portletcontainer.internal, ID: 135, State: 2
Bundle Name: com.ibm.ws.runtime.mqjms, ID: 142, State: 32
Bundle Name: WAS7Monitor, ID: 161, State: 8
```

Although there is little you can learn from the services in this enumeration, pay particular attention to bundles that have fragments (indicated by Fragments in the name). These are additional bundles that are to be treated as if they are part of the core bundle. In the preceding list, you can see that IBM has extended the Java Development Tools from the base Eclipse, which makes sense because the runtime must dynamically support generation of artifacts such as servlets from JSP pages. Similarly, the com.ibm.cds bundle, which assists in class loading to allow the IBM J9 JVM to support its class cache, is treated as a fragment of the core system bundle. Finally, note the fragments that are added to the com.ibm.ws.runtime bundle—these are the core facilities of the application server itself.

Although the details have been removed from the output here, I also used the ability to query a service and use reflection in my monitor bundle implementation. If you wanted to extend the services offered by the WAS environment that were shown in your service changes as they were dynamically registered as your dynamic log output, you could use the same technique to get access to the APIs and generate your own implementations. You will use this technique in Chapter 4 when you write your own sample WAS extension component to load inside the WAS runtime environment.

Extending WAS

You have already seen two ways to extend the WAS runtime—using services and using extensions. There are IBM documents showing how to use the Eclipse Extension Registry on WAS, but it is unlikely that any extensions to WAS itself would be supported by IBM. However, you can use the techniques described in this chapter for further experimentation.

Suppose you were able to extend WAS in a supported manner. How would you go about it? Let's say I wanted to add the ability to fail over a virtual IP address in WAS, as I can in other environments. Well, I could have a JNI component to provide lower-level access to the sockets interface that this would require, wrap the component with a Java class, and then host the component in a plug-in that I load dynamically from a standard Java EE application. In reality, while I might be able to find services for the HA Manager to hook so that I would know when a failover was occurring, such as the HA Manager Bulletin Board Service, I would be sensitive to every change and it would be difficult to get my extension to function reliably without IBM help.

A more likely example is what I would do if I wanted to add my own web application filtering functionality to the existing web services or to add support for new web service facilities. The services and extension points for access to the various transport chains and threading used by the Axis2/Web Services Feature Pack engine were designed with this in mind, but for IBM's use. By providing the same extensions and using the same services as the other facilities, I could extend WAS with little effort and be able to tie into the core WAS runtime services. This could even be used to provide a WebSphere ESB SCA–compliant runtime using the Apache Tuscany engine, but this would probably not be worth doing because IBM is already doing it with the SCA Feature Pack for WAS 7.

Summary

This chapter started by looking at the Eclipse plug-in model and how plug-in components offer up extension points that other components use through extensions. It then looked at the newer OSGi model, in which components are shipped in the form of bundles, which, unlike the Eclipse plug-ins, can be loaded and unloaded dynamically through the use of the `activator` class. You saw how these bundles register services that others can use. In the examples, you created your own Eclipse-based browser and then looked at how the startup mechanism of this worked in the same way as the WAS startup itself. You then looked at the WAS use of Eclipse and created an OSGi bundle to monitor the dynamic behavior of the WAS runtime and its numerous bundles. Along the way, you learned how Eclipse and OSGi work, with the use of a few key tools like the OSGi Console that ships with every OSGi runtime environment. You saw why companies build on this platform to make their products dynamic in runtime component usage, to reduce the memory footprint, yet easily extensible.

Now that you understand the basics of Eclipse plug-ins and how they work, you are ready to discover some of the plug-ins supplied with WAS and what functionality they provide. The next chapter covers the internals of the core WAS 7 runtime. You will see how the Eclipse extension point model is used in the WAS runtime to partition the components that are loaded into each container; how the WAS runtime consists of Eclipse plug-ins and components that use the Extension and Service Registries; and how all of this fits together to create the containers that make up WAS 7.

CHAPTER 4

■ ■ ■

Underlying WAS Runtime

In the previous chapter we looked at the Eclipse/OSGi architecture and how it works, and then how it relates to the underlying infrastructure of WAS. While WAS is layered, pretty much like every other piece of software on the market, it is also componentized and split into subsystems, that is, systems of components. The components are defined using the Eclipse and OSGi technologies described in the previous chapter, with extensions, extension points, and services accessed via the underlying Eclipse/OSGi registries. This is, however, just one view of the architecture that allows WAS dynamic extensibility. There are other views or perspectives that are just as valid.

In this chapter we look at the underlying WAS runtime from more than one perspective to see how the components fit together. This chapter is limited to covering the core functions of WAS underlying the base application server runtime on which the rest of the Java Enterprise Edition (JavaEE) environment builds. This includes facilities such as threading, socket management, transaction management, and so on, that cross the boundaries of the various JavaEE containers and subsystems. It includes the core container facilities on which the EJB and web containers build, but does not include the policies under which these containers offer their individual facilities. Thus, WAS is like many other large software systems, with a core layer providing function, which I will describe here, on top of which the policies seen externally are executed. The core WAS 7 runtime referred to in this chapter is found in the plugin JAR file `com.ibm.ws.runtime.jar` from the WAS `plugins` directory. The fragments are in separate plugin JAR files that extend the core runtime plugin code, but are treated as part of it by the Eclipse/OSGi environment. The core WAS runtime referenced in the `MANIFEST.MF` file for the `com.ibm.ws.runtime.jar` plugin refers to the following plugins:

- `com.ibm.ws.runtime`
- `com.ibm.ws.ejbportable`
- `com.ibm.ws.security.crypto`
- `com.ibm.ws.runtime.dist`
- `com.tivoli.pd.amwas.tai`

All of these are treated as one core unit by the Eclipse/OSGi runtime, as shown in the code listing in Chapter 3, in which the bottom four entries in the list of loaded OSGi bundles declared themselves as external fragments of the core `com.ibm.ws.runtime` component. However, some other component plugins are accessed along the way to provide some other key functionality. These are separated from the core runtime because the functionality is large enough that a separate library is necessary.

The majority of this chapter examines one key plugin, `com.ibm.ws.runtime`, because the others have only a minor part to play in the orchestrating of the WAS subsystems that provide what JavaEE developers see as the application server. This is a suitable abstraction on which to build, but it can be misleading because there are numerous other plugins that are loaded and play a major part, particularly the `com.ibm.ws.wlm` and `com.ibm.ws.webcontainer` plugins.

The previous chapter considered how Eclipse-based extension points and extensions are declared in the `plugin.xml` file and how they are read for each plugin and loaded into the Eclipse extension registry. Thus, when the Eclipse registry is queried to load the extensions for a particular extension point relating the components for a particular container, *all* extensions that extend it from *all* plugins loaded from the plugins subdirectory are returned.

This chapter considers only the components loaded in the key containers from the `com.ibm.ws.runtime` plugin. Although I will ignore those components loaded from the numerous other plugins shipped with WAS, I will point out when they have external references. This abstraction will help you to understand the relationships between containers and components. The components loaded from the `com.ibm.ws.runtime` plugin are the key ones, but this representation is only a simplification we use in this chapter, because many containers, components, and subsystems mentioned in the execution flow in this chapter and other chapters are implemented in other plugins. We will see more of this and the relationship between containers and the components they load in subsequent chapters.

While we examine the runtime, keep in mind that there are multiple chains of execution through the runtime startup that periodically join and separate at various touch points. By *chain* I mean groups of threads and their related environmental artifacts. The startup command line for WAS highlights how this comes about, with the Java Virtual Machine (JVM) starting the Eclipse/OSGi environment, which then starts the various bundles, followed by the named application entry point that the Eclipse/OSGi runtime starts. So, as explained in the previous chapter, the command line refers to `com.ibm.ws.runtime.WsServer` and the Eclipse runtime runs the `com.ibm.ws.runtime.eclipse.WSStartServer` as the named class for the extension ID `startWsServer`, extending the `org.eclipse.core.runtime.applications` extension point. Just to make it even more complex, the core WAS runtime `MANIFEST.MF` file declares a bundle activator of `com.ibm.ws.runtime.component.RuntimeBundleActivator` to handle the OSGi side of bundle startup. Thus, there are three separate "entry points" to understand: one referenced on the command line (`com.ibm.ws.runtime.WsServer`); one started as part of the Eclipse-specific initialization via extension-point-related functionality (`com.ibm.ws.runtime.WSStartServer`); and one started as part of the Eclipse Equinox OSGi bundle activation (`com.ibm.ws.runtime.component.RuntimeBundleActivator`). Fortunately, this initialization converges.

The Runtime Base Server Functionality

All JavaEE application servers—and WAS 7 is no different—have an expected set of services and facilities dictated by adherence to specifications. At the core of these standards is the reuse of many of the existing Object Management Group (OMG) CORBA Object Request Broker (ORB) standards for communications, security, and remote object access. Additionally, the fact that the JavaEE specification outlines separation of concerns into containers suggests that some underlying layer should provide common facilities to these containers for thread pool management and TCP/IP socket management. These facilities provide the building blocks upon which the required JavaEE services should be built. These components and services that form the building blocks require monitoring and management facilities to enable enterprise-level qualities of service.

These facilities together underpin the behavior of application servers and we should expect to see them at the base of the WAS 7 runtime architecture.

Core WAS Infrastructure Services

WAS builds upon an Eclipse Equinox implementation of the OSGi standard that is based around the concept of looking up services in a registry to find the implementation. Dynamic binding from the caller is then used to allow access to that service. Though web services are the most commonly referred to technologies in the service-oriented architecture (SOA) arena, OSGi was designed around the same concepts, so OSGi and technologies built with it are arguably service oriented.

As WAS is becoming more service oriented, the core base facilities on which the rest of the application server is built are offered as services by the runtime. These services are accessed via a getService request to the internal WebSphere Application Server (WAS) service registry (WsServiceRegistry). This is not pure OSGi but it slightly extends it. These service facilities are implemented by components that make use of lower-level classes to do much of the work. The components offering the services are implemented using the OSGi and Eclipse technologies, but the services offered from the WsServiceRegistry are WAS rather than pure OSGi services.

Services perform an addService to register themselves with the internal WAS service registry so other services can find and access them. A service name in the form of a class name is used as the key in the registry lookup. This is the most important part of the application server—its core. The following are key JavaEE-related infrastructure services that are visible to the administrator and application developer that you will see referred to throughout this book and that you should pay particular attention to:

- *Thread Pool Mgr Service*: The thread pool manager handles pools of threads for other subsystems to use.

- *Channel Framework Service*: This handles the layered chains of connections for TCP/IP communications into and out of the application server, which underpins many other services. Essentially, this is the network layer of the application server runtime.

- *ORB Service*: This provides the CORBA ORB engine that underpins much of J2EE/JavaEE.

- *Multibroker Domain Service*: This supports the Data Replication Services (DRS) that support some of the high-availability (HA) facilities, with this being a messaging-style service similar to Java Message Service (JMS). Officially the term Multibroker is deprecated, but internally the service still exists.

- *Core Stack Service*: This initiates the core HA facilities and acts as the main controller for the WAS HAManager.

- *Cluster Runtime Service*: This handles more of the clustering for scalability and high availability.

- *Security Service*: This provides the coordination and control for the security facilities in WAS.

- *Tx Service*: This provides the control for transaction management. This is also known as the Transaction Service.

- *Name Service*: This supports the Java Naming and Directory Interface (JNDI) facilities that underpin J2EE and its object bindings.

These services permeate much of the WAS implementation and underpin the subsystems that provide the JavaEE functionality. There are some less evident, but core and fundamentally important, services that provide enterprise-level qualities of service that make up the runtime too. These provide runtime facilities on which the other services are built, to manage configuration of the applications, the server, and access to the administration facilities. They include the following:

- *Meta Data Service*: This provides runtime access to the deployed application code and is used by services to open JARs, WARs, and EARs, examine their manifests, and provide any necessary adjustments to support the running environment. This is a fundamental service that is used throughout the runtime environment. There are facilities for subsystems and service implementations to provide listeners so they can adjust their facilities when the deployed code changes.

- *Config Service*: This provides runtime access to the XML files that support the cell, cluster, core group, and node configuration and is used by services to look up configuration information for themselves or other services.

- *Admin Service*: This provides access to the administration facilities and the ability for subsystems to listen for and monitor any administration requests that would result in their needing to perform reconfiguration.

- *Application Mgr Service*: This provides access to the modules that make up an application and support for listeners for deployed object events for services, components, and subsystems to detect changes in the deployed applications and their state.

- *Server Service*: This provides the ability for a component to register a listener to monitor for state changes in the application server environment, such as its starting or stopping.

Many of the services and components use listeners registered with other services so they can be notified of environmental and application changes. They install collaborators (essentially hooks) into the EJB container and web container to monitor what is running and provide facilities to them, for example, adding web services support.

The WAS Runtime Implementation and Its plugin.xml File

Before delving any deeper into the runtime, you must understand the tools for the journey. A JAR file is nothing more than a zip file with a particular structure and a manifest file. A manifest file, which is a MANIFEST.MF file for traditional Java JAR files and OSGi bundles or a plugin.xml file for Eclipse plugins, details the contents of the JAR file itself and the relationship between the constituents. We will merely unzip the main com.ibm.ws.runtime.jar JAR file (and its related files) or examine it in Windows Explorer and look at its structure, the names of files, and the `plugin.xml` and `META-INF/MANIFEST.MF` files that declare how the components are bound and used together.

The first thing to understand about the technical structure of the WAS runtime is the design pattern that IBM uses to implement WAS to support changing underlying implementations without changing interfaces and that defines the approach to coding. The strategy development pattern (see Figure 4-1) is used extensively, with interface classes and interfaces providing public interfaces used by other components, and implementation classes providing the private implementation of each of the methods exposed on these interfaces, which aids maintenance. The implementation classes have the same core name as the interface class or interface with the suffix `Impl` in the name. Similarly, IBM has subsystems that provide the high-level functionality for WebSphere products using the path `ws` in the class package name, and that make use of Service Provider Interface (SPI) implementations using the path `wsspi` in the class package name. Some WebSphere-specific components and subsystems are zOS-specific and thus use `ws390` in the package name.

Strategy Pattern Implementation

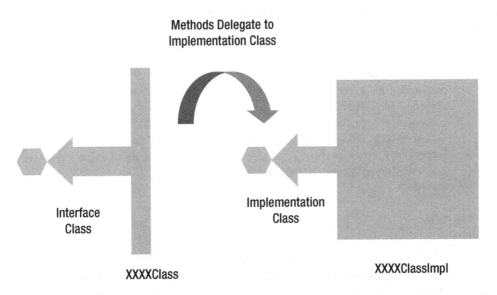

Methods Delegate to Implementation Class

Interface Class

Implementation Class

XXXXClass

XXXXClassImpl

Figure 4-1. *The strategy pattern and WAS class naming*

Start by unzipping the `com.ibm.ws.runtime.jar` file and opening the `plugin.xml` file that controls the Eclipse startup and some of the management of the componentization. A lot of the same component-loading information can be seen through the use of listeners on the Eclipse/OSGi runtime, through debuggers and stack dumps where components fail during startup, or through looking at entries in the `SystemOut.log`. You saw the use of listeners in the previous chapter, which looked at Eclipse plugins and how the `plugin.xml` file is used. This chapter concentrates on the extension points used by the WAS container management and Eclipse code to load components into each container, ensuring the components are loaded in the correct order with all the necessary dependencies validated. These WAS extension points used to control component loading into a container are represented by the name `com.ibm.wsspi.extension.XXX-startup`, where XXX identifies the type of container it refers to. For example, the JavaEE specification-level application server container–owned components are defined in the section of the `plugin.xml` file within the bounds of the `com.ibm.wsspi.extension.applicationserver-startup`. Similar sections of this `plugin.xml` file exist for the base server underlying the application server, the EJB container, and the scheduler container. The extension point for the web container that controls the loading of the components it owns is defined in the `plugin.xml` file for the `com.ibm.ws.webcontainer.jar` plugin file, but the way it works is the same. Listing 4-1 shows a sample entry from `plugin.xml` for the application server container components. The `plugin.xml` file for the core WAS runtime JAR file is large, so you will have to scroll through it to find the `com.ibm.wsspi.extension.applicationserver-startup` extension point section when we refer to its contents later in this chapter.

Listing 4-1. *Sample Entry from plugin.xml*

```
...
<extension point="com.ibm.wsspi.extension.applicationserver-startup">
   <components>
...
       <component startup="2147483647"
           class="com.ibm.ws.runtime.XXXX"
           component-id="WS_XXXX"
           startup-mode="dependency">
           <dependency type="service"
               name="com.ibm.ws.runtime.service.ApplicationMgr"/>
           <dependency type="service"
               name="com.ibm.ws.runtime.service.AdminService"/>
       </component>
...
     <components>
<extension>
...
```

In Listing 4-1, the component WS_XXXX, which has an implementation class of `com.ibm.ws.runtime.XXXX`, is loaded by the application server container with a startup value of `2147483647`, which is probably one of the last components to load. It is dependent on the Application Manager Service and the Admin Service. In the past, with version 6.1, WAS declared the layers as separate extension points, with sub-elements for each component making up the layer that gave a startup order. Some additional attributes identified which platforms the component was targeted to and the class providing the functions for that component. Each component class implemented the WsComponent interface for state and lifecycle management (i.e., starting, stopping, etc.).

This behavior led to the careful wording used by IBM that says the same binaries for WAS run on all platforms. However, not necessarily the same code executes on each platform, because some of the attributes mark code as specific to one platform or another from OS400 (iSeries/System i), zOS (zSeries/System z), or distributed (everything else). Components for System z also can run as servants, control, region, or adjuncts with similar recovery types, an organization that handles the different architectural structure of the zOS operating system.

Each WAS layer is referred to as a container, which is similar to a J2EE container, with a related WsContainer class using an implementation from WsContainerImpl to enumerate all the component sub-elements from the section of the plugin.xml file for that container. The runtime then loads and starts the component via its declared class name.

Each container is passed an identifier for the section of the plugin.xml file to read to identify the required components that it loads and contains. The core server base is identified by com.ibm.wsspi.extension.server-startup, which then loads the application server container that then itself contains the EJB container, client services, HAManager, the web container, and then the scheduler container. Finally the administration services start.

WAS 7 has the same features and behavior as WAS 6.1, but uses a new com.ibm. ws.runtime.service.ComponentManager/ComponentManagerImpl class combination loaded via the com.ibm.ws.runtime.WsServer/WsServerImpl class combination. WAS 7 adds a new variation on the component entries that identifies them with a component ID and lists service and component dependency attributes. The reason for this is simple: it allows different components to be started in the same manner from the same base runtime set of code for different roles, such as a standalone application server, a clustered application server, Node Agent, Deployment Manager, Admin Agent, Job Manager, roles in a zOS control region, and so on. The components required to make up a specific WAS build for a specific role are also grouped and configured for that role in the plugin.xml file. For example, the com.ibm.wsspi. extension.job-manager-components-CR extension point groups together all of the components that are required for the WAS 7 Job Manager role for a WAS 7 zOS control region. The plugin.xml file also lists other specific groupings of components and services separately to allow additional configuration. This functionality will form the basis of the role-specific WAS builds in WAS.NEXT.

WAS Base Server Container Startup and Primordial Components

Essentially, the WsServer main method, called on the command line for the WAS JVM startup, delegates to the WsServerImpl main method implementation. The next four parameters from the command line that follow the com.ibm.ws.bootstrap.WSLauncher are processed to identify the profile configuration path, the cell name, the node name, and the server or process name for initializing logging and basic configuration, before booting the component manager followed by the base server container via the bootServerContainer method.

As for all containers, the extension point for the given container startup is used to read the list of components for that container, as declared in the plugin.xml files for all of the plugins and loaded into the Eclipse Extension Registry. An internal loadComponents method is called to enumerate the entries and initialize each component in turn. It is at this point that the WAS core runtime starts up. If the configurations are not found for the cell, node, and server definitions, XML-related or file-related errors will occur before the plugin.xml file data is read by the Eclipse/OSGi and WAS runtime combination to load the components.

For the base server runtime container, at the point when the components start to load for the base environment, the Config Service (com.ibm.wsspi.runtime.config.ConfigService) is registered with the OSGi service registry (which will already have the IBM wrapper for it loaded in com.ibm.ws.runtime.service.Repository). Some of the primordial components, meaning those already loaded by the startup before the base server container extension point is processed and that support the base operations, will be loaded and in operation (i.e., the VariableMap in com.ibm.ws.runtime.service.VariableMap and the TraceService in com.ibm.ws.runtime.service.TraceService). The bootServerContainer method uses the ComponentManager/ComponentManagerImpl and other WsServerImpl methods as outlined previously. Some of this was covered in the previous chapter when the service changes were logged. Note that all of these services are registered from the bundle com.ibm.ws.runtime. The following base server components and facilities are found in the plugin.xml file in the section marked by the extension point com.ibm.wsspi.extension.server-startup, with the components considered part of the environment within the element sub-tree for the base server container:

```
Service Reference: {com.ibm.ws.runtime.service.Repository}={service.id=34},
Bundle: com.ibm.ws.runtime, Bundle ID: 73 REGISTERED.
Service change at: Mon Dec 08 12:09:09 GMT 2008
Service Reference: {com.ibm.wsspi.runtime.config.ConfigService}={service.id=35},
Bundle: com.ibm.ws.runtime, Bundle ID: 73 REGISTERED.
Service change at: Mon Dec 08 12:09:09 GMT 2008
Service Reference: {com.ibm.ws.runtime.service.VariableMap}={service.id=36},
Bundle: com.ibm.ws.runtime, Bundle ID: 73 REGISTERED.
Service change at: Mon Dec 08 12:09:09 GMT 2008
Service Reference: {com.ibm.ws.runtime.service.TraceService}={service.id=37},
Bundle: com.ibm.ws.runtime, Bundle ID: 73 REGISTERED.
Service change at: Mon Dec 08 12:09:14 GMT 2008
Service Reference: {com.ibm.ws.runtime.service.ComponentManager}={service.id=38},
Bundle: com.ibm.ws.runtime, Bundle ID: 73 REGISTERED.
Service change at: Mon Dec 08 12:09:15 GMT 2008
Service Reference: {com.ibm.ws.runtime.service.Server}={service.id=39},
Bundle: com.ibm.ws.runtime, Bundle ID: 73 REGISTERED.
```

Note that the primordial components do not need to be started because they have already been identified by a startup value of 0 and a startup-mode of primordial.

Each of these primordial components is still attributed by a component ID, to allow some builds to not use the component if it isn't required. In all, nearly 90 components are started up by the base runtime as part of this initialization phase, with five primordial components already started, as outlined in the previous listing, for which the class attribute is ignored. The real loading of components starts at the value identified in the ws-container-startup.xml file.

From the perspective of the plugin.xml file, WAS is started up in groups of component and service subsystems referred to as containers, made up of individual base components and services. The initial base server, with its services supporting the application server functionality, is started first. The core containers and startup phases related to extension points in the plugin.xml file are shown in Figure 4-2 with some of the key components loaded in each phase.

The following are key components and facilities started by the base startup:

- Host and endpoint management

- Communications

- Thread pool management and monitoring

- Logging

- Reliability and failover services

- Performance metrics gathering

- Transport channel management

- Web services base support

- Debugging services

- The Object Request Broker infrastructure underpinning JavaEE

- High-availability HAManager clustering

- Recovery management

- Transaction management

- Cache management

- Security

- Scheduling

- Some JMS facilities

- Some JMS message queuing facilities (referred to as JFAP throughout WAS)

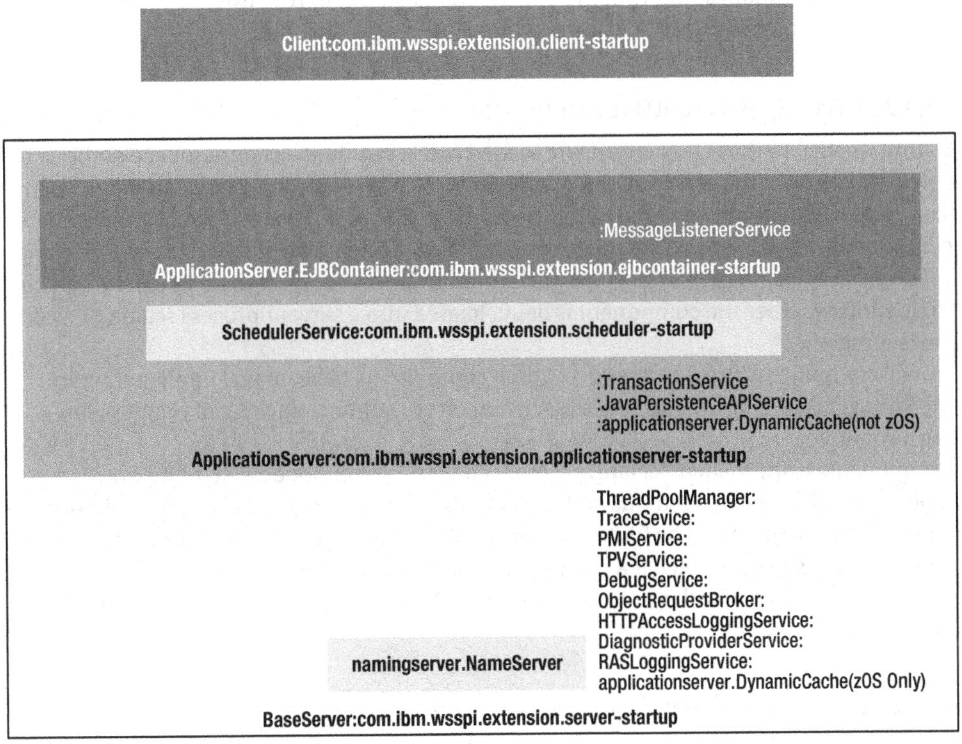

Client:com.ibm.wsspi.extension.client-startup

:MessageListenerService

ApplicationServer.EJBContainer:com.ibm.wsspi.extension.ejbcontainer-startup

SchedulerService:com.ibm.wsspi.extension.scheduler-startup

:TransactionService
:JavaPersistenceAPIService
:applicationserver.DynamicCache(not zOS)

ApplicationServer:com.ibm.wsspi.extension.applicationserver-startup

ThreadPoolManager:
TraceSevice:
PMIService:
TPVService:
DebugService:
ObjectRequestBroker:
HTTPAccessLoggingService:
DiagnosticProviderService:
namingserver.NameServer   RASLoggingService:
applicationserver.DynamicCache(zOS Only)

BaseServer:com.ibm.wsspi.extension.server-startup

Figure 4-2. *Core WAS containers and components initialized through plugin.xml entries*

Toward the end of this phase of initialization, the next container-loading phase is started via the component named in the type attribute for the Application Server entry at startup value 12000, for the containerExtensionPoint value com.ibm.wsspi.extension. applicationserver-startup, which then loads the base application server facilities using configuration in another section of the plugin.xml file, that is, com.ibm.wsspi.extension. applicationserver-startup, with the help of references in the com.ibm.wsspi.extension. server-components section. The type attribute entry is used as a key to look up the implementation class in the com.ibm.wsspi.extension.server-components section of plugin.xml to retrieve the implementation class com.ibm.ws.runtime.component.ApplicationServerImpl, and this class is loaded as a component that acts as a container that loads and runs the components listed in the com.ibm.wsspi.extension.applicationserver-startup section of plugin.xml. The same process is repeated later for other containers.

Other complex containers and subsystems work in a similar way. For some subsystems (e.g., ORB, NameServer, EJBContainer, etc.) that require more complex startup of other components, other separate sections of the plugin.xml file are used. With the component entry in the base server and application server startup extension sections (com.ibm.wsspi.extension. server-startup and com.ibm.wsspi.extension.applicationserver-startup), com.ibm.wsspi. extension.server-components is used, giving a component name and type, but no class. The class is used to initialize the subsystem and its components named under an entry for the component, using the type as a reference in the com.ibm.wsspi.extension.server-components section of the plugin.xml file. Thus, for these subsystems, there is a two-stage lookup required for the component initialization, with the type reference in the startup extension section used as a lookup in the components extension section of the plugin.xml file.

Component Loading and Services

Some components for the zOS platform are loaded twice, but this is a consequence of the multiprocess nature of the zOS implementation of WAS, with control regions handling system type code and listeners and servant regions handling application-level type code and listeners. The components often load in different ways, depending which type of JVM process is loading them. The processType and recoveryType attributes on the component-loading entries can be used to identify whether the component is being loaded into a servant process region or a control process region.

Not all components provide a service. Some components have no real implementation, and the entries in the plugin.xml file are place markers to support tracking of progress for loading a container.

Components being loaded declare any other services or components that they are dependent upon, with any specific methods and mandatory requirements, and where any additional configuration information can be found via dependency child elements of the component element and attributes, respectively. If a component offers one or more services, they are declared in services child elements with a provide interface child element that declares the interface implementation file.

Base Server Container Components Loading via com.ibm.wsspi.extension.server-startup

To understand how the base server that provides pure infrastructure services to the application server works, you need to examine the core components that it loads from com.ibm.ws.runtime. Components loaded by the WAS base server container in the server startup initialization phase from the com.ibm.ws.runtime plugin are outlined in Table 4-1.

Table 4-1. *Base Server Container Components and Their Load Order*

Component	Class	Startup	Target	Services
WS_Repository	RepositoryImpl	0		Repository
WS_RCS	ConfigServiceImpl	0		ConfigService
WS_VariableMap	VariableMapImpl	0		VariableMap
WS_ComponentMgr	ComponentManagerImpl	0		ComponentManager
WS_Server	ServerImpl	0		Server
WS_VirtualHostMgr	VirtualHostMgrImpl	1000	zOS only	VirtualHostMgr
WS_ThreadMonitor	ThreadMonitorImpl	1999(I)		ThreadMonitor
WS_EndPointMgr	EndPointMgrImpl	2000(I)		EndPointMgr
WS_FirstChannelActions	FirstChannelActions	2000(I)	Distributed only	FirstChannelActionsService
WS_ThreadPoolMgr	ThreadPoolMgrImpl	2000(I)		ThreadPoolMgr
WS_TransportChannelLoader	TransportChannelLoaderImpl	2000(I)	Distributed, OS400	TransportChannelLoader
WS_WsByteBufferPoolMgr	WsByteBufferPoolManagerServiceImpl	2499		WsByteBufferPoolManager
WS_TraceService		3000		TraceService
WS_RAS		3500		
WS_FFDC	FfdcProvider	3500		FfdcProvider
WS_EnvironmentType	EnvironmentType	4000		
WS_SecurityConfig	SecurityConfigComponentImpl	4100		
WS_DiagnosticProvider		4400		
WS_PMI		4500		PMI
WS_TPerfViewer		4600		
WS_ChannelFrameworkService	ChannelFrameworkServiceImpl	4600		ChannelFrameworkService
WS_SOAPContainerChannel	SOAPContainerChannelComponentImpl	4900	zOS only	SoapContainerService
WS_SOAPAcceptorChannel	SOAPAcceptorChannelComponentImpl	4901	zOS only	
WS_SystemWebServices	WSSysServerImpl	4990	zOS only	WebServicesSystemService
WS_DebugService		5000		DebugComponentImpl

Table 4-1. *Continued*

Component	Class	Startup	Target	Services
WS_ORB		5000		ORB
WS_HAManager	ProxyImpl (zOS) CoordinatorComponentImpl (not zOS)	5400		CoreStack
WS_J2CHAProxy	J2CHAProxyControllerComponentImpl	5401	zOS only	
WS_WLM	ProcessRuntimeImpl	5504		WLM
WS_ClusterRuntime	ClusterRuntimeImpl	5505		ClusterRuntime
WS_ChannelSelectionAdapter	ChannelSelectionAdapterImpl	5506		ChannelSelectionAdapter
WS_ClusterMemberService	ClusterMemberServiceImpl	5506		ClusterMemberService
WS_HealthMonitorManager	HealthMonitorManagerImpl	5507		HealthMonitorManager
WS_RecoveryLog	RecLogServiceImpl	5550	zOS only	
WS_NameServer		6000		
WS_ActivityServiceCR	ActivityServiceComponentImpl	6000	zOS only	
WS_NameServer	ServantNameServiceImpl	6001	zOS only	
WS_NameSpaceInitializer	NameSpaceInitializerImpl	6002		
WS_MDBRoutingService	MDBRoutingServiceImpl	6400	zOS only	
WS_HandlerFramework	HandlerFrameworkServiceImpl	6500		HandlerFrameworkService
WS_DRS	MultibrokerDomainImpl	6500		MultibrokerDomain
WS_TxController	TxControllerComponentImpl	6500	zOS only	
WS_CacheResourceMgr	CacheResourceMgrImpl	6550	zOS only	CacheResourceMgr
WS_Dynacache		6600	zOS only	CacheService
WS_Dynacache_object	ObjectCacheServiceImpl	6600	zOS only	
WS_CFSBinder	CFSBinder	7000		
WS_WSBBSBinder	WSBBSBinder	7000		
WS_WLMChainEventListener	WLMChainEventListener	7001		WLMChainEventListener
WS_HTTPAccessLog		7100		HTTPLoggingService
WS_server_services		9000		
WS_ExtensionHelper	ExtensionHelperServiceImpl	9500		ExtensionHelper
WS_CustomService	CustomServiceImpl	10000		
WS_ODCManagerService	ODCManagerService	11400		ODCManager
WS_ODC	ODCService	11500		ODCService

Component	Class	Startup	Target	Services
WS_Security	SecurityComponentImpl	11500		SecurityService
WS_JMSRegistration	JMSRegistration	11550		
WS_WebServicesSecurity	WSSecurityComponentImpl	11600		WSSecurityService
WS_SchedulerConfig	SchedulerConfigServiceImpl	11999		SchedulerConfigService
WS_PMIRequestMetrics	PmiRmImpl	12000	zOS only	
WS_ApplicationServer		12000		ApplicationServer
WS_CompositionUnitMgr	CompositionUnitMgrImpl	12000	zOS only	CompositionUnitMgr
WS_Transaction	TXServiceImpl	12000	zOS only	TXService
WS_DRS	MultibrokerDomainImpl	12000	zOS only	MultibrokerDomain
WS_RecoveryLog	RecLogServiceImpl	12001	zOS only	
WS_ProductRegistration	ProductRegistrationComponentImpl	13000	zOS only	
WS_server_components		13000		
WS_ODCProxyManager	ODCProxyManager	13010	zOS only	
WS_JFAPProxy	JFAPProxyComponentImpl	13500	zOS only	
WS_ControllerCacheService	ControllerCacheServiceImpl	14500	zOS only	
WS_SfControllerService	SfControllerServiceImpl	15000	zOS only	
WS_JmsAdminService	JmsAdminService	15000		
WS_ECAChannel	ECAChannelComponentImpl	15500	zOS only	
WS_ESIChannel	ESIChannelComponentImpl	15600	zOS only	
WS_ESIInvalidator	ESIInvalidatorComponentImpl	16000	zOS only	
WS_ServerSecurity	ServerSecurityComponentImpl	20000	zOS only	
WS_Transaction	TXServiceImpl	25000	zOS only	TxService
WS_TaskMgmtServiceMapper	TaskManagementServiceMapper	100000		TaskManagementServiceMapper
WS_TaskMgmtMBean	TaskManagementMBean	100100		TaskManagementMBean
WS_TaskConfigMonitor	TaskConfigMonitorImpl	6006000		
WS_UserManagement	UserManagementProcess	999999		
WS_WLC	WLCImpl	2147483647	Distributed, OS400	WLC
WS_SOAPMonitorChannel	SOAPMonitorChannelComponentImpl	2147483647	zOS only	

Base Server Container Components

Table 4-1 shows the components loaded by the base server container that provides infrastructure services to the rest of the application server. We will now look at what these components do. You will see that for the most part they are fine-grained infrastructure services that enable the JavaEE level of functionality that underpins the application server container to provide enterprise-level qualities of service.

Primordial Components

The components with a value of 0 are primordial components that were already underway in their startup before the component enumeration began. Those with 1999–2000 values marked with an I are immediate components that must be started straight away. The rest of the components are dependency components that depend on others that are already started or must be started.

There are a few important points to be aware of. Note that there are many components specific to the System z platform and its zOS operating system. This is because of the large number of architectural differences on the platform and the structure the JVM exposes, along with the need to tie some of the WAS system services to some of those of the platform. Although IBM may ship a common set of binary components for all platforms in the form of the JAR files, the code paths through those binaries and the services that are started are very different between the System z and other platforms and, to a much lesser extent, the System i platform (signified by the OS400 platform type). Attributes specific to the process types on zOS were covered earlier in this chapter.

Before considering how the application server runtime fits together, let's get an understanding of what some of the components are and the relationships between them. In most cases, the ordering of the components shows the underlying layering. The first five components are primordial components that control the rest of the environment.

As outlined earlier in this chapter, the primordial components are created, loaded, and initialized by the WsServerImpl class and then brought together by the bootServerContainer method. This is all a direct result of the Java process command line and Eclipse/OSGi startup.

The first component used by the base was the primordial Repository component that handles the WebSphere internal service registry (WsServiceRegistry) and provides the Repository Service. This component effectively acts as a service repository based on the OSGi model that is internal to the WAS runtime for a configuration, cluster, node, and so on. The service that is registered is essentially a type of traditional JavaBean that has a defined interface that can be bound to dynamically at runtime. The Repository component needs to be started first to handle the registration of other WAS components. This isn't directly related to the OSGi service repository, but builds upon it. Most subsequently loaded components register with this component and access it to find other components that have already been loaded.

The RCS (Runtime Configuration Service) component builds upon the Repository component and its underlying repository of registered components. It manages the configuration of the cell, cluster, node, and other information for the runtime environment. This component creates and registers the Config Service that is used by other components to access configuration data. Access to the configuration data is handled by the Repository and RCS components. Many of the configuration elements are defined using the Eclipse Modeling Framework (EMF). When this component loads you can see the EMF bundles being accessed in the monitor plugin discussed in the previous chapter. This component does not register with the `Repository` component directly because a reference to the `Repository` component is passed to its constructor as the two are intertwined. Many later components list their configuration data as being managed by `rcs` in the `plugin.xml` file, which refers to this component, as can be seen in the `configurationData` attribute of the `ThreadPoolMgr` component, for example.

The `VariableMap` component is in many ways similar to the environment variables manager of a traditional operating system. It reads the configuration using the two previously loaded components and then performs substitution of variables from the values in the `variables.xml` file. Substitutions are registered with the Config Service. The `VariableMap` component registers and provides the Variable Map Service.

The `ComponentMgr` component that provides the Component Manager Service is in many ways the core of the WebSphere runtime for configuring containers. It uses the `Repository` component under the covers, but also interacts with the Eclipse runtime and registry for loading plugins and working with extensions and extension points. It reads the given section of the `plugin.xml` file for the invocation, enumerates and loads the components with the appropriate attributes for the component using an internal class, and handles the requested registration. It is this component that has been responsible for handling the base server runtime components listed in Table 4-1 and ensuring that dependencies are met, including checking that the component is appropriate for the target platform. Later, in the base server container-loading phase, this component will be used to load the application server container runtime components.

The `Server` component starts the transition from a traditional Java application to an enterprise-class application server environment. It ensures that the necessary thread-monitoring and failure-handling settings are in place for the application server environment for the provided configuration and starts the provision of the underlying setup for the EJB container environments. This component handles the starting and stopping of the application server environment and performs recovery when required. This component also registers and offers the interface for the Server Service that is used by components to check for state changes when the runtime is starting or stopping.

Basic Infrastructure Components

After the primordial components, the first of the System z and zOS platform's specific components is loaded: the `VirtualHostMgr` component. As the name suggests, this component registers the virtual host aliases and port information for the zOS environment based on the configuration in the `virtualhosts.xml` configuration file. It uses the Variable Map and Config Service components to read the configuration and make appropriate substitutions. It runs as a control region and provides the Virtual Host Mgr Service.

The first immediate component to load for all platforms is the `ThreadMonitor` component, which does what the name implies. It monitors the threads in the environment for hung threads and raises the alarm when it finds them. Property files configure the detection parameters. This is the component that provides the Thread Monitor Service to other components and that alerts hung threads to the WAS logs and is used by administration facilities and infrastructure (i.e., JMX) for monitoring the behavior of the threads in the environment.

The `EndPointMgr` component, which sets up the End Point Mgr Service, reads the `serverindex.xml` file for the given cell, cluster, and nodes configuration and sets up the endpoint configuration. It is an immediate load component.

The FirstChannelActions component sets up the necessary transport channel sockets for the given configured endpoints for the environment, along with any buffering. A lot of the TCP/IP work performed by the underlying WAS runtime is initialized by this immediate load component, although later management is handled by the Channel Framework Service. Look out for configuration items in WAS in the server.xml file that are identified by TCPChannel, as the initialization of these relates to the FirstChannelActions component. This component provides the First Channel Actions Service.

The ThreadPoolMgr component has a different configuration for the System z zOS platform from other platforms but has a common implementation. It is a true thread pool manager in that it manages a pool of threads where a thread is borrowed and later returned, with different thread pools supporting the different containers and subsystems within WAS. The thread pools are configured in server.xml. This component collaborates closely with the Thread Monitor component and provides the Thread Pool Mgr Service.

The TransportChannelLoader component, which is an immediate load component, sets up the connection between the channel lists and the JAR file handling the transport channels. It doesn't do much in itself but is part of the overall Channel Framework Service environment and offers the Transport Channel Loader Service. This is the last of the immediate load components. It runs on the distributed and System i (i5OS) platforms only and not zOS.

The WsByteBufferPoolMgr component is used to provide a set of byte buffer pools for file channels. The code follows a different path than on other platforms when run on a zOS platform. For size management it keeps a close eye on the thread pools it relates to. The configuration is handled by entries in server.xml. The component provides the Ws Byte Buffer Pool Manager Service.

As the name suggests, the TraceService component implements the interface for control of tracing. It also provides the Trace Service interface. The configuration set up by an administrator to trace through components and subsystems is handled through this component. Individual components and subsystems use tracing components to trace through their behavior at various key points in their running. If this component has tracing configured for a registered component, the details are output to the trace log. This service uses component class details listed in the com.ibm.wsspi.extension.server-components for its initialization.

The RAS (Reliability, Availability, and Serviceability) component controls the RAS Logging Service MBean for JMX and the logging of service messages (i.e., AUDIT, WARNING, SERVICE, etc.). This service uses component class details listed in the com.ibm.wsspi.extension.server-components for its initialization.

The FFDC component, which loads the FFDCProvider implementation class and provides the FFDC Provider Service, is part of the IBM FFDC (First Failure Data Capture) strategy for handling unexpected errors. Incidents and environment summaries are logged to the PROFILE/logs/ffdc directory for later use by IBM when raising a PMR. The Apache Commons logging facilities are used under the covers.

The EnvironmentType component merely acts as a placeholder for the environment to determine what is running as a client and as a server.

The SecurityConfig component monitors the configuration of the environment for changes and manages the related security configuration.

The DiagnosticProvider component provides the interface for use for registration and control of diagnostic providers. These can be accessed via JMX. The beauty of diagnostic providers, which were introduced in WAS 6.1, is that they allow components and subsystems to generically provide an instrumentation object to output configuration or state, or to even run self-diagnostics. Configuration of the component uses the `DiagnosticProviderService` reference in the `com.ibm.wsspi.extension.server-components` section of the `plugin.xml` file.

The `PMI` component that registers the PMI service acts as an interface to control the performance-metrics gathering at the JVM and WAS levels and to interface to the performance-metrics MBean for JMX. Control is via the `pmi-config.xml` file. This service uses component class details listed in the `com.ibm.wsspi.extension.server-components` for its initialization.

The `TPVService` component controls the Tivoli Performance Viewer components within WAS for performance monitoring. It sets up the service, the engine, the JMX MBean, and the performance advisor. This service uses component class details listed in the `com.ibm.wsspi.extension.server-components` for its initialization.

The `ChannelFrameworkService` component that provides the Channel Framework Service is one of the most important core components in the base of the WAS runtime. This component provides the base communications infrastructure for WAS and its JavaEE facilities. It uses the `server.xml` configuration to set up transport channels, factories, and chains with their related thread pool settings, with listeners on the configuration, thread pools, and chains ensuring resources are used appropriately. The `TransportChannelLoader` component loaded earlier is used to assist. This fundamental communications management within WAS allows connections to an endpoint to be built up to provide higher levels of service; an HTTPS connection is built from an HTTP connection that has SSL added, and this HTTP connection is built from a TCP connection, all of which forms a transport "chain." Transport chains need threads to monitor them and handle requests and responses, so a tight coupling to thread pool management is needed. The configuration used by this component is the major part of the `server.xml` file for a given node, cluster, and cell configuration. There is a different configuration of the component for zOS and other platforms, but the implementation is essentially the same.

The `SOAPContainerChannel` component configuration loaded here is zOS-specific and sets up a core system web services "engine" and router for the platform to handle SOAP/HTTP interactions. This intercepts, routes, and handles web services requests on the zOS platform and loads the system web services engine support. This runs as a control region and provides the SOAP Container Service.

The `SOAPAcceptorChannel` component that provides the SOAP Acceptor Channel Service works with the `SOAPContainerChannel` component on the zOS platform to handle inbound requests and set up a virtual channel. It enumerates the channels and chains managed by the Channel Framework Service to apply the appropriate configuration before setting up the HTTP channels required. This runs as a control region.

The `SystemWebServices` component on the zOS platform that runs in a control region is the web services engine that handles JAX-RPC and works with the previous two zOS-specific component configurations to support web services. It interacts with and collaborates with the web container and EJB container for runtime integration but handles many of the XML and web services support functions itself. It provides the Web Services System Service. The WAS JAX-WS web services support merely uses the Axis2 implementations under the covers in the Web Services Feature Pack support code, with core integration into WAS, but the underlying transport management is shared between both JAX-RPC and JAX-WS implementations. It uses the Meta Data Service to get information about the requirements to support the applications and applies the necessary configuration. The real web services implementation is provided by the WSServerImpl class that provides the Web Services Service and collaborators for the web and EJB containers, along with appropriate security support, so the SystemWebServices component delegates to it.

The DebugService component merely handles the external interface mappings from TCP/IP ports for debugging for the environment to the underlying internal service interfaces, including those for the Bean Scripting Framework (BSF). The BSF was originally developed by IBM and donated to the open source community to support scripting languages in accessing Java code. The DebugService component provides the Debug Component Impl Service. This component is a generic component that runs on all platforms. The service provided uses component class details listed in the com.ibm.wsspi.extension.server-components for its initialization.

The ORB component service is a thin wrapper for the CORBA ORB implementation that underpins a large amount of the JavaEE services in the WAS runtime. The use and exposure of some CORBA services, such as for EJB remote access via the Internet Inter-Orb Protocol (IIOP), is a requirement of the JavaEE specification. The component merely gives access to the ORB runtime, some of which is provided by the base JVM, and the rest of which is provided by the CORBA and orbimpl classes within the WAS runtime, with these latter features supplementing the core features with application server–level qualities of service. An interface to the thread pool management facilities of the runtime environment are required by the component because it is thoroughly tied into many services, such as EJBs, as is a tie into the channel services that support the IIOP/GIOP communications facilities of CORBA. The ORB component loads at this point because it underpins many of the services that follow in the load sequence, but it requires many of the recently loaded facilities. The component provides the ORB Service and uses component class details listed in the com.ibm.wsspi.extension.server-components for its initialization, using a type of orb.ObjectRequestBroker as its key.

The HAManager component that provides the Core Stack Service is unusual in that it has one interface but has two completely different implementations: one for the zOS platform and one for the rest of the platforms. On the zOS platform, the servant region code acts as a proxy and delegates to the HAManager subsystem GroupManager class implementation and issues messages for any unsupported methods, with the GroupManager handling membership of the core group and status of the members to allow appropriate takeover in the event of failure of a member. The non-zOS and zOS control region implementation is more substantial, consisting of a number of classes that watch for failure, check for changes in the core group topology from an administration point of view, and generally provide part of the HAManager subsystem implementation. In Chapter 9, we will look more thoroughly at how the HAManager subsystem works. The target HAManager component starts as a servant region for the HAManager proxy on zOS and a control region for the actual core HAManager implementation.

The J2CHAProxy component is a zOS-specific component that makes use of the Core Stack Service to implement high-availability control of J2C/JCA adapter resources, but builds upon and handles group membership and state management via the underlying GroupManager class implementation. It provides the Core Stack Proxy Service. This component runs as a control region.

The WLM component provides the WLM Service and is loaded via the ProcessRuntimeImpl class from the com.ibm.ws.wlm.jar plugin. The WLM stands for Workload Manager, but the component is more of an interface used by and for traditional workload management than a workload manager itself. The interface is used to get details of the cluster, member details, and resource locations. However, there is a lot more to the loading of this component than is immediately apparent. One of its key functions is to provide clustering support for IIOP artifacts such as remote EJBs, so code is dedicated to decorating the ORB Service interface with the clustering functionality. When this component loads to provide the interface, the ServerWlm component, from the plugin com.ibm.ws.wlm, is providing the implementation for the cluster ProcessRuntimeImpl class. Remember that the Eclipse/OSGi runtime has already enumerated all of the bundles at this point and knows where to find the classes they offer for use elsewhere. The component management within the container initialization code makes use of this knowledge to load the ServerWlm component that provides a number of the clustering facilities that get loaded at this point. The ProcessRuntimeImpl class provides a lot of the cluster management used in the Network Deployment edition of WAS in that it makes use of the cell, core group, and cluster information for the environment, reads the cluster.xml and server.xml files to validate and control the configuration, and then interfaces to the HAManager (particularly the bulletin board) and the ORB to ensure the appropriate load balancing and resilience are maintained. EJBs are particularly dependent on the ORB/IIOP functionality and thus are highly dependent on the functioning of this component.

The components and classes in the com.ibm.ws.wlm.jar file form the basis of the resilience and clustering features of the WAS runtime, monitoring the cluster health and responding to configuration and failure events. Many of the components within it pay particular attention to the Admin Service that monitors the environment for configuration changes as a result of administration, so when you change the configuration from the WAS administrative System Console, it is these components that are performing much of the work in responding to your requests.

The ClusterRuntime component that provides the Cluster Runtime Service is next to load, with the initialization and control handled via the ClusterRuntimeImpl class. The WLM and ClusterRuntime components together are key to the runtime resilience of applications throughout their runtime execution. The ClusterRuntime component checks to see if it is running in an Admin Agent or Job Manager environment and drops out if it is because these administration deployment constructs are designed to reply on platform HA features rather than those within WAS. These types of checks are duplicated in many other components. The ClusterRuntime component is also found in the com.ibm.ws.wlm bundle. This works with the WLM component implementation outlined previously to support clustering. The two components together watch for configuration changes and ensure that the necessary JMX support is maintained. Various listeners and monitor threads used by some of the classes used by this component look out for failures and take remedial action.

The ChannelSelectionAdapter component that offers the Channel Selection Adapter Service uses appropriate criteria to select the appropriate endpoints and channels to support the WLM and clustering functionality outlined previously. It loads immediately after the ClusterRuntime component under the control of the ChannelSelectionImpl class.

As can be expected by the name, the ClusterMemberService component offers the Cluster Member Service for managing cluster membership and is again a part of the com.ibm.ws.wlm bundle. This is just a simple component initiated by the ClusterMemberServiceImpl class for managing the internal configuration for runtime high availability and load balancing rather than acting as a functional component of that HA and load-balancing implementation.

The name of the HealthMonitorManager component describes what it does. It monitors the health of the environment and conformance of the environment to the desired topology.

It runs background threads to make the checks. It is part of the `com.ibm.ws.wlm` bundle with an implementation class of `HealthMonitorManagerImpl` and offers the Health Monitor Manager Service.

The `RecoveryLog` component is loaded at this point as a zOS-specific service component that controls the recovery log and handles recovery of transactions in the event of failure, at least for the zOS platform. The component implementation is controlled by the `RecLogServiceImpl` class. On other platforms, it loads as part of the application server container, rather than the base server container. For its role at this point it must monitor the configuration and topology of the cell and cluster and respond to ensure that the appropriate cluster member recovers in-doubt transactions. This component is found in the base `com.ibm.ws.runtime` bundle rather than the `com.ibm.ws.wlm` bundle and runs as a control region.

The next component to load is the `NameServer` component, which is a major subsystem in its own right. It interfaces to the ORB, the administration, the security, and the configuration subsystems for the cell and maintains the namespace lookups for the objects within the environment. The `namestore.xml` file is used by this component. The CORBA CosNaming support and the related Interoperable Object References (IORs) used in the WAS world require the support of this component to allow communication with remote objects using the CORBA IIOP standards that underpin JavaEE, in particular EJBs. This subsystem uses component class details listed in the `com.ibm.wsspi.extension.server-components` for its initialization. When running on zOS it runs as a control region.

The `ActivityServiceCR` component is another zOS-specific component and is implemented by the `ActivityServiceComponentImpl` class. *Activity* means some work or function is done, but in J2EE and CORBA terms, the activities are a way of coordinating multiple one-phase units of work to create a higher-level transaction-like unit of work. The principles come from the OMG Activity Service for CORBA and the JSR95 specification for J2EE that builds upon it. This component provides some of the functionality to support these specifications. The *CR* refers to the *control region*, which is a process type on the zOS platform that handles the infrastructure setup for WAS, for example, TCP/IP ports, and so forth. The control region runs in its own JVM. *Servant* regions are where the application code runs. The component interfaces with the ORB to collect activity information and to build upon the OMG specification implementation directly. The `ActivityServiceCR` component uses a recovery log manager and recovery director to control recovery from failure to handle in-doubt units of work and uses other classes to collect local, user, and process information.

On the zOS platform, a separate implementation of the `NameServer` component environment runs next, this time as a servant process, and provides management for the naming service facilities. The `ServantNameServiceImpl` class provides the implementation.

The next component to load is the `NameSpaceInitializer` component that uses JNDI to initialize the namespace for WAS for Java. This component is implemented by the `NameSpaceInitializerImpl` class.

The `MDBRoutingService` component is a zOS-specific component that is implemented by the `MDBRoutingServiceImpl` class. It runs in both control and servant regions. Components such as this are necessary for the zOS platform due to its very different architecture. The mix of servant regions running application code and controller regions that handle the infrastructure tasks means that requests must be routed between them to get to the correct application code that handles a message. This component is part of a set of components and classes that handles this routing.

The next component to load is the `HandlerFramework` service component that provides the Handler Framework Service and is implemented by the `HandlerFrameworkServiceImpl` class. This is a component that is important for all platforms. Many other things inside the "WebSphere" domain are built on it, and it is usually used in conjunction with the Channel Framework Service that provides the infrastructure communications for WAS. The handler framework is a framework for declaring a chain of handlers for a request, whether that request is for a JMS message or services in the Service Integration Bus. The chain is declared using IBM-specific XMI file extensions, `ws-handlerlist.xmi` or `ws-handler.xmi`. A good example is for developing an ESB using plain WAS and its SDO functionality, because handlers can be used to declare mediations that examine and transform a message. Handlers can be in EJBs or plain old JavaBeans. For more details, the IBM DeveloperWorks web site gives some good examples. This component and service provides the management of the handler lists.

The `DRS` component handles the configuration and management of the WAS Data Replication Services. It is implemented by the `MultibrokerDomainImpl` class and provides the Multibroker Domain Service. Configuration for a cell is handled via the `multibroker.xml` file, which is a legacy name from earlier releases where multibroker domains were supported. The Data Replication Services are used to replicate data in the form of "replicas" between multiple nodes in a domain for high availability. The session manager, stateful session beans, and caching make use of this service. Periodic data transfers take place between nodes on background threads, with the different "brokers" keeping any changes to the data being replicated in sync by sending update messages when a change occurs. An internal JMS-style mechanism underpins the replication transport.

The `TxController` component is loaded next specifically for zOS at this point as a control region. It is part of the implementation of the Java Transaction API (JTA) support for the platform. The platform implementations, such as the use of recovery logs and the handling of the Open Group Distributed Transaction Processing XA standard, provide the underlying functionality. The `TxControllerComponentImpl` class provides the implementation that initiates the component.

The next component to load is the `CacheResourceMgr` that is implemented by the `CacheResourceMgrImpl` class and provides the Cache Resource Mgr Service. This sets up the providers, resources, and bindings necessary to support caching. As such, it is part of the underlying services to support the WebSphere Dynacache mechanism. Servlet and JSP fragments caching and data access "commands" are handled by this mechanism. This component manages the providers and resources to underpin the caching. On zOS, this runs as a control region.

For the zOS platform only, once the `DRS` and `CacheResourceMgr` components are started, the `Dynacache` component and its Dynacache mechanism is next to start. The `Dynacache` component registers and provides the Cache Service and makes extensive use of the `DRS` and `CacheResourceMgr` components. The first entry in `plugin.xml` uses component class details listed in the `com.ibm.wsspi.extension.server-components` for its initialization, and the second declares a class for initialization. The first entry handles the basic core cache initialization and replication itself, particularly of the WebSphere Common Configuration Model (WCCM) configuration, and the second declares and configures the object cache built upon it. The `Dynacache` component runs as a control region on the zOS platform. If WAS is running as a proxy server, the component uses the Cache Resource Mgr Service to bind. When WAS is running as a conventional application server, it runs the Resource Mgr Service to bind. Dynacache

MBeans are set up, cache providers are loaded and configured, and servlet support is enabled. All of this uses lower-level WCCM- and Cache-related classes to do the work. The DRS Multibroker Domain Service and associated listeners support cache replication.

Also on the zOS platform, to support the Dynacache mechanism on that platform, the Dynacache_object component is loaded next as a control region. It is implemented by the ObjectCacheServiceImpl class that supports object management facilities for the Dynacache subsystem.

The CFSBinder component that loads next for all platforms is part of the Channel Framework Service that underpins the communications within the WAS runtime. This component binds the services with JNDI and sets up some of the MBean support. It is implemented by the CFSBinder class.

The WSBBSBinder component relates to the WAS Byte Buffer Pool Manager, which supports the TCP channel facilities within the Channel Framework Service. This component binds the services with JNDI to support later lookup. The WSBBSBinder class provides the implementation.

The WLMChainEventListener component that loads next is part of the com.ibm.ws.wlm bundle and adds an event listener to the transport chains for the Channel Framework Service. Its implementation class is WLMChainEventListener and it provides the WLM Chain Event Listener Service. The Channel Framework Service handles the communications for WAS that components and subsystems will need to monitor for events related to those communications.

The HTTPAccessLog component is the next to load and it provides the HTTP Logging Service. This service uses component class details listed in the com.ibm.wsspi.extension. server-components for its initialization. In this case, the HTTPLoggingServiceImpl class is loaded using this configuration information, and if it is run on the zOS platform, it is configured to run as a control region. The component provides an access logging service in front of the existing National Center for Supercomputing Applications (NCSA) standard, Fast Response Cache Architecture (FRCA), and debug logging mechanisms for the HTTP channel.

All of the components listed previously support or provide infrastructure services either to support the implementation of the JavaEE functionality or to provide reliability, availability, and serviceability features that make WAS fit for enterprise use.

Server Container Service Components and the Application Server Container Initialization

The next set of components to load provides services to the environment rather than the core infrastructure. The distinction is not clear so there is a large gray area as to what is core infrastructure and what is a service. This phase of loading in the server container also includes the initialization of the application server container.

The next component to start is the Server_Services component. This has no class implementation named and is essentially just a placeholder in the plugin.xml file. There is a com.ibm.ws.runtime.service.Server class that supports a Server Service that provides information about the server configuration such as cell name, cluster name, node name, recovery information, and the running state. This is in the "catch all" section of the startup that just covers loosely related services and components that are required to start up in this phase but have not been started yet.

The ExtensionHelper component naming does not accurately relate to the function of the component. It aids in the management of database access and transactions for other container components. It provides the Extension Helper Service and is implemented by the ExtensionHelperServiceImpl class.

The CustomService component provides configuration support for custom services defined externally to be loaded and managed in the same way as other components and services. The service essentially provides a way for application-level code to declare hooks that are invoked when the application server starts up or shuts down. These can be used to initialize components and services. Configuration for the custom service is defined externally via a URL. Any related JMX support in the external component is treated as any other internally loaded service. The component is implemented by the CustomServiceImpl class.

Next, two components load that are part of the WebSphere On-Demand Configuration (ODC) functionality that allows WAS components and configurations, such as the WAS Proxy Server configuration, to build the information needed to route requests without any specific configuration for those requests.

The first component to load to support the ODC functionality is the ODCManagerService component, which loads the necessary components to support ODC and is implemented by the ODCManagerService class. The ODCManagerService component provides the ODC Manager Service. ODC returns configuration information for the cell, cluster, WAS, and the server platform itself. The relationships between the information retrieved for ODC support can be found within the com.ibm.ws.runtime plugin in the META-INF directory in the ODCSchema.xml file.

After the ODCManagerService component is loaded, the ODC component itself is loaded, which is implemented by the ODCService class and provides the ODC Service. This component has a different configuration on the zOS platform than on the other platforms. This ODC component is responsible for using a number of related classes to obtain the information tree for the configuration to be used by the ODC consumers. This is a complex and busy part of the environment, with listeners for configuration changes in multiple areas.

The Security component is next to start, with its SecurityComponentImpl implementation class, and provides the Security Service. This is the core of security for WAS, with different implementations for zOS and other platforms. It includes listeners, checks for SSL, and realm checks at its interface. Under the covers, it starts and configures the WebSphere Common Configuration Model (WCCM) environment, Java 2 Security, Java Authentication and Authorization Service (JAAS), the security configuration, and the WAS support for single sign-on (SSO) via the Trust Association Interceptors (TAI). There are hooks into the ORB itself, which is no surprise, given the use of the CORBA Common Secure Interoperability (CSI) v2 standard in J2EE, and the EJB container. Lookups are performed against the user and administration repositories configured for WAS to get a common representation of the relevant user principle object for the security task at hand for the given context. Role-based authorization checks are performed by this service when required. Finally, listeners for configuration changes are in place to identify any changes that affect security. How and whether security is enabled for WAS and for the applications running on top of it affects how this component and its service perform their work but not the general functions performed. The security.xml, domain-security.xml, and app-security.xml files control the configuration, along with property files and configured providers.

The next component to start is the JMSRegistration component, which is controlled by the JMSRegistration implementation class. This sets up JMS to use whatever provider is configured for the environment, either the internal Service Integration Bus Messaging Engine, provided via WebSphere Platform Messaging, or WebSphere MQ. If it is WebSphere MQ, the version is checked and the appropriate classes are loaded to tie into JMS. To monitor the environment, MBeans are also configured.

Next to load is the WebServicesSecurity component, which handles the use of certificates, keys, tokens, and nonces for security for web services and also provides the WS Security Service. Its implementation class is WSSecurityComponentImpl. This component also configures management for web services security via JMX. Configuration is handled via the ws-security.xml file for X509 certificate management of key stores and use of LDAP certificate repositories to manage certificates and related certificate revocation lists. Any hardware cryptographic support is configured at the high level via this component.

The SchedulerConfig component that loads next performs the function its name suggests: it handles configuration for the Scheduler Service within WAS. It provides the Scheduler Config Service. The implementation class is SchedulerConfigServiceImpl.

Next is the PMIRequestMetrics component, which at this point is targeted at the zOS platform only and runs as a control region. The implementation class that controls the component is PmiRmImpl. This is part of the Performance Monitoring Infrastructure (PMI) for WAS that covers the gathering of performance metrics, including database connection pool threading, connections and waits, EJB method call response times and bean concurrency, JCA connection pools and response times, JTA transaction timings, JVM memory and CPU usage, ORB concurrency and response times, thread pool sizings, servlet response times, JMS and web services connections and threads, async beans, and session management sizings and timings. To get this information, it monitors the configuration of the environment for changes, loads the appropriate ARM monitoring implementation for the configuration, and then monitors the configured metrics. Particular attention is paid to the EJB container. The pmirm.xml file is used for configuration for this component. Underlying the implementation is the Application Response Measurement (ARM) infrastructure that can be provided by Tivoli tools, such as ITCAM or the Enterprise Workload Manager (EWLM) infrastructure, with different configuration and implementation for each.

After the preceding set of components has been loaded, the next phase of runtime startup is initiated by the loading of the ApplicationServer component that loads the application server container atop the base runtime container. The details of what loads are covered in the next section of this chapter. This loading proceeds asynchronously from this point because the base services that are needed to support it have been loaded: the configuration management, the transaction management, the connection management, the thread management, the monitoring facilities, the HA and recovery facilities, and the ORB. Essentially, these are just base infrastructure components that could support other Java-based functions and applications rather than just an application server. It is the application server container runtime that turns these infrastructure functions into a JavaEE application server by applying the JavaEE policies to the underlying functionality to build new functionality for higher-level containers. The service provided by this component to the higher-level parts of the runtime includes classloader and property listener facilities, although the components it runs are key parts to the rest of WAS.

The code to start the application server container references the com.ibm.wsspi.extension. applicationserver-startup section of the plugin.xml file in its containerExtensionPoint attribute. The class that starts this loading is referred to in the related entry for the component applicationserver.ApplicationServer in the com.ibm.wsspi.extension.server-components section of the same file. Thus, the reading of the initial entry to load this component spawns two additional accesses to other parts of the file. The Application Server Service is provided by the ApplicationServer component that is loaded by this configuration. This is covered in more detail in the next section of this chapter.

While the application server container is being loaded, the base server runtime continues to load components. The CompositionUnitMgr component for the zOS platform, implemented by the CompositionUnitMgrImpl class, is next to load and loads as a control region. It provides the Composition Unit Mgr Service. WAS 7 introduced support for Business Level Applications (BLAs), groups of JavaEE-level applications and archives that are combined to provide an application service that is meaningful to business users. This component reads the configuration for the BLAs and "composes" them within WAS to build up the BLA relationship. The CompositionUnitMgr component loads the Composition Unit instances, for which there is a separate class and component; it is these composition units that make up the BLAs.

Next to load on the zOS platform only is the Transaction component to support the Tx Service, which is implemented by the TxServiceImpl class. This is the first time this component tries to load on the zOS platform. It checks the configuration, particularly with respect to the HA facilities for the cell and cluster, checks that the recovery log is available, sets up the required interfaces to the zOS Resource Recovery Services (RRS), sets up the necessary transaction management and timeout parameters for the environment and the Open Group Distributed Transaction Processing XA standard implementation, interfaces to the Work Manager, Workload Manager, and Recovery Directory environments (for failure recovery), sets up the thread pooling required for transaction management, interfaces to zOS-specific transaction logging, and then sets up JMX management for the service. Lower-level components are used to enlist XA transaction management resources from the platform environment for use from the WebSphere Application Server environment with its own interfaces and functions. Its recovery type is that of a servant region.

At this point the DRS (Data Replication Services) component service is reloaded on the zOS platform only as a control region. This provides, as before, the Multibroker Domain Service and is implemented by the MultibrokerDomainImpl class. The DRS component allows synchronization with components that are started later than the previous invocation. There are control and servant regions required for the environment that have different functions.

On the zOS platform, the RecoveryLog component is again reloaded, for the same reasons as outlined for the DRS component; but this time, its recovery type is that of a servant region. It is implemented by the RecLogServiceImpl class.

Next, the ProductRegistration component is loaded on the zOS platform only. The zOS platform has its own product registration service that is accessible from the Java environment. While there is no implementation component available as part of the base WAS runtime, eventually the platform product registration service Java support is accessed. Its recovery type is that of a control region, although its process type is more general. The implementation class for this component is ProductRegistrationComponentImpl, which is external to the com.ibm.ws.runtime plugin.

Server Container Components

The server_components plugin.xml entry and the components that load following it address the loading of core infrastructure components that are part of the server runtime, providing key JavaEE-level functionality. Most, but not all, of the components that are loaded are specific to the zOS platform and are required due to its unusual architecture, which requires multiple process types to achieve the same ends as a single JavaEE JVM process on other platforms. Also, most of the components loaded in this phase of loading do not provide services that are registered with the WAS service registry (WsServiceRegistry).

The `server_components` component, as it is listed in the `plugin.xml` file, is not a true component because it has no direct implementation. It is another "catch all" entry that demarcates the base server startup, and it is the next to "load."

Again on the zOS platform only, the `ODCProxyManager` component loads next and is implemented by the `ODCProxyManager` class. This is a proxy for the ODC listener and tree management for the ODC support to work on zOS. The zOS implementation of control and servant regions to support the WAS environment leads to a requirement for this proxy that is not necessary for other platforms that run within a single JVM process. This loads as both control and servant regions.

On the zOS platform, the next component to start is the `JFAPProxy` component. This does not offer up a service. JFAP is the *Java Formats and Protocols* connectivity proprietary standard from IBM, more commonly known as the Java JMS transport of messages over a WebSphere MQ-like transport. WebSphere MQ itself usually uses an RFH2 header and special flags in the communications to provide the variant known as MQFAP. So FAP is the transport at one level, on which the JFAP and MQFAP higher-level transports and protocols build. MQFAP differs in a number of ways, some related to its need to provide synchronization status flags in the transport to keep each end of a transport channel working together in tandem, and others related to the different failover characteristics of WAS and WebSphere MQ. On zOS, the multiprocess nature of the WAS environment, coupled with the likelihood of WebSphere MQ also being present, leads to this proxy component being required. There is no implementation in the base `com.ibm.ws.runtime.jar` archive environment. This runs as a control region. The implementation for the component is provided by the `JFAPProxyComponentImpl` class.

The `ControllerCacheService` component, as implemented by the `ControllerCacheServiceImpl` class, is next to load on the zOS platform only. This controller component ties together `DRS` and `Dynacache` service components on the zOS platform. It also has to take account of the multiprocess-type nature of WAS on the zOS platform and thus runs as a control region.

The `SfControllerService` component, which is again zOS-specific, is next to load as a control region. It is implemented by the `SfControllerServiceImpl` class. This component controls how state is replicated between WAS instances on the zOS platform, using DRS to support the EJB container. Listeners watch for events that require state updates to the caches and for failures that HAManager is handling. It is part of the EJS Container managed services that underpin the EJB container.

The `JmsAdminService` component is a multiplatform component. This simply sets up the JMX MBeans that manage the JMS providers configured for the cell and node environment. It gets the cell and node names from the server and uses this information to query the Admin Service for the environment. From this it determines the JMS configuration, which it uses to set up the MBeans. The component implementation is provided by the `JmsAdminService` class.

The `ECAChannel` component runs next, as a control region for the zOS platform only. This provides some of the asynchronous I/O (AIO) functionality for WAS on the zOS platform where ESCON Channel Adapter (ECA) cards are in use by providing channels and TCP transport chains for the Channel Framework Service. The `ECAChannelComponentImpl` class provides the component implementation.

Next, the `ESIChannel` component is started up, again only for the zOS platform and as a control region. The `ESIChannelComponentImpl` class provides the implementation for the component. This provides the Edge Side Include (ESI) transport channel and inbound HTTP chain to the web container from the ESI Processor. The ESI Processor is inside the WAS proxy plugin, running inside the HTTP server that caches specifically configured markup to avoid repeated unnecessary hits on the application server. To handle the caching of web content, a dedicated channel to WAS from the plugin is required, and this component starts it.

The ESIInvalidator component is another zOS-specific component that must run only in a control region. It acts as an interface to a proxy controller instance for ESI to provide cache invalidation support to the Edge Side Includes for which that channel was previously set up. Again, the implementation of this component in the ESIInvalidatorComponentImpl class is a direct consequence of the zOS implementation of WAS across multiple different types of processes. This component can be considered as part of the Dynacache environment for zOS.

The ServerSecurity component is the next to start on the zOS platform as a control region. The implementation of this component is provided by the ServerSecurityComponentImpl class. This is a complex component that manages the security for the environment at the channel level and at the application level. First, it checks to see if server security is enabled and, if so, continues. It gets the virtual host and endpoint details from their respective services and other details from the Config Service for the server.xml file and sets the appropriate security configuration. The Security Service is started and the SSO facilities are configured. Any changes to EAR, WAR, or EJB JAR files result in appropriate security configuration and roles and permissions being applied, so the component monitors for installs and uninstalls for these modules. Manipulation of the HTTP transport chains to support SSL is handled here.

Next, the Tx Service as run by the Transaction component, started earlier as a servant region on the zOS platform, is started as a control region for the zOS platform. The TxServiceImpl component provides the implementation.

The TaskMgmtServiceMapper component is a multiplatform component that starts next and that essentially provides an e-mail sending service to administrators in response to task management notifications and administrative events. When running on zOS, it starts as a control region. This component does provide and register the Task Management Service Mapper Service. The implementation is provided by the TaskManagementServiceMapper class.

The TaskMgmtMBean component is a multiplatform component that provides much of the management of the Task Management Service in that it handles the interface to the core of the Task Management Service, sets up the MBean for the environment, and sends appropriate notifications. Tasks run in their own "container" to a schedule, have alarms set on them, and have their configuration and state persisted. When running on zOS, it starts as a control region. The component provides the Task Management MBean Service and is implemented by the TaskManagementMBean class.

The TaskConfigMonitor component is the third component of the Task Management Service environment to start, and it ensures the notification policies are handled, interfaces to the previous two components to do its work, and monitors configuration changes. When running on zOS, it starts as a control region. The component implementation is provided by the TaskConfigMonitorImpl class.

Next the UserManagement component starts. This component starts the JMX management MBean for user management and, as such, needs to escalate its privileges in several places to get appropriate access to the administration service and to set up notification listeners for changes. This is a multiplatform component. The implementation for the component is provided by the UserManagementProcess class.

The WLC (Workload Controller) component is next to start, but only for distributed and System i (i5OS) platforms. The implementation is provided by the WLCImpl class. This sets up the WLC Service for other components to use to stop or quiesce the WAS environment. It uses a separate WorkloadController class to do its work, which is usually used to regulate workloads and resources within a WAS cluster, and makes use of the ORB in order to quiesce the resources when the service is used. This is the final component to start for non-zOS platforms for this phase of the base server initialization.

For the zOS platform, the last component to start is the SOAPMonitorChannel component, which is implemented by the SOAPMonitorChannelComponentImpl class and starts as a control region. At the highest level, this sets up a new SOAP Request Monitor Manager for the SOAP Monitor Channel. The SOAP Monitor Channel is a Channel Framework Service–managed transport chain into the web container. The zOS platform needs this in a control region to act as a conduit to the servant regions and is a consequence of the architecture of WAS on zOS.

The startup of the base runtime services is now complete. The base server that provides the supporting infrastructure for the JavaEE-level application server functionality is loaded as groupings of enterprise-level qualities of service components, service-related components, and key general infrastructure components. Also, the application server container that provides the basis for the JavaEE functionality is started asynchronously during the service component initialization, and this builds on the core infrastructure and service-related components that load before it. This phasing of loading within the container is shown in Figure 4-3.

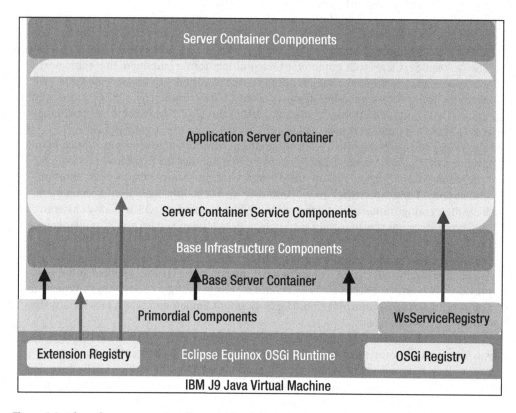

Figure 4-3. *Phased component loading within the base server container*

The Runtime Base Application Server Functionality

We have looked at the base server container startup and the components that make it up. Now the application server container is started in a similar manner. When the WS_ApplicationServer entry is read in the previous base startup, at value 12000, the containerExtensionPoint attribute is used to identify which section of the plugin.xml file to read to enumerate the components and services for this container. The startup of this entry starts the initialization of the application server container services proper, and the two initialization sequences then continue concurrently. As would be expected, the startup declares a dependency on the component manager service being available to perform its initialization. The list of components started can be found under the extension point com.ibm.wsspi.extension.applicationserver-startup section of the plugin.xml file, which is the section named by the containerExtensionPoint attribute. The class initiating this loading phase, ApplicationServerImpl, is identified in the entry for component applicationserver.ApplicationServer in the com.ibm.wsspi.extension.server-components section of the plugin.xml file.

The class starting the loading sets up the Application Server Service, sets up its classloader policies, uses the Library Manager and Server Services to set up some configuration, and checks the ws-applicationserver-startup.xml file for components it needs to load. The WsContainer class initialization handles the section of the plugin.xml file for the components loaded here. Additional components from the ws-applicationserver-startup.xml file can be referenced in the com.ibm.ws.runtime plugin, but these are not important as part of the initialization at this point.

While various services are subject to a second lookup from other sections of the plugin.xml file, the most significant is the EJB Container, which is loaded asynchronously when the startup value 7000 is reached and the containerExtensionPoint attribute is read. This attribute identifies the section of the plugin.xml file with extension point com.ibm.wsspi.extension.ejbcontainer-startup, which lists components that are owned by the EJB container and are started by it during its asynchronous startup phase. The web container is not referenced as part of this initialization in the com.ibm.ws.runtime plugin file, but it does start in this phase. It declares its own entries for the com.ibm.wsspi.extension.applicationserver-startup extension in the com.ibm.ws.webcontainer plugin file in plugin.xml. The Eclipse runtime will read this plugin.xml file to initialize the extension registry. It will be started at this phase of startup. This is addressed in the web container initialization coverage in Chapter 6.

Application Server Container Components Loading via com.ibm.wsspi.extension.applicationserver-startup

We now need to consider the list of components loaded in the application server phase of loading. They provide the base JavaEE services that support the other key JavaEE subsystems and containers. These components and their load order are outlined in Table 4-2.

Table 4-2. *Components Loaded in the applicationserver-startup Initialization Phase*

Component	Class	Startup	Target	Services
WS_ObjectPoolService	ObjectPoolServiceImpl	1000		ObjectPoolService
WS_MetaDataMgr	MetaDataMgrImpl	1000		MetaDataService
				MetaDataFactoryMgr
WS_VirtualHostMgr	VirtualHostMgrImpl	1000		VirtualHostMgr
WS_PMEMetaDataHelperService	MetaDataHelperServiceImpl	1001		MetaDataHelperService
WS_TransportMap	TransportMapImpl	1050		TransportMap
WS_ServerSecurity	ServerSecurityComponentImpl	1100		
WS_WorkManager	J2EEServiceManager	1500		AsynchBeansService
WS_Transaction		2000		TxService
WS_ActivityService	ActivityServiceComponentImpl	3000		
WS_CompensationRecovery	CScopeComponentImpl	3100		
WS_Compensation	CScopeAppComponentImpl	3100		
WS_RecoveryLog	RecLogServiceImpl	3200		
WS_J2CHAProxy	CoreStackProxyImpl	3300	zOS Only	CoreStackProxy
WS_ResourceMgr	ResourceMgrImpl	3500		ResourceMgr
WS_RALifeCycleMgr	RALifeCycleManagerImpl	3700		
WS_ActivitySession	ActivitySessionComponentImpl	4000		
WS_ActivitySessionWebApp	ActivitySessionWebAppComponentImpl	4000		
WS_AppProfile	AppProfileComponentImpl	4000		
WS_WorkArea	WorkAreaServiceServer	4000		
WS_ConnectionMgr	ConnMgrImpl	4000		
WS_TransactionRecovery	TxRecoveryServiceImpl	4000		
WS_WorkAreaPartition	WorkAreaPartitionServiceServer	4001		
WS_WSBA	WSBAImpl	4100		
WS_SOAPContainerChannel	SOAPContainerChannelComponentImpl	4900	Distributed, OS400	SOAPContainerService
WS_SOAPAcceptorChannel	SOAPAcceptorChannelComponentImpl	4901	Distributed, OS400	
WS_SystemWebServices	WSSysServerImpl	4990	Distributed, OS400	WebServicesSystemService

Component	Class	Startup	Target	Services
WS_Addressing	WSAWSComponentImpl	4990		
WS_Dynacache		4991		CacheService
WS_Dynacache_object	ObjectCacheServiceImpl	4992		
WS_Dynacache_servlet	ServletCacheServiceImpl	4993		
WS_applicationserver_services		5000		
WS_LocalTransaction	LTCCallbacksComponentImpl	5000		
WS_JaxRpcWebService	WSServerImpl	5000		WebServicesService
WS_InjectionEngine	InjectionEngineImpl	6400		InjectionEngine
WS_Scheduler	SchedulerServiceImpl	6500		SchedulerService
WS_ApplicationHandlerMgr	ApplicationHandlerManagerService	6500		ApplicationHandlerManagerService
WS_JPAComponent	JPAComponentImpl	6500		
WS_ExtensionRegistry	ExtensionRegistryService	6800		
WS_EJBContainer		7000		EJBContainer
WS_LocalHttpChainFactory	LocalHttpChainFactoryImpl	7500		LocalHttpChainFactoryImpl
WS_TxRecoveryMode	TxRecoveryModeServiceImpl	8000	Distributed, OS400	
WS_PMIRequestMetrics	PmiRmImpl	8500		
WS_ThreadPool	ThreadPoolImpl	8700		
WS_applicationserver_components		9000		
WS_ServerRuleDriver	ServerRuleDriverMBean	10000		
WS_ApplicationMgr	ApplicationMgrImpl	10000		ApplicationMgr
WS_LibraryMgr	LibraryMgrImpl	10000		LibraryMgr
WS_ClusterServerRuntime	ApplicationServerRuntimeImpl	10001		
WS_StartupService	StartUpService	10001		
WS_RRAHPPropertyLoader	RRAHPPropertyLoaderImpl	10002		
WS_I18N	I18nServerComponentImpl	11000		
WS_DebugServer	DebugAppServerComponentImpl	15000		
WS_EEXQuery	QueryComponentImpl	20000		
WS_J2EERequestProfiler	J2eeRequestProfilerService	53534		
WS_CompositionUnitMgr	CompositionUnitMgrImpl	100001		CompositionUnitMgr

Application Server Container Components

Table 4-2 lists the components loaded by the application server container that provide functionality to support the JavaEE specification as it relates to the other JavaEE containers running with enterprise-level qualities of service and the components that support startup of other JavaEE-level subsystems. We will now look at what each of these components does to support the environment.

Core Application Server Container Components

The first component to start is the `ObjectPoolService` component that provides the Object Pool Service. The implementation is provided by the `ObjectPoolServiceImpl` class. This sets up the Object Pool Manager implementation class environment that provides facilities for getting and managing multiple pools of objects of a particular class and the related JMX MBeans.

The `MetaDataMgr` component is the next to start, and this provides both the Meta Data Service and the Meta Data Factory Mgr Service. The WAS runtime keeps metadata on applications, modules, components, EJB components, web application components, custom containers, and related methods in metadata "slots" and maintains listeners for changes to be monitored and notified. This component sets up this metadata management environment and the service for access to the data from elsewhere. The implementation class for this component is `MetaDataMgrImpl`.

Next to load is the `VirtualHostMgr` component that provides the Virtual Host Mgr Service. The implementation is provided by the `VirtualHostMgrImpl` class. This component was previously loaded for zOS only as a control region, but now it loads for all platforms, this time in the application server container. This component registers the virtual host aliases and port information based on the configuration in the `virtualhosts.xml` configuration file. It uses the Variable Map Service and Config Service components to read the configuration and make appropriate substitutions.

The `PMEMetaDataHelperService` component is the next to load inside the application server container to provide the Meta Data Helper Service for PME and is implemented by the `MetaDataHelperServiceImpl` class. After the WAS 4 Enterprise Edition release introduced a number of extensions to J2EE, some of which were precursors to later versions of the specification, IBM started moving these Programming Model Extensions (PME) into the base WAS runtime from WAS 5.*x* onward. This component creates helpers to map PME-related metadata to that of the standard slots and types supported by the Meta Data Service and stores the information for a consistent view. It makes extensive use of the Meta Data Service provided by the `MetaDataMgr` component.

The `TransportMap` component that is the next component to start is implemented by the `TransportMapImpl` class and provides the Transport Map Service. This component utilizes the Config Service to get access to the `server.xml` information to maintain "maps" of the transport chains configured. This configuration includes the virtual hosts and endpoint hosts and ports, TCP, IP, SSL, HTTP, and HTTPS inbound and outbound transport channels at the base, and web container levels. Details of the endpoints are provided by the End Point Mgr Service. The Transport Map Service allows for these mappings and the ports to be accessed by other components.

Previously, the `ServerSecurity` component was started on the zOS platform as a control region as part of the base server startup. Now it is started for other platforms in the application server container and as a servant region on zOS. This is a complex component that manages the security for the environment at the channel level and at the application level. First, it checks to see if server security is enabled and, if so, continues. It gets the virtual host and endpoint details from their respective services and other details from the Config Service for the `server.xml` file and sets the appropriate security configuration. The Security Service is started and the SSO facilities are configured. Any changes to EAR, WAR, or EJB JAR files result in appropriate security configuration, roles, and permissions being applied, so the component monitors for installs and uninstalls for these modules. Manipulation of the HTTP transport chains to support SSL is handled here. The component is implemented by the `ServerSecurityComponentImpl` class.

JavaEE-Level Service Components and Enterprise-Level Quality of Service Components

The `WorkManager` component that sets up a service known as the Asynch Beans Service is started next. The functionality handled by this is known in some documentation as the Work Manager Service or J2EE Service Manager, but this refers to the user-level facilities rather than the code level being examined here. The component maintains a stack of async beans service information and uses the Object Pool Service, Thread Pool Mgr Service, and Security Service to get contextual information for the EJB and web containers. The work manager implementation and timers it sets up perform the core work for the async beans, using its own thread and object pools to handle the requests for the beans. Essentially, the Work Manager Service exists because it is against the JavaEE and J2EE specifications to create threads, because the application server cannot track resources, so a mapping to a thread pool thread is provided by the Asynch Beans Service to allow similar types of use cases to be implemented. Thus, asynchronous beans provide a means by which application daemon-like or background-threaded activities can be performed on threads from the `WorkManager` thread pool using the `startWork` method, and if a listener is provided, the application can be notified when that task is complete. The contextual information obtained is important to ensure the right JNDI context is used for lookups. This component sets up the engine for this set of activities. The implementation of the component is provided by the `J2EEServiceManager` class.

Next to load is the application server container side of the `Transaction` component to support the Tx Service. The class handling this, `TxServiceImpl`, is identified in the entry for component `applicationserver.TransactionService` in the `com.ibm.wsspi.extension.server-components` section of the `plugin.xml` file. It checks the configuration, particularly with respect to the HA facilities for the cell and cluster from `server.xml`, checks that the recovery log is available, sets up the required interfaces to the zOS Resource Recovery Services (RRS) on zOS only, sets up the necessary transaction management and timeout parameters for the environment and XA, interfaces to the Work Manager, Workload Manager, and Recovery Director subsystem environments (for failure recovery), sets up the thread pooling required for transaction management, interfaces to platform-specific transaction logging, and then sets up JMX management for the service. Lower-level components are used to enlist XA transaction management resources from the platform environment for use from the WebSphere Application Server environment with its own interfaces and functions.

Previously, in the base server runtime on the zOS platform, only the `ActivityServiceCR` component was loaded as a control region to handle the Activity Service support. Now, the true `ActivityService` component loads on other platforms and as a servant on zOS, but this time as part of the application server container. The implementation class, `ActivityServiceComponentImpl`, is the same as for the CR control region version. The WAS

Activity Service subsystem, as mentioned earlier in this chapter, is an implementation of the JavaEE JSR95 Activity Service standard to coordinate multiple units of work that builds upon the CORBA OMG Activity Service implementation in the CORBA ORB. The component interfaces with the ORB to collect activity information and provide a direct mapping to the ORB implementation and uses other classes to collect local, user, and process information.

The CompensationRecovery component, implemented by the CScopeComponentImpl class, is started next, which handles the recovery of compensating transactions in the event of a failure. This is part of the JavaEE-level Compensation Service. Essentially, compensation can be thought of as a logical transactional concept, so in the event of a failure, similar activities as those for transactional recovery using recovery logs is needed, with the complication that compensation can take more time to execute because of its nature. In this case, this is part of the PME for WAS that includes the Activity Service but has subsequently been standardized in other products or subsystems in WAS. In this case, the WS-BPEL facilities in WebSphere Process Server have replaced this implementation. Since it may not be possible for the compensation recovery to take place on the same system, this component interfaces to any platform provided Peer Restart and Recovery (PRR) services, such as on zOS, to control the XA resource managers handling any parts of the transactions in doubt, to lock them where necessary until their state can be resolved. It makes extensive use of the Meta Data Service and Application Manager Service to add listener facilities to watch for changes to EJBs, PME extensions, and so forth, as these may also require compensation facilities. It also listens for EJB container changes for the same reason. The recovery log manager and recovery director subsystem facilities are key to this component's functionality, so it creates an agent to manage the relationship. The Config Service is used to look up the server-pme51.xml file for configuration for this component. It interfaces to the Activity Service because the two are closely related and this compensation facility is an essential part of its function.

The previously loaded component supports compensation recovery for the JavaEE-level Compensation Service subsystem, so the next component to load is the Compensation component, with its CScopeAppComponentImpl implementation. Note that no WsServiceRegistry Compensation Service interface is provided by this component because the Compensation Service is a JavaEE-level subsystem. In fact, this component does very little because most of the work is handled by the previous two components and the EJB container itself.

The RecoveryLog component was loaded previously in the base server runtime as a zOS-specific service that controls the recovery log and handles recovery of transactions in the event of failure, but now it is loaded for other platforms as part of the application server container. The implementation is provided by the RecLogServiceImpl class. For this role, the component must monitor the configuration and topology of the cell and cluster and respond to ensure that the appropriate cluster member recovers in-doubt transactions. It creates or uses a recovery log, a recovery log manager, and a recovery director set of classes to handle the real recovery log functionality.

The J2CHAProxy component is a zOS-specific component that handles group membership and state management via the underlying Group Manager subsystem implementation. It is implemented by the CoreStackProxyImpl class. The component is loaded as part of the base runtime container as a control region, but this time loads as a servant. It ensures the appropriate management of J2C/JCA adapter resources and provides the Core Stack Proxy Service. The architecture is a consequence of the zOS platform implementation of WAS with multiple processes.

Next, the `ResourceManager` component loads. It is implemented by the `ResourceMgrImpl` class and provides the Resource Mgr Service. This component essentially manages the binding of resource providers, resource binders, and resources, such as JCA Resource Adapters, JMS providers, and various other resources with JNDI and the ORB. It also handles associated listeners for receiving and notifying changes. The high-level installation of a resource or a resource provider in WAS as part of administration is handled at the highest level via this component. It is, thus, a complex component that makes use of many other services and components, particularly for accessing configuration and application information for which the Config Service and Application Manager Service are used. Resources are named in the `resources.xml` file and other variations of this file name for IBM WebSphere extensions from earlier versions. Each resource type has a resource binder that handles the binding, so a collection of binders is maintained. The WAS resource binders available are declared later in the `plugin.xml` file via the `com.ibm.wsspi.extension.resource-binders` extension point declaration.

As the name suggests, the `RALifeCycleMgr` component, which is the next component to load, manages the high-level life cycle of J2C resource adapters, i.e., their starting, stopping, and so on. To do this it makes use of a number of other services. It sets up access to the thread pool manager provided by the Thread Pool Mgr Service for use by the JavaEE-level Work Manager Service, registers event listeners with the Resource Mgr Service for J2C Resource Adapters, JDBC providers, and JMS providers, makes use of the Meta Data Manager Service to manage metadata, and uses the Application Manager Service to monitor the applications deployed. When required, it uses the resource manager to install resource providers and sets up the JMX MBeans for monitoring them, with the triggers being application deployment events. The application of any configuration that a J2C resource adapter requires at runtime and the JNDI name bindings (i.e., connection factories, etc.) are handled by this component when the adapter is started, using various lower-level helper classes. This component underpins a lot of the key functionality for WAS because many of its functions, such as JDBC, JMS (including WebSphere MQ), and other resource adapters, are handled via its functions.

A grouping of components is started next to provide more of the functionality for the JavaEE-level Activity Service subsystem. The first is the `ActivitySession` component that is part of the JSR95 implementation that builds on the OMG Activity Service for CORBA. This is implemented in the `ActivitySessionComponentImpl` class. Other key functions and subsystems within WAS build upon the Activity Service subsystem. The component handles some of the configuration for the Activity Service and watches for changes in application or PME-based application metadata for the environment using the Meta Data Service because it needs to be aware of the applications and their environmental requirements. The component installs activity session listeners in the web container specifically and looks for changes in web modules.

The next component to load, the `ActivitySessionWebApp` component, is a small component that merely calls into the `ActivitySession` component to initiate the web container monitoring. The implementation is provided in the `ActivitySessionWebAppComponentImpl` class.

Effectively, the previous two components loaded together provide configuration and monitoring for the `ActivityService` component loaded earlier, but all of the related components are necessary to provide the JavaEE JSR95 Activity Service support for WAS.

The `AppProfile` component is the next to start, and is another WAS extension to the JavaEE specification. Application profiling allows access to methods on EJBs to be fine-tuned in terms of concurrency, prefetch, and read ahead to maximize performance, with some variations in the facilities in previous versions of WAS requiring different paths through the implementation to maintain compatibility. The access intents also relate to units of work, so this component follows on from the previous one in building upon the unit of work support provided by the Activity Service. The component is implemented in the AppProfileComponentImpl class. It uses the JavaEE Activity Service subsystem support for unit of work management and ties into the EJB and web containers and the asynchronous beans service using collaborator classes. The implementation accesses the serverindex.xml file via the Config Service to determine the server configuration and then examines the WAS-specific deployment.xml file for that application module. The application module is generated by WAS when an application is deployed for application-specific settings where profiling has been applied and ensures the requests are honored through the collaborators installed earlier.

The WorkArea component that uses the WorkAreaServiceServer implementation class starts next. Work Areas are another WAS PME like those in the previous components, but with this being an implementation of the JSR149 specification rather than being something IBM-specific. Components such as EJBs and servlets normally pass data through interfaces while the application server infrastructure provides shared information such as security and transactional context to all components behind the scenes. The Work Area facilities within WAS allow applications to make use of a user-shared storage area. This facility is implemented using thread local storage for local components and IIOP for remote components, for sharing contextual information between components that can be accessed via a JNDI lookup. This component runs on multiple platforms but only as a servant on zOS. The component sets up configuration information for the storage areas, called Work Area Partitions, and sets up a management component for them that is registered with JNDI that does the real work of running the service with the help of the separate Work Manager Partition Service and its implementation. Collaborator components for the EJB and web containers are set up along with a collaborator interface to the Asynch Beans Service.

The ConnectionMgr component does very little. It merely loads a data source factory handling class to create and destroy data sources, manages the transactional environment for these data sources, and checks configuration for the component metadata for EJB and web modules making up the deployed applications. The implementation class for this component is ConnMgrImpl.

The TransactionRecovery component starts next, which in this case has no associated service and is implemented by the TxRecoveryServiceImpl class. This just sets up the JTA (Java Transaction API) Recovery Manager subsystem, which itself handles the replaying of transactions from transaction logs, transaction log management, XA and J2C RA transaction support, and replay of partner transaction logs after failure. While the TransactionRecovery component has a minimal implementation, the complex JTA RecoveryManager class (com.ibm.tx.jta. RecoveryManager) it uses is the key component in WAS transaction and transaction log recovery, so in the event of transaction log recovery support issues, this class is the first port of call for investigation.

The WorkAreaPartition component is next to start, and it is this that manages the Work Area storage referred to earlier. It is implemented by the WorkAreaPartitionServiceServer class and configures each of the required partitions for the Java-EE level Work Area Service that are then used by its management component.

The WSBA component is next to load, which provides the Web Services Business Activity (WS-BA) support in WAS for compensating transactions as part of the OASIS (Organization for Advancement of Structured Information Standards) WS-Transaction specification. As expected, this makes use of the JavaEE-level Compensation Service facilities loaded earlier, with asynchronous threading facilities provided by the WorkManager component and Asynch Beans Service support. Essentially, this implementation in the WSBAImpl class is a thin wrapper that delegates to the Compensation component CScope implementations.

Previously, web services support was loaded for zOS only in control regions, but now it loads for the distributed and i5OS environments only. The SOAPContainerChannel component configuration loaded here sets up a core system web services "communications engine" and router for the platform to handle SOAP/HTTP interactions. This intercepts, routes, and handles web services requests on the platform and loads the system web services engine support. The implementation for this component is handled by the SOAPContainerChannelComponentImpl class that provides the Soap Container Service.

The SOAPAcceptorChannel component works with the SOAPContainerChannel component to handle inbound requests and set up a virtual channel. It enumerates the channels and chains managed by the Channel Framework Service to apply the appropriate configuration before setting up the HTTP channels required. The implementation class for the component is SOAPAcceptorChannelComponentImpl.

The SystemWebServices component, as implemented by the WSSysServerImpl class, is part of the web services engine that handles JAX-RPC and works with the previous two components to support web services at the system level. It interacts with and collaborates with the web container and EJB container for runtime integration but handles many of the XML and web services support functions itself. It provides the Web Services System Service. The JAX-WS support within WAS 7, which most new web services implementations will use, merely uses the Axis2 implementations under the covers in the Web Services Feature Pack support code, with its core integration into WAS. The JAX-RPC support in WAS 7 has been upgraded from the J2EE 1.4 level. The component implementation uses the Meta Data Service to get information on the requirements for the environment to support the applications and applies the necessary configuration. The real JAX-RPC web services implementation is provided by the WSServerImpl class that provides the Web Services Service, which starts soon after this component to provide the core of the JAX-RPC handling. The Web Services Service implementation component includes collaborators for the web and EJB containers, along with appropriate security support, so the SystemWebServices component delegates to it to implement its functionality.

Next, the Addressing component to handle the WS-Addressing web services standard implementation is loaded, with configuration as a servant on the zOS platform and a separate configuration for the distributed and i5OS platforms. The component itself is simple in its implementation in the WSAWSComponentImpl class because it delegates to other implementation classes to do the real work. It registers an implementation class as a *WS Addressing Base Service* service provider and another implementation class as an *End Point Map Service* service provider. The component uses the Meta Data Service to register an endpoint mapping listener to provide support for changes to the deployed applications, although the services registered are not declared in the plugin.xml file.

The Dynacache component for the Dynacache caching subsystem mechanism is started next. This is implemented in the CacheServiceImpl class referenced in the com.ibm.wsspi. extension.server-components section of the plugin.xml file for the DynamicCache entry. It provides the Cache Service and sets up the providers, resources, and bindings necessary to support dynamic caching for the WebSphere Dynacache mechanism. Caching of servlet and JSP fragments and data access "commands" are handled by this mechanism. The entry in plugin.xml uses component class details listed in the com.ibm.wsspi.extension.server-components for its initialization. The class handles the basic core cache initialization and replication itself, particularly making use of the WebSphere Common Configuration Model (WCCM) configuration. The component registers the Cache Service, and if WAS is running in a proxy server role, it uses the Cache Resource Mgr Service to bind. When running as a standard application server instance, the component uses the Resource Mgr Service to bind. Dynacache MBeans are set up, cache providers loaded and configured, and servlet support enabled, all of which uses lower-level WCCM and cache-related classes to do the work, with the use of the DRS Multibroker Domain Service and associated listeners to support cache replication.

The next component to start is also part of the Dynacache mechanism and is the Dynacache_object component that is implemented in the ObjectCacheServiceImpl class. This takes the cache units from the component above and adds object caching support.

The last part of the Dynacache mechanism to start is the Dynacache_servlet component that adds support for servlet, portlet, web service, and static content cache units based on the Dynacache subsystem component implementations outlined above, if servlet caching is enabled for the web container environment and applications. The implementation is provided by the ServletCacheServiceImpl class.

Application Server Container Services

A placeholder for the application server container services rather than a component is loaded next, as the component with the ID ws_applicationserver_services is read at a startup value of 5000.

The LocalTransaction component loads next, which handles Local Transaction Containment (LTC) for WAS applications with components (i.e., EJBs) operating outside of a global transaction to avoid the leaking of JCA managed connections. With LTC, the web container creates an LTC context when a servlet is invoked. This is used with JDBC and other similar calls and used by the connection pooling code to hold and access the same resource until the servlet doService call ends, which can lead to a shortage of connection-related resources in times of heavy load. This is a simple component that creates callbacks for user transactions and user activity sessions using a class called LTCUOWCallback. It is this complex lower-level class that handles the high-level operations of managing local transaction units of work. The implementation class for this component is LTCCallbacksComponentImpl.

Next to start is the JaxRpcWebService component that initiates the actual JAX-RPC Web Services Service engine provided by the WSServerImpl class referred to earlier in this chapter when we looked at the SystemWebServices component. The implementation class for this component is complex and interfaces to a number of key WAS subsystems to provide the WAS support for JAX-RPC JSR109 web services. The component makes use of the Application Mgr Service to get access to the deployed application code to "adjust" it to fit in with the application server runtime implementations for the web and EJB containers, the Meta Data Service to add a listener to watch for application changes, and both the EJB Container Service and the Web Container Service to install collaborators to provide the supporting hooks for web services. It also installs MBeans for monitoring and managing web services and the engine. The component implementation makes use of the Channel Framework Service to ensure the appropriate transport chains and channels are available, with the required buffering provided by the WS Byte Pool Buffer Manager Service. Security hooks provided by the Web Services Security Service are also installed. When applications are deployed, this component is used to adjust the code deployed, based on the WSDLs, XML, and any IBM-specific XML extensions provided and any JAX RPC code to handle the appropriate bindings. The setup of endpoints is also managed through this component. When JAX-RPC web services are deployed and used this code is at the core. This component and the underlying subsystem implementation is examined in more depth in Chapter 7 when the handling of web services in WAS is covered.

The next component to load is the `InjectionEngine` that provides the Injection Engine Service with an implementation in the `InjectionEngineImpl` class. With the introduction of Java 5 with WAS 6.1, annotations were introduced to allow markers to be placed into executable code that could be read by other Java code. This allowed the introduction of dependency injection (DI) facilities with Java Platform, Enterprise Edition 5 (JavaEE 5) to support the EJB 3 specification and Java Persistence API (JPA). With EJB 3, the code is annotated to highlight points where references to other objects are required, such as to use the Entity Manager for EJB 3 entity beans. WAS handles injection through the injection engine setup by the `InjectionEngine` component. It installs metadata listeners and watches for events triggered by metadata changes that signify that code requires injection of references. When injection is required, the component uses lower-level classes to handle JNDI, resource references, and EJB link references before interfacing to the JIT compiler, then processes annotations or XML configuration of dependency injection references as required. Ultimately, the methods, fields, and objects of the executing environment are updated to inject the reference at the desired point.

The Scheduler Service Component

The `Scheduler` component provides the Scheduler Service. The higher-level WAS Scheduler Service, in a functional context for running batch jobs and events, first appeared as a PME in the high-end WAS Enterprise product, and then a variant was introduced into the J2EE specification. It allows tasks to be configured against a calendar that can invoke methods on a Session Enterprise JavaBean or that can send a JMS message and that can receive event notifications during its task life cycle. The EJB 2.1 timer service is built upon the internal Scheduler Service.

The `Scheduler` component that provides the Scheduler Service interface is also a container in WAS runtime terms and is implemented in the `SchedulerServiceImpl` class. It extends the base container implementation class and declares the `containerExtensionPoint`, with two components loaded within it, declared elsewhere in the `plugin.xml` file in the `com.ibm.wsspi.extension.scheduler-startup` section. One component is for handling beans and one is for handling messages.

There are two entries for the loading of the component in the application server: one for zOS as an adjunct and the other for general multiplatform usage, with differences in the configuration rather than the implementation.

The component declares its own service but makes use of the Security Service, the Resource Mgr Service, the Meta Data Factory Manager Service, the Extension Helper Service, the Application Server Service, the Thread Monitor Service, the Server Service, the EJB Container Service, the Web Container Service, the Variable Map Service, and the Application Mgr Service. In other words, it is a complex component with a lot of dependencies. A map of scheduler instances is maintained based on a JNDI name, and methods are used to maintain the map, with each instance having its own configuration. When a new instance of the Scheduler is started, a listener into the Security Service is used to allow the maintenance of role-based authorization and the new instance is created. The Meta Data Factory Manager Service is used to access the J2EE application context and the other services are used to set up the Scheduler container, using the `META-INF/ws-scheduler-startup.xml` component declarations and the `containerExtensionPoint` component declarations with the right configuration for the server. It includes hooks into the EJB container and web container environments for the applications. The Thread Monitor Service is used to provide the hung thread monitoring and qualities of service expected of a container. Other methods inside the component support the service interface and the declaration and management of tasks to be run.

Additional Application Server Container Components and Services

The next component to be started after the `Scheduler` component is the `ApplicationHandlerMgr` component. This component is implemented in the `ApplicationHandlerManagerService` class and declares the Application Handler Manager Service interface. This essentially uses the Application Mgr Service to get access to the application modules (i.e., JAR files, WAR files, EJB JAR files, etc.) deployed to the environment. It then builds on the functionality in the original Handler Framework Service that was started as part of the base server container for handling chains of handlers for a request by delegating to it. The application modules are examined and opened to find the `META-INF/ws-handler.xmi` file declaring the handlers. This is processed as for the lower-level service. Event monitors check to see when the applications stop or start so the handler chains can be controlled.

New in JavaEE 5 is the Java Persistence API (JPA), which underpins the entity bean support for the EJB 3 specification. The next component to start, the `JPAComponent`, supports this, and although there is no service interface declaration here, the type describes this as supporting the `jpaservice.JavaPersistenceAPIService`. The component is implemented by the `JPAComponentImpl` class and loads providers for the JPA subsystem support. The JTA, if required for EJB support, sets up the JPA Entity Manager pool capacity, adds a listener to monitor application deployments via the Application Mgr Service, and then registers injection processors for the `PersistenceUnit` (a set of classes that the Entity Manager maps to the database data) and `PersistenceContext` (the in-memory representation of the data in the database) classes using the Injection Engine Service covered earlier in this section. The listener callback methods respond to application startup and stopping events and use lower-level classes to apply the necessary support for JPA to the deployed modules via the classloaders. This support includes making use of and accessing the Entity Manager.

Chapter 3 looked at the Eclipse runtime environment and the Eclipse extension registry that allows plugins to look up and extend extension points provided by other plugins. This is the internal system-level extension registry provided for the use of WAS itself and its components. WAS also offers a public extension registry to support application-level plugins and extension points, only this one is accessed via a JNDI lookup rather than via the Eclipse `Platform.getExtensionRegistry` method, even though the rest of the extension interfaces are supported. This public registry is part of the *Workplace* (`wkplc`) structure within WAS to support this and is set up by the `ExtensionRegistry` component that loads next. This uses the `ExtensionRegistryService` implementation class but does not declare that it exposes a service. The component implementation makes use of a number of classes to provide a fairly complete implementation of the Eclipse plugin extension facilities, including support for listeners. It uses the Meta Data Service to look for changes to applications that may provide plugins by adding itself as an ExtensionRegistryMetaDataListener reference.

EJB Container Initialization and Application Server Container Services

Next to load is one of the most important parts of a JavaEE application server environment, the EJB container. This is loaded by the EJBContainer component that exposes the EJB Container Service, which has different dependency configurations for zOS and for other platforms. Like the other containers before it, this container uses the containerExtensionPoint attribute value to identify the components to load, and then these are loaded asynchronously while the rest of the components in this phase continue to load. In this case, the value com.ibm.wsspi. extension.ejbcontainer-startup identifies the section later in the plugin.xml file to read the entries required to load components into the EJB container. No implementation class for this container is named in either of these sections of the plugin.xml file. As with the application server container, a lookup for the com.ibm.wsspi.extension.server-components extension point for the applicationserver.ejbcontainer.EJBContainer entry suggested by the type attribute gives an implementation class named EJBContainerImpl, which at the highest level doesn't just initialize the EJB container, but provides much of the EJB container functionality to support EJBs with the help of some additional classes, most important of which is the EJSContainer class that supports some of the lower-level container and bean operations. We will look at this more in the EJB container initialization section.

The LocalHTTPChainFactory component controlled by the LocalHttpChainFactoryImpl class registers a LocalInboundChainFactory service with the internal WAS service registry, but declares the Local HTTP Chain Factory Impl Service in the plugin.xml file entry. The service offers facilities to create local HTTP chains, that is, layers of communication infrastructure facilities required to facilitate HTTP transport. It uses the Channel Framework (e.g., ChannelFramework and ChannelFrameworkImpl classes) to create either an HTTP or HTTPS inbound chain, using the appropriate factory depending on whether security is required, for a requested port and hostname. It updates the configuration for the appropriate access logs. As for many other components, much of the code inside the component is used to support the FFDC facilities.

The TXRecoveryMode component starts next via the TxRecoveryModeServiceImpl implementation class, but only for the non-zOS platforms, that is, the i5OS and distributed platforms. This component supports the use of WAS in recovery mode (i.e., *RECOVERY MODE* in the code). When a failure has occurred and there are in-doubt transactions identified in the transaction log, WAS starts with limited facilities in recovery mode and processes those transaction log entries to bring the environment data into a consistent state and release any resource locks before shutting down. This is a simple component that checks if WAS is running in recovery mode via the Server Service, and then makes use of the Channel Framework Service to start only the required transport chains if WAS is in recovery mode.

Previously, the PMIRequestMetrics component was started for zOS only as a control region, but now it starts for other environments. It is implemented by the PmiRmImpl class. This component is part of the Performance Monitoring Infrastructure (PMI) for WAS that covers gathering of performance metrics, including database connection pool threading, connections and waits, EJB method call response times and bean concurrency, JCA connection pools and response times, JTA transaction timings, JVM memory and CPU usage, ORB concurrency and response times, thread pool sizings, servlet response times, JMS and web services connections and threads, async beans, and session management sizings and timings. To get this information, it monitors the configuration of the environment for changes using a combination of the Admin Service and Config Service, loads the appropriate ARM monitoring implementation for the configuration, and then monitors the configured metrics. Particular attention is paid to the EJB container and async beans, for which it accesses the EJB Container Service and Asynch Beans Service, respectively, and registers collaborators. The pmirm.xml file is used for configuration for this component. Underlying the implementation is the Application Response Measurement (ARM) infrastructure support that can be provided by Tivoli tools such as the IBM Tivoli Composite Application Manager (ITCAM) or the Enterprise Workload Manager (EWLM) infrastructure, with different configuration and implementation for each.

The ThreadPool component starts next under the control of the ThreadPoolImpl class. This component accesses the ORB Service and EJB Container Service and ties the thread pool underlying the ORB IIOP facilities into the EJB container to support the CORBA Servant infrastructure that underlies remote EJBs.

Application Server Container Components

Within the plugin.xml file section for this loading phase there is a placeholder component called applicationserver_components that doesn't have any implementation. It does, however, signify that the components loaded after it are considered components rather than service providers, although this distinction is not a clear one.

The ServerRuleDriver component is next to start, which has the ServerRuleDriverMBean implementation class controlling it. This component is part of the PMI and Runtime Performance Advisor infrastructure that supports the WAS performance advisors and provides the ServerRuleDriverMBean for JMX management. It loads details of diagnostic provider properties from the AdvisorDiagnosticProvider.xml file that ships inside the runtime (along with other performance-tuning XML files) and applies these as a configuration to the performance-tuning infrastructure. Then it responds to diagnostic events, looks for patterns in the data, and dumps appropriate state data and heap dumps in response to the events. It essentially acts as a controller for the PMI engine that monitors the WAS internals. While it is a complex component, much of the functional work is provided by other classes and the PMI engine itself. Performance tuning classes are part of the com.ibm.ws.performance.tuning package inside the com.ibm.ws.runtime.jar file, and the performance-tuning-related XML files also sit within this package structure in the JAR file. The ServerRuleDriverMBean.xml file provides some configuration for the component.

The ApplicationMgr component as implemented by the ApplicationMgrImpl class and that controls the Application Mgr Service is next to load. This is often known as the Application Manager Service and is one of the most important infrastructure services within WAS. It essentially controls and monitors the deployed applications and their status and "adjusts," or allows others to use it to adjust, the runtime configuration of these deployed applications where necessary. It particularly interfaces to the class-loading facilities. It has listeners on the application objects; installs, starts, and stops the applications and modules; and supports the Business Level Applications (BLA) facilities. One of the unexpected features of this component is the finalization and garbage collection it drives via the JVM. But this is logical, given that the application state is being controlled. The service supports notification of changes to the deployed applications, listeners for changes, and the ability for registering "adjusters" that allow other services to provide modifications to the deployed application environment to support the runtime facilities. It makes use of the Server Service, the Configuration Service, the Variable Map Service, the Virtual Host Mgr Service, the Resource Mgr Service, the ORB Service, the Composition Unit Mgr Service, and the Library Mgr Service to perform its work. This is one of the fundamental services that supports much of the runtime WAS environment.

The `LibraryMgr` component that provides the Library Mgr Service is the next to start. It is implemented by the `LibraryMgrImpl` class. This supports the management of libraries, library paths, classpaths, and classloader environments for the deployed applications. To perform its work, it makes use of the Server Service, the Config Service, the Variable Map Service, the Composition Unit Mgr Service, and the Resource Mgr Service. This component is important in a traditional JavaEE environment but also underpins some of the BLA facilities through the use of the Composition Unit Mgr Service.

The name of the implementation class for the next component to load may cause confusion. The `ClusterServerRuntime` component's implementation class in the `com.ibm.ws.cluster.runtime` package is named `ApplicationServerRuntimeImpl`. This is *not* the class that implements the application server runtime and is not in the correct package, or even in the `com.ibm.ws.runtime.jar` file, but is in the `com.ibm.ws.wlm.jar` file loaded earlier. It is a particularly heavy user of the Cluster Member Service. It uses it to perform its main purpose, which is to join and leave ("disjoin") clusters and handle events caused by deployment that affect the cluster. It also makes use of the Admin Service and the Server Service to understand its role within the cell and cluster configuration and the Application Mgr Service to monitor the deployment events.

The `StartupService` component, which is implemented by the `StartUpService` class, is the next to load. This component provides a means for applications to be notified when they or their modules are being started or stopped so they can perform any initialization or shutdown of dependent services and components. To perform its work, it needs to monitor the state of the applications and their modules. It provides itself as a `MetaDataListener` reference that is registered via the Meta Data Service to monitor for application configuration changes, a `DeployedObjectListener` reference that it registers with the Application Mgr Service to monitor the state of the application modules, and a `PropertyChangeListener` reference registered with the Server Service to monitor for changes in the state of the server environment. Applications register startup beans to receive the notifications so the component also interfaces to the EJB container to access the beans via their registered interfaces.

The `RRAHPPropertyLoader` component starts next, which is implemented in the `RRAHPPropertyLoaderImpl` class. This supports the JCA adapters that specifically support relational DBMS systems, known as Relational Resource Adapters (RRA), and is part of the data source/data store adapter management within WAS. This provides support for loading properties to support the required configuration, with particular attention paid to Container Managed Persistence (CMP) entity beans. To support its task, the component monitors the EJBs deployed into the EJB container and uses the Application Mgr Service to install listeners to monitor for deployed object changes and to access the EJB JAR modules. WAR and EAR files are also monitored for other data sources used in a similar way. For all module types, the deployment descriptors are examined and resource references to get the appropriate configuration information for the given application environment.

The `I18N` component supports internationalization within WAS and is implemented in the `I18nServerComponentImpl` class. It interfaces to the EJB container and the web container to tie i18n support into them and makes use of the Meta Data Service, the Meta Data Helper Service, and the Asynch Beans Service. A singleton I18nServiceServer instance object is created when the component is created, started, and used by the component for the rest of its work until the component, and thus the singleton, is stopped. The services used by this component are stored as instance variables within it and made available to the I18nService instance.

The DebugServer component is started by the DebugAppServerComponentImpl class and provides support for running WAS in debug mode, with most of the real work delegated to a service component called DebugComponentImpl that sets up the listeners on the appropriate ports and controls some of the configuration. It installs collaborators into the EJB container and web container so it can interact with them, sets up a daemon thread, creates a DebugAgent object, and, if required, creates a DebugAttachAgent object for remote access. Filtering is used to control what is debugged. The DebugAgent object handles command interactions for debugging. Commands are passed using XML, and specific support exists throughout this component and the classes it delegates to for use of the Bean Scripting Framework (BSF).

The EEXQuery component as implemented by the QueryComponentImpl class is next to start, which provides some of the support for query plan management to support the Object Query facilities within WAS. This is a simple component that installs a collaborator into the EJB container and watches for starting and stopping events. On a stop event it merely flushes the query plan from the template cache.

The J2EERequestProfiler component is next to load and is implemented by the J2eeRequestProfilerService class. It is not in the com.ibm.ws.runtime.jar library, but in the com.ibm.ws.prereq.olt.jar file. It adds collaborators to the EJB container and web container, if J2EE Request Profiling is enabled, and the J2EERequestProfilingLogger singleton is loaded. This provides support for J2EE Request Profiling.

The final component to load in the application server container phase of startup is the CompositionUnitMgr as implemented in the CompositionUnitMgrImpl class. This loaded previously for zOS only as a control region as part of the base server runtime startup. WAS 7 introduced support for Business Level Applications (BLAs); groups of JavaEE-level applications and archives that are combined to provided an application service that is meaningful to business users. This component reads the configuration for BLAs and "composes" them within WAS to build up the BLA relationship. The CompositionUnitMgr component loads the CompositionUnit instances, for which there is a separate class and component, and it is these composition units that make up the BLAs. It offers the Composition Unit Mgr Service for use by other components and subsystems.

The application server phase of startup is now complete and the main WAS runtime support that underpins the JavaEE-level containers is in operation. Much of the functionality of the EJB and web containers have been loaded, but there are some components that still need to be loaded. As for the base server container, core components and services load to provide infrastructure to support the initialization of the containers and subsystems along with related qualities of service. Then core application server containers and subsystems are started with related services. Finally, core components to support the container once the other containers and subsystems are loaded are brought to life. The distinctions for groupings of components is not a clear one because the load order is based on subsystems, component, and container dependencies rather than real groupings, although markers do exist in the plugin.xml file to indicate desired groupings. This phased loading is shown in Figure 4-4.

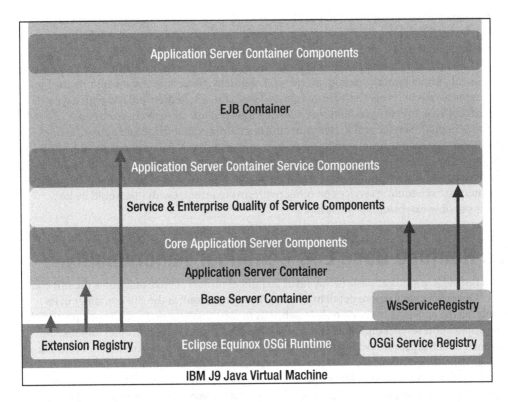

Figure 4-4. *Phased component loading in the Application Server container*

The Scheduler Container

The Scheduler container, which is implemented as a container rather than a component so it can load other components, is loaded as part of the application server runtime phase of initialization before the EJB container is loaded. The component entry at this point declares an implementation class that was covered earlier, in the application server container component loading section, and declares the containerExtensionPoint of com.ibm.wsspi.extension. scheduler-startup to identify components to load. This list of components can be found elsewhere in the plugin.xml file. From the point of initialization in the application server runtime loading phase, the component loading within this container proceeds asynchronously, albeit only for two components from the com.ibm.ws.scheduler.service package. The Scheduler Service supports user-provided calendars and can call back notifications of the task status.

The first component to load in this container is the BeanTaskInfoSvc component that is implemented by the BeanTaskInfoServiceImpl class. It registers with the Scheduler Service and then leaves it up to that service to call back into the methods that form the BeanTaskInfoService and TaskInfoRegistry interfaces. These return IDs and descriptions and *Task Info* implementations and interfaces. Essentially, this component supports the facility for applications to deploy stateless session beans with methods that are scheduled and run with a type ID of 1, with the Task Info unique identifier allowing the service to be used to control it.

The next and last component to load is the `MessageTaskInfoSvc` component, which is implemented by the `MessageTaskInfoServiceImpl` class. It registers with the Scheduler Service and then leaves it up to that service to call back into the methods that form the `MessageTaskInfoService` and `TaskInfoRegistry` interfaces. These return IDs and descriptions and Task Info implementations and interfaces. Essentially, this component supports the facility for applications to receive a JMS message that is sent to a schedule and run with a type ID of 2, with the Task Info unique identifier allowing the service to be used to control it.

The Scheduler Service and its container are not complex, but the implementation does allow IBM to extend this functionality easily in future versions. Most importantly, the implementation allows the execution of JavaEE functionality in a batch mode within the standard environment without additional support. Allowing the Tivoli Workload Scheduler that underpins enterprise scheduling services on other platforms to interact with this would be an obvious possible extension for the future.

The Runtime Base EJB Container Functionality

One of the most important parts of any JavaEE application server environment is the EJB container. This is covered in more detail in Chapter 5 where we look at the EJB container in its entirety, so the coverage here will only look briefly at the initialization from the perspective of the application server container. The entry in the application server runtime initialization in its section of the `plugin.xml` file references the `containerExtensionPoint` entry of `com.ibm.wsspi.extension.ejbcontainer-startup`. This extension point configuration can be found in the `plugin.xml` file after that for the `applicationserver-startup` and `client-startup` sections. A lookup for the `com.ibm.wsspi.extension.server-components` extension point for the `applicationserver.ejbcontainer.EJBContainer` entry referenced by the `type` attribute in the original entry refers to an implementation class named `EJBContainerImpl`.

The component loading entries in this container are limited to one real component entry for the `MDBListener` component that sets up the Message Listener Manager Service and one placeholder with no implementation for `ejbcontainer_services`. The Message Listener Manager Service has no implementation class referenced at this point, but under the entry in the `com.ibm.wsspi.extension.server-component` extension point section of the `plugin.xml` file the `MessageListenerImpl` class can be identified.

The `MDBListener` component that provides the Message Listener Manager Service essentially sets up the listeners for message-driven beans (MDBs), as the name would suggest. It initially makes use of the Thread Pool Mgr Service to access its thread pool and then makes use of the `DurableSubscriptionManager` and `ExtendedMessagingService` classes to set up its underlying infrastructure for subscriptions, logging, and JMS before creating an `MDBListenerManager` object that does the main work of the component. Factory classes are used to create the appropriate underlying classes. It then installs a listener from the `MDBListenerManager` object to the Admin Service to watch for configuration changes that might affect it before finally adding itself as a service for other components to use. The Server Service and Config Service are used to support configuration appropriate for the environment, with the endpoint configuration for the applications read from `serverindex.xml`. A listener is also installed with the Application Mgr Service to watch for deployed object state changes, such as when the application server or modules start or stop so it can perform any tidying up. The events then drive the behavior of this service so appropriate changes can be made when the environment or application state changes as triggers through calls back into the methods of the listener interfaces. The classes that perform most of the work for MDB support are part of the `com.ibm.ejs.jms` packages within the `com.ibm.ws.runtime.jar` file,

With the EJB container, most of the core functionality for the container comes from just a few classes. The underlying container behavior is controlled by the infrastructure code provided by the `EJSContainer` class and the `com.ibm.ejs` packages for JMS, persistence, resource adapter management, and security. The `EJSContainer` class, with an implementation that can be found in the `com.ibm.ws.runtime.jar` file, can be thought of as providing the underlying infrastructure to support the EJB container. EJS stands for Enterprise JavaBeans Server or Enterprise Java Services depending on which older documentation is used, but regardless, it provides the infrastructure for handling EJBs in WAS. The `EJBContainerImpl` class provides the initialization, the tie into the `EJSContainer` class support, and the high-level methods and listener support expected of the EJB container by the specification. The ORB Service provides much of the communications and interface support. Chapter 5 looks more at the EJB container implementation and functionality.

Web Container Initialization

By this point, you have probably noticed what looks like a glaring omission, although it has been referred to briefly. Where does the web container start?

The contents of this chapter so far may be a little misleading. Remember that the runtime environment is using an Eclipse/OSGi environment at its base with the service and extension registries. I listed only the entries in the `com.ibm.ws.runtime.jar` `plugin.xml` file, but the containers don't load from that directly; instead they use the Eclipse extension registry.

In the previous chapter, we looked at the Eclipse runtime and noted that it looks in the `plugins` directory and loads the `plugin.xml` file from every component when it initializes, but loads the components themselves when they are accessed. This `plugin.xml` file is loaded into the Eclipse runtime itself and used to underpin the registries, and this is repeated for all components. So when the WAS runtime container implementation enumerates the entries for the `containerExtensionPoint` attributes for the different phases of container loading to load individual components, it doesn't just see the entries in the `plugin.xml` file from its own plugin (`com.ibm.ws.runtime.jar`) but the entries for the same extension point in other plugins as well. This helps WAS to be extensible, because expanding the WAS environment is as simple as dropping a new plugin into the `/plugins` directory with the appropriate extension declaration, and the component runtime will load it.

For the web container, the implementation can be found in the `com.ibm.ws.webcontainer.jar` file, and in this there is a `plugin.xml` file with a similar structure to that of the base runtime, but it has a limited number of entries. This declares an entry for the `com.ibm.ws.wsspi.extension.applicationserver-startup` phase with a value of 8000 that starts the `WebContainer` component just after the EJB container and that offers the Web Container Service. It refers to a later entry under the extension point `com.ibm.wsspi.extension.server-components` for a component `WebContainerImpl` and a new `containerExtensionPoint` of `com.ibm.wsspi.extension.webcontainer-startup` that lists another small set of three components for JavaEE servlet session management, Java Server Faces (JSF) handling, and JSP handling.

Similarly, the web container is also loaded as a control region on the zOS platform via the `com.ibm.wsspi.extension.server-startup` extension point to form part of the base server container runtime.

The `WebContainerImpl` implementation class is a complex class. At startup it registers itself as a provider for the Web Container Service and adds listeners to the Application Server Service to listen for state changes, the Meta Data Factory Manager Service to look for changes in the application environments, and the Application Mgr Service to look for any changes to the deployed applications and their modules, and then loads extension points to support its running. It supports collaborators being added to it and adds them to a list. The changes and the operation of the web container are handled by the `WSWebContainer` class object that is loaded by this component and many of the methods invoked by the listeners delegate to it.

We will look at the details of the web container and how it works in Chapter 6. This chapter only considers the initialization from the perspective of the application server container.

How Is a Component and Service Created for WAS?

We have looked at how the components and services work and collaborate within the WAS runtime environment to provide the base application server facilities and the containers, but we haven't looked at how these are implemented or how we might provide our own components and services to run inside WAS.

To build our own components and services we first need to make the `com.ibm.ws.runtime.jar` file available inside the Eclipse IDE runtime to provide the `WsComponentImpl` class and the tracing facilities that the components subclass. If we wanted to create a container we would subclass the `WsContainerImpl` class. Similarly, we need to make the `com.ibm.ws.bootstrap.jar` file that is part of the startup for WAS available since this includes the `WsServiceRegistry` class that we use to register our service. For convenience, although this isn't recommended, we can copy these JAR files to our Eclipse IDE `plugins` directory. We then create a `Plug-in Project` for Eclipse 3.2 and change the `Project Properties` to include the two IBM WAS JAR files in the build path. Then we need to update our `MANIFEST.MF` file to include these IBM files as dependencies.

For our services we need to have an interface so create an interface that declares a method. This method on the interface is our service that can be seen by other WAS components. Our `MyComponentInterface` public interface with its single `sayHello` method is shown in Listing 4-2.

Listing 4-2. *MyComponentInterface Interface Definition*

```
package mywas7component;

public interface MyComponentInterface {

    public abstract void sayHello();
}
```

Next, we need to create our component class that implements this interface and extends the `WsComponentImpl` class, and if we use the Eclipse wizards to do it and have the IBM libraries set up in the classpath for the Eclipse Plug-in Development Environment (PDE) environment we will get the necessary methods generated automatically. Most of these methods, as for many of the simple WAS components, aren't used, but the initialize and start methods are used by most components. The initialize method is called when the component is created and it is usually used to set up dependencies and to register its service with the WAS service registry provided by the WsServiceRegistry class. Most of the methods use the RAS TraceComponent facilities to log their entry and exit points so their behavior can be seen when WAS tracing is enabled. We should end up with an implementation component like the following in Listing 4-3, although in practice the use of System.out.println is definitely a bad thing:

Listing 4-3. *MyComponent implementation class, a WsComponentImpl subclass*

```
package mywas7component;

import com.ibm.ejs.ras.Tr;
import com.ibm.ejs.ras.TraceComponent;
import com.ibm.ws.exception.ComponentDisabledException;
import com.ibm.ws.exception.ConfigurationError;
import com.ibm.ws.exception.ConfigurationWarning;
import com.ibm.ws.exception.RuntimeError;
import com.ibm.ws.exception.RuntimeWarning;
import com.ibm.wsspi.runtime.component.WsComponentImpl;
import com.ibm.wsspi.runtime.service.WsServiceRegistry;

@SuppressWarnings("deprecation")
public class MyComponent extends WsComponentImpl
implements MyComponentInterface {
    private static final String MyComponent =
        "mywas7component/MyComponent";
    private static final String MyComponentInterface =
        "mywas7component/MyComponentInterface";
    private static TraceComponent tc = Tr.register(MyComponent);

    // Our service interface method declared in the
    // MyComponentInterface Service Interface File
    public void sayHello() {
        System.out.println("Hello World!");
    }

    // All methods below are from the WsComponentImpl class.
    // Typically, all WAS components and services use the
    // TraceComponent facilities to declare their entry and
    // exit points for use when tracing is enabled inside WAS.
    public void destroy() {
        if(tc.isEntryEnabled()) {
            Tr.entry(tc, "destroy");
        }
```

```java
            System.out.println("Destroying MyComponent");

        if(tc.isEntryEnabled()) {
            Tr.exit(tc, "destroy");
        }
    }

    public String getName() {
        // TODO Auto-generated method stub
        return null;
    }

    public String getState() {
        // TODO Auto-generated method stub
        return null;
    }

    // Components are initialized before use
    public void initialize(Object arg0)
        throws ComponentDisabledException,
        ConfigurationWarning, ConfigurationError {
        if(tc.isEntryEnabled()) {
            Tr.entry(tc, "initialize");
        }

        System.out.println("Initialising MyComponent and " +
            "adding service");

      // To make our Service interface available to other
        // callers we use the addService method of the WAS
        // Service Registry to declare this object as
        // as providing the given interface.
        try {
            WsServiceRegistry.addService(this,
                Class.forName(MyComponentInterface));
        } catch (ClassNotFoundException e) {
            e.printStackTrace();
        } catch (Exception e) {
            e.printStackTrace();
        }

        if(tc.isEntryEnabled()) {
            Tr.exit(tc, "initialize");
        }
    }
```

```
    public void start() throws RuntimeError, RuntimeWarning {
        if(tc.isEntryEnabled()) {
            Tr.entry(tc, "start");
        }

        System.out.println("Starting MyComponent");

        if(tc.isEntryEnabled()) {
            Tr.exit(tc, "start");
        }
    }

    public void stop() {
        if(tc.isEntryEnabled()) {
            Tr.entry(tc, "stop");
        }

        System.out.println("Stopping MyComponent");

        if(tc.isEntryEnabled()) {
            Tr.exit(tc, "stop");
        }
    }
}
```

This isn't all we have to do though. For the runtime to load the component into the appropriate container we need to create a plugin.xml file that includes the extension point and startup value. We haven't declared our service here but will cover that in the next two chapters. In reality, this needs an XSD to be validated to generate our plugin properly using the official Eclipse generation, but the definition would be as follows as in Listing 4-4.

Listing 4-4. *Extension point entries in plugin.xml for MyComponent*

```
<?xml version="1.0" encoding="UTF-8"?>
<?eclipse version="3.2"?>
<plugin id="MyWAS7Component" name="WS_MYCOMPONENT"
    provider-name="WebSphere Application Server 7 Pro Internals"
    version="1.0.0">
    <extension
        point="com.ibm.wsspi.extension.applicationserver-startup">
        <components>
            <component startup="8197" component-id="WS_MYCOMPONENT"
                class="mywas7component.MyComponent"
                processType="Servant" startup-mode="dependency" >
            </component>
        </components>
    </extension>
</plugin>
```

Just to finish off we need the `MANIFEST.MF` file to make sure that we have a singleton that is loaded when the first class is accessed. This is shown in Listing 4-5.

Listing 4-5. *MANIFEST.MF for the MyComponent Plugin / Bundle*

```
Manifest-Version: 1.0
Bundle-ManifestVersion: 2
Bundle-Name: MyWAS7Component Plug-in
Bundle-SymbolicName: MyWAS7Component;singleton:=true
Bundle-Version: 1.0.0
Bundle-Activator: mywas7component.Activator
Bundle-Vendor: WebSphere Application Server 7 Pro Internals
Bundle-Localization: plugin
Require-Bundle: com.ibm.ws.runtime, com.ibm.ws.bootstrap,
 org.eclipse.core.runtime
Eclipse-LazyStart: true
```

We have created our own component that loads into the WAS runtime and offers services via the WAS service registry. Like other components it could install collaborators with the web container and EJB container or use the other services to install listeners that call back into its methods. The component needs merely to be copied into the plugins directory of the WAS runtime to become part of WAS.

Creation of a new container is a little more complex, but not greatly so. For this the `WsContainer` class or `ContainerImpl` class are sub-classed, which are essentially special types of components that support the same methods, and in the initialization the appropriate section of the `plugin.xml` file is read to load all the components for that extension point in a `loadComponents` method. Each of the components loaded must be a subclass of the `WsComponentImpl` class, or the deprecated `ComponentImpl` class.

Now we know how to create our own components, services, and containers to extend the WAS runtime.

Transport Channels and Chains

One of the most important parts of the base server runtime is the Channel Framework Service that supports the transport chains and channels. Essentially, a transport chain can be thought of as the network stack required to support a particular connection.

At the end of the `plugin.xml` file the extension point `com.ibm.wsspi.extension.channel-framework-channel-type` can be found that declares the available types of channels, the classes that configure them, and the classes that support them at runtime.

A channel is essentially a pool of similarly configured sockets and listeners, with related code and threads, to support a particular protocol implementation, i.e. TCP, HTTP, SSL, etc. The chains are built by combing these as layers such that an HTTPS connection needs an SSL channel that builds on an HTTP channel that itself builds on a TCP channel. Specific channels are then built up to support IIOP to support the EJB container and the ORB, MQFAP and JFAP to support JMS for SIB, and for internal services such as DRS. Channels, and the chains that build upon them, can be inbound or outbound, with the separation necessary as a result of asynchronous communications and to better scale with improved throughput. So, a request comes into the chain and passes through each channel type in the chain until it arrives at an input queue for a given container or component. Similarly, the container or component puts the response on an outbound queue where it passes through the outbound chain for returning to the caller.

Configuration of the transport chains for a particular environment is handled via mappings for each particular usage (e.g., SIB_SSL_JFAP_SSL_OUT, etc) in the server.xml file that are based on the generic mapping types in the plugin.xml file. The services section sets up the thread and connection management mappings and the transportChannels entries declare the channels used in combination by the chains entries to form the chains. An example of how the Channel Framework Service provides the transport chains from the channels in support of the Service Integration Bus is shown in Figure 4-5.

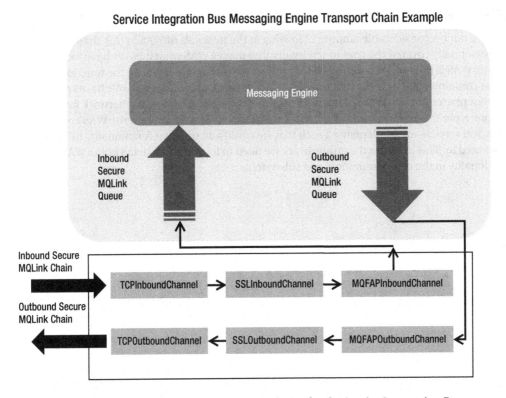

Figure 4-5. *Channel Framework Service transport chains for the Service Integration Bus*

The Base Runtime in Operation

The majority of this chapter has looked at component initialization for individual components and subsystems within the com.ibm.ws.runtime.jar sphere of control that provides the base WAS runtime, yet little has been said about how it functions in operation. This is by design. Most of components provide a service and install listeners that respond to events or state changes. Other components inside WAS, either inside the com.ibm.ws.runtime.jar plugin or other plugins, make use of the services or components or classes that they have created, or they are brought into play through the operation of one of the events that trigger a method call on one of the listeners installed by the components installed here. What we have loaded here as the core runtime provides the functions that are WAS, but not all of the higher level policy that makes use of them that is provided elsewhere in a typical WAS installation.

Later on in the plugin.xml file there are a number of different listings of components for different categories of installation. These show the components that are required to support a typical role within this core runtime. Most are needed for all cases. The existence of this section should show the future for WAS and application services in general, i.e. custom installations to suit particular roles. The componentization of WAS and the use of the OSGi and WAS internal component registries are what has made this possible.

Summary

We have done a considerable amount of looking at the internals of WAS in this chapter, and have essentially covered the core functionality that makes WAS what it is. We have looked at the way WAS is formed of containers filled with components that make up the functionality of that container, and how the functionality is declared as a set of services. We have seen the different phases of the startup of the WAS runtime Java code, and how the network facilities that underpin these phases are structured. Finally, we have looked at how the WAS components and services are implemented such that we could add our own functionality to WAS if we wanted to. This provides the groundwork we need to look in more detail at the WAS JavaEE functionality in the other containers and subsystems.

CHAPTER 5

■■■

The EJB Container

The Java EE specification introduces the concept of the Enterprise JavaBeans (EJB) container for the express purposes of running business logic in the form of session beans, data access logic in the form of entity beans, and message handling logic in the form of message-driven beans. The typical behavior envisioned by the Java EE specification is that a developer writes an Enterprise JavaBean, a simple component, and the EJB container adds the necessary infrastructure for communications, transactions, and data access to turn that business logic into something that executes. In addition, the EJB container provides the lifecycle management for the component to ensure that its creation, usage, and destruction are both efficient and in accord with the specification. To do this, the underlying infrastructure is expected to build on the functionality of a CORBA ORB for the security and interoperability, but this still leaves a large gap in the required infrastructure that is left for an application server vendor to develop. For WebSphere Application Server, the additional infrastructure built on the ORB to support the EJB specification is provided by the Enterprise Java Services (EJS) container layer that underpins the EJB container itself.

Chapter 4 provided a brief, high-level overview of the services that the EJB container uses and the underlying EJS container that it works with to build its services. This chapter drills down into the implementation to give you an understanding of the detailed relationships between the components and subsystems, although you will also see some of the support for external subsystems to interact with and influence the behavior of the EJB container runtime.

When the EJB container is started, it has, at its highest level, the EJBContainerImpl class as its controller, which is a subclass of the generic ContainerImpl class. EJBContainerImpl implements the EJBContainer service interface, and has listeners for changes to the deployed application modules and other parts of the environment.

As you saw when looking at the WAS runtime in Chapter 4, the deprecated ContainerImpl class and the WsContainerImpl class that is used in other areas both support the interaction between the underlying Eclipse OSGi-based WAS runtime and methods to allow the base runtime to tell the component to initialize itself (initialize), to start itself running once it is initialized (start), to inform it that it is about to be stopped or destroyed so it can tidy up (stop), and to cause the destruction itself to be performed (destroy). These are component and container lifecycle methods.

You will look now at how a generic container functions, such as that underlying the EJB container, before you look at the specifics of the EJBContainerImpl class itself.

Creating the EJB Container

It takes nothing more than a little Java reflection to see the inheritance dependencies, methods, and interfaces that define the EJB container. So, a good place to start is at the beginning, the EJB container class hierarchy, and work upward to find what is generic. Then you can use Eclipse itself and the WAS plugins directory to generate your own EJB container so that you can see what it looks like to the outside world.

As you can see in Figure 5-1, the EJBContainerImpl basic class diagram, the implementation class for creating and running the EJB container is EJBContainerImpl, which is a subclass of the deprecated ContainerImpl class, which itself is a subclass of the ComponentImpl class introduced in Chapter 4. The deprecated ComponentImpl class itself extends the WsComponentImpl class and implements a number of interfaces, most notably the Component interface that extends the WsComponent interface. You previously generated code from this, but if you look at the WsComponent interface, you can see some key methods that explain how the components, and therefore the container, are controlled by the WAS runtime environment (see Figure 5-2). The ContainerImpl class is a subclass of the ComponentImpl class, so it can be treated like any other component by the loadComponents calls of the outer container that initializes it. This is how the base server starts, controls, and interacts with the EJB container.

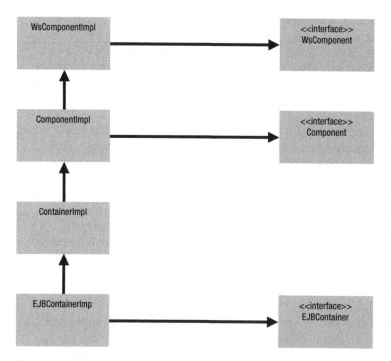

Figure 5-1. *EJBContainerImpl basic class diagram*

In the interface, the methods initialize, start, stop, and destroy are key for control, and the getName and getState methods allow monitoring from elsewhere that is particularly used on startup and shutdown. The strings exposed by the interface are used by the getState call to inform callers of the running status of the component.

Figure 5-2. *The WsComponent class methods and state management constants*

The `initialize` method is called first to ensure that the necessary underlying components are created and executed before starting the component. The `start` method actually runs the component, `stop` gets the executing parts of the component to shut down, and `destroy` does the tidying up. The states and their transitions are shown in Figure 5-3. So, the key methods for understanding the execution of a component, and a container, are the `initialize` and `start` methods and any additional interfaces that the component implements. Most components expose a number of interfaces, but particular emphasis is placed on the listeners and the events that allow communication with the runtime.

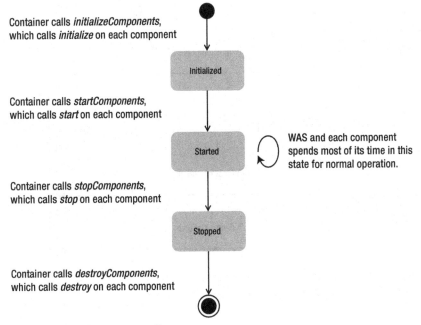

Figure 5-3. *Component state diagram*

As discussed in Chapter 4, for containers, the Eclipse Extension Registry is used to enumerate all of the components that expose the extension point associated with the container and that are declared in all of the plugin.xml files. This is handled by methods that the ContainerImpl class exposes; the loadComponents method handles the initial creation and loading of components in the configured collection for the declared container extension point, and then one of the initializeComponents methods is used to handle initialization of each individual component in turn by calling one of the initializeComponent methods in the ContainerImpl class for the given target component. Ultimately, the initialize method of each component gets called, but at this point the component is loaded but not running.

With WAS and its runtime, it all starts with the bootServerContainer call that initializes first the server container and then the application server container, which then starts the other containers you expect such as the web container and the EJB container (as described in some detail in Chapter 4). A simplified sequence diagram showing how the components fit within the container startup is shown in Figure 5-4. When the container gets to a properly executing state via the start method of the WsComponent-derived start method call, the container calls the startComponents method that uses helper classes to start each component. Similarly, when the stop method is called on shutdown, the stopComponents method is called, and on a destroy call into the container, the destroyComponents method is called, which results in a destroy call to each component.

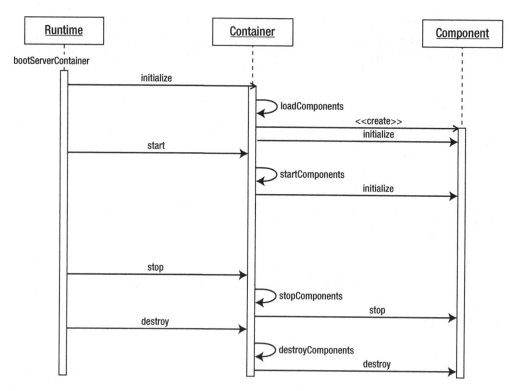

Figure 5-4. *WebSphere Application Server container creation sequence diagram*

The EJB Container Implementation Class

The EJBContainerImpl class is a complex class with many dependencies, as shown in Figure 5-5. Some of the dependencies are structural and inheritance related, and some are dynamic and collaborative in nature.

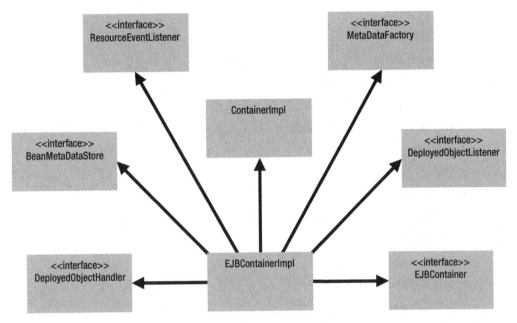

Figure 5-5. *EJBContainerImpl inheritance—classes and interfaces*

As you read previously, the generic container class handles such things as loading components and starting them, with the interfaces that are declared providing the specific behavior. Using reflection, you can see the interfaces that the EJBContainerImpl class uses. Next look at each interface and the methods it exposes, paying particular attention to how things appear in terms of the Java EE EJB specification and the underlying implementation. The interfaces are as follows:

- EJBContainer: This is the most important interface that the EJBContainerImpl class exposes. It supports both integration with the rest of the environment and the core Java EE EJB functionality. The methods that are used to handle the interfaces to the rest of the environment are

  - addCollaborator: There are a number of these to provide mechanisms for other components to add their own "hooks" into the EJB container.

  - createWebServiceEndpointManager: This is used to tie to the EJB container implementation the web services functionality that allows EJBs to expose services with mechanisms as simple as an annotation.

  - getPersistenceManagers: This simply returns an enumeration of the engines that support persistence, e.g., JPA providers, etc.

The methods that directly or indirectly underlie the Java EE EJB functionality include

- `enlistInvocationCallback`
- `getAccessIntent`
- `getBasicEJBInfo`
- `getCMRHelper`
- `releaseCMRHelper`
- `getClassLoader`
- `getCurrentInvocatonToken`
- `getEJBDynamicQueryHelper`
- `releaseEJBDynamicQueryHelper`
- `getEJBHome`
- `getEJBLocalHome`
- `getIsolationLevel`
- `getJ2EEName`
- `getServantManager`
- `getAccessIntent`
- `setEJBAccessIntent`
- `setRollbackOnly`

The `EJBContainerImpl` class implements each of these key methods, using underlying services such as the ORB Service and the EJS container facilities.

There are other methods, such as `flush` and `setClusterNameService`, but these are not so key to the functionality of the container.

- `DeployedObjectHandler`: This class implements the `start` and `stop` methods that pass a `DeployedObjectEvent` object. These events notify the container that a new module has been deployed so that the container has an opportunity to examine the module to check for any EJBs it needs to handle. The metadata-related service facilities are used to perform this examination.

- `DeployedObjectListener`: This listener has the `stateChanged` method that receives a `DeployedObjectEvent` object, as above, that tells the EJB container that a deployed EJB module or some related component has been started or stopped.

- `BeanMetaDataStore`: This interface has simple `get`, `put`, and `remove` methods that handle the relationships between JNDI names and beans and are used to store the relationships in the internal EJB container collection variables.

- `MetaDataFactory`: This interface has the `createMetaData` and `destroyMetaData` methods that take a `MetaDataFactoryMgr` object and `DeployedObjectEvent` object. These methods are used to allow the EJB container to scan newly deployed components for annotations and other deployment artifacts to obtain the metadata that allows the components to be managed and accessed.

- ResourceEventListener: This listener includes the resourceFactoryEvent and resourceProviderEvent methods. The resourceProviderEvent method does nothing, but the resourceFactoryEvent method is used to allow the EJB container to handle changes in the resources used in the environment and update the underlying Variable Map Service data for it.

Generating Your Own EJB Container

By generating an outline EJB container in Eclipse and filling in just a small part of the interface code to the base runtime, you can get an understanding of how the EJB container is controlled and interacts with its application server container environment.

As in Chapter 3, create a project and make sure that all the WAS plug-ins are on the classpath and all are listed as project dependencies. Then simply create a new class that declares the appropriate interfaces outlined previously and is a subclass of ContainerImpl, and remember to generate all the abstract methods. You will add to the generated code some of the high-level calls that you know the container must implement. You may need to use the Eclipse editor's "add unimplemented methods" operation to add some additional methods if they are not automatically generated. Some dependencies may not be met using this mechanism, so expect to see some errors.

When the code is generated, you can see all the package dependencies within the WAS runtime itself. This demonstrates some of the complexity of the EJB container infrastructure.

In your container, you will have initialize, start, stop, and destroy methods to implement, because a container is a component in its own right, but one that loads other components, so you will need code within the lifecycle calls to the container methods that then makes the necessary lifecycle calls to the components so that they can handle their own state and any components they may need to load.

In this example, you will leave much of the code unimplemented for the interface into the wider subsystems, but pay particular attention to the code for handling collaborators that allows other subsystems to interact with and control this one. In addition to the methods for handling the EJB lifecycle in accord with the Java EE specification, there are listener methods that allow dynamic interaction and behavior based on changes in WAS and its environment.

Now take a look at the code itself.

First consider the large number of packages imported. This shows the complexity of the implementation and the interfaces, and some of the important underlying classes for the implementation.

```
package myEJBContainerPackage;

import java.lang.reflect.Method;
import java.rmi.RemoteException;
import javax.ejb.EJBException;
import javax.ejb.EJBHome;
import javax.ejb.EJBLocalHome;
import javax.ejb.EntityContext;
import javax.xml.ws.Provider;
import com.ibm.ejs.cm.portability.PortabilityLayerExt;
import com.ibm.ejs.container.EJBConfigurationException;
```

```
import com.ibm.websphere.appprofile.accessintent.AccessIntent;
import com.ibm.websphere.cpmi.PersistenceManager;
import com.ibm.websphere.csi.AfterActivationCollaborator;
import com.ibm.websphere.csi.BeanMetaDataStore;
import com.ibm.websphere.csi.BeforeActivationAfterCompletionCollaborator;
import com.ibm.websphere.csi.BeforeActivationCollaborator;
import com.ibm.websphere.csi.CSIException;
import com.ibm.websphere.csi.CSITransactionRolledbackException;
import com.ibm.websphere.csi.EJBCallbackCollaborator;
import com.ibm.websphere.csi.EJBComponentInitializationCollaborator;
import com.ibm.websphere.csi.EJBContainerException;
import com.ibm.websphere.csi.EJBDynamicQueryHelper;
import com.ibm.websphere.csi.EJBModuleInitializationCollaborator;
import com.ibm.websphere.csi.EJBServantManager;
import com.ibm.websphere.csi.J2EEName;
import com.ibm.websphere.csi.J2EENameFactory;
import com.ibm.websphere.csi.PMTxInfo;
import com.ibm.websphere.csi.RemoveCollaborator;
import com.ibm.ws.appprofile.accessintent.EJBAccessIntent;
import com.ibm.ws.cpmi.association.CMRHelper;
import com.ibm.ws.csi.EJBClusterNameService;
import com.ibm.ws.ejbcontainer.BasicEJBInfo;
import com.ibm.ws.exception.RuntimeError;
import com.ibm.ws.exception.RuntimeWarning;
import com.ibm.ws.runtime.component.ContainerImpl;
import com.ibm.ws.runtime.deploy.DeployedObject;
import com.ibm.ws.runtime.deploy.DeployedObjectEvent;
import com.ibm.ws.runtime.deploy.DeployedObjectHandler;
import com.ibm.ws.runtime.deploy.DeployedObjectListener;
import com.ibm.ws.runtime.metadata.MetaData;
import com.ibm.ws.runtime.metadata.MetaDataFactory;
import com.ibm.ws.runtime.resource.ResourceEvent;
import com.ibm.ws.runtime.resource.ResourceEventListener;
import com.ibm.ws.runtime.service.EJBContainer;
import com.ibm.ws.runtime.service.MetaDataFactoryMgr;
import com.ibm.ws.util.InvocationCallback;
import com.ibm.ws.util.InvocationToken;
import com.ibm.wsspi.ejbcontainer.WSEJBEndpointManager;
import com.ibm.wsspi.ejbcontainer.WSEJBHandlerResolver;
```

The class definition, as shown next, for your EJB container itself shows the class hierarchy by which the WAS EJB container is implemented. The EJB container extends the ContainerImpl class that itself is a special type of component. It also implements the functionality required by an EJB container through the EJBContainer interface and a number of other interfaces that support interaction through other subsystems.

```
@SuppressWarnings("deprecation")
public class MyEJBContainer extends ContainerImpl implements
  DeployedObjectHandler, DeployedObjectListener, BeanMetaDataStore,
  MetaDataFactory, ResourceEventListener, EJBContainer {
```

The initialize, start, stop, and destroy methods, shown in the next listing, are responsible for handling the component, and therefore the container, life cycle. For a container implementation of initialize, the state is set up, the components to be loaded are read from the XML configuration, and a method is used to call initialize on each component loaded. For start, a method is used to call the start method of each component, and for stop and destroy there are methods that similarly pass the lifecycle method on to each component loaded.

```
// Component Initialization called by core runtime
public void initialize(Object arg0) throws
  ComponentDisabledException,
  ConfigurationWarning, ConfigurationError {
    setState("INITIALIZING");
    loadComponents("META-INF/ws-ejbcontainer-startup.xml");
    initializeComponents();
    setState("INITIALIZED");
}

// Startup of component after initialization
public void start() throws RuntimeError, RuntimeWarning {
    setState("STARTING");
    startComponents();
    setState("STARTED");
}

// Stopping of running component before destruction
public void stop() {
    setState("STOPPING");
    stopComponents();
    setState("STOPPED");
}

// Destruction of stopped component
public void destroy() {
    setState("DESTROYING");
    destroyComponents();
    setState("DESTROYED");
}
```

The collaborator methods allow external subsystems to listen for events and then affect the handling of the event within the EJB container itself:

```
// First of a number of collaborator methods to allow external
// components and subsystems to interact with the EJB container.
// Other container subsystems work the same way.
public void addCollaborator(AfterActivationCollaborator arg0) {
}

public void
  addCollaborator(BeforeActivationAfterCompletionCollaborator arg0)
{
}

public void addCollaborator(BeforeActivationCollaborator arg0) {
}

public void addCollaborator(EJBCallbackCollaborator arg0) {
}

public void addCollaborator(RemoveCollaborator arg0) {
}

public void
  addCollaborator(EJBComponentInitializationCollaborator arg0) {
}

public void
  addCollaborator(EJBModuleInitializationCollaborator arg0) {
}
```

The methods used by the listeners allow the EJB container to respond to changes in its environment. This includes being notified of deployed applications being stopped and started, which triggers the EJB container to examine the deployed components and modules for EJB deployment descriptors and annotations that require the EJB container to perform some configuration and be prepared to take on some work.

```
public void stateChanged(DeployedObjectEvent arg0) throws
  RuntimeError, RuntimeWarning {
}

public MetaData createMetaData(MetaDataFactoryMgr arg0,
                               DeployedObject arg1)
  throws RuntimeError, RuntimeWarning {
    return null;
}
```

```
public void destroyMetaData(MetaDataFactoryMgr arg0,
                            DeployedObject arg1)
  throws RuntimeError, RuntimeWarning {
}

public void resourceFactoryEvent(ResourceEvent arg0)
  throws RuntimeError, RuntimeWarning {
}

public void resourceProviderEvent(ResourceEvent arg0)
  throws RuntimeError, RuntimeWarning {
}
```

The remaining methods directly relate to the functionality required for handling EJBs:

```
public Object get(J2EEName arg0) throws CSIException {
    return null;
}

public void put(J2EEName arg0, Object arg1) throws CSIException {
}

public void remove(J2EEName arg0) {
}

public WSEJBEndpointManager
  createWebServiceEndpointManager(J2EEName arg0, Method[] arg1)
    throws EJBException, EJBConfigurationException {
    return null;
}

public WSEJBEndpointManager
  createWebServiceEndpointManager(J2EEName arg0,
                                  Class<Provider<?>> arg1)
    throws EJBException, EJBConfigurationException {
    return null;
}

public void enlistInvocationCallback(InvocationCallback arg0,
                                     Object arg1)
  throws IllegalStateException {
}

public void flush() throws RemoteException {
}

public AccessIntent getAccessIntent(EntityContext arg0) {
    return null;
}
```

```java
public BasicEJBInfo getBasicEJBInfo(Object arg0) {
  return null;
}

public CMRHelper getCMRHelper() {
    return null;
}

public ClassLoader getClassLoader(J2EEName arg0) {
    return null;
}

public InvocationToken getCurrentInvocationToken() {
    return null;
}

public PMTxInfo getCurrentPMTxInfo()
  throws CSITransactionRolledbackException {
    return null;
}

public EJBDynamicQueryHelper getEJBDynamicQueryHelper() {
    return null;
}

// Standard EJB container interaction methods
public EJBHome getEJBHome(J2EEName arg0)
  throws EJBContainerException {
    return null;
}

public EJBLocalHome getEJBLocalHome(J2EEName arg0)
  throws EJBContainerException {
    return null;
}

public int getIsolationLevel(int arg0) {
  return 0;
}

public int getIsolationLevel(Object arg0,
                             PortabilityLayerExt arg1) {
    return 0;
}
```

```
public J2EEName getJ2EEName(Object arg0)
  throws EJBContainerException {
    return null;
}

public J2EENameFactory getJ2EENameFactory() {
    return null;
}

public PersistenceManager[] getPersistenceManagers() {
    return null;
}

public EJBServantManager getServantManager() {
    return null;
}

public void releaseCMRHelper(CMRHelper arg0) {
}

public void releaseEJBDynamicQueryHelper(
    EJBDynamicQueryHelper arg0) {
}

public void setClusterNameService(EJBClusterNameService arg0)
  throws EJBContainerException {
}

public void setEJBAccessIntent(EJBAccessIntent arg0) {
}

public void setRollBackOnly() {
}

public void
  setWebServiceHandlerResolver(WSEJBHandlerResolver arg0) {
}
```

This gives you some idea of the structure of the EJBContainerImpl class. Much of the functionality required for EJBs is provided by the ORB subsystem and the EJS container, the collaborators that provide hooks into the environment, and the event-related methods. The next section explains what some of these methods do in the real implementation.

EJBContainerImpl Methods

Upon initialization, when the initialize method is called, a check is made to see if the platform is zOS using the EJSPlatformHelper class, and the object that manages the metadata for the EJB container is created, EJBMDOrchestrator. The container then sets its state to "initializing" and initializes its collaborator lists that are used later to integrate with other environments to monitor EJB and module statuses. The `EJBComponentImpl` component then registers itself with the outer container registry as supporting the EJB Container Service and reads the default data source JNDI name for later use. Next, the behavior that makes the EJB container a standard WAS container is executed as the components specified by the Extension Registry for the EJB container are loaded using the `loadComponents` call using the entry in the `META-INF/ws-ejbcontainer-startup.xml` file as a parameter to control the loading. Ultimately, the `com.ibm.wsspi.extension.ejbcontainer-startup` extension point is used.

As for other containers, the `initializeComponents` call is then executed to initialize the components that have just been loaded. The initialization accesses the Resource Manager Service to install listeners for factory resources to watch for `CMPConnectorFactory` or `DataSource` resource changes. Finally, the EJS container class `ContainerProperties` `InitializeEJBsAtStartup` method is called to configure the properties for the EJB container and save or apply them to the EJB container configuration. When system properties for the EJB container are set, it is the `com.ibm.ejs.container.ContainerProperties` class that manages them.

The next step is that the now-initialized EJB container starts when the controlling container calls the `start` method exposed by the underlying `WsComponent` interface. This is a complex process:

1. Upon entry into the `start` method, the EJB container accesses the Meta Data Factory Manager Service and registers itself as a Meta Data Factory with it. This makes sense, because the EJB container needs to monitor changes in the application environment and the deployment of modules. Callbacks will come into the `createMetaData` and `destroyMetaData` methods, as outlined earlier.

2. The code uses the ORB Service to save a reference to the ORB itself, before creating the underlying EJS container and saving a reference to this underlying engine for later use after registering an EJB Access Intent Service and Cluster Name Service with it.

3. The world of CORBA now comes to light in this `start` method as a root Object Adapter from the ORB is created and tied to the EJS container. Object Adapters mediate between requests to the ORB and the actual underlying implementation servant objects that the client doesn't have direct access to that perform the request.

4. The appropriate Container Extension Factory is created, depending on whether the Activity Session Service is in use, whether Programming Model Extensions are required, and whether a Unit of Work Controller is required.

5. A security collaborator object is created and loaded into the container to handle security for requests.

6. The passivation directory is created and used to initialize the file bean store depending on the cluster configuration obtained from the Server Service, with different behavior for the zOS platform from other platforms.

7. The Pool Manager that handles object pooling and the EJB Cache are created and the cleanup and caching parameters are set for these, including complex eviction and least recently used (LRU) strategy components to handle what is in the cache and what gets kicked out.

8. Collaborators are created and added to the collaborator lists to monitor activation, component metadata, EJB callbacks, removal, and module and component initialization. These collaborators are the mechanism that the EJB container uses to tie into

the rest of the environment and monitor application and environment behavior that affects it (e.g., the starting of an EJB module), and conversely the collaborators are provided by outside components and subsystems to allow them to "hook" into the EJB container. The term *collaborator* is appropriate if you consider the example of a session bean that declares its methods as web services methods using annotations. In this case, the EJB container and Web Services engine must collaborate when the EJB module is loaded and the annotation is read to generate the web service inside the web services engine.

9. Some of the underlying components to support the container are created:

   a. The Performance Monitoring Infrastructure factory object that creates the beans supporting PMI is created.

   b. The MDB Listener Manager is created to provide the support for MDBs to be created and managed using the appropriate interface to a provider with an appropriate listener. This makes use of the Message Listener Manager Service.

10. One of the most important facilities of EJB 3 is created, with the Persistence Manager implementation class loaded and passed a reference to the EJB container to support collaboration.

11. The EJB Scheduler configuration is loaded—that is, the `jdbc/DefaultEJBTimerDataSource` and associated settings.

12. The configuration of the EJB passivation policy for the environment is loaded using the `ContainerProperties` class, with specific configuration for the zOS platform, with all of this tied into the Data Replication Services (DRS) settings for the container and environment to ensure that any passivated components are replicated between instances in a cluster for high availability if clustering is enabled. Again, a considerable amount of different configuration is provided for DRS for the zOS platform. The Multibroker Domain Service that supports DRS is used to apply the settings.

13. The ordering of the operations within this method is important. A Container Configuration object is created to relate all of the configuration performed so far, and this is then provided to the `initialize` method of the EJS container object to support its configuration, and the DRS Cache component is then initialized to support the EJS container object with the DRS settings obtained earlier.

14. The root object adapter is used to create an object adapter, with the EJS container providing a wrapper manager to handle the adapter.

15. A management runtime collaborator object is created for the EJB container and an MBean is registered for it.

16. All the operations so far have happened without the components being started that the EJB container loaded earlier. You have now reached the point at which the components need to start, but the EJB container has yet to install the facilities for the callback methods that allow the monitoring of the deployed objects. The Application Manager Service is accessed and used to register the `EJBContainerImpl` object as a deployed object handler and deployed object listener to allow monitoring of newly deployed modules and their starting and stopping.

17. The startComponents method can be run to execute the start methods of each component the EJB container runs.

18. The WebSphere EJB container services are registered with JNDI.

19. To complete the start method functionality, diagnostic modules for the EJB container and the associated metadata are created and registered with the first failure data capture (FFDC) facilities, and environment variables and values are registered and passed to an initial context to create the EJB local namespace.

At this point the EJB container is running and all functionality is being handled through the events and callback methods, but the detailed implementation is largely provided by the underlying EJS container.

We won't examine the stop or destroy methods because they are simple implementations, as outlined in the container sequence diagram presented earlier (see Figure 5-4).

■**Note** The destroy method calls the terminate method on the EJS container object, so it's not as simple as stop.

Now, the deployment event–related methods that support the deployed object handler and deployed object listener have simple, high-level implementations within the EJB container that use a number of complex, low-level public and private methods to respond to the events. Essentially, these methods use the deployed event object to identify what is being deployed, open the modules and examine manifest and metadata information and annotations for the components, and call into the appropriate EJS container facilities to install the appropriate support for the given module. The Java EE components are loaded, named, and bound to JNDI as appropriate, and any binding to message destinations or creation of real EJB objects is performed as appropriate. The hooks into the EJS container are pre-invoke, post-invoke, before-activation, post-activation, etc.

Similarly, most of the EJB container interface methods that are related directly to the handling of EJBs are simply delegated by the EJB container methods down to the EJS container object or result in calls to or the creation of lower-level artifacts or helper classes. Thus, to understand more about the EJB container you need to understand the EJS container.

The EJS Container

The EJB container is the official container that provides the public face of EJB handling, while the Enterprise Java Services (EJS) container provides the private functionality that WAS uses to make it work. When the EJB container starts, it creates the EJS container object and initializes it, and then delegates to it many of the implementation tasks that do the work required by the public EJB container methods. When writing EJB-related code in an IDE such as Rational Software Architect (RSA) or Rational Application Developer (RAD), the EJB deployment code generation step can target WAS specifically and exploit the WAS infrastructure. Similarly, when deploying EJBs to WAS using the normal administration tooling, code generation is required. You must remember that the code that actually runs within the EJB container isn't the code that the developer writes but rather a subclass of it or a wrapper for it that brings in support for the underlying infrastructure to support scaling, transactions, etc. It is for this reason that much of the generated code related to deployment of EJBs from WAS, RSA, or RAD includes methods and classes with the EJS prefix rather than the EJB prefix, and why stack traces and dumps have a predominance of EJS-prefixed methods. It is the EJS container that does the real work of handling Enterprise JavaBeans and its underlying persistence mechanisms.

When the EJB container calls the EJS container `initialize` method from its `start` method, it passes a `ContainerConfig` object that is used by the EJS container to store references to factory, persistence, cache, object adapter, unit of work, MDB Listener Manager, and data store objects that are used to do its work. The `ContainerConfig` object also passes in this object the references to the collaborator collections of each type that are maintained by the EJB container. The EJB container is the public interface to other subsystems and components that need to collaborate with it, but it is the EJS container that handles the details of relationships. There are after activation, before activation, before activation-after completion, EJB callback, component initialization, and remove collaborator collections maintained.

The initialization-, remove-, and activation-related collaborators relate to phases in an EJB life cycle and are used by other WAS components to get notification of and assist in the handling of these phases of the life cycle. The configuration object also contains references to the infrastructure objects created by the EJB container, such as the DRS Cache, PMI bean factory, persistence managers, and the Pool Manager. The configuration object uses the passed-in references to create a Stateful Passivator for session bean passivation, an Activator to handle the contents of this, and an Activator Strategy class to control how these relate. It then registers an underlying class with an internal Unit of Work Controller to handle transactions, and creates a JPA component to handle EJB 3 persistence before completing its initialization. From this point, all operations within the EJS container take place as a result of delegated calls from the EJB container or events triggered by a call into one of the container interfaces.

One of the key ways in which the EJS container operates is through EJS wrapper classes that encapsulate the relationship between the EJB bean component interface, the underlying CORBA servant, and the home, local, and remote interfaces for the servant object. As an example of how this works, consider the request to the EJB container for a local home for a given bean name. This request is immediately delegated to the equivalent call in the EJS container, which then gets an internal home interface wrapper, and from this a local wrapper interface is returned to the EJB container and then on to the caller. Similarly, the web service endpoint manager EJB container access is delegated: a wrapper is created from the underlying bean implementation and is returned.

Lifecycle operations for EJBs, after the configuration of the EJS container is completed, are essentially quite simple. For example, a bean reload results in a `stopBean` and a `startBean` call, a passivate operation results in a call to the `passivate` method on the activator object for the given bean, and a `passivateAll` call is delegated to the activator object `passivateAll` method. There is a little more to it, though, as the `stopBean` call results in a bean being uninstalled, which then results in notification of the associated collaborators. These patterns of operations are typical of the way in which the EJS container functions, so the key remaining mechanisms to understand are the activator, the EJS Wrapper, and ORB classes and services. Transaction management is also implemented in terms of lower-level UserTransactionWrapper and ContainerTX wrapper classes.

The EJSWrapper class has a number of related classes for specific uses. A WrapperManager class acts as a controller at one level, and at the other end of the spectrum are the EJSLocalWrapper and EJSRemoteWrapper classes that serve specific functions at the Java EE specification level. Specific wrapper classes are used for MDBs and to represent User Transactions, and at the CORBA level there are _EJSRemoteWrapper_Stub and _EJSRemoteWrapper_tie classes. When making use of an EJB, all of these classes are important for the EJS container to provide the functionality necessary to support the requirements of the EJB container. At the top level of control is the WrapperManager class that was used to create the root Object Adapter for the EJB container, and then, from the perspective of the EJB container, most operations take place using the EJSWrapperBase and EJSLocalWrapper objects. So, what are these wrappers? See Figure 5-6.

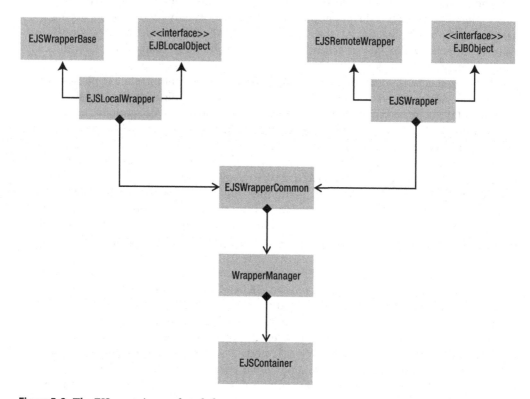

Figure 5-6. *The EJS container–related classes*

The EJSWrapperBase class is an abstract class that is used as the base class for many of the other classes involved in the EJS container EJB functionality, and has no real operations. The EJSLocalWrapper, EJSRemoteWrapper, WSEJBWrapper, TimedObjectWrapper, and BusinessLocalWrapper classes all extend it. This allows the WrapperManager operations to be implemented in terms of just the abstract EJSWrapperBase class yet support operations on all subtypes. The EJS container is a little more fussy, and uses specific wrapper subclasses where required, but uses the EJSWrapperCommon class where common functionality is required and the EJSWrapperBase class when interacting with the collaborators that have been set up via the EJB container.

The EJSWrapperCommon class acts as a single point of call for the EJS container because it contains placeholder variables for local, remote, implementation, and business interfaces and objects and the wrapper class objects they relate to for a particular EJB, which allows a simple lookup for everything to do with a bean.

The WrapperManager class handles bringing a bean into an operational state from the cache, providing access via a key, and discarding objects. It is this class that pins an object in memory before operations on it are called and unpins it after the calls, so it is a class that handles some of the EJB life cycle that is visible to EJB developers. The class implements the DiscardStrategy, FaultStrategy, and EJBServantManager interfaces that the EJB container and EJS container classes use for control. Using interfaces in this way does allow a more flexible change policy if the feature requirements change.

As is to be expected, the EJSLocalWrapper class provides the EJB standard EJBLocalObject functionality using the underlying facilities of the WrapperManager to access the real bean. It supports getEJBLocalHome, isIdentical, getPrimaryKey, and remove methods using the underlying WrapperManager functionality. The EJSHome class that underlies EJBHome support handles the CORBA object creation and narrowing to support remote IIOP interaction.

So far I haven't explained what creates your bean implementation object. A class called BeanO is the base class for all EJBs, and this is extended by SessionBeanO, which is extended by StatefulBeanO and StatelessBeanO, and the same type of relationships exist for MessageDrivenBeanO extending BeanO, and EntityBeanO extending BeanO. Each of these has a factory class to manage its creation. Also, each of these has additional subclasses for bean-managed interaction with the container called BMXXXXBeanO and container-managed interaction with the container called CMXXXXBeanO.

These classes are all created and managed by a class called ContainerAS that again handles some of the lower-level lifecycle elements of bean behavior, with support for finding beans and calls before and after methods and activations. This is combined with the ContainerTX class, which has similar lifecycle support methods but with the support provided at the transaction boundaries. The EJS container class creates the ContainerAS object as part of the unit of work management, and this brings the ContainerTX object into play. These all interplay, under the initial control of the EJS container, to create and manage the EJB objects.

The BeanO class contains the generic behavior of beans, and each of the specific classes adds its own functionality specific to that type of bean. A set of CMR classes supports Container-Managed Relationships for entity beans. This is what makes beans behave the way they do.

The Channel Framework Service

To understand what the Channel Framework Service provides to the ORB that underpins the EJB and EJS containers, and much of the Java EE standards, you can look in the config/templates/servertypes/APPLICATION_SERVER/servers/default/server.xml file. This template is used to provide specific configuration for a particular implementation. The configuration file declares inbound channels for TCP, SSL, and the ORB (i.e., IIOP), and these channels are used to create an unsecured inbound chain by combining the TCP and ORB channels; and a secured inbound chain by combining TCP, SSL, and ORB channels. So, you have both secured and unsecured inbound chains underpinning the ORB Service.

The EJS layer provides additional functionality, such as the JMS interfaces and management. Similarly, there are classes for interaction with the ORB.

The ORB that underpins the EJB and EJS containers is that started by the ORBImpl class that creates the ORB Service. The ORBImpl class provides a scalable CORBA ORB function within WAS, and is similar in architecture to the EJB container. The implementation class handles threading and connections for ORB functions. An underlying EJSORB implementation provides the enterprise services to support the ORB. Ultimately, under the covers, operations are mapped to CORBA objects, ties, and skeletons that are scaled along with the operations within the application server. Remote EJB invocations are mapped to CORBA remote method calls in accord with the EJB specification.

Java Persistence API and EJB 3

Java EE 5 introduced the Java Persistence API (JPA) and EJB 3 persistence into the application server environment. WAS 7 handles this with the help of the Apache OpenJPA implementation that it wraps and integrates with the core WAS runtime in the same way as the Apache Axis2 web services engine is integrated. I will not present the operation of the OpenJPA implementation because that information is publicly available, but I will explain how it is integrated into the WAS environment.

The Apache OpenJPA engine is shipped with WAS 7 as part of the com.ibm.ws.jpa.jar plug-in. The component name within the plugin.xml file contains the name JPAProviders.

The JPAComponentImpl Controller and Integration Component

This component provides to the base WAS runtime (and through it, integration with the EJB container) the dynamic monitoring of deployed applications to add the JPA support that underpins the EJB 3 persistence mechanism. At startup, this component loads the com.ibm.ws.jpa.jar plug-in that integrates the engine for the default JPA provider, OpenJPA, into the environment. When a deployment state change occurs, this component is notified to read the persistence.xml file for the module and enable JPA for the module. Lower-level classes map the standards-based JPA support to the default provider—i.e., the OpenJPA engine.

When the main WAS 7 runtime com.ibm.ws.runtime.jar plug-in starts, the WAS runtime loads the JPAComponentImpl component that supports the jpaservice.JavaPersistenceAPIService. This loads just after the Injection Service component is loaded that provides the support for integrating the EntityManager references into JPA-based applications in place of annotations. The component loads providers for JPA and, if required for EJB support of the Java Transaction API (JTA), sets up capacity for the entity manager pool. The component then adds a DeployedObjectListener listener to monitor deployments through the Application Manager Service. The component registers injection processors using the Injection Engine service component for the PersistenceUnit and the PersistenceContext. When an application is deployed and the DeployedObjectListener callback method is invoked, it integrates the JPA support into the application environment and provides the tie in with the Entity Manager.

Part of this component is dedicated to finding and loading the default JPA provider, which in this case will result in the com.ibm.ws.jpa.jar plug-in being loaded to get access to the OpenJPA engine. The system property com.ibm.websphere. jpa.default.provider identifies the provider to load, and the class name is identified by the property com.ibm.websphere.persistence.PersistenceProviderImpl. A private method, discoverServerScopePersistenceProviders, that is loaded by a call from the getEffectiveDefaultJPAProviderClassName method, which itself is called from the component initialize method, loads the bundle com.ibm.ws.jpa.jar that results in the OpenJPA engine being brought into memory, and the bundles' META-INF/services/ javax.persistence.spi.PersistenceProvider identifies what else is to be loaded.

When the DeployedObjectListener stateChanged method is notified from the Application Manager Service, it passes the DeployedObjectEvent reference. This is examined to work out the transition state. Whether for modules or components, a JPAApplInfo class reference is used with the deployed object application name as a parameter. This class constructor loads the application module or component to get access to the META-INF/persistence.xml file that controls the JPA persistence for the application.

The com.ibm.ws.jpa.jar Implementation

This plug-in is structured a little differently from most in that the plugin.xml file doesn't say much and there is no bundle activator. Essentially, this plug-in acts more as a library of classes than as a directly executable bundle. The principle on which it works is to ship a number of IBM-specific classes for persistence and the complete Apache OpenJPA implementation, and have the IBM implementation classes subclass IBM interfaces that subclass OpenJPA interfaces and then wrap the OpenJPA code using delegation.

Consider the key EntityManager interface that provides the main functionality of the JPA solution that is usually included within an application's code by annotations and dependency injection. The IBM class that implements this functionality is the com.ibm. ws.persistence.EntityManagerImpl class that extends the org.apache.openjpa.persistence. EntityManagerImpl class and implements the IBM-specific com.ibm.websphere.persistence. WsJpaEntityManager and com.ibm.ws.persistence.WsJpaEntityManager interfaces. The former of these IBM interfaces extends the OpenJPAEntityManager interface. The latter of these extends the OpenJPAEntityManagerSPI interface, which is the OpenJPA service provider interface that supports its integration into the wider application server, and also implements the former IBM interface. The method implementations do use their own IBM code that performs some validation of parameters, and use other IBM wrapper classes for the OpenJPA code, but ultimately the requests are handled by OpenJPA. See Figure 5-7 for the class diagram.

The QueryImpl class that does much of the underlying work of handling query requests extends the org.apache.openjpa.persistence.QueryImpl class and mostly leaves the work to it through small wrapper methods that either do a small amount of work and then call super or just have no implementation and leave the work to the parent.

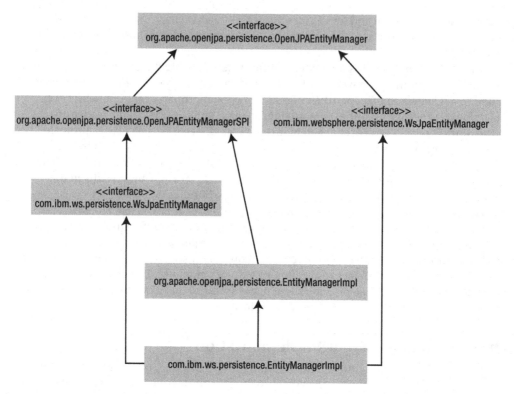

Figure 5-7. *IBM EntityManagerImpl class and interface hierarchy*

Summary

EJBs are complex objects with a well-defined life cycle. To support the behavior required by the Java EE APIs, the EJB container provides a public interface that is implemented on the facilities provided by an underlying EJS container. A number of classes interact under the control of the EJS container to handle scalability, passivation, etc. Other support is required by the container to support message-driven beans, i.e., JMS, or entity beans, i.e., JPA. The JPA functionality is provided through inheriting from and delegating to the Apache OpenJPA implementation that is shipped with WAS from some IBM-specific wrapper classes.

CHAPTER 6

■ ■ ■

The Web Container

Thus far in the book you have looked at the structure of WAS from the base upward and, in the last chapter, at how to create a generic container like the EJB container. Now that you are familiar with the details of how the EJB container works, you are ready to tackle the web container. As part of this analysis, you will also examine how other components and subsystems within WAS integrate their support into a container in general (using the web container for a detailed example) to allow them to monitor, manipulate, or redirect the normal operations, all of which requires use of a collaborator class.

The web container is one of the most important subsystems within any Java EE application server, as is evidenced not just by the Java EE specification but also by the success of the Tomcat stand-alone reference environment as a runtime environment in its own right. Ultimately, despite its complexity, the concepts behind the web container are simple: support HTTP listeners and pass requests to and from Java classes that expose the servlet interface or one of its descendents. Even JSP pages and portlets are a special class of servlet, but are specialized to add additional functionality. While the generic Servlet interface is not HTTP specific, in reality only the HttpServlet interface is commonly used, so when I use the term "servlet" in this section, I am referring to the HttpServlet interface and related classes rather than the more general parent classes.

This chapter begins by describing how the web container is started. It then introduces the key classes that the web container relies on to process a web request. After that, you will look at a collaborator for the web container and create a simple implementation of your own. Underpinning the web container is the communications support for HTTP and HTTPS provided by the Channel Framework Service, so you will examine that and how it links with the web container. Finally, you will briefly examine the extensions to servlets, such as JSP, and how they build upon the base HttpServlet support provided by the web container.

WAS Runtime Web Container Initialization

When you last looked at the web container, you saw that it is largely implemented in the com.ibm.ws.webcontainer.jar file, but is initialized by the application server startup when it performs its loadComponents call and loads, initializes, and starts all components that extend the appropriate extension point. This behavior is common to all of the containers within WAS.

The web container is loaded as a component container in the application server startup phase because its own `plugin.xml` file declares the `com.ibm.wsspi.extension.application-server-startup` extension point, rather than relying on an entry for that extension point in the `plugin.xml` file in `com.ibm.ws.runtime.jar`. One of the extensibility features of Eclipse/OSGi is that the `plugin.xml` files of all plugins are read from the appropriate locations and made available as part of the Eclipse Extension Registry so that when the WAS containers enumerate a particular extension point, they find all extensions extending it and not just those that are part of their plug-in JAR file. The web container entry declares a component, `WebContainer`, with a startup value of 8000 that provides the Web Container Service, a type of `components/applicationserver.webcontainer.WebContainer`, and a `containerExtensionPoint` of `com.ibm.wsspi.extension.webcontainer-startup`. This is confusing, but essentially if you look up the implementation class for the type as declared in the `com.ibm.wsspi.extension.server-components` in the JAR file `plugin.xml`, the class referenced provides the base web container implementation. This referenced implementation will load all of the components referenced in the `plugin.xml com.ibm.wsspi.extension.webcontainer` child elements and provides the controlling web container functionality. So, to understand the web container, you need to look at the implementation class, `WebContainerImpl`, and the components it loads and references. The `WebContainerImpl` class contains a lot of the controlling functionality for the web container, but, as you will see later in this chapter, much of the core functionality is delegated to the `WSWebContainer` and `WebApp` classes.

On the zOS platform, a separate component implementation for the web container, `WebContainerCRImpl`, loads as a control region as part of the base server startup, so the details here pertain to the distributed and IBM Series i OS (formerly known as i5/OS) platforms and the zOS platform as servants.

The WebContainerImpl Class

The `WebContainerImpl` class is a subclass of the `WsContainer` class and implements the `DeployedObjectHandler`, `VetoableChangeListener`, and `WebContainerService` interfaces. These are important interfaces, with the `DeployedObjectHandler` interface providing a callback mechanism for the Application Manager Service to notify the web container of deployed module changes; the `VetoableChangeListener` interface allowing a callback from the Application Server Service to notify the environment of changes in the runtime state (e.g., startup or shutdown); and the `WebContainerService` interface providing the exposed functionality used by other subsystems to access the web container. The `WsContainer` class is provided as part of the `com.ibm.ws.runtime.jar` file that provides the base WAS runtime, and that itself extends the `WsComponentImpl` class that implements the `WsComponent` interface. The `WsContainer` class provides functionality to load components to supplement the base functionality; and the `WsComponentImpl` class provides the initialize, start, stop, and destroy lifecycle functionality that allows the container to be loaded by another container (the application server container). Figure 6-1 shows the class diagram for the `WebContainerImpl` class hierarchy.

The `WsComponent` interface exposes the `initialize`, `start`, `stop`, `destroy`, `getName`, and `getState` methods, and the `WsComponentImpl` class implements them, at least to some extent. The implementation provides an asynchronous initializer, sets up MBeans, and listens for property changes and fires events when they occur.

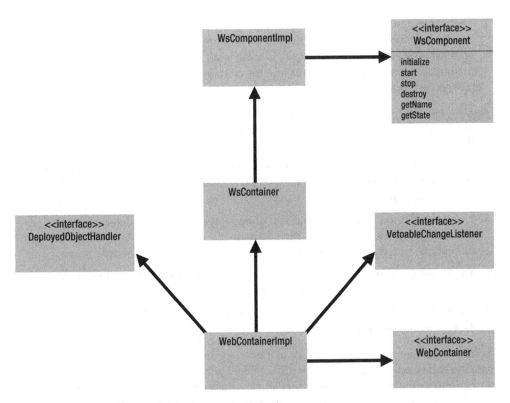

Figure 6-1. *WebContainerImpl class diagram*

The WsContainer class is where the action happens in making the web container behave like a container. Its implementation is similar to that of the EJB container, albeit with a different class hierarchy. As before, the methods build upon those in the WsComponent interface, but with implementations to handle the loading of components within the container. As before, there is a sequence of calls that handles startup and shutdown, with the initialize method handling the configuration of the environment before it is started, the start method starting the container and all of its components, the stop method being called on shutdown to stop the components the container has loaded, and the destroy method destroying all of the now stopped components.

Container and Component Lifecycle Management

The WebContainer component is both a component loaded by the application server container and a container in its own right that loads other components. This relationship makes understanding the lifecycle interactions important. The following explains how the container and component life cycles are managed:

1. The WsContainer initialize method starts with a call to the loadComponents method, which takes the plugin ID as a parameter that enables it to find the extension point it needs to enumerate in the Extension Registry. This extension point is used to build a list of declared extensions populated from the plugin.xml entries that identify the components that should be loaded within this container.

2. The initialize method takes a configuration object as a parameter that it next uses to check what kind of container configuration is required, if any, and then extracts more granular configuration from it for use in a call to an internal initializeComponents method that loads the components into the container. If no container configuration is passed, an empty configuration is used for the component initialization.

3. The loadComponents call that is called from the initialize method is a simple one that merely uses a helper that gets a list of components for the given extension point from the Eclipse Extension Registry and returns the list to the caller.

4. The initializeComponents call simply uses the given list with a helper class and the configuration information to call the initialize method on each of the components in the list of loaded components.

5. The start method uses an internal startComponents method that delegates to a helper class to call the start method on each component with any provided startup configuration data, with that startup data tidied up when it is no longer needed.

6. The stop method merely calls a stopComponents method that uses a helper class that calls the stop method on each component.

7. The destroy method calls a destroyComponents method that uses a helper to call the destroy method on each component.

So, as you can see, the general behavior of the WsContainer class that underlies the WebContainerImpl class is the same as for the EJB container, although with a different class hierarchy. It is now time to look at how the WebContainerImpl class that is specific to the web container works.

The WebContainerImpl class uses an underlying WSWebContainer class that provides some of the core functionality in the same way as the EJSContainer class underpins the EJBContainer class operation. It exposes the WebContainer interface and declares a WebContainerService class interface to the internal WebSphere service registry.

1. The initialize method call of the WebContainerImpl class builds upon that of the underlying WsContainer class. The start of the method handles getting the appropriate configuration information to pass to the subordinate methods. It then makes specific checks for the zOS platform. It first checks if the web container is running as a control region and throws an exception if it is because a zOS-specific class (WebContainerCRImpl) exists for that. It then checks if the web container is running in a servant-handling configuration that allows multiple web container instances to be run—which is very different from the implementation on other platforms.

2. The state is checked to ensure that it should go to a STARTED state and the Application Service is called to add a vetoable change listener on the state so the web container knows when to start up and shut down as part of the application server environment.

3. The Web Container Service class is then registered with the WebSphere service registry.

4. To handle monitoring of changes in the application environment that affect the web container, a new WebMetaDataFactory object is created and registered with the Meta Data Factory Manager Service.

5. Next, the WsContainer parent class initialize method is called to load and initialize the components for the web container, and a check is made to see if the web container transport chains have been started; if not, a flag is set.

6. The `initialize` method then ends, but the underlying `WSWebContainer` class has yet to be created, and you will see later in the chapter why this is.

7. The `start` method calls its parent class `start` method, which starts all of its loaded and initialized components, and uses the Application Manager Service to register itself as a `DeployedObjectHandler` to monitor the modules that are deployed to the environment. It then calls the `loadServletContextFacadeRegistry` private method that creates a `ServletContextFacadeExtensionPoint` extension point object and loads the extension point, and follows this by a call to the `loadExtensionFactoryRegistry` private method that creates a web container `ExtensionFactoryExtensionPt` extension point object and loads the extension point. These extension points are part of the web container OSGi functionality.

8. A web container diagnostic provider MBean is created, diagnostic provider properties are set, and a helper class is used to register the MBean with the diagnostic service. Still, the underlying `WSWebContainer` web container functionality is not loaded, so how does it get initialized?

Web Container Functionality

The `WebContainerImpl` class exposes the `DeployedObjectHandler`, `VetoableChangeListener`, and `WebContainerService` interfaces. Through the `DeployedObjectHandler` interface, it sees what applications are deployed and whether any of these need the underlying web container functionality.

The `DeployedObjectHandler` interface, which can be found in the `com.ibm.ws.runtime.jar` plug-in, simply offers the `start` and `stop` methods that receive deployed object events so that the implementor of the interface can see which modules in the runtime have been started and stopped and then take appropriate action.

When the `WebContainerImpl` class receives a start call from the runtime environment, due to its registration with the Application Manager Service, it checks from the deployed object event contents whether the deployed object module file is a WAR file; if it is, it calls its `install` private method, which performs the magic of initializing the real functionality of the web container:

1. The `install` method passes control to an `init` method, which returns immediately if an underlying `WSWebContainer` web container object already exists. This is where the `WSWebContainer` singleton object gets created.

2. In the `init` method, a call is made to the `WSWebContainer` static method `getWebContainer`, which checks to see if it already exists and, if not, calls its private constructor to get created and immediately passes as a reference to the configured session registry.

3. The collaborators are set up, which enable other containers and subsystems to interact with and control the web container operation, with a list of initialization collaborators created to allow interaction on web application initialization and a list of invocation collaborators created to allow interaction on web application invocation.

4. You finally initialize the underlying `WSWebContainer` object with a call to its `initialize` method, passing a web container configuration object, which the next section examines.

5. The internal startTransports method is called, which gets a Variable Map Service reference and a Thread Pool Manager Service reference and passes them to the underlying WSWebContainer object startTransports method.

6. Finally for the init method, the internal registerMBean method is called to create a runtime collaborator for the underlying web container and activate an MBean for it using an Admin Service MBean factory helper class. The init method then completes and returns to the install method.

7. The install method proceeds by creating a DeployedModule object based on the deployed object passed in the event to the start method, i.e., the module that is being started that it has already confirmed is a WAR file module.

8. The next step in the process is to create any collaborators that are required and add them to a set of arrays of different types of collaborators.

9. A call is then made to the underlying WSWebContainer object's addWebApplication method, passing the WAR module reference and collaborator references to ensure the underlying web container functionality is properly configured.

10. If the transport chains for the web container have not been initialized the internal startEndpoints method is called, which calls the startTransports method previously outlined, if required, and the startChannels method.

11. The startChannels method calls the init method if the underlying web container object does not exist and then it calls the startChains method of the underlying WSWebContainer object.

I previously covered the processing that happens in the WebContainerImpl class when the DeployedObjectHandler install method is called, i.e., the install method is called as a result of a WAR file being deployed to the environment. Essentially, if the underlying WSWebContainer object has not been created and initialized, this triggers its creation. Most of the real functionality of the web container then happens in the underlying WSWebContainer object.

Before leaving the WebContainerImpl class, we should briefly look at some of the other methods.

When an event triggers the uninstall method, a deployed object module reference is created and passed to the removeWebApplication method of the underlying web container object.

The stop method calls the shutdown method on the underlying web container object and then calls stopComponents to shut down the components it is hosting.

The destroy method delegates responsibility to the destroy method in its parent class.

Most of the interesting functionality exists in the listener and extension factory methods that delegate to the underlying containers, and in the methods that add collaborators. The methods that add collaborators simply add the appropriate type of collaborator to a collection for passing to the underlying web container when required.

The VetoableChangeListener interface method, vetoableChange, is used to trigger a call to the startEndpoints internal method, outlined previously, to start the channels and transports of the underlying web container when the triggering change notification indicates that the web container is to be started. The reload and restart method calls for web applications are passed on to the underlying web container to take the appropriate action on the web module.

The view of the web container at the top level, as provided by the WebContainerImpl class, is now complete, but as yet you have seen very little of the functionality you would expect of the web container from the Java EE specification. That functionality is provided by the combination of the WSWebContainer class and the related WebApp class that relates to the applications deployed within it. To help you to understand this more, let's take a little detour to briefly look at how a request into the web container is handled at the functional rather than the communications level (which I will cover later).

Web Container Request Processing

Before looking at the underlying WSWebContainer class that provides the core functionality that the WebContainerImpl class delegates to, you need to see where it fits in the architecture of a web request.

Essentially, the WebContainerImpl class provides the initialization and the interface to the outside world via the exposed WebContainer interface. It delegates all of the real work to the WSWebContainer class, which provides the handleRequest method that is called to route all requests to the correct application module for a given URL.

The web application modules are grouped together into a WebGroup object that consists of a number of WebApp objects, with the WebApp objects representing the underlying servlets that provide the HttpServlet request that performs the application functionality. Each of these objects has a handleRequest method that routes the request until it reaches the service method of the underlying servlet. This is shown in Figure 6-2.

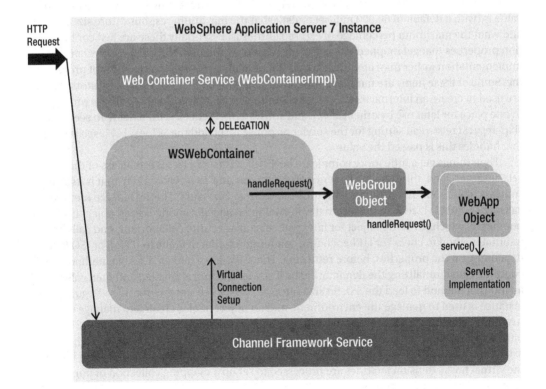

Figure 6-2. *Web container request processing*

The WSWebContainer Class

The WebApp class represents the functionality that a web application provides; i.e., it is a wrapper class for the underlying servlet that does the real work of the application. The WSWebContainer class provides the functionality to route requests to the appropriate WebApp object, and thus to the underlying servlet object, for each web application that runs within it, and to support the public web container view, allowing interaction with other WAS subsystems represented by the WebContainerImpl class. Some of the underlying functionality for the WSWebContainer class is itself provided by a WebContainer parent class (not the interface of the same name), particularly in the long and complex handleRequest method.

Earlier you saw that the WSWebContainer class is a singleton that is created when the static getWebContainer method is called from the init method when a deployed object is installed in WebContainerImpl as a result of the start method of the DeployedObjectHandler interface being called. Once the list of collaborators has been set up, the initialize method of this WSWebContainer class is called, and it is here that some of the real web container infrastructure starts to become visible.

WSWebContainer Lifecycle Methods

The initialize method first checks the configuration passed to it to set up its environment. There are checks for the default virtual hostname, whether servlet caching is enabled, whether pooling is disabled, whether asynchronous request dispatching is allowed, what the timeout value is (with a default of 60,000 milliseconds), what the maximum response store size is, and what the maximum percentage of expired entries is. Essentially these are just configuration properties that get mapped to underlying attributes and data within the WSWebContainer implementation rather than anything that fundamentally alters the internal flow of processing. Some of these items are familiar configuration parameters for WAS administrators. These are used to create an internal WSWebContainer configuration object that holds these properties in one place for later use by other classes and subsystems. A check is then made to see if the skip-InputStream-read setting for the servlet response is set and the SRTServletResponse class that handles this is passed the value.

Then things get a little more complex. The WSWebContainer class is a subclass of the WebContainer class, this time the generic class from com.ibm.ws.webcontainer that is itself a subclass of BaseContainer, rather than the WebContainerImpl class. The initialize method calls super.initialize with the internal web container–specific configuration object it populated, which saves the object for later use, sets up a security collaborator, and calls an internal method to check for URI encoding configuration that defaults to UTF-8 or ISO 8859-1, depending on the properties, before returning. The WSWebContainer initialize method then continues, first initializing the dynamic cache if servlet caching is enabled and then calling an internal method to load the SSL bit size settings. Next, a WebContainerWorkloadRegular instance is used to manage the environment, and an object pool is created to manage connections. Properties are examined to configure settings for the reaper interval and the URL plus-sign handling, before the virtual host handling is configured through the virtual host extension factories. Security properties are read for WAR and EAR boundary handling before the virtual host extension factories are processed to set up a mapping collection of ports and contexts to handle the requests.

So far, you haven't seen any real handling of requests, merely configuration. You will look at a few more methods next before seeing how requests are handled, but to give you an appetizer, keep in mind that this class is a subclass of the WebContainer class, and it is in this parent class that the magic happens.

In the destroy method of the WSWebContainer class, the chains that handle the communications are stopped and then the underlying WebContainer class destroy method is called to tidy request mappers and temporary directories before the reaper alarm that causes tidying up to happen is cancelled.

WSWebContainer WebApp Management and Request Forwarding

The intializeDynamicCache method merely calls the initialize method on the configured CacheManager class reference.

Virtual Host handling is configured via the loadVirtualHost method that handles the mapping of aliases to ports and addresses.

It is again through the methods of the event-driven and public interfaces that the real functionality you expect can be seen. The WSWebContainer class extends the WebContainer class and implements the Runnable and WebContainerConstants interfaces. The WSWebContainer class does indeed have a thread that executes a run method, as this signature would suggest.

When an application is added to the web container, the addWebApplication method is called, which has an implementation in the WSWebContainer class and in its WebContainer parent class. In the WSWebContainer class, the implementation is quite different for the zOS platform than it is for other platforms, in that for zOS a separate thread is created to handle the loading with a separate class loader, but for other platforms the code merely calls the private addWebApp method passing the module and collaborator details.

The addWebApp method extracts the virtual host information from the deployment module, sets up methods for the base web container with extension factories, and then calls the addWebApplication method for the virtual host before saving a mapping between the module and virtual host into a mapping table for later use. The virtual host class used here is based on the VirtualHost and VirtualHostImpl classes and details are obtained from the Virtual Host Manager Service. It is in the VirtualHost/VirtualHostImpl class hierarchy, as VirtualHostImpl extends VirtualHost, that the mapping to the WebApp class, which represents the true web application functionality, happens.

The VirtualHost class addWebApplication method splits the deployment module into its constituent parts and creates a WebGroup, with the WebApp parts that make it up, and saves a virtual host mapping of the context root to web group. The web group is initialized and contains the WebApp objects that represent the deployment module contents. It is the WebGroup and its collection of WebApp objects that runs to create what the user sees as a complete web application, with the WebApp objects representing the finer-grained servlets and JSP pages. The VirtualHost class also extends the BaseContainer class and has the addWebApplication and removeWebApplication methods, along with a handleRequest method that takes the ServletRequest and ServletResponse as parameters for dispatching via the RequestProcessor class.

Returning to the WSWebContainer class, the removeWebApplication method finds the mapping for the application in the virtual host mapping table and removes it, getting a reference to the VirtualHost object for that mapping along the way and calling removeWebApplication on that. In the VirtualHost class, the removeWebApplication call again involves the splitting up of the deployment module into constituent parts, the removal of mappings in its internal tables, and then a call to the WebGroup removeWebApplication method to handle the removal of the WebApp object. It completes its processing by calling the removeSubContainer method of the AbstractContainer class, which is much higher in the class hierarchy, to remove any lower-level elements and artifacts within that container.

The restartWebApplication method calls removeWebApplication and then addWebApplication for the given deployed module.

The getConnectionHandleCollaborator returns the existing connection handle collaborator or creates one if it doesn't exist.

The handleRequest method is an important one and takes IRequest and IResponse references as parameters. These interfaces passed are created by the WCChannel and servlet-handling mechanisms to represent inbound and outbound communications, respectively. The method does handle some request and response processing, but primarily captures metrics and displays some internal exceptions.

The reap method, which is called when the reaper alarm expires, trawls the list of web groups and web apps and tidies up to release resources.

WSWebContainer Transport Management

The remaining methods in the WSWebContainer class are mainly thin wrapper methods for other methods or handle the transport chains.

There are two startTransports methods. The first startTransports method, which takes no parameters, merely delegates to the startChains method, which checks to make sure it isn't running in a zOS control region before performing its magic, starting with getting access to the Channel Framework Service interface. The startChains method checks to see whether it is running as a proxy server or on-demand router, or if the property for enabling in-process connections is set. If any of these is true, it gets access to the Local Inbound Chain Factory Service and calls its createLocalChains method, passing the reference to the Channel Framework Service interface, in order to create the underlying communications for use by the web container. At the end of the startChains method, the Channel Framework Service startChainsByAcceptorID method is called, which gets up and running the communications that underpin the WSWebContainer mechanisms.

The stopChains method undoes the work of the startChains method if it isn't running as a zOS control region, calling the Channel Framework Service to get access to its interface, on which it then calls stopChainsByAcceptorID to shut down the communications underlying the container.

The second startTransports method is a little more interesting in that it is the one called by the install method of the WebContainerImpl class. It takes variable map and thread pool manager instance parameters and then immediately passes these to the complex transformTransportsToChains method. In the transformTransportsToChains method, the object is simple—it reads the configuration for the transports and thread pools and the properties, and then uses the Channel Framework Service interface to create the underlying channels that serve the web container, relating the connections to the threads that handle them.

The thread pool manager instance is used to get access to the threads, and the Channel Framework Service addChannel method is used to get the channels running by passing in a name, a reference to the factory class that handles that type of channel (i.e., SSL or TCP), the properties to apply, and the number to create (usually 100).

The flattenProps method inside the WSWebContainer class is used to access the properties for the web container and make them more usable. Checks exist throughout the transformTransportsToChains method for different handling for zOS control regions and servant regions, once again showing the considerably different behavior of the zOS platform from other distributed platforms. Hosts, ports, timeouts, and other properties for HTTP and HTTPS are set here, building on the TCP and SSL functionality. It is this class that applies the values from the server.xml file.

The WebContainer Class and the WebApp Classes

The WebContainer class, which the WSWebContainer class (previously described) extends, itself extends the BaseContainer class, and this implements the aptly named RequestProcessor interface that has one simple method called handleRequest that actually handles the requests. This is shown in the class diagram in Figure 6-3. It has some of the underlying implementation for the WSWebContainer class, with particular emphasis on handling listeners.

It is also the WebContainer class that has implementations of the addWebApplication method, previously outlined, that calls into the addWebApp internal method to open up the deployment module, get a virtual host reference from it, and call into the addWebApplication method of that virtual host reference to deploy that module to the virtual host implementation that runs it. This was described earlier in the chapter.

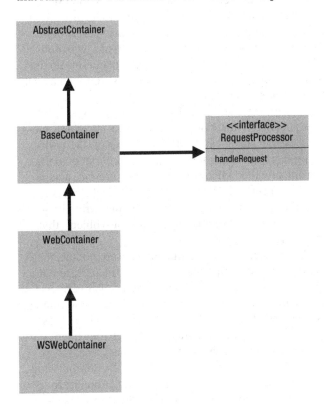

Figure 6-3. *WSWebContainer class diagram*

Let's look at some key methods:

- removeWebApplication: This method reverses the deployment process and removes the web application deployed module.

- restartWebApplication: This so-called restarting of the web application is simply a combination of removal of the application running the deployment module via removeWebApplication and adding it again via addWebApplication.

- handleRequest: This is an important method for processing web requests because it gets the request and response objects from the connection context, having first invoked the security collaborators, handles any URI mappings and caching, and then gets access to the WebApp object for the call from the wrapper it obtained from the cache map. The context and path information are then set for the wrapper, including query string information, and then the handleRequest method of the wrapper or a RequestProcessor is called, i.e., that for the WebApp object. After this processing, the connection context is released and the security collaborators are notified. Connection contexts are important for resource management and at some levels can lead to resource difficulties, deadlocks, and hung threads through the local transaction context management.

The WebContainer class also handles cache management for the requests and responses in that it provides the interface to the cache manager.

The WebApp class relates to a web application and related modules (i.e., WAR and JAR files), extends the BaseContainer class, and provides the ServletContext and IServletContext interfaces. It maintains session context, servlet context, servlet attribute, session attribute, and servlet request listener lists and the JSP class loader list. On initialization of a web module, WebApp checks the requirements of the target servlet specification version and sets up the appropriate handlers, listeners, class loaders, context path, and collaborators, and then installs any servlet filters via a WebAppFilterManager class object reference.

As part of the initialization, the session context is created, lifecycle listeners are installed to monitor the boundaries of the interface between the servlets (including JSP pages as a special category of servlet) that are part of the servlet specification, and mappings of URL path to handling class are initialized. The mappings include the setting up of the interfaces to the JSP processor that creates a servlet from any provided JSP pages. A wrapper interface acts as the boundary between this class and any JSP or servlet. The RequestMapper object addMapping method creates the relationship between the given URL path and the particular wrapper or processor object to call for it, which applies for JSP and servlet objects, and also objects that represent static files included as part of the web application.

Most of the code inside the WebApp class handles decomposition of the web module, mapping of its constituents to the appropriate process or wrapper for the given URL path, and the setting up of listeners and class loaders that apply for the given module and constituent. As the class maintains the listeners and collaborators, it also handles the notification and calling of these when appropriate boundaries are reached or lifecycle events occur. This is the class that handles some of the key servlet specification interface methods, although they might not be exposed directly, such as getServletContext, getSessionContext, getRequestDispatcher, getNamedDispatcher, sendError, and getResourceAsStream, and these access the internal wrappers and facades for the underlying workings that map the web container functionality to the web application implementation in the servlets and JSP pages. While the class consists of a large and complex implementation, it is in essence conceptually simple and would seem familiar to most experienced servlet developers as having implemented what is implied by the documented servlet specification.

It is the handleRequest method of the WebApp class that handles redirection, forms authentication via looking for the j_security_check URL, mapping between relative and absolute paths, and sending standard HTTP notifications such as the infamous 404. The method creates a RequestProcess object to which it passes the request and response objects, and it uses the RequestMapper object map method to direct to the appropriate wrapper. As part of the method, the web container addToCache method is called to handle caching, which benefits performance. A call to the invokeFilters method, which enumerates the filters maintained by the filter manager instance held by the WebApp object, is used to ensure the servlet filter chains are respected and called appropriately at the right processing points.

The WebAppImpl class extends the WebApp class to add more listener handling, MBeans, and namespace initialization for the deployment modules. The key handling is in the parent class.

Three classes mentioned repeatedly thus far are ServletWrapper, RequestProcessor, and RequestMapper, which comprise an important part of the processing, so you need to understand the relationship between them. The BaseContainer class, which the WebApp class and other classes extend, implements the RequestProcessor interface and manages the RequestMapper object for its subclasses. This container handling is more complex than for other containers inside WAS because the web container has subcontainers, such as that for portlets and SIP (Session Initiation Protocol) handling, so parent-child relationships have to be maintained for containers and their associated request and response handling.

The RequestMapper reference stored by the BaseContainer class is an interface that is implemented by classes such as URIMapper that returns a RequestProcessor for a given request and path mapping, with the RequestProcessor returned being appropriate for handling one of the different types of requests. The relationship between these classes is best understood by looking at a specific usage combination.

For example, the JSPExtensionProcessor extends the AbstractJSPExtensionProcessor that handles compiling the JSP file, having processed any tag libraries, and provides a wrapper along the way. Then JSPExtensionProcessor, in its handleRequest method, delegates much of the real processing to that wrapper for the underlying servlet it created. A lot of other processing takes place along the way, mainly to extract the information for the mapping. Ultimately, the runtime entity that is created maps to the HttpJspBase class that is the special type of servlet that offers the interfaces the JSP specification dictates (i.e., jspinit, service, etc.). HttpJspBase delegates some of its functionality to the Jasper engine from the Apache Tomcat reference implementation. The wrapper class for JSP pages at this level is AbstractJSPExtensionServletWrapper, which acts as the interface to the higher-level classes that abstract the type of servlet created.

A Collaborator of Your Own

One the key features of the major containers within WAS is how they work with other containers and subsystems. This is of particular importance for the web container and the EJB container because they underpin many of the Java EE features. As you have seen, the mechanism they use is to support collaborators, a mechanism whereby registered subsystems exposing a particular interface can be called before and after normal container operations are performed, allowing them to react to or modify those operations. In this section you will create a simple collaborator component of your own that logs the operations performed by the web container (i.e., calls to the Servlet interface of a registered web application). You will also include in this component support for a key service of WAS that underpins its extensible runtime, the Application Manager Service, so that you can see and log the starting and stopping of the applications deployed.

The Web Container Service interface includes an addWebAppCollaborator method that takes a WebAppCollaborator object reference to install a collaborator into the web container. The collaborator allows interaction between the web container and other components and subsystems. To generate a collaborator of your own, you create a component and service in Eclipse, as you did earlier in this book, but support the requirements of the WebAppCollaborator interface. This interface is just a marker interface that has no methods, so you should use a subclass interface such as WebAppInvocationCollaborator. You need to add the appropriate extension point to the plugin.xml file, with a declaration so WAS knows where to load it, and then export it all as a plug-in and drop it into the WAS plugins directory. Obviously, this isn't supported by IBM, so don't do it on a production system. But you can use this as an example of how other subsystems work with the WAS web container.

First, consider what a collaborator does: it supports true collaboration. So, the WebAppInvocationCollaborator is called before and after the invocation of a web application by the web container, and information is passed to allow the invocation to be monitored or modified. In this case, the web container deals with servlets, as even JSP pages are a special case of servlets at runtime, so before and after a servlet is called the collaborator is passed the ServletRequest and ServletResponse objects to allow them to be monitored and even modified. This sort of functionality can be used to add layers of new facilities to the environment without modifying the web container code itself, and hides the details of some of these services from the web container, which allows easier maintenance. Along with your collaboration, you are also going to copy what a typical container does (as collaborators are often implemented as part of a container) and look for modules starting and stopping by registering an interface for the DeployedObjectHandler with the Application Manager Service.

To start, create a new plug-in project in Eclipse (see Chapter 3) and add all of the plug-ins in the WAS 7 plugins directory and the j2ee.jar file from the WAS 7 lib directory to the project build path as external JAR files. A plugin.xml file must be created with the appropriate component name, class, and startup value, and you will see how that is done a bit later, in Listing 6-2. Listing 6-1 creates a new class, myCollaboratingComponent, which does all of the work—it subclasses WsComponentImpl and exposes the methods of the desired interfaces. The methods will output data that gives a view as to what the collaborators and deployed object handlers can do.

Listing 6-1. *A Web Container Collaborator Component with Application Manager Service Support*

```
package testcollaborator;
import java.io.FileWriter;
import java.io.IOException;
import java.util.Date;
import javax.servlet.ServletRequest;
import javax.servlet.ServletResponse;
import com.ibm.ejs.ras.Tr;
import com.ibm.ejs.ras.TraceComponent;
```

```java
import com.ibm.ws.exception.ComponentDisabledException;
import com.ibm.ws.exception.ConfigurationError;
import com.ibm.ws.exception.ConfigurationWarning;
import com.ibm.ws.exception.RuntimeError;
import com.ibm.ws.exception.RuntimeWarning;
import com.ibm.ws.runtime.deploy.DeployedObjectEvent;
import com.ibm.ws.runtime.deploy.DeployedObjectHandler;
import com.ibm.ws.runtime.service.ApplicationMgr;
import com.ibm.ws.webcontainer.WebContainerService;
import com.ibm.ws.webcontainer.metadata.WebComponentMetaData;
import com.ibm.ws.webcontainer.webapp.collaborator.WebAppInvocationCollaborator;
import com.ibm.wsspi.runtime.component.WsComponentImpl;
import com.ibm.wsspi.runtime.service.WsServiceRegistry;
@SuppressWarnings("deprecation")

public class MyCollaboratingComponent
    extends WsComponentImpl
    implements DeployedObjectHandler, WebAppInvocationCollaborator {
    private static final String MyCollaboratingComponent =
        "testCollaborator/MyCollaboratingComponent";
    private static TraceComponent tc =
        Tr.register(MyCollaboratingComponent);

    // The start method with a DeployedObjectEvent parameter is one
    // of the key methods on the DeployedObjectHandler
    // listener interface called by the Application Manager Service
    // for registered components. It is called when a deployed object
    // is started.
    public boolean start(DeployedObjectEvent doe)
        throws RuntimeError, RuntimeWarning {
        showStatusMessage("start", doe);
        return true;
    }

    // Similarly, the Application Manager Service calls the stop
    // method of the DeployedObjectHandler when a deployed object
    // stops.
    public void stop(DeployedObjectEvent doe) {
        showStatusMessage("stop", doe);
    }

    // This private method merely logs that something has changed
    // status and what that something is
    private void showStatusMessage(String status,
        DeployedObjectEvent doe) {
        try {
```

```
            FileWriter outlog = new FileWriter(
                "/tmp/logs/WAS7Collaborator.log", true);
            outlog.write("***************" + "\n");
            outlog.write(status + " with DeployedObjectEvent at: " +
                new Date().toString() + "\n");
            outlog.write("Deployed Object Name is: " +
                doe.getDeployedObject().getName() + "\n");
            // Make sure that things get written
            outlog.flush();
            outlog.close();
        } catch (IOException ioe) {
            ioe.printStackTrace();
        }
    }


    // The WebAppInvocationCollaborator interface is called before
    // and after an invocation of a web application by the web
    // container. There are two types of parameter sets; one with
    // just metadata as to the details of the web application and
    // the other with servlet request and response objects.
    // The collaborator can react to these parameters or
    // manipulate them as part of the collaboration.
    // We just log the information but could do more.
    public void preInvoke(WebComponentMetaData wcmd) {
        showCollaboratorMetadataMessage("preInvoke", wcmd);
    }


    public void postInvoke(WebComponentMetaData wcmd) {
        showCollaboratorMetadataMessage("postInvoke", wcmd);
    }


    private void showCollaboratorMetadataMessage(String method,
        WebComponentMetaData wcmd) {
        try {
            FileWriter outlog = new FileWriter(
                "/tmp/logs/WAS7Collaborator.log", true);
            outlog.write("***************" + "\n");
            outlog.write(method + " with WebComponentMetaData at: " +
                new Date().toString() + "\n");
            outlog.write("J2EE Module Name is: " +
                wcmd.getJ2EEName().getModule() + "\n");
            outlog.write("Name is: " + wcmd.getName() + "\n");
            outlog.write("Web Component Description is: " +
                wcmd.getWebComponentDescription() + "\n");
            outlog.write("Implementation Class is: " +
                wcmd.getImplementationClass() + "\n");
```

```java
        // Make sure that things get written
        outlog.flush();
        outlog.close();
    } catch (IOException ioe) {
        ioe.printStackTrace();
    }
}

public void preInvoke(WebComponentMetaData wcmd,
    ServletRequest req, ServletResponse resp) {
    showCollaboratorHandlerMessage("preInvoke", wcmd, req, resp);
}

public void postInvoke(WebComponentMetaData wcmd,
    ServletRequest req, ServletResponse resp) {
    showCollaboratorHandlerMessage("postInvoke", wcmd, req, resp);
}

private void showCollaboratorHandlerMessage(String method,
    WebComponentMetaData wcmd, ServletRequest req,
    ServletResponse resp) {
    try {
        FileWriter outlog = new FileWriter(
            "/tmp/logs/WAS7Collaborator.log", true);
        outlog.write("****************" + "\n");
        outlog.write(method +
            " with WebComponentMetaData " +
            "& servlet request/response at: " +
            new Date().toString() + "\n");
        outlog.write("J2EE Module Name is: " +
            wcmd.getJ2EEName().getApplication() + "\n");
        outlog.write("Name is: " + wcmd.getName() + "\n");
        outlog.write("Web Component Description is: " +
            wcmd.getWebComponentDescription() + "\n");
        outlog.write("Implementation Class is: " +
            wcmd.getImplementationClass() + "\n");
        outlog.write("Servlet Request Content Length is: " +
            req.getContentLength() + "\n");
        outlog.write("Servlet Request Remote Host is: " +
            req.getRemoteHost() + "\n");
        outlog.write("Servlet Response Content Type is: " +
            resp.getContentType() + "\n");
        // Make sure that things get written
        outlog.flush();
        outlog.close();
    } catch (IOException ioe) {
```

```
                ioe.printStackTrace();
        }
    }

    public String getName() {
        return null;
    }

    public String getState() {
        return null;
    }

    // All methods below are from the WsComponentImpl class. These are
    // used to control the life cycle of the component when loaded by
    // the WAS runtime container support.
    // Typically, all WAS components and services use TraceComponent
    // facilities to declare their entry and exit points for use when
    // tracing is enabled inside WAS.
    public void destroy() {
        if (tc.isEntryEnabled()) {
            Tr.entry(tc, "destroy");
        }
        System.out.println("Destroying MyComponent");
        if (tc.isEntryEnabled()) {
            Tr.exit(tc, "destroy");
        }
    }

    // Components are initialized before use
    public void initialize(Object arg0)
        throws ComponentDisabledException, ConfigurationWarning,
        ConfigurationError {
        if (tc.isEntryEnabled()) {
            Tr.entry(tc, "initialize");
        }
        System.out.println(
            "Initializing MyCollaboratingComponent " +
            "and adding collaborator");

        // To declare this object as a collaborator to the web
        // container get access to the Web Container Service and
        // pass it a reference to our web app collaborator method.
        // Then we will get called before and after calls into the
        // Servlet interface methods.
        try {
```

```java
            WebContainerService service =
                (WebContainerService) WsServiceRegistry.getService(
                    this, Class.forName(
                    "com.ibm.ws.webcontainer.WebContainerService"
                    ));
            service.addWebAppCollaborator(this);
        } catch (Exception e) {
            e.printStackTrace();
        }
        // Now do the same to get called when deployed objects start
        // or stop but use the Application Manager Service
        try {
            ApplicationMgr appmgr =
                (ApplicationMgr) WsServiceRegistry.getService(
                    this, Class.forName(
                    "com.ibm.ws.runtime.service.ApplicationMgr"));
                    appmgr.addDeployedObjectHandler(this);
        } catch (Exception e) {
            e.printStackTrace();
        }
        if (tc.isEntryEnabled()) {
            Tr.exit(tc, "initialize");
        }
    }

    public void start() throws RuntimeError, RuntimeWarning {
        if (tc.isEntryEnabled()) {
            Tr.entry(tc, "start");
        }
        System.out.println("Starting MyCollaboratingComponent");
        if (tc.isEntryEnabled()) {
            Tr.exit(tc, "start");
        }
    }

    public void stop() {
        if (tc.isEntryEnabled()) {
            Tr.entry(tc, "stop");
        }
        System.out.println("Stopping MyCollaboratingComponent");
        if (tc.isEntryEnabled()) {
            Tr.exit(tc, "stop");
        }
    }
}
```

You have to provide a `plugin.xml` file for the component, and add support for WAS to use it, as shown in Listing 6-2. In order to make your component load as part of the web container, you need to use the web container extensions extension point `com.ibm.wsspi.extension.webcontainer-startup`, so you need to add an extension declaration to the `plugin.xml` file for your component. If you wanted this to load as part of the normal application server container, you would use the extension point `com.ibm.wsspi.extension.applicationserver-startup` instead. The runtime reads all `plugin.xml` entries to see what to extend before the container enumerates its components, so you add this to your own `plugin.xml` file and it will be enumerated when the container asks the registry for its components in the `loadComponents` call, and your component will receive the `initialize`, `start`, `stop`, and `destroy` lifecycle method calls as would any other component deployed with WAS. The same happens for the components shipped with the Web Container plug-in, but their extension entries are added to the `plugin.xml` file of the Web Container plug-in itself.

You have declared your component as being dependent on the Application Manager Service and the Web Container Service because you are using both, so if they aren't started, then neither will your component start.

Listing 6-2. *Extension Declaration to Be Added to Component plugin.xml*

```
<extension point="com.ibm.wsspi.extension.webcontainer-startup">
    <components>
        <component startup="2147483647"
            class="testcollaborator.MyCollaboratingComponent"
            component-id="MyCollaboratingComponent"
            startup-mode="dependency">
            <dependency type="service"
                name="com.ibm.ws.runtime.service.ApplicationMgr"/>
            <dependency type="service"
                name="com.ibm.ws.webcontainer.WebContainerService"/>
        </component>
    <components>
<extension>
```

In this collaborator component, you have also seen the use of the Application Manager Service. This service is used throughout the WAS code via either the `DeployedObjectListener` or `DeployedObjectHandler` interface. The overuse of this service and interface pair is one of the reasons that application deployments to the WAS 7 environment can be slow, because so many components register with it. For example, subsystems such as the Web Services Axis2 integration component need to examine applications deployed to see if the modules are of the correct type to hold web services (using the Eclipse models for all Java EE module types), and then any deployed descriptors and annotations need to be examined for each component module, i.e., a WAR file within an EAR file. Similarly, WebSphere ESB needs to look for SCA modules and WebSphere Process Server needs to look for modules containing WS-BPEL and process declarations. When building upon WAS, the Application Manager Service is almost always required, although it should be said that the WAS extensions and subsystems often overuse it by having listeners registered from multiple parts of a single subsystem.

In summary, you can monitor the web application modules to see when they start and stop, and can see the invocations of the applications. There is more to this than shown here, but the core functionality shows what can be achieved. Using this technique, you can even intervene and amend the request and responses. The functionality here could easily be built up to provide extra features, such as for a Web Application Firewall. When exploring the internals of WAS or building upon it, Listings 6-1 and 6-2 show the basic framework of what is required to develop a collaborator with a DeployedObjectHandler for the web container and other subsystems.

The Web Container and the Channel Framework Service

You've seen how the web container is structured, with its key components and subsystems, and how other subsystems in WAS collaborate with it to add their own functionality or to monitor the web applications. This section reviews how the web requests for service by the web applications hosted by the web container are received and passed into the web container for processing. As with all WAS communications, the listeners and transport handling are under the control of the Channel Framework Service. The relationship between the web container components and the Channel Framework Service when handling a web request is shown in Figure 6-4.

The WSWebContainer method transformTransportsToChains method used the Channel Framework Service to set up the layered TCP/IP communications referred to earlier in this book, i.e., TCP is layered upon to create SSL and HTTP, and HTTP has SSL added to create HTTPS. The addChannel method called passed in a factory object that handles the creation of the underlying implementation objects that handle the communications channels into the web container. These underlying objects that are created are called the WCChannel, WCChannelLink, WCCRequestImpl, and WCCResponseImpl objects.

The WCChannel class extends the InboundApplicationChannel class and creates the WCC Channel Links object pool of 100 objects. It reads the configuration and properties to handle the appropriate buffering for the connection. It maintains the WCChannelLink objects to represent the connections in the pool and handles adding and removing the objects as required for individual virtual connections.

The objects that are maintained in the pool are of the WCChannelLink class that extends the InboundApplicationLink class. They relate to a particular WCChannel and virtual connection. Most of the work is handled by the parent class that handles request and response and internal queues and buffering, but when the destroy method is called, the object returns itself to the pool. When a particular link object is closed, it checks to see whether it is to be reused; if it is not and is to be destroyed, it creates new WCCRequestImpl and WCCResponseImpl objects to assign to its parent request and response variables, respectively, to speed up its reuse when it is later retrieved from the pool. When its ready method is called with a virtual connection reference by the underlying Channel Framework Service handling, it initializes itself for the given connection. It then calls into the web container handleRequest method, passing the request and response objects created earlier, which relates the low-level WCCRequestImpl and WCCResponseImpl to the HTTPRequest and HTTPResponse objects that ultimately pass through layers of processing to enter the service method of a servlet. After the handleRequest method returns, the WCChannelLink ready method flushes any buffers and tidies up. This class handles the sending of headers and the writing of responses from the buffers.

The WCCRequestImpl class handles many of the methods that are required of the HttpRequest class, and it implements the IRequest interface so that it can be handled generically by the WAS subsystems. The implementation saves the channel, request, and response references passed to it on initialization along with the HttpInboundServiceContext reference, with the references being set to null so that they can be tidied up when the finish method is called. It then implements standard HttpServletRequest methods as getQueryString, getRemoteUser, getServer, getMethod, getRequestURI, getHeader, getContentLength, getRemoteHost, getSessionID, getInputStream, getCookies, etc., using simple string manipulation on the underlying request buffer. It also handles X509 certificates and its own security "armor" in a similar way. One of its methods is used to return an interface to the underlying related response object.

Similarly, the WCCResponseImpl class, which has a simple implementation, extracts the request and response references from the passed-in WCChannelLink reference and delegates to these to provide some of the implementation required of the HttpServletResponse class.

The factory mappings that handle the relationships between these classes can be found under the com.ibm.wsspi.extension.channel-framework-channel-type extension point section in the plugin.xml file from the com.ibm.ws.webcontainer.jar file. Specific configuration for a deployment can be found in the server.xml file.

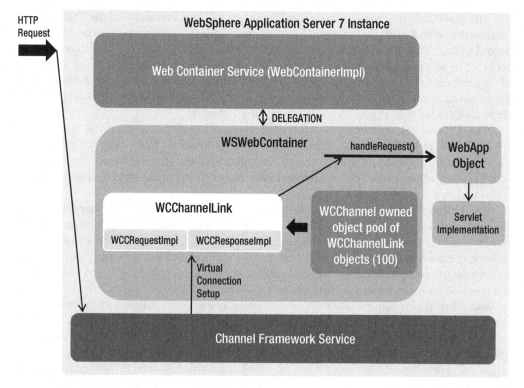

Figure 6-4. *Web container communications using the Channel Framework Service*

Java Server Pages and Java Server Faces

You have seen how the web container handles servlets and how other subsystems integrate with the web container to amend the processing to add their own support using collaborators, but I haven't yet shown you how other types of web application components play a role. Fortunately, from the perspective of the Java EE specification, everything is, to some extent, an HttpServlet or some sort of derivative of it. JSP pages have their own life cycles, but when they run they are handled like servlets, and JSF pages are the same. One thing does differ for both JSP and JSF pages from the standard HttpServlet processing: both need to be compiled from their base XML-derived tag-based source files with their tag libraries and expression language statements and turned into the underlying servlets that run, and because this can happen at runtime, the web container needs support to detect the arrival of or changes to a JSP or JSF source file and perform that compilation. From the Java perspective, the Eclipse JDT is used for the compilation itself, but the translation to the HttpServlet derivative that is to be compiled requires additional components. This section examines the components that turn JSP pages and JSF pages into the HttpServlet derivatives.

I have already mentioned how JSP pages are handled by the WebApp, RequestMapper, and RequestProcessor classes and interfaces. You do have to remember, however, that the original web container loading also included some classes to handle this.

The web container starts up the component com.ibm.ws.jsp.runtime.JspComponentImpl class. This component sets up a JSP string buffer and extension factory, and configuration and caching for tag libraries when it starts, with a listener on the thread pool manager. It also registers a listener with the Meta Data Service so it can detect when a new web module is deployed that may contain JSP pages that need to be compiled and installed. The listeners are in specific classes, the JspThreadPoolListener and JspMetaDataListener classes, respectively. The JspThreadPoolListener performs tidying up of WebApp resources for JSP pages when the thread handling it is destroyed, with particular attention paid to tidying up tag libraries. The JspMetaDataListener looks for deployments, opens any WAR files deployed, and extracts JSP pages and related tag libraries to set up the necessary context and environment; as a result, the necessary WebApp object is created to allow the treatment of the compiled JSP page as an HttpServlet derivative that can be executed by the WebContainer.

Also started by the web container is the class that handles JSF, com.ibm.ws.jsf.extprocessor.JSFComponentImpl. This merely creates a JSFExtensionFactory class for use by the web container when it starts up and registers it with the Web Container Service. The factory object creates a JSFExtensionProcessor that extends the standard WebExtensionProcessor that handles JSF applications.

Summary

The web container support required by the Java EE specification is a complex interplay between the WebContainerImpl class and the WSWebContainer class it delegates to, which inherits some of its implementation from its parent classes. The WebApp, RequestProcessor, and RequestMapper classes and interfaces are used by the web container classes to handle the mapping between the web application implementations and the runtime environment that handles providing the support for the specifications. The Channel Framework Service has specific web container–related classes, WCChannel, WCChannelLink, WCCRequestImpl, and WCCResponseImpl, that take the underlying communications and tie them to the runtime implementation of the web container and the servlet specification interfaces.

CHAPTER 7

■ ■ ■

Web Services

With web services support in WAS, we really have two subsystems to consider instead of one, as in other areas. The JAX-RPC standard support initially specified in J2EE 1.4 and shipped in WAS 6.x is provided in one subsystem, for which the WAS 7 implementation raises the JAX-RPC compatibility level to version 1.2. The other subsystem is the implementor of the JAX-WS standard from Java EE 5; the support is provided by a wrapper component that makes use of the open source Apache Axis2 core engine for JAX-WS and the Apache Sandesha2 module to add WS-ReliableMessaging support to the engine. Web services is a big subject, with a core SOAP/HTTP standard on which a number of other standards build, but for the purposes of this book we will concentrate on only the core itself.

In Chapter 4, we covered how the WAS runtime components fit together to provide services. One component described is the JAX-RPC Web Service component that provides the Web Services Service, which is implemented in the WSServerImpl component that starts the JAX-RPC web services facilities. (Note that in this case the S after the W in WSServerImpl is capitalized to distinguish it from the WsServerImpl component that bootstraps WAS itself.) The WSServerImpl class covers JAX-RPC web services, and the controlling component is named JaxRpcWebService for this reason, but JAX-RPC and the WSServerImpl class that supports it cover only one part of the Java web services standards and not anything JAX-WS related.

This chapter examines how the WSServerImpl component is built upon to provide the complete JAX-RPC web services implementation. It also describes the Axis2 integration at the core of the web services support within WAS that supports JAX-WS.

Prepare for a little confusion caused by some of the naming within WAS; some of the key functionality is provided by the com.ibm.wsfp.main.jar file, where "wsfp" stands for "Web Services Feature Pack," which was the WAS 6.1 name for the JAX-WS support extension that evolved into that in WAS 7.

Figure 7-1 provides a high-level overview of the major components of the two web services stack implementations.

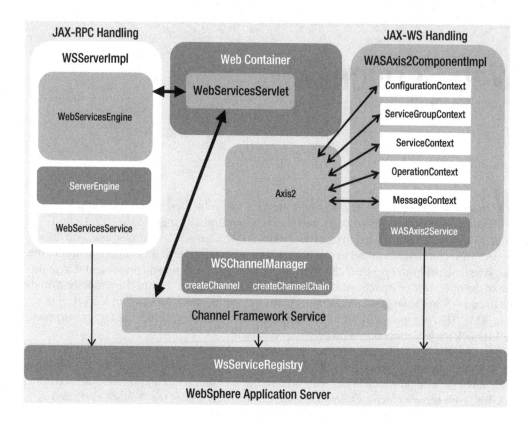

Figure 7-1. *The JAX-RPC and JAX-WS web services major components*

JAX-RPC Support and the WSServerImpl Class

Chapter 4 provided a brief look at how the JAX-RPC web service implementation is started. This section examines in a little more detail the JAX-RPC functionality, the components underlying it, and the classes it relates to.

The WSServerImpl class extends the ComponentImpl class for lifecycle management under the control of the runtime or containers (as you have seen in other chapters), which means it implements the initialize, start, stop, and destroy methods that allow the runtime to control it; and it implements the DeployedObjectAdjuster, MetaDataListener, and WebServicesService interfaces. The first two of these interfaces allow the component to monitor the runtime environment for new deployments and respond to them accordingly when the deployed applications contain web services; the last of the interfaces allows the Web Services Service programming interface to be offered that allows callers to query the runtime web services metadata, web services engine configuration, and some service reference information. When I refer to "web services" when describing this implementation, I'm referring only to JAX-RPC services, as the JAX-WS implementation is very different.

As you will see throughout the classes in the JAX-RPC implementation, the key classes involved in request handling are handler classes derived from the BasicHandler class, and the key method is the invoke method that finds its way through coarse-grained objects down to fine-grained objects that eventually make use of the underlying deployed application web service implementation.

WSServerImpl Component Initialization and Startup

The WSServerImpl component, like all components loaded inside containers by WAS, has lifecycle methods to control its initialization, starting, stopping, and destruction. This section explains the function of the initialize and start methods that handle bringing the component into a running state.

The initialize Method

Starting with the component initialize method, i.e., the point when it starts its work, the WSServerImpl component checks its environment and disables itself if it is running inside a Deployment Manager instance or in a zOS control region. Otherwise, it then registers the WebServicesService as a runtime service with the WebSphere WsServiceRegistry, and sets itself as the reference to the current WebServicesService implementation for the WebServicesServiceHome class, which allows IBM some flexibility to change this implementation.

The start Method

With the start method, which gets the component actually running, the Protocols WAS runtime class init method is first called to perform any protocol package registration to get any specific protocol handlers running, although the actual implementation of the method is empty, and then the class registers itself with the Application Manager Service as a DeployedObjectAdjuster listener object so that it can see and manipulate any code that is deployed as it pertains to web services.

In the same way, the WSServerImpl component registers itself as a MetaDataListener with the Meta Data Service for the purpose of monitoring deployments, although more for the reason of getting notified of changes to the application environment than for controlling what is deployed. It passes the Meta Data Service reference to a WASWebServicesServerMetaDataImpl class to allow this class to register the application, module, and component metadata slots with the service, and then this class can handle control of this metadata on deployment. If the component has references to the Web Container Service or EJB Container Service at this point (although the same happens whenever it gets these references later on if these containers are subsequently started), it registers a WebCollaborator and EjbCollaborator reference, respectively with each to allow coordination and control with these containers for the related web services deployment information.

The component then registers and activates an MBean for the Web Services Service before getting references to the Web Services Security Service, Variable Map Service, and Security Service for later use in its operation. Before completing its startup, it enables its communications by getting access to the Channel Framework Service and WS Byte Buffer Pool Manager Service and passing these to its internal WSChannelManager singleton class that handles communications for this web services implementation.

The WSChannelManager class handles the creation, pooling, and management of the channels, chains, and links for the web services support in the same way as described for the web container. Factory classes control the creation of the inbound and outbound HTTP and HTTPS client and server connectivity, and read the configuration to apply for this. Finally, the SecurityHooks class startup method is called to get running the complex components that tie the web services security and general security services and components with the ports, bindings, etc. of the deployed web services.

Stopping and Destroying the WSServerImpl Component

This section covers the lifecycle methods that handle taking the component from a running state and removing it from memory.

The stop Method

When the stop method is called, the SecurityHooks class cleanup method is called to release the service interfaces it uses and tidy up, and the services used directly by the WSServerImpl class are also released.

The destroy Method

When the destroy method is called, the WebServicesEngineConfigurationGenerator class destroyConfigGenerator call is made to perform tidying up.

These methods conclude the lifecycle method descriptions required by the general WAS runtime to treat this as a component in accord with the ComponentImpl parent class.

Running State Methods

During a running state, the listener, service, and adjuster interface methods become significantly more important. These allow the JAX-RPC web services engine implementation to respond to changes in its environment.

The adjust Method

The adjust method is called as a consequence of registration with the Application Manager Service, and the call supplies a DeployedObjectEvent reference. This reference is interrogated to get access to deployed object WAR or EJB JAR files to perform any required "adjustment." The adjust method passes a WAR file to its private warAdjust method for handling and passes an EJB JAR file to its private jarAdjust method.

The warAdjust Method

In the warAdjust method, the first operation required to work with the internals of a WAR file is to open it and understand its contents, so the Eclipse JST LoadStrategy class (from com.ibm.ws.wccm.jar) is used for the deployed object module to get a wrapper for accessing the individual constituents. Next, a WebApp object reference is obtained from the deployed object module reference and its deployment descriptor. The operation of the WebApp class was discussed in Chapter 6, with the key operation being the handleRequest method.

Next, a JAXRPCMetaDataHelper class and a JAXRPCMetaDataWrapper class are created from the deployed object reference information to get access to the module contents, the classloader setup, and the configuration. If the wrapper isn't created or the WAR file contains no JAX-RPC web services, the method exits and returns to the caller because there is nothing for it to do, but if there are services, the method continues. The wrapper is then used to get access to the web service description and port information, if it contains configuration for a JAX-RPC specifically configured port, and the "servlet link" Service Implementation Bean name is extracted and passed to the WebApp reference to get access to the servlet that implements the service.

The servlet reference is then passed to the bindServiceBeanToServlet method, which simply looks for a service class name of a service bean in its mapping. If it doesn't find one, it gets the web type class name reference for the servlet and stores the com.ibm.ws.webservices. engine.transport.http.WebServicesServlet class name in it, and stores the servlet and service class name in the service bean mapping, thus binding the service bean to the servlet. So, this handles all of the magic of configuring the WebApp servlet to tie into the web services engine, and the web services functionality itself is handled by the WebServicesServlet class. The WebApp class and its handleRequest method that ultimately calls the underlying servlet service method were discussed in Chapter 6.

The jarAdjust Method

The jarAdjust method is a little different from the warAdjust method in that it is used to provide JAX-RPC web services interfaces for pre-J2EE 1.4 EJBs in an EJB JAR file. Like the warAdjust method, the Eclipse JST LoadStrategy class is used to get access to the constituents of the module file, and the deployment descriptor is used to get an EJBJar file reference to work with. The rest of the method only executes if the J2EE version of the EJB JAR file is less than version 1.4, otherwise the method simply returns.

Next, a JAXRPCMetaDataHelper and a JAXRPCMetaDataWrapper are created from the deployed object reference information to get access to the module contents, the classloader setup, and the configuration. If the wrapper isn't created or the EJB JAR file contains no JAX-RPC web services, the method exits and returns to the caller because there is nothing for it to do, but if there are services, the method continues.

The wrapper is then used to get access to the web service description from the WSDD information and the port information. If this information contains configuration for a JAX-RPC specifically configured port, the "EJB link" Service Implementation Bean name is extracted, from which an enterprise bean reference is obtained from the EJB JAR file reference. A Java class reference is created for the web service endpoint obtained from the wrapper earlier, and this is passed to the setServiceEndPoint method of the enterprise bean reference once it has been typecast to a session bean reference.

Next, the EJB JAR file reference (named EJBJar) and the enterprise bean reference are passed to the copyRemoteMethodTxns method, which then enumerates the assembly method transactions to get the signatures. For each signature obtained from the enumeration a new SERVICE_ENDPOINT_LITERAL method element is created and inserted into the EJB JAR reference for that enterprise bean.

Metadata Management Methods

You previously looked at the adjust method that is called when deployment events trigger the Application Manager Service to notify components registered with it, and then you looked at how this results in WAR and EJB JAR files being handled. For the interface called as a result of being registered with the Meta Data Service, there are a number of methods that can be called. There are lots of different types of metadata that are manipulated and used to control the configuration when a deployment occurs.

The metaDataCreated and metaDataDestroyed Methods

A metadata event can be triggered through some change to a deployment module. When the metaDataCreated method is called, the module metadata, if available, is extracted to get access to the deployed object and the module file it contains, and if it relates to an EJB JAR file, the deployed object and metadata are passed on to the ejbJarMetaDataCreated method, and if it is a WAR file, it is passed on to the warMetaDataCreated method.

If the metadata isn't module metadata but component metadata, the reference to the deployed object is extracted along with the module file it contains. If the component metadata relates to an EJB JAR file, the ejbMetaDataCreated method is called, and the metadata and deployed object reference are passed to it. There are, thus, three lower-level methods that do the real work of handling the metadata creation notification.

When the metaDataDestroyed method is called with a metadata event notification, if the metadata is for a component or application, its reference within the web services environment is simply destroyed, but if it is for a module, then the MBean representing that application and module is unregistered before the reference is destroyed.

As described, the metadata-created event led to different underlying methods being called, so let's look at each of these methods in turn.

The ejbMetaDataCreated Method

The ejbMetaDataCreated method is called on component metadata creation events if the module referred to is an EJB JAR file. In this method, the component name and module metadata are extracted and used to get at the client module metadata. The deployed object reference obtained from the event is used to get at the module file itself, and its LoadStrategy class reference is added to the client module metadata so that too can extract the individual module constituents.

A client entity metadata reference is then obtained from the client module metadata using the component name as a lookup, and this reference then has its bindBindingsAndExtensions method called with the META-INF/ibm-webservicesclient-bnd.xmi and META-INF/ibm-webservicesclient-ext.xmi files as parameters, which is followed immediately by a call to its loadNow call. Once again, you can see the importance of these XMI files in directing the appropriate configuration of the web services environment. The two method calls use the WSModels class support, which essentially provides static wrappers to read the module XML files, to access and then load the client bindings, client extensions, service references, and WSDL.

The ejbJarMetaDataCreated method is called for a server module, rather than client component metadata, and again gets passed the metadata and the deployed object references. This method does a lot more in the way of providing web services support. It first gets access to the module file, the LoadStrategy class (allowing access to the module constituents), the classloader, and an EJB JAR reference (derived from the deployment descriptor) using the deployed object reference.

The application and module name are then extracted from the module metadata passed to the method and, with the classloader, are used to create a JAXRPCMetaDataHelper reference that is then used, via its loadJAXRPCMetaData method, to create a JAXRPCMetaDataWrapper class to give access to the underlying service information. If the wrapper identifies that the module contains JAX-RPC Services, the web services are extracted and then the port components are extracted. The META-INF/ibm-webservices-bnd.xmi and META-INF/ibm-webservices-ext.xmi files are then passed to the loadWebServicesBindingXML and loadWebServicesExtXML methods (described later) along with the LoadStrategy reference to obtain the web service binding and extension references.

Again you can see the importance of the IBM-specific files in addition to the standard META-INF/webservices.xml file that is used as the standard web services deployment descriptor (WSDD). If there is a web service binding, then an EJB JAR binding is obtained from the deployed object reference and the context root, and a router module iterator is obtained from the web service binding. The router modules and router module names are extracted, and then the names are used to extract the module files.

A ServerModuleMetaData reference is then generated for the application and module names (not the router module name) and this is then given the router module name and related to the URL absolute path from the deployed object reference and the EAR file. The web service descriptions are then used with the loadJavaWsdlMappingXML method to get the JAX-RPC mapping file. The WSDL file and port component are then loaded and from the port component the service implementation bean EJBLink reference is obtained and used to generate an enterprise bean reference.

The service endpoint is then obtained from the port component and used to get the service endpoint interface for the enterprise bean itself that has been typecast to a session bean, but if there isn't one and the target EJB version is 3 or later, then a Java class is created for the typecast enterprise bean and interface created for the given service endpoint description. The enterprise bean EJB class name is then extracted to get the implementation class name for the web service. The web service description, its file name, and the WSDD port obtained from the server module metadata are used to create a temporary WSDL file that is used with the createWSDDGen call (described later), or an existing WSDL file is read and passed to it. Then the setupWsddPort is used with these newly created artifacts.

The JNDI name and home interface for the EJB are obtained along with the methods. These are all passed to the WSDD port reference and tied into the WAS EJB service type handling. Security and properties are added to the service handling along with ports and the URL pattern for the service, and the endpoint is created by passing everything to the generateEndpoint method. An MBean relating the metadata and context root is then created. This concludes the server-side service handling of the module; the client-side handling in this method now happens.

As before, the client module metadata is used to create a client module reference, and the LoadStrategy reference and classloader are provided to it. An Eclipse JST WebServicesClient reference is generated using the META-INF/webservicesclient.xml file name as the reference key. For each of the enterprise beans in the EJB JAR file provided in the deployed object reference, the bindJ2EE13ComponentServiceRefs call is used to attempt to bind against the entries in the webservicesclient.xml file. The bindBindingsAndExtensions call is then used with the META-INF/ibm-webservicesclient-bnd.xmi and META-INF/ibm-webservicesclient-ext.xmi files to bind against the WSServerImpl class (i.e., the web services engine controller implementation) itself.

The warMetaDataCreated Method

The warMetaDataCreated method is called next with a module metadata reference and deployed object reference as parameters. As in the other methods, the module is obtained from the deployed object parameter and the LoadStrategy reference is set up for it to allow access to the constituent components, along with the appropriate classloader reference. The JAXRPCMetaDataHelper class is used with the module and classloader to create a JAXRPCMetaDataWrapper object to allow decomposition of the JAX-RPC-related constituents of the module, which is used to check if the module contains an JAX-RPC web service, and if not the method exits. If there are web services, a reference to them is obtained and the loadWebServicesBindingXML and loadWebServicesExtXML methods are used with the IBM XMI files as for EJB modules.

A WebApp reference is created from the deployment descriptor constituent of the deployed object, and, as for the web container, this represents the mapping between URLs and underlying servlet implementations that handle requests. The context root is saved for later use and then each web service description in the web services collection is enumerated and the loadJavaWsdlMappingXML call is used to get a JAX-RPC mapping file, i.e., the data usually found in WEB-INF/webservices.xml.

As before, the port components and bindings are enumerated, and from the port components the target servlet implementation name is obtained and used as a lookup with the WebApp reference to obtain the servlet implementation reference, which is then used to get a service bean reference implementation name. The target URL mapping and servlet name are stored into a ServerPortMetaData object and various other parameters are stored with it, with a call to buildWSDLPath and setupWsddPort to add to the population. Methods and security are added before an endpoint reference (EPR) is generated and added to the endpoints collection. A call to the JavaBeanDispatcher sets the class name for this port to relate to the servlet implementation for it, before the next iteration of the web services. An MBean is then set up for the endpoints collection.

Next, client module metadata is extracted from the original metadata and any web services client configuration from WEB-INF/webservicesclient.xml is extracted using the LoadStrategy reference as before, which is then bound using a call to bindJ2EE13ModuleServiceRefs followed by a call to bindBindingsAndExtensions with the IBM-specific XMI files as parameters. The structure of the handling for WAR metadata creation is very similar to that for EJB metadata creation and adjustment, as you would expect.

Web Services Service Interface Methods

There are Web Services Service interface methods that are either static or simple methods, often accessors and mutators, and there are some methods that are key to the functions of web services deployment. I will concentrate on the methods that are important to JAX-RPC operation, but will briefly refer to others that are commonly used and may be visible in stack dumps.

Simple, Accessor, and Mutator Methods

The isClientWebServiceEnabled and isServerWebServiceEnabled methods merely get access to the metadata for the client entity and server module, respectively, and return whether there are any services or whether there is any service configuration.

CHAPTER 7 ■ WEB SERVICES   **207**

The getClientEngineConfig method gets the client entity metadata and returns its configuration, and the getServerEngineConfig method gets the server module metadata and the configuration from it along with a map of WSDL module data.

The getPMIServicesModule method returns the PMIServicesModule reference from the server module metadata and the getPMIEndointsModule method returns the PMIEndPointsModule reference from the server module metadata, both of which are used by the performance metrics facilities inside WAS.

The bindServiceRef Method

The bindServiceRef public method is important to web services client operation, and it only does anything if there are any service references in the list that is passed to it. In addition to the list of service references, it takes a J2EE name reference, a classloader reference, a LoadStrategy reference, module metadata, and an environment context. It first tries to extract any client module metadata from that passed in, to create a ClientModuleMetaData reference, and if there isn't any it creates some and adds to it the LoadStrategy reference that gives access to constituents of the module and the classloader.

The component name is then extracted from the J2EE name and used to check if the client module is already bound. If the component is not already bound, the component module metadata reference bindServiceRefs method is used to tie the service references and environment context to the module and the result is synchronized with the passed-in module metadata reference before a check is made to see if the module is a WAR file. If the module is a WAR file, the client module metadata reference bindBindingsAndExtensions call is used to tie together the component name, the IBM extension files WEB-INF/ibm-webservicesclient-bnd.xmi and WEB-INF/ibm-webservicesclient-ext.xmi, and the client module metadata reference. These XMI files that are generated by the IBM client tools for web services are important because they give information to the WAS runtime to improve the operation of the environment.

Loading Web Service References

The loadWebServicesXML, loadWebServicesBindingXML, loadWebServicesExtXML, and loadJavaWsdlMappingXML methods are used to load into the engine the XML for the web services. There is a lot of commonality in the implementation of each in the way the WSModels class provides the base functionality. The static loadWebServicesXML method uses the WSModels class getWebServices method to return a set of web services references for a given LoadStrategy reference that gives access to the constituents of a module and an XML file name, and the loadWebServicesBindingXML does the same but uses the WSModels getWSBinding method. Similarly, the loadWebServicesExtXML method uses the WSModels getWSExtension method and the loadJavaWsdlMappingXML method uses the WSModels loadFromFile method. So, what are we getting from the WSModels class? This delegates to a WSModelsLoader object that is created via static initialization and allows the WSModels class to offer static methods, but this mechanism also offers the advantage that the given loader can be overridden.

The WSModelsLoader class takes the LoadStrategy object and uses it to get access to the constituent parts of a module, so most of the methods read and return the XMI or XML file from the module, but pay particular attention to the WSModelsLoader getWebServices method used by the loadWebServicesXML method because it returns a WSDD file, i.e., the WSDD that maps the services down to the underlying Java class and methods.

The WSModelsLoader also returns the WebApp and EJBJar object references used elsewhere in the implementation of the web services support to access the underlying code that the developer has produced and shipped as part of their application. So, these static methods are important for callers because they support the key configuration that maps the web services runtime down to the deployed code.

Working with WSDDs

The static createWSDDGen methods are used to generate the reference to the WSDDGen generation object that leads to the WSDD. They use the mapping metadata (MappingMetaData) reference and a WSDL path or context, with various other parameters, to do their work. They are protected methods.

The static setupWsddPort method takes the WSDD port, the web service description binding, classloader, implementation class name, port component, and WSDDGen references as parameters, and gets the port component WSDL port, the local port, and the namespace URI, and adds these, the WSDDGen reference, the WSDL file (obtained from the WSDDGen reference), and the implementation class to the WSDDPort reference. If there are port component handlers, it creates a WSDDJAXRPCHandlerInfoChain and then enumerates the handlers to access the SOAP roles, SOAP headers, and handler classes to add to a list. It creates a QName headers array from the SOAP headers obtained in the enumeration and then a hash map of the initialization parameters for each handler.

Then, still inside the handler enumeration, the remaining parts of the setupWsddPort method create a WSDDJAXRPCHandlerInfo object to hold the handler class name, the classloader, the headers, and the handler map, and then relate these to infrastructure handler maps before adding this to the handler list and the list to the WSDDJAXRPCHandlerInfoChain object. The thread context and classloader are then set before returning. Essentially, this method relates the WSDD and implementation to the underlying JAX-RPC handler infrastructure.

This concludes our look at the WSServerImpl class key methods that support the JSR109 JAX-RPC web services functionality inside WAS, but I haven't really explained what goes on at a high level to route and provide web services. Essentially, when an application is deployed to WAS, notifications go out via the interfaces registered with the Application Manager and Meta Data Services, and the EJB-JAR and WAR files are decomposed and "adjusted." A WebApp object is used to represent the call with a URL mapping to an underlying servlet or session bean implementation for the web service, with a generated service bean implementation handling the tie in to the web services engine infrastructure within WAS.

The WSChannelManager Class

One of the key requirements of a web services infrastructure is support for HTTP communications. The Channel Framework Service underpinning WAS provides TCP, SSL, and HTTP support for the core containers and subsystems, and is key to the WSServerImpl functionality in coordinating channels, chains, links, and pooling for inbound and outbound communications.

WSChannelManager Creation

The WSChannelManager class is a singleton with a private constructor, so an object gets created when its static getInstance method is called to return a reference. The private constructor checks to see what Web Services Service type is running, and then creates references to the factory object for TCP channel creation. The WSTCPChannelFactory class is used to create the factory object, except when used with the Web Services System Service, in which case the ZAioTCPChannelFactory class is used to create the factory object. This Web Services System Service adds a loadConfiguration method to the methods exposed by the Web Services Service interface. The private constructor then gets a reference to a ConfigSSLProvider singleton object reference that handles JSSE and certificate low-level handling for SSL support.

WSChannelManager Methods

Many of the methods within the class are simply getter and setter wrappers for references for the WS Byte Buffer Pool Manager and Channel Framework Service interfaces, but there are important methods that are essential for normal web services operation.

The createChannel Method

The createChannel method is important for setting up the communications channels for the JAX-RPC handling. It checks for the type of channel that it is being requested to create, and whether SSL is required, and either creates a factory object to handle the creation or calls the Channel Framework Service addChannel method directly for simple cases. If the requested channel type is httpclient-ssl-outbound and SSL properties have been supplied, either the WSSSLChannelFactory or SSLChannelFactory class is used to create the channel, depending on the environment it is running in, and any SSL alias is applied to the channel name.

If a call to the Channel Framework Service reference doesn't find that a channel of the requested type, including the alias if required, already exists, a check is made on the requested channel type:

- If the requested channel type is httpclient-http-outbound, the HttpOutbound ChannelFactory class is loaded and the Channel Framework Service addChannel method is called with the target type name and the factory object reference passed as parameters to create that channel.

- If the requested channel type is httpclient-ssl-outbound and the SSL channel factory reference chosen earlier exists, then the Channel Framework Service addChannel method is called with the channel type and any requested alias passed as parameters along with the SSL channel factory reference chosen earlier to create the channel.

- If the requested channel type is httpclient-tcp-outbound, an attempt is made to load an existing TCP channel factory reference, and if this fails, the TCPChannelFactory class is used and passed as a reference to the Channel Framework Service addChannel method along with the httpclient-tcp-outbound type parameter. This method really chooses the factory method appropriate for the channel and delegates to the addChannel Channel Framework Service mechanism.

The createChannelChain Method

The createChannelChain method is a wrapper for a number of calls to the createChannel method that is used to combine the channels in a layered manner to create a chain that is registered with the Channel Framework Service. It takes the channel chain name, an indicator of whether SSL is required, and SSL properties as parameters. It then checks to see if the target channel chain name exists with the Channel Framework Service, and if not it sets about creating the chain.

So, if SSL is required it creates the following in order:

1. An `httpclient-tcp-outbound` channel for the given SSL properties using the `createChannel` method

2. An `httpclient-ssl-outbound` channel for the given SSL properties that returns an SSL channel name

3. An `httpclient-http-outbound` channel for the given SSL properties

A String array is then set up containing `httpclient-http-outbound`, the returned channel name, and the `httpclient-tcp-outbound` chain and this is passed to the Channel Framework Service `addChain` method to register the originally passed-in channel chain name as a `FlowType.OUTBOUND` chain.

If SSL isn't required, the `httpclient-tcp-outbound` and `httpclient-http-outbound` channels are created using the `createChannel` method and a standard `HTTP_CHAIN_ARRAY` `FlowType.OUTBOUND` chain is passed to the Channel Framework Service `addChain` method to create the chain.

From this you can see how protocol handling in WAS using the Channel Framework Service is based on chains, which are layered communications built upon channels that handle different levels of the communication in an OSI standard–like manner.

Target Cluster Member Identification Methods

The next group of methods in this class handles identification of the target cluster member to route the service call to for handling. These methods can be complex because they use current loading metrics and endpoint data to help make decisions. External routing facilities, such as the On Demand Router component of WebSphere Virtual Enterprise, make use of these methods to make their routing decisions.

The clusterIdenFromEPR Method

The `clusterIdenFromEPR` method returns the identity of an appropriate cluster instance to route a request to based on the service EPR as part of the WS-Addressing standard support. It first loads a `javax.xml.rpc.handler.MessageContext` class that is used to decompose the message and then loads a Unified Clustering Framework (UCF) class from the IBM WS-Addressing handling that handles the routing itself. The method uses this latter class to get access to the HA cluster member ID for the given destination EPR and then calls `invoke` on it. If an ID isn't returned, an attempt to invoke a Workload Manager (WLM) cluster ID member for the message is made, then if this fails an attempt is made to get a fragile cluster member ID and call its `invoke` method, and then the same is repeated for the virtual host ID method.

The clusterIdenFromDWLMClient Method

The `clusterIdenFromDWLMClient` method is conceptually similar to the previous method, taking a `WSAddress` reference address to connect and an endpoint criteria reference, but is of interest because of the checks it performs. It loads a `DWLMClientFactory` reference and gets a Dynamic Workload Manager (DWLM) client reference. The client is used to perform session rebalancing based on workload, and is one of the mechanisms used by WebSphere XD/WebSphere Virtual Enterprise On Demand Router to move loads from overloaded instances to newly created instances. If you want to write your own service load balancer, the clusterIdenFromDWLMClient method is important.

In the method, the getRequestMapper and createRequestFlowInfo methods are called on the DWLM client reference to get a RequestMapper reference, and then the isEnabled method on the RequestMapper is called, and if the RequestMapper is not enabled a null ID is returned. If the RequestMapper is enabled, its mapRequest method is accessed to obtain a remote method reference (using the class getMethod call) and the previously created RequestFlowInfo reference is obtained and is used to get the cluster name, virtual hostname, and the cell name references for the request flow (actually, references to the getters/accessors for them are saved).

The WSAddress reference is then interrogated to get the hostname, port, schema (i.e., HTTP or HTTPS), and URI path and this and the RequestFlowInfo reference are passed to the RequestMapper mapRequest method, which is then invoked. The RequestInfo reference is then used to get the mapped cluster name and virtual hostname and these are used to update the endpoint criteria reference. The mapped cell name is also saved for later use. A cluster IdentityMapping reference is then used with the mapped cell name and the cluster name to get the cluster identity that this method then returns. This is how some of the web service routing is performed inside WAS.

The identityToCFEndPoint Method

The identityToCFEndPoint method is again used for request routing. It takes a given ID, endpoint criteria, and a context map. This uses the following pair of underlying helper classes that are part of the com.ibm.ws.wlm.jar plugin that handles high availability and clustering:

- ChannelSelectionAdapterImpl: Handles selection through a number of variations of its select method

- ChannelSelectionCriteria: Is a key parameter for these methods. The class has attributes used to select an appropriate channel, such as availability of the service, state and affinity requirements, etc.

The endpoint criteria are examined to see if session affinity must be maintained, and then matching takes place to identify a cluster target for receipt of the call. This matching compares the endpoint criteria with the attributes of that target in terms of endpoints, endpoint versions, etc. using a lower-level SelectionService class and a set of underlying rules that are used to control comparison of the endpoint attributes with the criteria. The results are cached for later use in a map. The identityToCFEndPoint method uses these classes but also checks properties such as timeouts before returning a target identity.

Connection Lookup Methods

The following methods are used to select the appropriate connection to use for a given WSAddress reference.

The getVCFactory Method

The getVCFactory method takes a WSAddress reference for the address to connect to and returns a VirtualConnectionFactory object reference for creation of virtual connections.

It checks the transport configuration for the given address properties (i.e., whether SSL is required) and the endpoint, and then calls the createChannelChain method to create the target transport chain. The Channel Framework Service is then used to return an outbound virtual connection factory (VirtualConnectionFactory) reference for the given transport chain. If this fails, a web services fault is thrown.

The getWSOutboundConnection Method

The getWSOutboundConnection method takes a transport chain, virtual connection factory, and WSAddress reference for the address to connect to as parameters, so it is paired with the getVCFactory method. This uses the virtual connection factory reference createConnection method to create the OutboundVirtualConnection reference that is used to create a WSOutboundConnection reference that is returned, by creating an HttpOutboundChannelConnection or an HttpsOutboundChannelConnection for the given outbound virtual connection, WSAddress reference, and transport chain. This is how web service client connections are set up.

The WebServicesServlet Class

This is one of the classes at the core of the WAS web services support because it interfaces to the core web services engine and extends the WebServicesServicesBase class that itself is a true servlet that extends HttpServlet. It implements the com.ibm.ws.webservices.engine. MessageContext.OneWayListener interface, where the OneWayListener is an inner class of the MessageContext class that implements that oneWay method with a MessageContext reference parameter. As for any other servlet, the key entry point to the classes being considered is the service method, although in this case the simple forwarding of requests to doGet and doPut methods isn't used and complex code decides how a request should be handled.

The WebServicesServletBase Class

The WebServicesServletBase class implements the methods expected of an HttpServlet, but adds some key ones of its own. It holds a reference to a ServerEngine, but when queried for a reference to the engine, it returns a typecast reference to itself or a reference to a passed-in servlet reference. Its service method simply handles thread safety and calls the service method on its parent HttpServlet class. Other methods handle extracting ports, server names, and paths from requests for use by child classes.

The MessageContext Class

The MessageContext class takes a WebServicesEngine reference in its constructor and handles schema mappings, SOAP versions, encodings, attachments, etc. On startup it gets the currently set options from the web services engine, sets the default SOAP version (1.2 by default) and related constants, and either creates a specific directory for attachments or uses the system temp directory.

It has methods to manage messages, and related attachments, thread contexts, type mappings, ports, sessions, and operations. To handle the operations, it has to drill into the SOAP envelope (SOAPEnvelope) reference of the passed in message and manage the body, request, response, encodings, SOAP headers, and faults. Many of the properties passed to the web services engine for WAS are handled by the setProperty method of this class.

Security for web service interactions (i.e., processing of the username and password) is handled here too using properties, i.e., the javax.xml.rpc.security.auth.username and javax.xml.rpc.security.auth.password properties. Some operations internally also break down the WSDL to get the QName and port (SOAPPort) information. The SOAPEnvelope Message class provides a Java wrapper for the SOAP document, and the native message is handled by the Message class.

The QName Class

The QName class is a standard Javax XML namespace class that represents the relationship between a namespace URI, its local part, and its prefix.

The Message Class

The Message class extends the IBMSOAPMessage class and implements the Serializable interface marker to support persistence. It merely wraps the message content and provides access to its parts, properties, attachments, and key constituents. It also provides access to the underlying output stream and XML.

The SOAPEnvelope Class

The SOAPEnvelope class, like the Message class, wraps the SOAP content of the message and provides access to the headers, body, attachments, and the individual XML elements.

The WebServicesEngine Class

The WebServicesEngine class handles sessions, options, and other configuration. Its most important method is the invoke method, which takes a MessageContext reference as a parameter. Ultimately, classes called PivotHandlers wrap the sending mechanisms for HTTP and JMS, and these are controlled by this class and used by this method. The method sets the message context for the thread to that passed in, nulls the response in the message context, sets the fault property to null, and gets access to the handler by calling its getMessageFlow method for the message context. The invoke method initializes the handler, clears some handler-related properties for the message context, and calls its invoke method passing the message context reference, i.e. the invoke method calls form a chain from one object to a more fine-grained object until it is handled.

The generateWSDL method works in a similar way but delegates to the handler generateWSDL method. The getMessageFlow method that returns the handler for the message context calls the createMessageFlow method to do its work, and this is provided by the ServerEngine class. Key to the whole processing is the getGlobalHandler method, which returns a SimpleTargetedChain object reference that has been configured for the engine that is the default for processing messages, and it is this engine reference that will handle most responses.

The ServerEngine Class

The ServerEngine class extends the WebServicesEngine class. Most of its methods handle configuration. The createMessageFlow method returns a handler that gets the message, envelope, and port. The handler is created dynamically using a WrapperHandler class, and this is passed to the PivotHandlerWrapper.factory method to be tied to the global handler and the transport.

The PivotHandlerWrapper Class

The PivotHandlerWrapper class that extends the BasicHandler class is used by the invoke method of the engines, and wraps requests and responses. In its invoke method it handles calling request and response handlers in handler chains, and handles any faults generated by replacing the SOAP Envelope body in the response through lower-level methods. There are calls to handlers to be invoked before the message is processed and afterward, but the core is the PivotHandler invoke method.

When the PivotHandlerWrapper class factory method is first called, the getGlobalHandler method is used to return the default SimpleTargetedChain class that is configured for the engine, so this is in the handler chain for all calls and will be used for most, but it merely delegates back to the wrapper class. So, what handles the messages? The JAXRPCHandler class exposes the invoke method so you might think that it eventually gets called for messages, but the handler chain hierarchy ends with the BasicHandler and its invoke method, although that is not the end of the story. This class reads a property, called com.ibm.ws.webservices.engine. PivotHandlerWrapper.ROOT_HANDLER_CHAIN, which declares the root handler. For now, we will look at some other important handler types in the chain that are referred to elsewhere.

The SimpleTargetedChain Class

The SimpleTargetedChain class extends the PivotHandlerWrapper class so that it can easily be typecast to it to be added to the handler chain. It has accessors and mutators to manage the handler chains for requests, responses, and general handling. The PivotHandlerWrapper class does most of the work of handling the chain and default configuration for the engine.

The JAXRPCHandler Class

The JAXRPCHandler class extends the SimpleTargetedChain class, which is why it can be treated the same. Again the key method is the invoke method. The class works in terms of actors (think of schemas) and bindings, and manages XML QNames and the handler chains.

The invoke method

The invoke method uses an underlying GreenDispatcher class dispatcher if the pivot handler is of that type, where it sets up the dispatcher environment, invokes the parent SimpleTargetedChain class invoke method, and then tidies up the dispatcher environment. If the pivot handler is not a GreenDispatcher derivative, it simply delegates to the parent class invoke method.

The JMSListenerMDB Class

The JMSListenerMDB class, on the ejbCreate method call, gets access to the ServerEngine for web services handling (described earlier) and then waits for its onMessage method to be called as for any MDB. In onMessage, it first checks to see if the message has transactions enabled and, if so, it enables the appropriate transaction handling. The message ID, correlation ID, reply to queue, and any specific properties of the message are extracted.

The End Point Manager bean may be notified for the target service. The target port for the engine is then related to the target service, and the message type determined so the appropriate message class can be applied to it. A Message class object is created for ByteMessage and TextMessage class messages, and this class is passed to the engine via the setRequestMessage call, which is followed by a call to the setTransportName and setProperty methods to set the message type as JMS.

Eventually, the serverEngine is invoked to handle the message, and the response is returned to any reply to queue, which may result in a lookup of the WebServicesReplyQCF queue connection factory and ultimately a writing of the response to the outbound message in the appropriate format. The rest of this class is essentially the same in concept to the WebServicesServlet in function, which you will see shortly.

The HTTPSender Class

The HTTPSender class extends the BasicHandler class and, as such, has an invoke method that is called as part of the handler chain in the WebServicesServlet.

The invoke method

The invoke method first gets access to the outbound connection cache and a WSChannelManager reference, and gets any properties for WS-Addressing redirection. It then gets the endpoint address URL from the message context and any endpoint criteria, and from the EPR uses the channel manager to get the identity of the target cluster member.

If the identity is null the invoke method gets a proxy address, gets the connecting address of the target URL from the WSAddress class, and checks to see what runtime engine should process the message. If this is the first time through and the IN_PROCESS_ENABLED variable has not been set by the enableinprocessconnections property, the method accesses the Web Container Service to first get its properties, and this property in particular to set the variable. The cluster member identity is checked for the WLM EPR using the WSChannelManager clusterIdentFromDWLMClient method along with checks of other properties before the session cookie is read for SSLJSESSIONID or JSESSIONID to set up session IDs and selection rules for them.

The WSChannelManager identityToCFEndPoint method is then called to get the endpoint, and the URL, hostname, port, and file are extracted to generate the target connection address using the WSAddress class, and the endpoint is set on this. The request message context (MessageContext) and its content is then used to create a Message class reference, an OutboundOutputStream object is created for the request content type, and the message is written to the stream using the writeto method.

The outbound virtual connection is then read from the outbound connection cache using the findGroupAndGetConnection method, passing the connecting address as a parameter. The connect method is called on this outbound virtual connection reference followed by the sendSOAPRequestAsync method with the outbound output stream reference, if the redirectFlag or asyncResponse flag is set, or the sendSOAPRequest otherwise. If an error occurs a WebServicesFault is thrown. SocketException and SocketTimeoutException handlers watch for the method success. If the sendSOAPRequest method was used, the receiveSOAPResponse method of the virtual connection is used to watch for a response and any handling is performed, including disconnecting the connection and returning it to the cache.

Note that in the handling of the message, any SSL configuration required is handled, redirections are performed, and the spnegoused and WWW-Authenticate properties are checked to see what security, if any, is required. Before exiting, the outbound output stream is reset. The security configuration for SSL uses a JSSEHelper class. Status codes, cookies, authentication, and headers are all handled using methods in this class.

The JMSSender Class

The JMSSender class is conceptually similar to the HTTPSender class in that it extends the BasicHandler, but its invoke method is much simpler. It checks to see that the message is for JMS and then calls invoke on either a JMSSenderHelperIBM class for MQFAP format messages (i.e., the protocol underlying the Service Integration Bus Messaging Engine or WebSphere MQ) or a JMSSenderHelperSPEC class for some other JMS provider. These helper classes get the connection, map the URL, access the message object, and then send the message to the target destination before closing the connection. Timeouts and properties are handled in the helper classes.

Now that we have covered the groundwork of what underpins the web services servlet, we can look at how it operates.

WebServicesServlet Operation

The WebServicesServlet class adds MBean handling to the base class and WSDL request processing, and the doGet method handles returning responses to requests for the WSDL for particular servlet paths. Tracing is also handled in this class. The key functionality is in the doPost method.

The doPost Method

The doPost method returns servlet exceptions if errors occur and in most ways behaves as a typical, but complex, servlet. A MessageContext reference is created using an internal method called createMessageContext that takes a reference to the WebServicesEngine, the request, and the response and sets properties based on the combination of the parameters. It extracts the request URL and sets this and the security provider reference on the message context as properties. It reads the input stream, content type, and Content-Location header and uses this to create a new Message reference that is then passed to the MessageContext reference using the setRequestMessage mutator method. It sets an action and session information in the MessageContext reference and calls invoke on the WebServicesEngine reference passing that MessageContext reference.

When this call completes, the response is extracted from the MessageContext reference using the getResponseMessage accessor method and then any fault handling is performed. If the fault is a 401 message, the WWW-Authenticate header is set and the response on the message context may be updated. Before returning the message context target endpoint address is checked to see if it starts with jms (in which case a JMS redirect is needed), and then it is checked to see if it is one way only or has a WS-Addressing NoneURI (in which case no response is sent).

If a JMS redirect is needed, the sendJMSResponse method is called, and if it is not needed, then the encoding is handled and response headers are set before calling the sendResponse with a Message reference and response message to return the response to the calling JAX-RPC web services client.

The oneWay Method

If the oneWay method is called, the response content-length is set to 0, and a 202 status is set if the response should be redirected.

The sendResponse Method

The sendResponse method handles the content length and gets the message context from the response message. It then gets access to the client engine configuration, as it needs this to create the appropriate QName for the given transport. The SimpleTargetedChain class is used to handle the response and, from it, an HTTPSender class reference is created and is passed the message context reference passed as a component of the Message reference. The Message reference writeTo method is used to write the response output stream to the caller using the underlying HTTPSender and SimpleTargetedChain.

The sendJMSResponse Method

The sendJMSResponse method takes the message context reference as a parameter. Again, it accesses the client engine configuration, which it uses to create a QName for a SimpleTargetedChain but this time to support JMS rather than HTTP. A JMSSender class is obtained from the SimpleTargetedChain reference, the URL is extracted from the message context, and the invoke call is made on the JMS sender to pass the message context.

JAX-RPC Support Summary

From the preceding discussion, you can see that JAX-RPC web services ultimately map down to a call to a servlet, albeit one that uses an underlying web services engine and the SimpleTargetedChain invoke method to process the message content. You have also seen how this processing supports WSDLs and the use of different handlers. The HTTPSender and JMSSender classes (with helpers) are the handlers at the base of the chain that do the work in the default case of handling messages in their invoke method for HTTP/HTTPS and JMS services, respectively.

JAX-WS Support, Axis2, and the Web Services Feature Pack

JAX-RPC was the original standardized web services support implemented by J2EE application servers, but it had a number of problems. One of the key problems was that the standard and its implementation, outlined in the Java Community Process JSR-109 specification, lent themselves to solutions with inherent performance problems largely caused by excessive serialization and deserialization between XML and the Java object counterparts. Thus, the JAX-WS standard was produced for Java EE 5. However, many application server vendors at the J2EE 1.4 standard level could see the benefits of JAX-WS support, due to its increased performance, and thus found ways of delivering it without the rest of Java EE 5.

IBM provided the Web Services Feature Pack for WAS 6.1 as a way of delivering a JAX-WS implementation on a J2EE 1.4 code base and this was built on a wrapper around the Axis2 engine. The Web Services Feature Pack code has been enhanced and extended for the WAS 7 engine, but many of the package names and much of the implementation are unchanged—which makes sense because the Web Services Feature Pack has been well proven in production environments in this earlier release.

New wrapper functionality, in the form of WS-Policy support, has also been provided but we will not examine this here because it doesn't form part of the core engine functionality. So, in this section we will examine the JAX-WS support wrapper integration with the underlying

Axis2 engine, but not the Axis2 engine itself, as this is documented by the Apache community. Most of the WAS code handles responding to deployments and manipulating the deployed object metadata to change the Axis2 configuration to support the application changes.

Axis2 in a Nutshell

Axis2 was introduced by the Apache Foundation open source community to replace the Axis1 implementation, which had a number of issues, mainly related to performance due to the standards on which it was built. Axis1 was aimed at the JSR109 JAX-RPC standard, whereas Axis2 targets JAX-WS.

Axis2 is much faster because it is built on its own high-performance, lightweight, pull-based XML object model, called Apache Axiom, for message processing in a manner that supports extensibility. The engine makes use of StAX (Streaming API for XML) parsing to improve its performance over the previous Axis iteration. Extensions can be easily inserted into the engine for custom header processing and management, but Axis2 supports specific extensions to enable new web services standards through the use of plugin modules, such as that for Sandesha2 to provide WS-ReliableMessaging functionality, Kandula2 to support WS-Coordination and WS-AtomicTransaction, and Rampart to provide WS-Security functionality (although addition of a module does require a restart because it changes the control flow in the core engine).

Unlike Axis1 the new engine was designed from the ground up to support asynchronous web services through non-blocking clients and transports, and to support hot deployment. This latter feature allows IBM to more readily integrate Axis2 into the IBM WAS deployment model. All this comes with a low memory footprint and a transport-independent framework that is used to allow IBM to add middleware integration for JMS (JFAP) and MQ (MFAP).

Axis2 supports both web services client/consumer and web services server/producer processing. Each is handled in phases and each may be on different platforms or the same platform. A SOAP processor must handle two actions, the sending and receiving of SOAP messages, which makes use of the send and receive methods that implement the flows named the Out Pipe and In Pipe, respectively. Handlers intercept and process parts of a SOAP message as it passes through the flows. An Out Pipe flow ends with a Transport Sender that sends the message to the target endpoint when the client API is used. A SOAP message is received by a Transport Receiver at the target endpoint that reads the SOAP message and places it into the flow of the In Pipe, where the handlers process it and a Message Receiver consumes it. Complex message exchange patterns are constructed using combinations of the In Pipe and Out Pipe.

With client processing, the client sender creates a SOAP message via an appropriate client API (such as JAX-WS, although there are alternatives supported by Axis2), and handlers intercept the message to perform any necessary actions, such as encryption, before passing the message on to the sender-side transport mechanism for transmission. Transport Senders and the Out Pipe are key to client processing.

With server processing, a Transport Listener detects the messages and passes them on to the handlers that perform any actions, such as unencryption, before passing the message on to dispatchers to dispatch the message on to the target application code. A Transport Receiver takes the incoming message when it is first detected by the Transport Listener and parses the transport headers before creating a message context from the SOAP message, with the message context containing the SOAP message, the transport headers, and other metadata inside it. The message context passes along the In Pipe flow from the Transport Receiver. The Axis2 In Pipe executes against the data in the message context, so expect to see the message context flowing through the WASAxis2Service interface methods into the Axis2 engine. Transport Receivers and the In Pipe are key to the server processing. The inbound and outbound Axis2 client and server processing is shown in Figure 7-2.

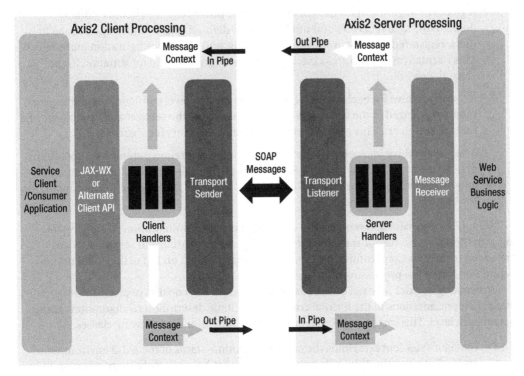

Figure 7-2. *Inbound and outbound Axis2 client and server processing*

The actions performed by Axis2, which are key to its extensibility, are broken down into phases. Each phase can have a number of handlers, some that are provided and some that can be added, which can be configured to execute in a particular order within that phase. The handlers come in the form of modules that can be plugged into the system, such as Sandesha2 for WS-ReliableMessaging. The following are the key phases:

- *Transport*: Transport-specific headers are processed and related data is added to the message context.

- *Pre-dispatch*: The message context is populated, ready for dispatching. Addressing headers of the SOAP message are processed and addressing handlers extract information to populate the message context.

- *Dispatch*: Routing and dispatch to the appropriate service and operation is handled.

- *User Defined*: Custom handlers execute.

- *Message Validation*: Checks are made to ensure that SOAP message processing has been properly executed.

- *Message Processing*: The SOAP message business logic is executed and as the last step of the phase the message receiver for the operation is executed.

Axis2 deployment artifacts consist of the following:

- A global configuration for the client and server processing that details globally defined message receivers and modules, user-defined phase names and related handlers, registered in and out transport channels, and global configuration parameters. This normally relates to an `axis2.xml` file. IBM represents the information in the `ibmaxis2.xml` file.

- A service archive for each service that contains service-level configuration parameters, modules engaged at the service level, operations inside the service, and service-specific message receivers. This normally relates to a `META-INF/services.xml` file.

- A module archive for each module with module configuration parameters, operations defined in the module, and the classes that implement the required module functionality. This normally relates to a `META-INF/module.xml` file. These provide the support for the handlers and extensions.

When Axis2 initializes, it requires the creation of an Axis Configuration reference, starting with the `axis2.xml` file for the global setup, and then the module and service archives are added to the Axis Configuration reference. Contexts are built on top of the configuration before SOAP message processing takes place.

Processing in Axis2 is based on an information model that consists of point-in-time dynamic representations in the form of contexts, and static description configuration information at each level. This can be seen in Figure 7-3 and consists of the following classes:

- `ConfigurationContext`: Holds the complete runtime status of the Axis2 environment and builds upon the `AxisConfiguration` object that holds all global configuration of transports, modules, parameters, and services.

- `ServiceGroupContext`: Holds the current usage state for a group of related services that can share information with the `AxisServiceGroup` class holding the deployment-time configuration information for the group.

- `ServiceContext`: Holds the usage information for multiple invocations of a single service and builds upon the `AxisService` class that contains the deployment configuration for the service and its operations.

- `OperationContext`: Holds the information about the current message-processing instance for that operation and builds upon the `AxisOperation` class that holds the deployment-time configuration for that operation.

- `MessageContext`: Holds all information about the message being currently executed and builds upon the `AxisMessage` class that contains the static configuration for that message, including the schema information that applies to it.

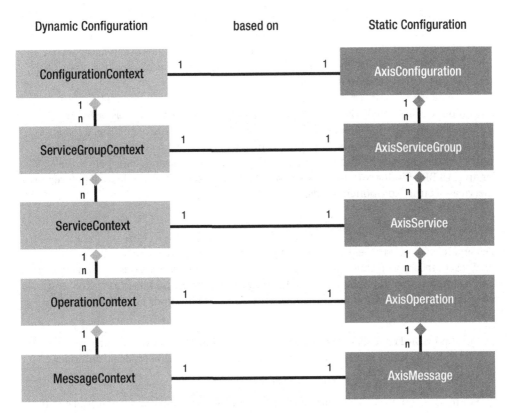

Figure 7-3. *Axis2 static and dynamic information model*

The key classes that you will see a lot of in the JAX-WS processing in WAS, in the integration between the WAS runtime environment and the Axis2 engine, are AxisConfiguration and ConfigurationContext, which are used to configure and control the environment, and MessageContext and AxisMessage, which relate to handling and handoff of a particular message. Thus, the WAS runtime deployment model controls the ConfigurationContext of the Axis2 engine and pushes it into the engine itself to control its operation, and the WAS runtime transports hand off the particular MessageContext for each service request. WAS maintains the ClientConfigurationContext itself, as this is not part of the Axis2 repository, but once pushed into the Axis2 engine, the ConfigurationContext is owned by it.

So, after that brief introduction to explain what the Axis2 engine does and how it works at a high level, let's look at how IBM has integrated it into WAS.

The com.ibm.wsfp.main.jar Plugin

This plugin provides much of the core JAX-WS web services functionality for WAS, but does this by integrating the Axis2 core engine. If you unzip it and examine the plugin.xml file, you get a picture of how it integrates with the rest of the runtime environment. The description in the plugin.xml file describes the component as the WebSphere Axis2 Integration Plugin, so, as the description suggests, it provides most of the functionality that takes the open source Axis2 library and integrates it as a subsystem into the WAS environment as a true part of the infrastructure, with all of the threading, resource, resilience, and memory qualities of service expected from the rest of the subsystems. Its `MANIFEST.MF` file lists `org.apache.axis2`, `com.ibm.jaxb.tools`, and `com.ibm.jaxws.tools` among its required bundles.

For the extension point `com.ibm.wsspi.extension.server-startup`, the Web Service Admin component is started. This has an implementation class of `com.ibm.ws.webservices.admin.component.WebServicesAdminComponentImpl` and a startup value of 6680, so it loads as part of the base server runtime just after the Cache Resource Manager component, and on zOS only after the Dynacache and Dynacache Object components, and loads before the CFS Binder and WS BBS Binder components are initialized. This component is loaded before the Web Services Security component loads.

The WebServicesAdminComponentImpl Class

The `WebServicesAdminComponentImpl` class implements the interfaces for the `WebServicesAdminComponent` and the `ConfigChangeListener`, and extends the `WsComponentImpl` class, so it supports the WebSphere Service Registry methods `initialize`, `start`, `stop`, and `destroy` that control the component life cycle. These lifecycle methods are implemented as follows:

- For the `initialize` call, the component implementation is registered with the WebSphere Service Registry as exposing the `WebServicesAdminComponent` interface.

- The `destroy` method unregisters this service.

- For the `start` method, if the process is a Deployment Manager or unmanaged stand-alone process, the Admin Service is accessed from the WebSphere Service Registry (`WsServiceRegistry`) and the component registers itself with it as supporting the configuration change listener interface. An Endpoint Central Manager runtime collaborator is then registered and activated as an MBean with the `EndPointCentralManager.xml` file controlling the configuration.

- The `stop` method does little but delegate to the parent implementation.

When the configuration changes, the `configChanged` method is called with a `ConfigRepositoryEvent` reference. The URI for each change is then checked to see if it applies to the cluster configuration in the `cluster.xml` file or deployment configuration in the `deployment.xml` file, and the application target cache entries are cleared for it. Thus, this component is a simple one that does nothing more than watch for configuration updates.

For the extension point `com.ibm.wsspi.extension.applicationserver-startup`, six components are started as part of the application server startup.

The JAX-WS Web Service component is first to start. It has a startup value of 5000, an implementation class of `com.ibm.ws.websvcs.component.WASAxis2ComponentImpl`, and provides the WAS Axis2 Service interface via the WAS runtime `WsServiceRegistry`. This again starts after the Dynacache, Dynacache Object, and Dynacache Servlet components, but at the same value as the JAX-RPC Web Service component and the `WSServerImpl` class previously outlined, showing the pairing of the two web services implementations.

The WASAxis2ComponentImpl Class

The operations relating the WAS server runtime event processing and the building and configuration of the underlying Axis2 engine are handled by the WASAxis2ComponentImpl class. This class extends the WsComponentImpl class and implements the MetaDataListener, Constants, WASAxis2Service, and DeployedObjectListener interfaces. It builds the ConfigurationContext used to control the Axis2 engine for a given set of service groups and services, and then the ConfigurationContext is maintained inside the engine. For client access to the engine, the component also maintains a store of ClientConfigurationContext references.

The key to understanding how the component works is to understand a few classes. For client communications, the WSChannelManager, described previously, sets up the appropriate underlying communications into and out of WAS to support the JAX-WS web services. The web services runtime not only allows for an asynchronous programming model but also for using WS-Addressing and for pushing asynchrony onto the wire. In those instances, the AsyncResponseServlet acts as the conduit or transport between the WAS integration component and the Axis2 engine when correlating inbound asynchronous responses to a client running in the WAS server process, with other transports used for other HTTP and JMS integration. WAS will store its configuration information for the client in the ClientConfigurationContext that conveys the deployment information.

The underlying web services handling is performed by Axis2, which supports dynamic deployment. When running on a server, changes to the deployment or management environment are notified through the MetaDataListener and DeployedObjectListener interfaces, and this results in the Axis2 engine configuration being built up and the Axis2 engine initialized using the ConfigurationContext. Arrays of client and server plugins and server and client module files are also maintained by the WAS Axis2 integration component as a means of providing the appropriate Axis2 configuration. Much of the code in the component handles the metadata events that arise from deployment, extract information from deployment object modules, or manage client configuration contexts. The call to load the Axis2 configuration context for an application is on the external public interface, so it comes from outside.

The ConfigurationContext is an Axis2 artifact that holds both static and dynamic configuration data used to start an instance of Axis2 to host web services for an application and at runtime is like an in-memory database, so its usage as part of the WASAxis2Integration component is to be expected, along with its associated AxisConfiguration object it keeps inside it to hold metadata such as Axis2-based deployment descriptors (i.e., axis2.xml, module.xml, services.xml).

Creation and Destruction of the WASAxis2ComponentImpl Component

To understand how the WASAxis2ComponentImpl component works to support its role as the handler for the WAS Axis2 integration, you must first see how it is installed; so, because it is a subclass of WsComponentImpl, you need to look at the initialize and start methods. Similarly, removal of the integration component is handled via calls to the stop and destroy methods.

- When the initialize method is called, the component checks it isn't running in a zOS control region, and then registers itself as supporting the WASAxis2Service interface in the WebSphere Service Registry.

- When the destroy method is called, the component unregisters itself in the WebSphere Service Registry.

- When the start method is called, a WASAxis2MetaDataImpl is registered with the Meta Data Service, the reference of which is obtained from the WebSphere Service Registry, and then the component registers itself with the Meta Data Service. Next, a new WebCollaborator is registered with the Web Container Service and a new EJBCollaborator is registered with the EJB Container Service. Next, new WASAxis2ExtensionFactory and AsyncServletExtensionFactory objects are created and registered as extension factories with the web container. The WASAnnotationCollector then gets annotation adapters registered and WSInjectionMetaDataListener and WSInvocationListenerFactory objects are registered with the InjectionEngineAccessor and InvocationListenerRegistry. The component then registers itself with the Application Manager Service with its reference obtained from the WebSphere Service Registry.

- When the stop method is called, the parent implementation is delegated to in order to tidy up.

The MetaDataListener Interface

As you have seen previously, much of the work of the containers is handled dynamically as the result of a call from some other service. With web services, which primarily make use of the web container, the same is true even though it isn't exactly a container environment. The key interfaces for this dynamic behavior are the DeployedObjectListener interface and the MetaDataListener interface. External control is provided via support for the WASAxis2Service interface. This section examines each of these in turn and how the component handles them. Much of what you'll see in the early parts of this section via the MetaDataListener pertain to the client side of JAX-WS handling, and much of the later part of the chapter relates to server-side JAX-WS handling, although the Axis2 engine handles both so there is some overlap.

The MetaDataListener interface description is in the com.ibm.ws.runtime.metadata package. It contains two methods, metaDataCreated and metaDataDestroyed, both of which take a metadataevent parameter. This interface is registered with the Meta Data Service, as you saw during the initialize method. The component also registered a WASAxis2MetaDataImpl class with the service to also receive the event notifications. It is when the WASAxis2ComponentImpl implementation of the listener methods is called that some of the magic happens.

The metaDataCreated Method

When the metaDataCreated notification is received, the first operation is a call to the initComponent private method that gets the environment running. A list of applications being handled by the WAS JAX-WS Axis2 combination is maintained in a set called applicationsProcessed, and this is handled in this method. The metadata event reference passed to the method is used to get access to an EAR file reference, if there is one. If there is an EAR file reference and there are one or more EJB JAR files within it, and if the application has not been processed before and added to the applicationsProcessed collection, a router module map is initialized using the metadata event via a call to initializeRouterModuleMap and the EAR file name is added to the applicationsProcessed collection maintained by the component.

A check is then made as to whether the metadata relates to a module and if that module is a WAR file. If so, the module information and the file name WEB-INF/ibm-webservicesclient-bnd.xmi are passed to the loadClientURLInfo method of the WASAxis2ClientImpl class to get a map of URL to service information. A ClientMetaData reference is then created from the passed in

MetaDataEvent reference and the URL information is set in it via its setClientURLInfo before the internal setClientModuleMetaData call that is part of the WASAxis2Service interface is used to relate this to the module metadata from the original event.

Following the WAR file handling, an attempt is made to extract an EJB JAR (EJBJar) module name. If there is one, an EJBJar file reference is extracted from the EAR file and passed to the Axis2Utils scanModule method, which returns a Boolean. For all other modules, the Axis2Utils scanModule method is called directly. If the Axis2Utils scanModule method was used and returned a true, the internal moduleMetaDataCreated method is called and the metadata event reference is passed to it.

If the original metadata event reference referred to a component, the module is again extracted and checked to see if it related to an EJB JAR file. If so, the module information and the file name WEB-INF/ibm-webservicesclient-bnd.xmi are passed to the loadClientURLInfo method of the WASAxis2ClientImpl class to get a map of URL to service information. A ClientMetaData reference is then created from the passed-in MetaDataEvent reference and the URL information is set in it via its setClientURLInfo method before the internal setClientComponentMetaData call that is part of the WASAxis2Service interface is used to relate this to the module metadata from the original event.

Pay attention to the fact that this implementation for EJB JAR file handling differs from that for WAR file handling in that the setClientComponentMetaData call is used rather than the setClientModuleMetaData call. For all component metadata notification events, the Axis2Utils scanModule method is called, and if it is successful, the internal completeClientComponentMetaData method is called and passed the original metadata event. This is all part of the JAX-WS client-handling functionality.

The metaDataListener interface metaDataCreated method, called above when new metadata is created on a deployment, calls a number of lower-level methods to do its work, so let's look at each in turn.

The initComponent Method

In the initComponent method, much of the key configuration of the core Axis2 engine and its modules is performed. This method is called when the metaDataCreated method is called through the listener registered with the Meta Data Service, so it is only if a web service is deployed that the Axis2 environment is initialized. As expected, the Axis2 initialization should only run once so the functionality of the method is embedded within an if statement that only runs if the engine isn't already initialized. The first operation creates an Axis2ServiceConfigPluginManager object and calls its discoverAxis2ServiceConfigPlugins method passing a true value.

The setManagedRuntime Method

The next step in the process is to integrate the underlying WAS communications through a call into the WSChannelManager (previously described) using the setManagedRuntime method, again passing a true value. Remember that Axis2 allows the addition of new transports to the core, so this is the first step of handling that integration. A ClientConfigurationContextStore reference is created to hold the client configuration for the integration mechanism for the response maps for the asynchronous response servlet. The Axis2 SVN information is then written out to debugging logs if debugging is enabled to allow the underlying Axis2 version to be determined.

The listChannelTransports Method

The listChannelTransports method is called next, which uses the Transport Map Service to get the HTTP and HTTPS virtual host to ports mappings and pass each to the AsyncResponseServlet in the setHttpHostandPorts and setHttpsHostandPorts calls. A number of factory classes are then created and registered with the FactoryRegistry via the setFactory call:

- ClassFinderFactory
- ResourceFinderFactory
- EndPointDispatcherFactory
- WSServiceInstanceFactory
- HandlerPreInvokerFactoryImpl
- HandlerPostInvokerFactoryImpl
- WSClientConfigurationFactory (which is registered with the MetadataFactoryRegistry)
- ExecutorFactory
- WSEndpointLifecycleManagerFactory
- WASWSDLReaderConfigurartor
- WSHandlerLifecycleManagerFactory

These factory classes are key to the nature of Axis2 in that it is designed for dynamic deployment. Thus, they must have access to factory objects to create the necessary support for a deployed web service at runtime whenever a service is deployed. To do this, the factories must exist to allow endpoints, classes, resources, and handlers to be created dynamically with the appropriate WSDL, client configuration, and application executable code support, which is all managed in accord with the standard life cycles.

Some of the factory classes can be found as part of the utils package for the component. Pay particular attention to the WASAxis2Executor class, which implements the Executor interface, that is the resultant class handled by the ExecutorFactory class and that runs the thread to handle the code deployed in the service. Once the factory classes are registered, the method returns to the caller, in this case the metaDataCreated method.

The initializeRouterModuleMap Method

The initializeRouterModuleMap method builds a map of EJB JAR files to the router modules for the application. It takes a MetaDataEvent reference as a parameter and, from this, extracts an EAR file reference, a module metadata reference, and an application metadata reference. It creates a WSApplicationMetaDataHolder reference and then iterates the EJB JAR files in the EAR file, creates a WSBinding reference for the EJB JAR file using the loadWSBinding call with the ibm-webservices-bnd.xmi file as an additional parameter to look for, accesses a router module for each WSBinding reference, and adds it to the WSApplicationMetaDataHolder reference using the addRouterModuleToEJBJarMapping call with the router module name as a key. Thus, one or more router module mappings is added to the application metadata holder reference for each EJB module.

The holder reference is then added to an application metadata slot for the application metadata reference. The loadWSBinding call uses the WSModels support referred to previously to access the constituents of a particular module.

The Axis2Utils.scanModule Method

The Axis2Utils.scanModule method indicates to the caller whether a module is to be scanned for annotations and performs different handling depending on the value of a server scan policy, which can emulate the policy of the WAS 6.1 Web Services Feature Pack or can take on new WAS 7 policies. It only runs its scans if the WASAxis2ComponentImpl is running, i.e., if the WAS Axis2 Service has been started. It accesses the manifest of the module and checks to see if it is a WAR file, an application client file, or an EJB JAR file and returns the required specification support to identify if JAX-WS should be supported, i.e., Servlet 2.5 for a WAR file, EJB 3.0 for an EJB JAR File, or Java EE 5.0 for an application client file.

If the file is not for a specification related to Java EE 5.0 and the UseWSFEP61ScanPolicy is set to true in the MANIFEST.MF file for the module, it will still be scanned for annotations. Generally, the Axis2Utils class is used to set up configuration, path, and classpath information, and return the link implementation file for a given service implementation for routing purposes.

The setClientComponentMetaData Method

The setClientComponentMetaData method called from the metaDataCreated method is simple. An internal reference to a WASAxis2MetaDataImpl object, which was registered with the Meta Data Service when the component start method was called, is merely passed references to the client metadata and component metadata references that were passed to this method, so the WASAxis2MetaDataImpl class performs the handling of these references.

The setClientModuleMetaData Method

The setClientModuleMetaData method is similar to the setClientComponentMetaData method in merely passing its references on to the WASAxis2MetaDataImpl object for handling.

The completeClientComponentMetaData Method

The completeClientComponentMetaData method is a little more complex in its operation. This method extracts the module file, component metadata, and module metadata from the passed-in metadata event reference. If the module is an EJB JAR file, the method uses the WASAxis2MetaDataImpl object reference to extract the client metadata and client service references. If any service references are incomplete, the method extracts the client service references and the server module metadata references using the WASAxis2MetaDataImpl object reference.

From the server module metadata reference, the service reference information map is extracted and passed to the completeServiceRefMetaData internal method. This method maps the client service references and client module metadata, which completes the service reference map.

The completeServiceRefMetaData Method

The `completeServiceRefMetaData` method simply checks the client service references for incomplete references. If it finds incomplete references, it creates a `ServiceRefPostProcessor` object with the client service, partial map, and module metadata references and then calls its `completeClientMetadata` method, which resolves WSDL locations, service and port QNames, using a `WebServiceRefMetaData` helper class. The `WebServiceRefMetaData` helper class reads the annotations and completes the references, including the handling for the identification of the need for use of the SOAP Message Transmission Optimization Mechanism (MTOM) for sending and receiving binary data.

The moduleMetaDataCreated Method

In the `moduleMetaDataCreated` method, the tying up of the Axis2 engine, the service implementation and servlet, and the underlying transport mechanism happens. This method relates the Axis2 configuration and the implementation code for the deployed services. Remember the `WebApp` class that underlies the web container? Well, that is referred to in this method. This is a complex method, but one that underpins the WAS use of Axis2.

At the start of the method, a reference to the deployed object is obtained from the metadata event reference passed into the method and, if it refers to a module file that is a WAR file, then the configuration is extracted from the metadata event object and typecast to a `com.ibm.wsspi.webcontainer.webapp.WebAppConfig` reference as used by the web container.

The module name, application name, and an EJB module name (if there is one) are extracted from the metadata event and the `Axis2Utils getContextRoot` method is used to extract the context root for the module. The application metadata and the server module metadata are also extracted using the EJB module name as a key, and the configuration context is returned—all within the `getModuleConfigContext` local call. If there is a context root, an Endpoint Manager bean reference is used and its `setContextRoot` method is called for that context root.

Next, the `storeModuleMetaData` is called for the metadata event reference and the configuration context. If there is no configuration context, a reference to the EAR file is extracted from the deployed object module file and a reference to the EJB module file is obtained and passed to a new `WASAxis2MetaDataProcessor` object, along with the metadata event reference and the `WebAppConfig` reference. The `processApplicationMetaData` method is called on the `WASAxis2MetaDataProcessor` object to generate the configuration context.

A new `WSRefInfoBuilder` object is then created and its `buildInfo` method is called to build the service reference partial metadata map for the module, and this is passed with the module metadata to the internal `setRefInfoForJAXRPC` call. If there is now a configuration context, an `EndpointManagerMBean` is created for the application name and EJB module and its context root set. The `Axis2Utils generateEndpoints` method is then called for the configuration context to get a list of endpoints, and this is used to initialize the endpoints for the MBean, and the `Axis2tils setEndpointManagerMbean` is used to relate the MBean and configuration context.

The metadata event reference and configuration context are passed to the internal `completeAxis2Configuration` and `driveJAXWSMetaDataListeners` methods to finish the Axis2 initialization, and then these references are also passed with the application name, module name, and partial metadata map for the module to the internal `storeMetaDataInApplication` method.

If the configuration context is null but the partial metadata map is not, then the `storeModuleMetaData` method is called with the metadata event reference, the partial metadata map, and a reference to the `WASAxis2MetaDataProcessor` object and the value returned from its call to `getDBCs`. A Description Builder Composite (DBC) is used as part of the JAX-WS description processing for the services to build up the metadata for use at runtime, including the map that allows the description to be looked up for a given URL.

If the EJB module name checked at the beginning of the method was null, then the module name and metadata event reference are passed to the internal `getModuleConfigContext` method to get the configuration context. If the configuration context is null, a new `WASAxis2MetaDataProcessor` object is created based on the module file, the `WebAppConfig` reference, and the metadata event reference, and the `processApplicationMetaData` method is called to get the configuration context followed by a call to `getDBCs` to get the DBC map.

If the deployed object is an EJB JAR file, the DBC map is used to create a new `WSRefInfoBuilder` reference and the `buildInfo` method is called on this to create a partial metadata map, which is passed to the internal `setRefInfoForJAXRPC` method with a reference to the module metadata. If there is now a configuration context, an `EndpointManagerMBean` is created for the application name and EJB module and its context root is set. The `Axis2Utils` `generateEndpoints` method is called for the configuration context to get a list of endpoints and this is used to initialize the endpoints for the MBean. The `Axis2tils` `setEndpointManagerMbean` is then used to relate the MBean and configuration context.

Next, the metadata event reference and configuration context are passed to the internal `completeAxis2Configuration`, which also has the partial metadata map passed, and `driveJAXWSMetaDataListeners` methods to finish the Axis2 initialization. If the deployed objected module is an EJB JAR file, these references are also passed with the application name, module name, and partial metadata map for the module to the internal `storeMetaDataInApplication` method. If there is not a configuration context but there is a DBC map, the metadata event, partial metadata map, and DBC map are passed to the internal `storeModuleMetaData` method. For any other case, the metadata event and the configuration context are passed to the `storeModuleMetaData` call.

We now have our Axis2 engine configuration for our deployed service implementation, with support for different functionality and implementation modules mapped to allow routing when requests arrive.

The storeModuleMetaData Method

The `storeModuleMetaData` method extracts the deployed object metadata, from which it extracts the application name and the module name and creates a new `ServerModuleMetaData` object based on this. It then adds the configuration context, partial metadata map, and DBC map to this object. The `ServerModuleMetaData` object reference and module metadata are added to the `WASAxis2MetaDataImpl` object held by the component via its call to the `setServerModuleMetaData` method.

The completeAxis2Configuration Method

The `completeAxis2Configuration` method ties the configuration, WS-Policy policy set, and security configuration into the engine. The deployed object is extracted from the metadata event and the policy set loader is obtained from the policy set loader manager, and if the policy set loader is an instance of the `WASAxis2PolicySetConfigurator`, the application class loader is set from the deployed object classloader. The policy set loader `associatePolicySets` method is called to associate the configuration context and configuration manager references.

The `storeModuleMetaData` method is called, passing the metadata event, configuration context, partial metadata map, and `dbc` map references as parameters. If the deployed object deployment descriptor is an instance of a `WebApp`, which is the class used to represent web applications to the web container, a `WebApp` reference is obtained from the deployment descriptor and this is passed with the configuration context to a new `WASAxis2SecurityConstrainer` object, and the `constrainURIs` method is called on the object to apply the appropriate security configuration.

If there is a configuration context but there is no `EndpointManagerMBean` set up for the Axis2 configuration, the application and module names are extracted from the deployed object and the context root is extracted using the `Axis2Utils getContextRoot` call for the module file name. The application and module names are used to create an `EndpointManagerMBean` reference using the `EndpointManagerMBeanFactory locateOrGenerateMBean` method and, if there is a context root, the `setContextRoot` method is called on the MBean reference.

The `Axis2Utils generateEndpoints` call is used for setup of the configuration context. A list of endpoints is generated and used to initialize the MBean. The `Axis2Utils setEndpointManagerMBean` method is called to relate the configuration context and MBean reference. The `Axis2Utils setContextRoot` method is called for the configuration context and module file to set the context root. Thus, this method uses the metadata and map along with the configuration context to complete the Axis2 configuration for the deployed object. It relates the underlying `WebApp` reference that wraps a web application deployment descriptor, as used by the web container, and applies security configuration to the URIs along with the WS-Policy policy sets.

The driveJAXWSMetaDataListeners Method

The `driveJAXWSMetaDataListeners` is a simple method that takes an indicator for whether the metadata was being created as the driver, the metadata event, and the configuration context. The set of `JAXWSMetaDataListener` references is then iterated, and if the created indicator is set, the `metaDataCreated` method on each listener in the list is called with the metadata event and configuration context as references; otherwise, the `metaDataDestroyed` method is called with the metadata event and configuration context references.

This facility allows all components that have registered listeners with the WAS Axis2 Service to be notified of the metadata event that has occurred through deployment, allowing them to take any additional action. The listeners are added to the `JAXWSMetaDataListener` list through calls into the public `addJAXWSMetaDataListener` method and removed using the `removeJAXWSMetaDataListener` method.

The storeMetaDataInApplication Method

The `storeMetaDataInApplication` method takes as parameters a metadata event, a key (usually an EJB JAR file or similar reference), an application name, a module name, a configuration context, and a partial metadata map. A server module metadata object is created using the application and module names as parameters, and the configuration context is passed to this using the setConfigurationContext method. The setServiceRefInfo method is then called on the server module metadata object, passing the partial metadata map that creates the service references as a parameter, and the setModuleKeyName method is used on it to set the passed-in key name to use for lookups.

The application metadata and server module metadata are then set on the WASAxis2 MetaDataImpl object reference held by the WASAxis2ComponentImpl object running the WAS Axis2 Service so the service has the appropriate metadata and configuration.

The metaDataDestroyed Method

Let's return to the MetaDataListener interface methods that are called by the Meta Data Service. We previously looked at what happens when metadata is created on deployment, so now let's look at what happens on destruction when the service calls the metaDataDestroyed method and passes a MetaDataEvent reference, as for creation.

First, if the metadata refers to module metadata, references to the deployed object, module, and module name are extracted from the metadata event, along with an application name if the deployed object is an EAR file. The application name and module name are then used in the unregisterMBean method of the EndpointManagerMBeanFactory class to unregister the MBean monitoring the application.

If the module is a WAR file, the warMetaDataDestroyed method is called with the metadata event reference to handle the tidying up. Then, irrespective of the type of metadata, a module file reference is extracted. If it is a WAR file or EJB JAR file module, the module and application name are extracted and passed to the internal getClientConfigurationContexts method to get a list of client configuration contexts, and this is passed to the terminateClientConfigurationContexts internal method to tidy them up.

An EAR file reference is then extracted from the module file reference and the EAR file name is passed to the remove method of the applicationsProcessed set that lists the applications for which there is a configuration of interest to the engine, thus removing the reference.

The warMetaDataDestroyed Method

In the warMetaDataDestroyed method, the metadata is extracted from the metadata event and, if it is a ServerModuleMetaData instance or a MetaDataHolder instance, its configuration context is extracted using getConfigurationContext and this is then passed to the internal shutdownModules method. The driveJAXWSMetaDataListeners method is then called to pass the information on to other registered components that the service has been stopped and the configuration context for the metadata is set to null.

The getClientConfigurationContexts Method

The getClientConfigurationContexts method merely delegates to a method of the same name on the client configuration context store that manages them.

The terminateClientConfigurationContexts Method

The terminateClientConfigurationContexts method effectively disables routing to the service being undeployed. For each client configuration context in the passed-in list, it calls the removeCCFromRspMap method on the AsyncResponseServlet instance with the client configuration context, and then calls terminate on the client configuration context reference and removes it from the list. The AsyncResponseServlet class is the router for and handles transport into Axis2 for inbound asynchronous responses to a client running in the WAS server process, so this removes the service. The client configuration context is the information shared between the Axis2 engine and WAS.

The shutdownModules Method

The shutdownModules method merely calls the terminate method on the configuration context reference to ensure it is shut down inside the engine.

The DeployedObjectListener Interface

The DeployedObjectListener interface relates to the Application Manager Service, which the WASAxis2ComponentImpl initialize method registered with. This has a single method, stateChanged, which is called whenever anything is deployed to the environment and receives a DeployedObjectEvent reference that allows the deployed object (i.e., EAR, WAR, EJB JAR, etc.) to be examined.

In the WASAxis2ComponentImpl class, the stateChanged method checks to see if there is a module and that its state is STARTED before getting its module metadata, by accessing the DeployedObject reference. This module metadata is used to see if it relates to a server module and has a configuration context. If so, it nullifies a module configuration map. This innocuous mechanism of handling the metadata gives access to the application and module names, service references, configuration, and injection targets—all through the ServerModuleMetaData class that is used to wrap the deployed object whose state has changed.

The WASAxis2Service Interface

The WASAxis2Service interface description can be found in the com.ibm.wsspi.websvcs. WASAxis2Service class. This has a number of methods for getting and setting module and component metadata, getting service reference information, loading the Axis2 configuration context, adding and removing JAXWSMetaDataListener references, maintaining the client configuration, and checking the server status.

We have looked closely at how client configuration contexts are managed by the WASAxis2Service component implementation as a form of communicating with the Axis2 engine but have yet to see how the client configuration contexts are deployed into the environment in the first place. The information is provided by one of the two loadAxis2ConfigurationContext methods, one of which takes an application name and module name and builds and returns the information, and the other of which takes a metadata event that extracts this information and calls the first implementation.

Controlling Axis2

When you first considered the WAS Axis2 integration functionality, I explained a little about the important classes used to control the Axis2 functionality within an application server.

The ConfigurationContext is used to start and control the behavior of an instance of Axis2, even when run inside an application server, as an in-memory configuration database of runtime static and dynamic data used to operate and manage the engine and services. It holds an AxisConfiguration object that represents the metadata (i.e., axis2.xml, services.xml, and module.xml). For use in an application server environment to load modules and services into Axis2, a war-based AxisConfigurator derivative is needed. These classes are all a core part of Axis2 functionality itself, and are merely used by the WAS Axis2 integration functionality.

One confusing aspect of examining how Axis2 configuration is controlled is the use of two methods that load the Axis2 ConfigurationContext object that have the same name, loadAxis2ConfigurationContext, but that have different signatures. We will look at both, starting with the version that takes an application name and module name, followed by the version that takes a metadata event.

The loadAxis2ConfigurationContext Method with Application and Module Name Parameters

The loadAxis2ConfigurationContext method that takes an application name and module name as parameters is public and returns a ConfigurationContext reference. The ConfigurationContext is stored inside the Axis2 engine in a repository and represents server-side JAX-WS handling, as opposed to the ClientConfigurationContext that is maintained by WAS and refers to client-side functionality. This loadAxis2ConfigurationContext method makes heavy use of a WASAxis2ConfigurationBuilder class and an AxisConfiguration class.

The method first creates a new WASAxis2ConfigurationBuilder object and passes in to the constructor the arrays of server and client modules and server and client plugins that it maintains. It then calls loadAxisServerConfiguration on the object to get an AxisConfiguration object returned. The ConfigurationContextFactory class is then used to create an empty configuration context, and the AxisConfiguration is passed to this. The internal setConfigParms method is then used with the configuration and application and module names to set the necessary parameters.

Next, the loadAxisServerModules method of the WASAxis2ConfigurationBuilder object is called for the AxisConfiguration and ConfigurationContext references, followed by similar calls to loadAxisServerTCMPPlugins and loadAxisServerACMPPlugins for the configuration context. TCMP plugins are thread context migrators and ACMP plugins are application context migrators, which are specific low-level plugins used to control the underlying message processing. The completed configuration context is then returned to the caller. Note that the arrays passed into the builder are updated by this processing.

The loadAxis2ConfigurationContext Method with a Metadata Event Parameter

The loadAxis2ConfigurationContext method that receives a metadata event extracts the deployed object and, from this, the module metadata; from the module metadata, the application metadata is extracted to get the application name. The application name and module name are passed to the preceding alternative loadAxis2ConfigurationContext method to get a ConfigurationContext to return to the caller.

The setConfigParms Method

The setConfigParms method is a simple one that uses the Axis2Utils class setApplicationName and setModuleName methods to put the application name and module name, respectively, into the AxisConfiguration object that underpins ConfigurationContext.

The WASAxis2ClientImpl Component

The WASAxis2ClientImpl component also extends WsComponentImpl for its lifecycle control, and therefore exposes the initialize, start, stop, and destroy methods, but it also exposes the WASAxis2Service interface just as the WASAxis2ComponentImpl class does.

- In its initialize method, the WASAxis2ClientImpl component adds the WASAxis2Service entry to the WebSphere Service Registry, registers annotation adapters via the WASAnnotationCollector registerAnnotationAdapters call, registers the WebServiceRefProcessor via its registerSelf method, and registers a message factory ClassFinderFactory from the Axis2 packages.

- The start method is used to get access to the application clients' Client Process Service from the WebSphere Service Registry, access its client file, create a new ClientMetaData reference, and get a map of client URL information via a call to the internal loadClientURLInfo method (which is also called from the WASAxis2ComponentImpl class for client handling). It then adds that map to the ClientMetaData reference via a call to its setClientURLInfo method. This supports service lookups.

- The destroy and stop methods are left to the parent implementations.

Most of the WASAxis2Service interface methods have little or no real implementation because this is a client representation rather than the full server representation. The getClientComponentMetaData and getClientModuleMetaData methods return the client metadata reference held by the component, and the addClientConfigurationContext method saves the Axis2 runtime engine ConfigurationContext reference for later use. The isServer method returns false to identify the implementation as a client representation.

The setClientComponentMetaData and setClientModuleMetaData methods are interesting in that they store references to the passed-in ClientMetaData and then call an internal processMetaData method.

The processMetaData Method

The processMetaData method is interesting in that it works initially with the archive file returned from the Client Process Service getClientFile call that was made in the initialize method and checks to see if it is an archive file. If so, it gets the DBC map via a call to getDBCs for the archive. Remember that a DBC is a Description Builder Composite that is used by the description processing for a service. If the processMetaData method gets a DBC map and the information is not partially initialized, then a ServiceRefPartialInfo reference is created via creating a WSRefInfoBuilder object for the given DBC map, and then its buildInfo method is called to update the partialInfoMap reference held by the component.

A new `ServiceRefProcessor` object is then created using the client metadata client service references and the partial information map, followed by a call to its `completeClientMetadata` method. This complete processing is used to build up the application client service map.

The `getDBCs` call takes a module file reference and a classloader reference as parameters and is used to build up a DBC map, i.e., the Description Builder Composite mapping metadata for service. It uses a `WASAnotationCollector` for its work and uses the classloader to extract the annotation information as it iterates the module contents to build up the map using a `WASAnnotationInputBuilder` helper to build the inputs. If the module is a WAR file, the `WEB-INF/webservices.xml` file is used; otherwise, the `META-INF` `webservices.xml` file is used, to get the WSDD definitions from the module.

A `WSServerMetadataMerger` object is used via its `mergeMetadata` method to put together all of the web service information, module information, and other map information and the resultant DBC map is returned to the caller. This is used both here in the `WASAxis2ClientImpl` component implementation and in the `WASAxis2ComponentImpl` component implementation.

The loadClientURLInfo Method

The `loadClientURLInfo` method takes a module file reference and XMI file references and creates a hash map of the URL information for a given module file name. It gets the client web service binding information using the Eclipse `WSModels` strategy support and then iterates them to get the component scoped references to build up a list of service references. It then calls the internal `processBindingRefs` method for the module, binding references, and client URL information before returning the client URL information hash map to the caller. This method is called by the `WASAxis2ClientImpl` implementation and the `WASAxis2ComponentImpl` implementation.

The processBindingRefs Method

The `processBindingRefs` method iterates the service binding references and for each extracts a list of port QName bindings and service QNames. It gets the endpoint URI URL for the port binding using this information, and for each entry it stores the URL in the client URL info hash map, keyed by the local part of the Service QName, a colon, and the local port QName. Thus, for a given service its endpoint URI can be looked up.

The getServiceRef Method

The `getServiceRef` method takes a module file reference, a service reference link, and component name as parameters. Its role is simply to return a service reference for a given component and service reference link in a module. The handling for a WAR file is easy because the service references are merely extracted from the deployment descriptor. For an EJB JAR file, the deployment descriptor is read and the enterprise bean identified by the component name is used to get the service references. For an application client file, the deployment descriptor is used to extract the service references. Then each returned service reference is iterated until the service reference identified by the service reference link is found, and this service reference is returned to the caller.

The WASAxis2MetaDataProcessor Class

The WASAxis2MetaDataProcessor class takes a module file, a WebAppConfig reference describing a web application configuration, a classloader reference, and a MetaDataEvent in its constructor, and then extracts the configuration information required to respond to that deployment event. In particular, it extracts the AxisServiceGroup and AxisService references for a given WebAppConfig reference and returns the ConfigurationContext necessary to handle the AxisServiceGroup and its AxisService references. Thus, this class is the glue between the Axis2 representation of JAX-WS web service information and the WAS representation. We will look only at a few key methods.

The processApplicationMetaData Method

The processApplicationMetaData method is particularly important and returns a ConfigurationContext. It accesses the WASAxis2Service interface, sets an application name from the EAR file and module name for the given module, and loads a web services metadata cache for fast lookups for the application. It then gets the class data objects needed to build the annotation DBC inputs if a cache exists. Otherwise, it processes the module metadata to extract the AxisServiceGroup information, which is then passed to the finishRuntimeConfiguration method to build the ConfigurationContext from the AxisConfiguration. At the end of the method, the AxisServiceGroup data is stored for later use using the internal storeMetaDataFileList method.

The storeMetaDataFileList Method

In the storeMetaDataFileList method, the services within the passed-in AxisServiceGroup reference are iterated, and for each iteration the composite WSDL is extracted. For each composite WSDL the WSDL references within it are added to a map and the XSD files are extracted. The servlet file mappings and the service names are all put into another mappings reference with the WSDL mappings. The mappings reference is stored in the ConfigurationContext reference maintained by the component, along with the module classloader information that is used to enable the servlet paths to be loaded.

The processModuleMetadata Method

The processModuleMetadata method loads the configuration, sets the web application name, builds the DBC inputs for the class data objects the module relates to, and then calls buildAxisServices to create an AxisServiceGroup reference to return to the caller. If the module is a WAR file, it calls locateJAXWSClassesForScan and passes the WebAppConfig reference and the AxisServiceGroup reference.

The loadConfiguration Method

The loadConfiguration method calls into the WASAxis2ComponentImpl WASAxis2Service Service interface to get the ConfigurationContext for the given application and module name.

The buildAxisServices Method

The buildAxisServices method just uses a WASAxis2DescriptionBuilder helper class for the module file and deployed object classloader and then calls its buildAxisServiceGroup method for the given service description list.

The finishRuntimeConfiguration Method

The finishRuntimeConfiguration method checks whether the passed-in AxisServiceGroup has services and, if so, adds it to the passed-in AxisConfiguration reference using the addServiceGroup method.

The locateJAXWSClassesForScan Method

There are two implementations of the locateJAXWSClassesForScan method. The first takes a WebAppConfig reference and an AxisServiceGroup reference and for each AxisService within that AxisServiceGroup object calls the other implementation of the same named method, which takes a WebAppConfig reference and an AxisService reference. This latter implementation gets the service implementation class for the given AxisService using the Axis2Utils class functionality and adds it and the classloader to a linked list. The EndpointDescriptors are extracted to get access to the HandlerChains and for each the handler class names are extracted and added to the linked list. The linked list is then added to the WebAppConfig reference list of classes to scan using its addClassesToScan method.

Other Key Classes

There are a few other key classes that deserve a brief mention because they play a small part in controlling the behavior of the JAX-WS runtime within WAS.

The Axis2ServiceConfigPluginManager Class

The Axis2ServiceConfigPluginManager class looks for Axis2 extension plugins and handles the lifecycle methods for adding them to the environment.

The WASAxis2MetaDataImpl Class

The WASAxis2MetaDataImpl class merely handles module, application, and component metadata slots in the WAS runtime Meta Data Service and maintains them, and then offers methods to extract and transform metadata of each of the appropriate types.

The WASAxis2ConfigurationBuilder Class

The WASAxis2ConfigurationBuilder class builds the configuration for the Axis2 engine. It maintains arrays of configuration modules and then applies the base configuration to them to build an AxisConfiguration reference for the combination of the base runtime and deployed services. For both client and server base configuration, the META-INF/config/ibmaxis2.xml file is used.

Server modules are loaded from

- com.ibm.wsfp.main.ibmaxis2-qos-module-server
- com.ibm.wsfp.main.custom-handler-server

Client modules are loaded from

- com.ibm.wsfp.main.ibmaxis2-qos-module-client
- com.ibm.wsfp.thinclient.ibmaxis2-qos-module-client
- com.ibm.wsfp.main.custom-handler-client
- com.ibm.wsfp.thinclient.custom-handler-thinclient

Each module is loaded, initialized, and then engaged with the runtime environment. The loadAxisCfg method used internally takes the ibmaxis2.xml file and creates a new AxisConfiguration object. The method then uses a builder to populate the AxisConfiguration and set up the configuration for each of the phases I mentioned earlier when I described how Axis2 works. Modules that are added to the Axis2 processing are each represented by the AxisModule class.

When I described how Axis2 works, I described how the runtime state of the environment and all of the service groups and services it is hosting, along with the dynamic configuration at a point in time, is represented by a ConfigurationContext reference. This uses the static base information in the AxisConfiguration object as its starting point.

Similarly, the MessageContext is the Axis2 dynamic representation of a particular SOAP message-processing flow, with the static representation of the content handled by the AxisMessage class.

AxisServiceGroup references describe the static description of a group of related services, each of which is represented by an AxisService reference. These map to the ServiceGroupContext and ServiceContext dynamic representations, respectively. The operations within each service are described by the AxisOperation object that has its dynamic representation handled by the OperationContext object.

The AsyncResponseServlet Class

This is a key class in the integration between WAS and the Axis2 engine for correlation of inbound responses to a client running inside the WAS runtime server process in that it provides the transport between the two for asynchronous communications. Essentially, it is a servlet that handles HTTP and HTTPS requests that looks in a provided End Point Reference map for each and, for a given context root, passes the requests and responses between WAS and the Axis2 engine itself.

The Axis2 configuration and the HTTP and HTTPS maps, set up by the WASAxis2ComponentImpl initComponent call, are read for each request to do the routing. A special URI, IBM_WS_SYS_RESPONSESERVLET, is used internally to name the "pipe" for use by Axis2 to represent the service transport. The communications between the application server integration component and the Axis2 engine for each service request and response take place using an Axis2 MessageContext object that the AsyncResponseServlet creates and manipulates for inbound requests into the engine and reads for outbound communications.

Other Related Components

The Web Service Init component, `WebServiceInit`, starts with a startup value of 5300 and an implementation class of `com.ibm.ws.websvcs.component.WebServiceInitImpl`. This class merely starts the `WebServiceRefProcessor` via a call to its `registerSelf` method. The `WebServiceRefProcessor` handles injection bindings for service references for JAX-WS and also JAX-RPC.

JAX-WS SOAP Message Flow

If you look at the Axis2 configuration used as the base for the `AxisConfiguration` object, which, as you saw previously, is loaded from the `META-INF/config/ibmaxis2.xml` file, you can see flow between the IBM WAS runtime under the control of the `WASAxis2ComponentImpl` file and the core Axis2 engine.

Remember the concepts of the In Pipe, Out Pipe, Transport Sender, Transport Receiver, Dispatcher handlers, and other handlers. The handlers execute in phases.

Under the section `Transport Ins`, three `TransportReceiver` classes are declared:

- `com.ibm.ws.websvcs.transport.http.client.WAShttpAsyncResponseListener`, listed as `http`

- `com.ibm.ws.websvcs.transport.http.client.WAShttpsAsyncResponseListener`, listed as `https`

- `com.ibm.ws.websvcs.transport.jms.AsyncTransportListener`, listed as `jms`

Similarly, under the section `Transport Outs`, the `com.ibm.ws.websvcs.transport.jms.JMSSender` class is listed with the name `jms`, and `com.ibm.ws.websvcs.transport.http.HTTPTransportSender` is listed with the names `http` and `https`.

For processing the EPR and choosing a server in a cluster, the IBM target `WSATargetResolver` and `OutboundURLResolver` resolvers are used.

First, let's consider the `InFlow` phase order. For the transport phase handlers, there are IBM `URLPatternBasedDispatcher` and `PortComponentBasedDispatcher` dispatchers. For the connection management phase, the IBM `HTTPConnectionHandler` is used. The `WASAxis2PMI-tc` and `WASAxis2PMI-pc` phases are additional IBM WAS-specific phases.

Next, let's look at the `OutFlow` phase order. The IBM `ClientEndpointHandler` is part of the `ClientEndpoint` phase. There are additional `WASAxis2PMI-pg` and `WASAxis2PMI-tg` phases.

The `InFaultFlow` and `OutFaultFlow` phase orders are similar to those just described. All other configuration is based on the standard Axis2 configuration.

As previously covered, the generic Axis2 inbound flow has six key standard phases:

- Transport

- Pre-dispatch

- Dispatch

- User Defined

- Message Validation

- Message Processing

The InFlow inbound flow consists of listening for a message on one of the Transport Listeners, such as the WAShttpAsyncResponseListener, and when a message is received, a MessageContext is created and it is passed on first to the Axis2 AddressingPreSecurityHandler in the ResolveOperation phase. In the Transport phase, where transport-specific headers are processed and related information is added to the message context, the IBM URLPatternBasedDispatcher is called first, followed by the IBM PortComponentBasedDispatcher, and then the Axis2 RequestURIBasedDispatcher and the SOAPActionBasedDispatcher.

In the PreDispatch phase, there are no handlers named, and in the Dispatch phase itself only the standard Axis2 handlers are named. After this, the IBM HTTPConnectionHandler is used in the ConnectionManagementPhase phase, and in the OperationVerifier phase the Axis2 handlers are again invoked.

The WAS and Axis2 message and processing flow are shown in Figure 7-4.

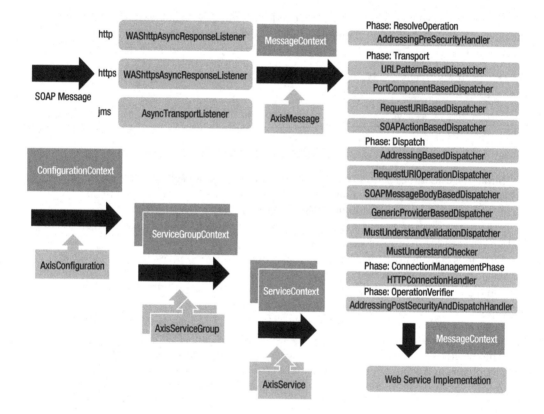

Figure 7-4. *WAS JAX-WS and Axis2 message and processing flow*

For the OutFlow outbound flow, the ClientEndpoint phase uses the IBM ClientEndpointHandler. The outbound transport is either the IBM HTTPTransportSender or the IBM JMSSender.

Summary

This chapter first examined the original standard web services functionality that has been in development for a number of WAS versions, i.e., the JSR109 JAX-RPC web service functionality as implemented in the `com.ibm.ws.runtime WSServerImpl` component. You saw how this works by having the `WSChannelManager` set up the inbound and outbound chains of communications that ultimately map to a servlet in a `WebApp`.

The second half of the chapter explained the JAX-WS functionality that first appeared in the WAS 6.1 Web Services Feature Pack. This is based on the `WASAxis2ComponentImpl` functionality that provides the WAS Axis2 integration, where WAS provides the core connectivity and the JAX-WS functionality is provided by the Apache Foundation Axis2 engine, an open source product designed for integration into application servers. Additional functionality is added to the environment using modules, with the Sandesha2 functionality for WS-ReliableMessaging being one such implementation.

CHAPTER 8

■ ■ ■

Service Integration Bus

One of the requirements of the J2EE specification is to support messaging via the Java Message Service (JMS) API. This is an API rather than a specification of message formats and protocols, but the API specification has some direction as to expected behavior in that interaction is asynchronous, supports publish-and-subscribe and peer-to-peer patterns, and supports both non-persistent and persistent messages. It has been suggested that IBM was behind the drive to get Message Oriented Middleware (MOM)–style interoperability into the application server arena due to a desire to integrate its MQSeries product functionality into WAS, with all of the functional benefits that come with it.

MQSeries was released by IBM as a mechanism for integrating disparate system types using messaging, and proved to be popular with large organizations due to its support on many different platforms ranging from PCs to Unisys mainframes to HP NonStop systems. So, to IBM the obvious answer was to support JMS on top of MQSeries.

The problem with just supporting JMS in a product externally to WAS is an obvious one, related to deployment and qualities of service: it is a separate product that consists of a number of separate processes yet WAS is just one process that runs different components inside a virtual machine.

In the early WAS 4.x releases, JMS support was provided by MQSeries itself with no real integration. With WAS 5.x IBM released a scaled-down version of the now renamed MQSeries, WebSphere MQ, that was called the WebSphere Embedded Messaging Publish and Subscribe (WEMPS) provider. This scaled-down JMS environment was essentially the same set of binaries as the full WebSphere MQ product, but through configuration, interoperability with remote WebSphere MQ nodes was prevented, leading to an installation of a full WebSphere MQ Server product being required.

Having an architecture with the main application server and its enterprise facilities running inside a single Java Virtual Machine (JVM) process working alongside a messaging engine consisting of upward of 11 processes is problematic for scalability. The WebSphere MQ environment processes are external to the single JVM process, but the two environments need to communicate to support JMS, so synchronization and interprocess communications are necessary. WebSphere MQ has processes to start queues, processes to create queues, and processes to listen on transports, but one key WebSphere MQ process is the amqppta process that manages threads, communications, etc. in a manner similar to that of the JVM, but using a different technology. Synchronization between the two products and their separate threading models requires the assistance of the operating system, which caused issues on some AIX environments. The solution is a simple and obvious one—re-implement the WebSphere MQ functionality inside the application server in Java.

With WebSphere Application Server 6.0, the reimplemented messaging functionality was released as the Service Integration Bus Messaging Engine. At its simplest it can be thought of as a Java implementation of WebSphere MQ with changes to support the active-active clustering facilities of WAS, but this is too simplistic and ignores the JMS-specific functionality. The WebSphere MQ Format and Protocol, known as MQFAP in the configuration files and WAS documentation, is supported, but a JMS-specific variation called JFAP is also supported as the default format and protocol to be more optimal as a JMS provider. The earlier WEMPS product can still be interoperated with and is known in configuration as the v5 messaging provider.

For users with a WebSphere MQ background, the Service Integration Bus Messaging Engine can seem entirely foreign. The terminology is different to accommodate the wider responsibilities of the Service Integration Bus (SIB) over pure WebSphere MQ, or is modified to fit with JMS facilities, or has been changed to support the concepts of WAS. Despite that, the core concepts of WebSphere MQ exist in the Messaging Engine and the implementation is mostly the same, apart from being in Java. For example, an MQ link consists of a sender channel and a receiver channel, which is completely analogous to a transmission queue in WebSphere MQ. This chapter concentrates mostly on the messaging implementation rather than the wider responsibilities, and will use the SIB naming for concepts with only a brief reference to the WebSphere MQ equivalents.

The SIB also provides the underpinning of a number of IBM products, notably the WebSphere ESB and WebSphere Process Server business integration packages, in that its implementation supports not only fast internal JMS messaging but also the use of mediations (i.e., format and protocol transformations) to be added to the message flow to support business integration facilities. The SIB mediation functionality is very different from that in the SCA (Service Component Architecture) model used in WebSphere ESB and WebSphere Process Server, but in one specific internal scenario in these two business integration products the SIB mediation implementation is built upon.

What Is the Service Integration Bus?

The internal SIB Service Provider Interface is JMS-like, so mapping to JMS itself is easy. A JCA Resource Adapter is used for delivery of inbound messages to MDBs. The activation specification is used for inbound messaging, and connection factories are used for outbound messaging.

SIB transcodes all messages (i.e., converts from one format to another) into a generic representation, which negatively impacts performance due to the associated overhead, but still it has been tested to handle up to 24,000 non-persistent messages per second at peak in a typical testing environment within IBM on high-end WAS configurations. For persistent messages, a database or the file system can be used, and for use of the database with messages in a single unit of work a one-phase commit can be performed.

There are five quality of service models in SIB that can be used. The list starts with the fastest, lightest, and least reliable quality of service and then increases in reliability at a cost of performance and complexity:

- *Best Effort*: Doesn't put much effort into delivery of messages and the messages can simply be discarded.

- *Express*: Will lose messages on a server failure, but will generally work hard to deliver the messages.

- *Reliable Non-Persistent/Acknowledge*: Will send acknowledgments that a message has been delivered but cannot guarantee results if a messaging engine fails.

- *Reliable Persistent*: Will send acknowledgments and will write the message to disk.

- *Assured Delivery*: Will write the message to disk on the sender's thread.

A bus exists within a cell and is a logical entity that is location transparent and contains destinations, with the destinations hosted on bus members on messaging engines. Applications connect to the bus that provides messaging facilities and can connect at any bus member within that bus, with the connections handled either as producer or consumer sessions. The connection is handled by the messaging engine, which then routes the messages to the destination while handling qualities of service functions such as persistence. Senders connect as message producers and attach to a destination. Receivers connect to a destination as message consumers. An application can deploy a mediation, i.e., a protocol or format transformation, to the bus independently of either producer or consumer, but this is more the realm of the WebSphere Enterprise Service Bus product that builds upon the SIB and the SCA standard. SIB does, however, support mapping between HTTP and JMS exposed services.

By default only one messaging engine in a bus is active at one time, to preserve message ordering, but multiple engines can be configured to be load balanced if ordering is not required. A cell can have multiple buses to provide isolation, and these buses can be linked to buses in the same cell or in a different cell via a foreign bus connection. A pair of messaging engines maintains the physical link. Messaging engines go into an HAManager-controlled grouping of singleton instances for high availability, an HAGroup, to ensure that a failure of one instance results in the work being picked up by another instance that was passively waiting to take over on a failure. Each bus member automatically connects to every other bus member. Multiple SIB buses can be connected via a SIBLink, and connections to a WebSphere MQ environment take place using an MQLink (essentially a sender and receiver channel pair similar to a WebSphere MQ transmission queue). Only one link is active between buses at a time. A SIB messaging engine instance can write to a foreign bus over an MQLink, but not read from it. However, for SIBLink connections a remote read is supported.

An MQLink has a sender channel and a receiver channel to facilitate communications to the WebSphere MQ Server environment in a manner it understands (i.e., transmission queues, sender channels, receiver channels, etc.), and to the WebSphere MQ side of things it appears to be a transmission queue connection. Inside the SIB the remote destination is represented by a proxy or a localization point to which messages are sent for forwarding.

There is a correlation between a bus in the SIB sense and a queue manager in the WebSphere MQ sense. A message sent to an MQServer in the SIB bus goes via the SIB and through an MQLink sender and receiver channel pair to the remote queue manager, but the remote WebSphere MQ Server does the work as the SIB messaging engine is a client of the WebSphere MQ Server node. The WebSphere MQ Server node sees the SIB as a remote WebSphere MQ Server node and the SIB destination as a remote queue.

In WebSphere MQ, messages that cannot be delivered go on the dead letter queue, but in the SIB environment the equivalent is the exception_destination. So, when errors occur these queues and destinations need to be monitored to determine what failed and with what messages.

The key concept to understand with the SIB is location transparency, because the users of a particular destination connect to the bus to access their destination but do not know where it is physically located. This concept is depicted in Figure 8-1.

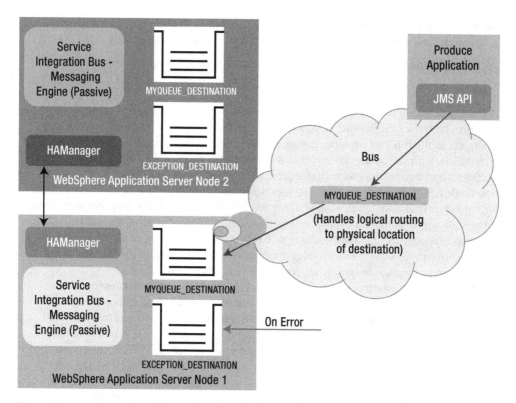

Figure 8-1. *JMS access to a destination on the Service Integration Bus*

SIB Communications from the Bottom Up

If you look at a typical server.xml file, you can see the communications set up by the Channel Framework Service to support the Service Integration Bus.

Two pools of threads do most of the work, one for inbound messaging and the other for outbound messaging. The inbound messages comes into a TCP/IP port for the particular type of messaging and the Channel Framework Service picks it up and passes it through the transport chain associated with that port. The TCP channel picks the message up first, any SSL handling is performed if required, and then the channel associated with the message type is used (i.e., MQ FAP or JFAP); and all of this uses a thread from the SIB FAP inbound thread pool.

For outbound messages, a thread is allocated from the pool used for outbound SIB FAP messaging and goes through the appropriate message handling format channel for the given chain (i.e., MQ FAP or JFAP), then any SSL handling is performed, and finally the message leaves the TCP/IP port associated with the outbound TCP channel. This can be seen for basic JFAP messaging in Figure 8-2.

JMS messaging is the lighter weight of the two types of messaging handled by the SIB, although much of the underlying functionality is the same. WebSphere MQ messaging, as provided by MQ links, has to handle the WebSphere MQ message descriptor (MQMD) and RFH2 headers. However, architecturally the communications are little different, with the key difference being in the use of semaphores on the communication stream to control the communications for WebSphere MQ (see Figure 8-3).

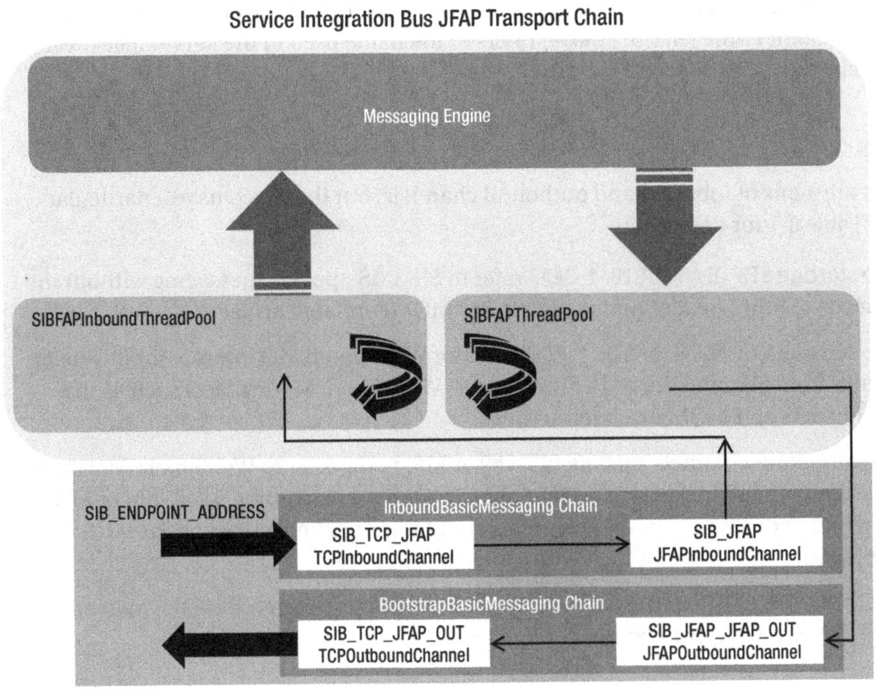

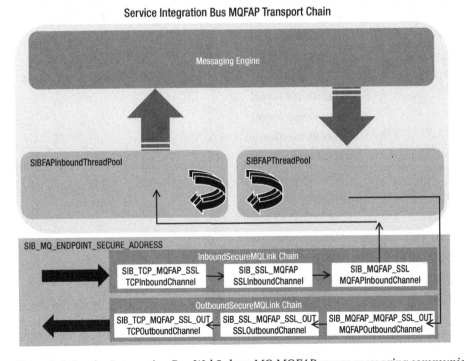

Service Integration Bus JFAP Transport Chain

Messaging Engine

SIBFAPInboundThreadPool

SIBFAPThreadPool

SIB_ENDPOINT_ADDRESS

InboundBasicMessaging Chain

SIB_TCP_JFAP
TCPInboundChannel

SIB_JFAP
JFAPInboundChannel

BootstrapBasicMessaging Chain

SIB_TCP_JFAP_OUT
TCPOutboundChannel

SIB_JFAP_JFAP_OUT
JFAPOutboundChannel

Figure 8-2. *Service Integration Bus JFAP basic message communications*

Service Integration Bus MQFAP Transport Chain

Messaging Engine

SIBFAPInboundThreadPool

SIBFAPThreadPool

SIB_MQ_ENDPOINT_SECURE_ADDRESS

InboundSecureMQLink Chain

SIB_TCP_MQFAP_SSL
TCPInboundChannel

SIB_SSL_MQFAP
SSLInboundChannel

SIB_MQFAP_SSL
MQFAPInboundChannel

OutboundSecureMQLink Chain

SIB_TCP_MQFAP_SSL_OUT
TCPOutboundChannel

SIB_SSL_MQFAP_SSL_OUT
SSLOutboundChannel

SIB_MQFAP_MQFAP_SSL_OUT
MQFAPOutboundChannel

Figure 8-3. *Service Integration Bus WebSphere MQ MQFAP secure messaging communications*

The following transport channels are set up by the Channel Framework Service to support the SIB. The end point name (endPointName) refers to the name used in the serverindex.xml file to map to specific TCP/IP ports.

Channels

The channels are a mix of inbound and outbound channels, but they each have a particular purpose (see Table 8-1 for details):

- Those starting SIB_JFAP or SIB_*_JFAP refer to SIB JMS-specific messaging without the overheads of RFH2 header management and MQMD-related artifacts.

- Those starting SIB_MQFAP or SIB_*_MQFAP are for WebSphere MQ interoperability using MQLinks from SIB, and these do fully support WebSphere MQ artifacts such as the RFH2 headers and MQMD-related settings.

- Those outbound channels starting SIB_RMQ or SIB_*_RMQ refer to WebSphere MQ client handling where SIB just acts as a WebSphere MQ client to a remote WebSphere MQ Server, and in this case inbound channels aren't required because this relates to client-only operations.

- Those with HTTP or HTC in the name refer to tunneled messaging where the message passes over an HTTP connection.

Table 8-1. *SIB-Related Channels*

Channel Name	Channel Type	End Point Name
SIB_TCP_JFAP	TCPInboundChannel	SIB_ENDPOINT_ADDRESS
SIB_TCP_JFAP_SSL	TCPInboundChannel	SIB_ENDPOINT_SECURE_ADDRESS
SIB_TCP_MQFAP	TCPInboundChannel	SIB_MQ_ENDPOINT_ADDRESS
SIB_TCP_MQFAP_SSL	TCPInboundChannel	SIB_MQ_ENDPOINT_SECURE_ADDRESS
SIB_SSL_JFAP	SSLInboundChannel	
SIB_SSL_MQFAP	SSLInboundChannel	
SIB_JFAP	JFAPInboundChannel	
SIB_JFAP_SSL	JFAPInboundChannel	
SIB_MQFAP	MQFAPInboundChannel	
SIB_MQFAP_SSL	MQFAPInboundChannel	
SIB_TCP_JFAP_OUT	TCPOutboundChannel	
SIB_TCP_JFAP_SSL_OUT	TCPOutboundChannel	
SIB_TCP_JFAP_TUN_OUT	TCPOutboundChannel	
SIB_TCP_JFAP_TUN_SSL_OUT	TCPOutboundChannel	
SIB_TCP_MQFAP_OUT	TCPOutboundChannel	

Channel Name	Channel Type	End Point Name
SIB_TCP_MQFAP_SSL_OUT	TCPOutboundChannel	
SIB_SSL_MQFAP_SSL_OUT	SSLOutboundChannel	
SIB_SSL_JFAP_SSL_OUT	SSLOutboundChannel	
SIB_SSL_JFAP_TUN_SSL_OUT	SSLOutboundChannel	
SIB_HTTP_JFAP_TUN_OUT	HTTPOutboundChannel	
SIB_HTTP_JFAP_TUN_SSL_OUT	HTTPOutboundChannel	
SIB_HTC_JFAP_TUN_OUT	HTTPTunnelOutboundChannel	
SIB_HTC_JFAP_TUN_SSL_OUT	HTTPTunnelOutboundChannel	
SIB_JFAP_JFAP_OUT	JFAPOutboundChannel	
SIB_JFAP_JFAP_SSL_OUT	JFAPOutboundChannel	
SIB_JFAP_JFAP_TUN_OUT	JFAPOutboundChannel	
SIB_JFAP_JFAP_TUN_SSL_OUT	JFAPOutboundChannel	
SIB_MQFAP_MQFAP_SSL_OUT	MQFAPOutboundChannel	
SIB_MQFAP_MQFAP_OUT	MQFAPOutboundChannel	
SIB_TCP_RMQ_OUT	TCPOutboundChannel	
SIB_TCP_RMQ_SSL_OUT	TCPOutboundChannel	
SIB_SSL_RMQ_SSL_OUT	SSLOutboundChannel	
SIB_RMQ_RMQ_SSL_OUT	RMQOutboundChannel	
SIB_RMQ_RMQ_OUT	RMQOutboundChannel	

Chains

The transport chains relate to the combination and ordering of channels that are required to support a particular type of communication. So, for InboundBasicMessaging a basic SIB JMS request would come into a TCP port and would be passed on up through the TCP/IP stack to the higher levels where it is recognized as a JFAP message. In the upper levels of the stack, it is translated and the JFAP protocol is applied. In this case, the protocol processing order in the stack is first for a TCPInboundChannel channel at the lower level followed by a JFAPInboundChannel channel built on top of this in the upper level.

Similarly, for an OutboundSecureMQLink, the request is coming down through the stack from the application layer and will start with the SIB handling for an MQ link, with the RFH2 headers and other WebSphere MQ artifacts, via an MQFAPOutboundChannel through an SSLOutboundChannel to add the Secure Sockets Layer (SSL) encryption and then out through a TCPOutboundChannel as it reaches the basic TCP/IP socket level. The combinations are shown in Table 8-2.

Table 8-2. *SIB-Related Transport Chains*

Chain Name	Channels
InboundBasicMessaging	TCPInboundChannel ➤ JFAPInboundChannel
InboundSecureMessaging	TCPInboundChannel ➤ SSLInboundChannel ➤ JFAPInboundChannel
InboundBasicMQLink	TCPInboundChannel ➤ MQFAPInboundChannel
InboundSecureMQLink	TCPInboundChannel ➤ SSLInboundChannel ➤ MQFAPInboundChannel
BootstrapBasicMessaging	JFAPOutboundChannel ➤ TCPOutboundChannel
BootstrapSecureMessaging	JFAPOutboundChannel ➤ SSLOutboundChannel ➤ TCPOutboundChannel
BootstrapTunneledMessaging	JFAPOutboundChannel ➤ HTTPTunnelOutboundChannel ➤ HTTPOutboundChannel ➤ TCPOutboundChannel
BootstrapTunneledSecureMessaging	JFAPOutboundChannel ➤ HTTPTunnelOutboundChannel ➤ HTTPOutboundChannel ➤ SSLOutboundChannel ➤ TCPOutboundChannel
OutboundBasicMQLink	MQFAPOutboundChannel ➤ TCPOutboundChannel
OutboundSecureMQLink	MQFAPOutboundChannel ➤ SSLOutboundChannel ➤ TCPOutboundChannel
OutboundBasicWMQClient	RMQOutboundChannel ➤ TCPOutboundChannel
OutboundSecureWMQClient	RMQOutboundChannel ➤ SSLOutboundChannel ➤ TCPOutboundChannel

Thread Pools

Each of the communications chains requires a thread pool to manage it. You can ignore the WMQJCAResourceAdapter thread pool that you may see referred to in the server.xml file, because that is specific to an external WebSphere MQ Server v7 installation accessed via a resource adapter that is completely external to the SIB. The thread pools vary in default sizes due to the different loads that are put on them in typical use. It is important to note that the thread pools referring to FAP are used for both JFAP and MQFAP, as the two protocols are closely related and the handling at the threading level is, therefore, generally the same. See Table 8-3 for a description of how each of the SIB/WebSphere MQ threads pools is set up.

Table 8-3. *SIB-Related Thread Pools*

Name	Minimum Size	Maximum Size	Description
SIBFAPInboundThreadPool	4	50	SIB FAP inbound channel thread pool
SIBFAPThreadPool	4	50	SIB FAP outbound channel thread pool
SIBJMSRAthreadPool	35	41	SIB JMS Resource Adapter thread pool
WMQCommonServices	1	40	WebSphere MQ common services thread pool

Communications Handling

Under the package path com.ibm.ws.sib are a number of packages, but two of particular interest for this area are the mqfapchannel and jfapchannel packages, which are associated with WebSphere MQ MQFAP handling and JMS JFAP handling, respectively.

JFAP Handling

Within the jfapchannel package tree is a package called framework, a subpackage of which is called impl. These contain the classes that open and manage the sockets, reading and writing, callbacks to notify when a write has completed, and buffering for the Channel Framework Service JFAP channels. The following interfaces are declared in the base jfapchannel package:

- The Conversation interface has quality of service and property management methods but also send, exchange, and close methods, as well as a method to set the default ReceiveListener for a Conversation object reference.

- The ReceiveListener interface has a dataReceived method that takes a buffer, flags, and a Conversation reference as parameters, and an errorOccurred method for error handling.

- The SendListener interface has a method called dataSent that takes a Conversation reference.

- The AcceptListener interface has an acceptConversation method that accepts a Conversation reference and returns a ConversationReceiveListener.

- The ConversationReceiveListener interface has a method called dataReceived, like the ReceiveListener interface.

- Various connection management interfaces, many of which have an errorOccurred method for use in error handling.

From this list you can see that much of the message queue handling is based around the concepts of listeners, asynchronous notifications, and sending and receiving through sockets, and that the higher-level parts of the stack between two nodes is handled via the concept of a conversation as provided by the Conversation interface. The Conversation interface includes the getHandshakeProperties method and various other methods to handle a handshake, an inner class to handle throttling, and priorities; so it is this interface that provides the SIB qualities of service at the lowest level, and you will see later that the BaseMessagingImpl class underpinning the SIB provides the high-level qualities of service that build on this.

The Conversation interface is implemented by the ConversationImpl class that handles the conversational state management, protocol management, and the management of the session between communicating messaging engines. In its constructor it takes a Connection reference that is used to handle the actual communications for the conversation (see the following list for details of Connection). It handles the setting up and tearing down of conversations, the higher-level parts of the protocol handling to close communications, the waking up of listeners, and key parts of the protocol management, but key are the send and exchange methods, which map down to the sendInternal method that handles buffering, and the use of the send method on the Connection object to actually send the data to a remote address and port.

Within the impl subpackage of the jfapchannel package are the classes that implement the preceding interfaces:

- The ClientConnectionManager class handles the setting up of a JFAP connection to a remote messaging engine.

- The ServerConnectionManagerImpl class handles the setting up of listeners on the channel with the appropriate qualities of service and the accepting of connections.

- The Connection class handles the actual buffering, sending, and receiving of data.

- The JFapChannelFactory class and its WSJFapChannelFactory subclass handle the creation of the individual channel instances of the JFapChannelInbound and JFapChannelOutbound channels, which themselves use the JFapInboundConnLink and JFapOutboundConnLink classes, respectively, and the VirtualConnection class that ultimately maps down to the sockets.

- The ConversationImpl class manages the detailed handshakes that set up, manage, and tear down the relationship between two communicating messaging engines and the state of a conversation at any point in time.

MQFAP Handling

Within the mqfapchannel package, things are a little simpler than within the jfapchannel package used for JFAP handling. At the top level are the key interfaces that follow, and under the impl subpackage are the implementation classes (introduced in the subsequent list):

- The Connection interface manages timeouts, bytes sent and received, buffers, SSL sessions, transport chains, network addresses, and ports; and has send and close methods.

- The ConnectionManager is an abstract class that handles an AcceptListenerFactory interface reference, and has a connect method that takes a socket address and a ReceiveListener reference to allow the setting up of a listener on a particular connection.

- The AcceptListener interface has an acceptConnection method that takes a Connection reference and returns a ReceiveListener for that connection.

- The AcceptListenerFactory interface has a manufactureAcceptListener method that merely returns an AcceptListener.

- The ReceiveListener interface has a dataReceived method that makes use of a Connection reference and a buffer.

- The DataSentListener interface has a dataSent method that takes a Connection reference, a list, and a flag.

Many of these interfaces also have an errorOccurred method for use in error handling. Note that the concept of a conversation doesn't exist here as it does for JFAP; the nearest equivalent is the more primordial connection that just relates to a network connection rather than higher-level concepts.

Within the `impl` subpackage things are handled in a similar manner as for JFAP, although without the client connection management:

- The `ConnectionManagerImpl` class handles the setting up of `AcceptListener` listener references on the channel with the appropriate qualities of service, the opening of remote connections to an IP address and port combination with a related `ReceiveListener` reference, the accepting of connections, and the setup and teardown of the `VirtualConnection` reference for a particular exchange.

- The `Connection` class handles the actual buffering, sending, and receiving of data and the SSL management.

- The `MQFapChannelFactory` and its `MQJFapChannelFactory` subclass handle the creation of the individual channel instances of the `MQFapChannelInbound` and `MQFapChannelOutbound` channels, which themselves use the `MQFapInboundConnLink` and `MQFapOutboundConnLink` classes, respectively, and the `VirtualConnection` class that ultimately maps down to the sockets.

Semaphores are used on the connection throughout the MQFAP code to notify components at each end of the current state, such as the `okayToSend` notification semaphore, and callbacks are also used for handling. MQFAP has far more low-level connection management than JFAP because of its need to maintain interoperability with older WebSphere MQ releases.

The Messaging Engine Relationship

The channel and chain handling just discussed is low level and part of the Channel Framework Service area of control. Above this in the SIB stack are the classes of the package `com.ibm.ws.sib.comms.server` and `com.ibm.ws.sib.commson.server.mesupport`. These classes implement the listeners previously outlined (i.e., the `ReceiveListener`, the `AcceptListener`, and so on) and manage the creation of connections, but also manage the relationship to the messaging engine itself.

The CommonServerReceiveListener Abstract Class

The `CommonServerReceiveListener` abstract class in the `com.ibm.ws.sib.comms.server` package is key to the functioning of the WebSphere MQ interoperability with the MQFAP protocol. In this `CommonServerReceiveListener` class, the constructor takes a flag to indicate if it is a client connection. The `rcvHandshake` method takes a communications request buffer, a `Conversation` reference, and other information and then sets various properties of the communication based on the passed data in the request buffer to control the FAP protocol and even sets up communications to the WebSphere MQ Resource Adapter, with the handshake including cell, node, protocol details, heartbeats, and FAP versions. The handshake may result in the communication being rejected.

The MEConnectionImpl Class

The `MEConnectionImpl` class in the `com.ibm.ws.sib.comms.server.mesupport` package handles the creating of connections in the `connect` method, where it creates an `METransportReceiveListener` receive listener object for a messaging engine and a `Conversation` object and then opens the connection to the remote host using a given chain, and handles the handshaking until the connection is established. The METransportReceiveListener class implements the ConversationReceiveListener interface from the jfapchannel package.

A JsMessagingEngine reference that is maintained by the MEConnectionImpl class is used to handle the connection between the endpoints via the jfapExchange method. Various other connection lifecycle methods are used to close and manage the connection and Conversation reference:

- The inboundSetup method sets up the state for the Conversation object.

- The send, sendChunkedMessage, and sendEntireMessage methods handle the sending of messages across open connections using the jfapSend method.

- The jfapSend and jfapExchange methods are both methods of the JFAPCommunicator abstract class that the MEConnectionImpl class extends via its extension of the ServerJFapCommunicator class, with these methods calling the send and exchange methods of the Conversation object reference once the necessary parameters are set up.

The METransportReceiveListener Class

METransportReceiveListener extends the CommonServerReceiveListener abstract class and provides the key to message handling in the dataReceived method that handles receiving of messages, exchanges, and connection close requests. When a request comes to close a connection, the MEConnectionImpl object representing the connection is notified and any buffers are released.

When a request for an exchange arrives, the MEConnectionFactory is used via the createMEConnection method to create a new MEConnectionImpl object reference. The conversational state is retrieved from the message attachment and passed to the MEConnectionImpl inboundSetup method to manage its state. The request is extracted and used to create a handshake reply and the MEConnectionImpl JsMessagingEngine reference is extracted to get at its message processor to handle the reply. The reply eventually returns through the Conversation send method and the buffer for the request is freed.

On receiving messages, the data is extracted, put into a JsMessage object, and then passed to the receiveMessage method of any listeners. Outbound setup uses the JsMessagingEngine messaging engine message processor and sets up a listener for the connection.

As you can see from the preceding discussion, the JsMessagingEngine class and its handling of message processors is important. We will look at this later on in this chapter.

Service Integration Bus Startup and Operation

The Service Integration Bus and messaging components are associated with a number of plugins within the WAS environment, but the core can be found in the com.ibm.ws.sib.server.jar file, which provides the core messaging engine functionality. If you look at the plugin.xml file inside this JAR file, you can see a number of extension points used, but the key class that initializes the environment requires following a few referred entries within the file. If you look at the base application server startup, as controlled by the com.ibm.wsspi.extension.server-startup extension, you can see the class com.ibm.ws.sib.admin.impl.JsAdminComponentImpl with a component name of SIB JS Admin Component is started before the real application server environment, but as the name implies this provides administration facilities.

The core of SIB itself is started under the `com.ibm.wsspi.extension.applicationserver-startup` extension point from `plugin.xml`, after the TCP Proxy Bridge is started up on zOS only. This SIB core is referred to as the SIB Service with an interface declared of `com.ibm.ws.sib.admin.impl.JsMainImpl`, but no implementation class is declared, and instead a type of `sibservice.SIBService` is declared. When you previously saw the subsystem under the control of the application server, when looking at the WAS runtime itself, you saw this type of configuration where the type name references an entry under the extension point `com.ibm.wsspi.extension.server-components`; the same is true here, because the reference refers to an implementation class that is the same as the interface class from the application server startup, `JsMainImpl`.

Other components are also started by the `com.ibm.wsspi.extension.applicationserver-startup` extension point that relate to the SIB, such as the SDO Repository, Web Services Gateway (`com.ibm.ws.sib.webservices.component.SIBWSComponent`), and the Web Services Notification component (`com.ibm.ws.sib.wsn.admin.impl.WSNComponentImpl`). The key components that make up the SIB architecture as it pertains to messaging are presented next. The top-level architecture is shown in Figure 8-4.

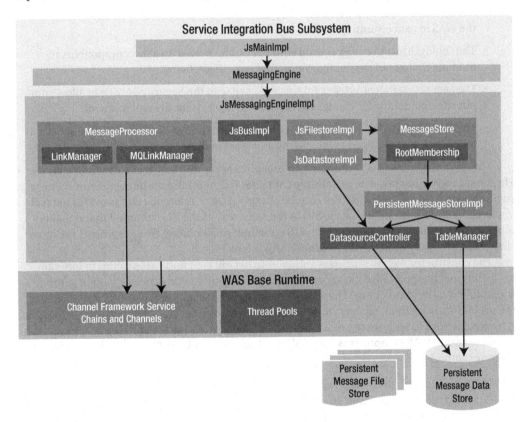

Figure 8-4. *The Service Integration Bus component architecture*

The JsMainImpl Class

This key SIB startup class, JsMainImpl, extends the JsConfigObject class that itself extends the ComponentImpl class that provides its lifecycle methods. The JsMainImpl class implements a large number of interfaces and is truly the core of SIB. It implements the following interfaces, which, apart from the first three, you have seen before used by a number of components and subsystems as part of the base WAS runtime:

- The JsMain interface does no more than expose the method getSibServiceStatsGroup.

- The JsMainImplMBean interface is a lot more interesting as it provides the control interface used for administration and includes a showMessagingEngines method that returns a list of messaging engines the SIB instance is looking after, a startMessagingEngine method that starts a messaging engine by name, and two stopMessagingEngine methods.

- The JsHealthMonitor interface merely exposes a reportLocalError method and a reportGlobalError method.

- The VetoableChangeListener interface is a standard Java bean interface that is used to notify state changes that can be accepted or refused. The Server Service uses this to allow components to say whether they can or cannot accept a change in state, such as the WAS instance shutting down.

- The ConfigChangeListener is used with the Config Service to allow components to monitor changes in the configuration that may affect them.

- The SecurityServiceListener interface is used with the Security Service to allow components to monitor for changes in the security context for the environment.

- The DeployedObjectListener interface is used with the Application Manager Service to monitor new or changed deployments and react to them.

The JsMainImpl class also contains the MessagingEngine and ComponentList inner classes. The MessagingEngine class acts as a simple container for the configuration of the messaging engine and to hold a reference to the core JsMessagingEngine reference that provides the real implementation functionality for the SIB in the same way as the EJS container functionality provides the real implementation of the EJB container functionality. The ComponentList inner class merely maps class names to internal components.

The constructor merely initializes variables to default null and false values before calling an internal method called constructorCode that does more initialization work in getting access to the JsAdminService and passing a reference to the running JsMainImpl instance to the setAdminMain method, registers a statistics template lookup class, and then sets various zOS-specific flags to indicate the mode the SIB instance is running in.

As for other WAS components, the real initialization work is performed in the initialize lifecycle method:

1. In this method, the JsMainImpl class passes a reference to itself as a SecurityServiceListener to the security service, saves the configuration passed into the method to a member variable for later use. Then, if the service is enabled and the server is not in recovery mode, the JsMainImpl class starts the PMI and statistics gathering.

2. The method then adds the `JsMainImpl` class instance reference to the Server Service as a `VetoableChangeListener` object for the server state, sets a flag to indicate if the HAManager is running, and registers itself as a service with the WAS `WsServiceRegistry` registry.

3. If the environment is running in a zOS control region or on any other platform, the method creates a `SIBJMSResource` object for later use to represent the MBean type. The method then loads various classes, and initializes any components with any configuration in the same way as the containers do, i.e., by calling the `initialize` method on each.

4. The `createMessagingEngines` internal method is called, which gets the `sib-engines.xml` file from the Config Service and, for each engine in the list, calls `createServerMessagingEngine` with the appropriate configuration object.

5. `createMessagingEngines` registers the engine before using the Config Service to get the `server.xml` file configuration for the SIB engines to be applied and registered with the dynamic configuration, and then repeats the procedure for other engines in the cluster via a call to `createClusterMessagingEngines` with the configuration object for that engine, with a check made for the `cluster.xml` file to check that the environment is in a cluster.

6. Both the `createServerMessagingEngine` and `createClusterMessagingEngine` methods pass the configuration reference passed to them to the internal `createMessagingEngine` method to get a `MessagingEngine` reference that they add to a server messaging engine list and cluster messaging engine list, respectively.

7. The `createMessagingEngine` method gets a `JsBusImpl` reference through a call to `getBusProxy` and then creates a new `JsMessagingEngineImpl` for zOS control regions and other platforms or `JsShadowMessagingEngineImpl` for zOS non-control regions. The reference to the `JsBusImpl` object is then passed to the constructor of the `MessagingEngine` inner class that is created to hold the reference and related configuration, and here the instance provided is added to an internal messaging engines list.

The rest of the methods in the `JsMainImpl` class are easier to explain:

- The `start` lifecycle method, as for other components, gets running the component, the components it uses, and, in this case, the messaging engines. The Application Manager Service is accessed from the WAS `WsServiceRegistry` registry and the `JsMainImpl` reference to itself is passed to its `addDeployedObjectListener` method. Each component loaded by the SIB is enumerated and its `start` method is called. Then the `MessagingEngine` references in the list saved during the `initialize` method are enumerated and the `startConditional` method is called on each after it is typecast to a `BaseMessagingEngineImpl` class. The `start` method is then called on the `DynamicConfigManager` configuration manager reference maintained by the SIB in the `JsMainImpl` class.

- The `serverStarted` method enumerates the `MessagingEngine` references in the list saved during the `initialize` method, and the `serverStarted` method is called on each reference after it is typecast to a `BaseMessagingEngineImpl` class.

- The serverStopping method enumerates the MessagingEngine references in the list saved during the initialize method and the serverStopping method is called on each reference after it is typecast to a BaseMessagingEngineImpl class.

- The stop lifecycle method uses the Application Manager Service to remove itself as a DeployedObjectListener reference. It then enumerates the MessagingEngine references in the list saved during the initialize method, and the stopConditional method is called on each reference after it is typecast to a BaseMessagingEngineImpl class. The method then enumerates all of the components loaded during the initialize method call and calls stop on each of them.

- The destroy lifecycle method enumerates the MessagingEngine references in the list saved during the initialize method and the destroy method is called on each after it is typecast to a BaseMessagingEngineImpl class. The method then enumerates all of the components loaded during the initialize method call and calls destroy on each of them.

- The getBusProxy method that takes a configuration object searches for buses in the list where the server is a member, and then searches for buses in the map where the server is not a member. If the method doesn't find a reference, it searches for and registers the bus member and adds it to a vector.

- The registerBusListener method simply uses the registerListener method of the JsBusListener class to register the dynamic configuration manager, bus name, and reference to the JsMainImpl object.

- The getBusProxy method that takes a bus name as a parameter searches for a bus in the list where the server is a member and returns a reference to it.

- The getBus method takes a bus name as a parameter and calls the getBusProxy method above with it as a parameter.

- The getDefinedBus method searches by bus name for a bus in the list where the server is a member, then searches for the bus in the map where the server is not a member, and finally calls searchForAndRegisterBus for the bus name and adds it to a list.

- The searchForBusInListWhereServerIsMember method uses the bus name to find the bus in a vector, and the searchForBusInMapWhereServerIsNotMember method uses the bus name to find the bus in a list by name.

- The searchForAndRegisterBus method searches for a configuration object for the bus and, if it finds it, creates a new JsBusImpl object and then calls registerBusListener for the configuration object.

- The getBusConfigObject method takes a bus name as a parameter and uses the Config Service to get the sib-bus.xml file for that bus and then searches for that bus.

- The getProcessComponent method takes a class name as a parameter and returns a component that has been run by the SIB environment.

- The getMessagingEngine method takes a messaging engine name as a parameter, searches the stored list of messaging engines, and, if it finds it, returns a JsMessagingEngineImpl reference for it.

- The listMessagingEngines methods return an enumeration of the messaging engines, either all messaging engines or just those in that bus.

- The getMessagingEngineSet method returns the set of messaging engines for the given bus name. It calls getBusProxy to get the JsBusImpl reference for the bus name, and, if it finds it, iterates the bus member list from the configuration object for the reference and adds each bus member to the set that is returned.

- The showMessagingEngines method calls the listMessagingEngines method to get an enumeration of the messaging engines and then creates a String array of bus names, member names, states, etc. by adding each to the array while iterating the enumeration.

- The startMessagingEngine method takes a bus name and a name and calls the getMessagingEngine method for the combination for which it typecasts the result to a BaseMessagingEngineImpl reference that it then calls the startConditional method on.

- The stopMessagingEngine methods—all of which take a bus name and name as parameters, and two of which take a node—end up with a call to the getMessagingEngine method for the combination of bus name and name, which returns a result that is typecast to a BaseMessagingEngineImpl reference that the stopConditional method is called on.

- The setAttributes method takes a BaseMessagingEngineImpl reference that the configuration is set on.

- The activateJMSResource method creates a new SIBJMSResource object, and the deactivateJMSResource method deactivates the MBean for it and sets its reference to null.

- The getService method uses the ComponentImpl parent to access the WsServiceRegistry to get access to a service. The releaseService method calls the parent releaseService method to free the object returned when the service is accessed.

- The vetoableChange method takes a PropertyChangeEvent reference and checks to see if the current application server process state is STARTED, and calls serverStarted if it is, or stops and calls serverStopping if the state is STOPPING as a result of the application server process shutting down. Thus, the messaging engines are started as a result of the call from the Server Service to say the state of the application server process is changing.

- The isServerStarting and isServerStopping methods return flags that indicate if the state is transitioning to the state indicated by the method name.

- The getHealthState method enumerates the components hosted by the SIB environment and returns the worst state of health it finds. The reportLocalError method and reportGlobalError method call the getLocalError and getGlobalError methods, respectively, for the JsHealthState class and pass the returned values to the recordedHealth moreSevere method. These methods all use the JsHealthState and recordedHealth classes.

- The configChanged method checks the passed-in ConfigRepositoryEvent for changes and enumerates them. It looks for changes to the sib-engines.xml file, which require a call to the engineConfigChanged method, or changes to the sib-mqserverbusmembers. xml file, which require a call to the mqServerBusMemberConfigChanged method. For each changed MessagingEngine reference, the reloadEngine method is called with a refer-ence to the BaseMessagingEngineImpl object for that engine and the configuration for it. The changed engines are then enumerated with a call to the engineReloaded method for the engine and the engine components.

- The reloadEngine method enumerates the localization points for the engine and the MQLink sender channels and updates them from the configuration. The reloadMQServerBusMemberEngine method is called with the engine implementation reference, and then the reloadEngine method is called on that reference.

- The getSibServiceStatsGroup and getSibEnginesStatsGroup methods return the internal references implied by the names.

- The isJsBusActivatable method returns a flag indicating if the Security Service is running on the given JsBus bus.

- The addJsBusActivatableListener method adds a JsBusActivatableListener listener for the given JsBus bus.

- The stateChanged method that takes a SecurityServiceEvent parameter checks the state of the parameter and sets the Security Service up flag to true and calls the dispatchActivationListeners private method.

- The dispatchActivationListeners method enumerates the JsBusActivatableListeners list maintained by the JsMainImpl class and calls the busIsActivatable method on each listener.

- The isServerInRecoveryMode method simply returns the flag used to indicate if the server is in recovery mode.

- The expandVariables method takes a String parameter and returns an expansion of it by calling the parent implementation of the method.

- The engineConfigChanged method uses the Config Service to get the sib-engines. xml file to obtain a list of messaging engines. For each MessagingEngine refer-ence in the list, the method calls the getBusProxy method. On the reference, if the isConfigurationReloadEnabled call returns true and the UUID for the engine is not in the messaging engine list, the createServerMessagingEngine method or createClusterMessagingEngine method is called dependent on the scope. In that call that creates a messaging engine of the appropriate type a BaseMessagingEngineImpl reference is used and the initialize method is called on that reference. The BaseMessagingEngineImpl reference is passed to setCustomProperties, setAttributes, and the MEsToStart list. If the engine UUID is in the messaging engine list, then its con-figuration is set and it is added to the list of changed messaging engines. If there are any messaging engines to start, the Resource Manager Service reload method is called, and for each engine reference the startConditional method is called. Some messaging engines may end up having their stopConditional methods called as a result of the con-figuration change, in which case they are destroyed and removed from the lists.

- The `mqServerBusMemberConfigChanged` method gets a list of messaging engines for the bus name that is iterated and if any messaging engine in that list has changed it is added to the list of changed messaging engines.

- The `reloadMQServerBusMemberEngine` method takes a `BaseMessagingEngineImpl` reference as a parameter, and if the reference is for a `JsMessagingEngineImpl`, the Config Service is accessed and a reference to the service interface is passed, with the bus name, to the `getMQServerBusMembersByBusName` method of the `SIBMQServerBusMemberHelper` class to get a `Hashtable` of MQ Server bus members for the bus name. The engine `getMQServerBusMembers` method returns a `Hashtable` that is iterated, and if the UUID for the engine is not in the set of MQ Server bus member engines, the `createMQServerBusMember` is called for the Config Service reference, the engine, and the MQ Server bus member being iterated. Then for the list returned from the `getMQServerBusMembers` call the entries are iterated and a `Config` object is obtained for each and passed with the engine reference and MQ Server bus member being iterated to the `deleteMQServerBusMember` method. Then for each of the iterated bus members the configuration is obtained and the `alterMQServerBusMember` method is called. After the iterations complete, the `setMQServerBusMembers` call is made on the engine, passing in the bus member list as a parameter.

- The `createMQServerBusMember` method iterates the localization points for the MQ Server bus member and adds each to the messaging engine, and the changed reference is returned to the caller.

- The `deleteMQServerBusMember` method iterates the localization points for the MQ Server bus member and each is deleted from the messaging engine, and the changed reference is returned to the caller.

- The `alterMQServerBusMember` method takes a Config Service reference, a `JsMessagingEngine` messaging engine reference, and `Config` object references for the engine MQ Server bus members and the configured MQ Server bus members. The method iterates the localization points for the configured MQ Server bus member instances and each is added to the messaging engine. The `alterMQServerBusMember` method then iterates the localization points for the engine MQ Server bus member instances and each is deleted from the messaging engine. If the two configuration object references are different, the localization points are altered for the messaging engine. The changed messaging engine reference is returned to the caller.

- The `asHashtable` method takes a configuration object for an MQ Server Bus Member and iterates its localization points to create a `Hashtable` that is returned to the caller.

- The `getBusEngineList` method takes a `Hashtable` of engines and a bus name, and it iterates the list looking for members of the bus; when it finds them, it adds them to a new list that is returned to the caller.

- The `areMQServerBusMemberDifferent` method takes two configuration object references and compares their UUID, name, virtual queue manager name, ports, transport chains, channels, etc., and if they are the same, it returns `false`. The `areMQLocalizationPointProxyDifferent` method does the same thing for localization points. The underlying `areDifferent` method just compares two strings.

- The parseConfigUri method breaks down a configuration URI by cells, nodes, servers, clusters, and buses into tokens to create a set of properties that is returned to the caller.

- The createScope method uses the Config Service and sets properties for node, server, cluster, and bus levels.

- The forceConfigReload method calls the forceReload method of the dynamic configuration manager reference for the environment.

- The stateChanged method that takes a DeployedObjectEvent, and is the method called as part of the DeployedObjectListener interface, checks to see if the server is started or if an application is being started and, if so, calls the forceConfigReload method.

- The listDefinedBuses method uses the Config Service to get a String array of buses and creates a list from the result and returns it to the caller.

- The JsBusListener class implements the ConfigChangeListener interface and watches for changes in configuration for the bus with a given bus name. It is notified via the configChanged method from a call from the Config Service and particularly looks for changes in sib-bus.xml, sib-mediations.xml, sib-destinations.xml, or sib-security-audit.xml. When those changes occur, it sets up the messaging engine configuration and refreshes the subsystems that require changing.

The BaseMessagingEngineImpl Class Implementation

This class is the placeholder for the components of messaging rather than communications, in that it holds the references to the components that do the real work. This section examines only the important functionality in the class, rather than its method details. This is the class that manages the relationships between classes that manage the higher-level qualities of service and the mechanisms for managing message persistence such as the file store or a database.

The class extends the JsEObjectImpl class and implements the following interfaces:

- JsEngineComponent

- JsMessagingEngineMBean

- JsHealthMonitor

The constructor initializes a number of member variables, such as references to the file store, caches, state variables, and messaging engine references, but also gets the ConfigObject from the messaging engine configuration for the dataStore and fileStore, which it uses to create new JsDatastoreImpl or new JsFilestoreImpl objects, respectively, to handle the persistence that the message store functionality will build upon.

The JsMessagingEngine Interface and the JsMessagingEngineImpl Class Implementation

The JsMessagingEngine interface is implemented by the JsMessagingEngineImpl class, and manages JsEngineComponents, the file store and the data store that underlie the message store, SIB destinations, SIB mediations, MQ links, gateway links, and locality sets.

The JsMessagingEngineImpl class extends the HAManagerMessagingEngineImpl class and implements the following interfaces:

- JsDefaultMessagingEngine

- JsEngineComponent

- JsEObject

- JsHealthMonitor

Technically, the JsDefaultMessagingEngine interface extends the JsMessagingEngine interface, and the JsMessagingEngineImpl class implements this, the JsEngineComponent, the JsEObject, and the JsHealthMonitor interfaces while also extending the HAManager MessagingEngineImpl class. The HAManagerMessagingEngineImpl class implements the HAManagerMessagingEngine interface and sets up the HAGroup properties for SIB's HAManager use (i.e., WSAF_SIB, WSAF_SIB_MESSAGING_ENGINE, and WSAF_SIB_BUS) and provides the activation and deactivation support to fail over messaging engine instances when the health check assessment isAlive method indicates.

While the JsStandaloneEngineImpl class used for simple standalone SIB messaging engines also implements the JsMessagingEngine interface, the JsMessagingEngineImpl class is a more complex implementation to account for high availability. The JsStandaloneEngineImpl class code gives a simple picture of the requirements of a messaging engine in that it sets up the MessageStore singleton reference for the messaging engine; applies the configuration to initialize it and then starts it; and maintains the datastore, filestore, and JsEngineComponent references. The datastore reference refers to a JsDatastoreImpl class and the filestore reference refers to a JsFilestoreImpl class in the same way as for the JsMessagingEngineImpl implementation.

The JsMessagingEngineImpl class constructor is passed a JsMainImpl reference, a JsBusImpl reference, and a messaging engine ConfigObject reference as parameters. It uses the ConfigObject reference to read the configured localization points and apply them, and then uses the Config Service with the bus name as a lookup to access a list of WebSphere MQ Server bus members, from which it creates a Hashtable object for later use.

Let's look at some of the implemented methods:

- In the initialize method, the implementation loads classes for security, mediation, WS-Notification, and WS-ReliableMessaging, loads a list of gateway links and WebSphere MQ client links, and then loads classes for the message processor and message store handling. It then enumerates and loads the JsEngineComponent components.

- The start method enumerates and starts the appropriate components depending on the mode (e.g., recovery mode), with a call to the start method on the components.

- The stop method enumerates and calls stop on each component.

- The destroy method enumerates and calls destroy on each component.

- Most other methods enumerate and manage the components, such as to perform a reload of the messaging engine, manage the configuration, or manage the WebSphere MQ client links or gateway links. For example, a reload may need the MQ links to be reloaded so the localization points, sender channels, etc. are re-created from the configuration. Similarly, the SIB link connections to other messaging engines are reloaded from the configuration. Underpinning this configuration is the Virtual Link Definition that includes details of any foreign bus configuration. Most other methods handle state notifications.

The `JsDatastoreImpl` and `JsFilestore` classes are not what they might seem to be, but rather are essentially marker classes that also hold the configuration for a data source or a file source, respectively, for the message store. The `JsMessagingEngine` class itself handles the control for persistence. The `JsDatastoreImpl` and `JsFilestoreImpl` classes are extremely thin wrappers, where most methods do nothing. The magic works as they extend the `JsEObjectImpl` class and implement the `JsEObject` and `JsEngineComponent` interfaces, so as the `JsDatastoreImpl` and `JsFilestoreImpl` classes have the data source or file source configuration, respectively, for the messaging engine passed in to them when they are created, they save that configuration and leave most of the work up to the parent class.

The `JsEObjectImpl` class maintains a hash map of children, maintains MBeans for management, and maintains configuration for which it has a number of accessors for different data types. The `loadClass` method is used to create new `JsEngineComponent` instances for use by the messaging engine.

The `MessageProcessor` class is one of the core worker classes of the SIB. It creates, removes, and maintains connections with the outside world for subjects and subscribers, destinations, foreign SIB bus links via the `LinkManager` class, and the links to foreign WebSphere MQ buses and MQ Links to WebSphere MQ queue managers via the use of MQ link definitions, localization definitions, and the `MQLinkManager` handler class. The `DestinationManager` class used by the `MessageProcessor` class wraps the details of the implementation of each link type. The `MessageProcessor` class also creates the default queues, such as the `exception_destination` queue for the bus. It also maintains system connections to neighbors on the same bus.

JsBusImpl Class Implementation

The `JsBusImpl` class extends the `JsEObjectImpl` class and implements the `JsBus` and `JsEObject` interfaces.

The `JsBus` interface itself extends the `JsEObject` interface and includes identification, configuration, remote connectivity, and messaging configuration methods and methods to add `ConfigChangeListener` references:

- For identification, the `getName` and `getUuid` methods are available.

- For communications configuration, the `getPermittedChains` and `getPermittedChainUsage` methods are available.

- For general configuration, the `getCustomProperty`, `isSecure`, `isBootstrapAllowed`, and `isBusAuditAllowed` methods are available.

- For remote connectivity and messaging configuration, the `getSIBDestination`, `getSIBDestinationLocalitySet`, `getSIBMediation`, `getSIBMediationLocalitySet`, `getForeignBus`, and `getForeignBusForLink` methods are available. Mediations are transformations of formats and protocols that are usually associated with ESBs, and this functionality is now more properly best handled within WebSphere ESB, so mediations in WAS 7 are intended more for legacy compatibility reasons.

- To watch for configuration changes, the `addConfigChangeListener` methods are available.

In the `JsBusImpl` constructor, member variables are initialized, a reference to the singleton `JsAdminFactory` object is obtained, new `JsMediationCache` and `JsDestinationCache` objects are created for use by the bus for mediation and remote routing purposes, respectively, and the

Config Service is accessed to check the allowAudit variable in the sib-security-audit.xml file to see if auditing is enabled.

Most methods in the JsBusImpl file are simple one-line wrapper methods that delegate to some lower-level object:

- The getName, getDestinationCache, and getMediationCache methods just return the values of their member variables.

- The getSIBDestination and getSIBDestinationLocalitySet methods delegate to the same method names on the destination cache member variable.

- The getSIBMediation and getSIBMediationLocalitySet methods delegate to the same method names on the mediation cache member variable.

- The isSecure method checks to see if the bus configuration is set for secure operation and accesses the WAS Security Service via the WAS Service Registry, and if both have security enabled, the method returns true; otherwise it returns false.

- The getUuid method creates a new UUID, if there isn't one, and stores it in a member variable and returns the value of the member variable.

- The getForeignBus method gets a list of foreign buses from the foreignBus part of the configuration, which it enumerates until it finds the passed-in foreign bus name, and then it uses the JsAdminFactoryImpl createForeignBusDefinition method on that configuration to create a foreign bus definition that it returns to the caller. If the foreign bus name isn't found a null is returned.

- The getForeignBusForLink method gets a list of foreign buses from the foreignBus part of the configuration, which it enumerates to examine the virtualLink part of the configuration until it finds the virtualLink value for the passed-in UUID, and then it uses the JsAdminFactoryImpl createForeignBusDefinition method on that configuration to create a foreign bus definition that it returns to the caller. If the VirtualLink UUID isn't found, a null is returned.

- In the refreshMediationCache method, a new JsMedationCache object is created and assigned to the member variable, and it is used to populate the destination cache via the mediation cache refreshDestinationCacheWithMediations method.

- In the refreshDestinationCache method, a new JsDestinationCache object is created and assigned to the destination cache member variable.

- The isConfigurationReloadEnabled method merely returns the value of the configurationReloadEnabled configuration variable if it exists.

- The setCustomProperties method iterates the configuration properties list and sets the configuration name-value pairs.

- The setCustomProperty method takes a name and a value and sets the combination as a custom property.

- The getCustomProperty method returns the value associated with a property name.

- The isEventNotificationPropertySet checks the value associated with the sib.event.notification custom property and returns true if it is set to enabled and false if it is set to disabled.

- The getPermittedChains method gets the list of chains from the permittedChains configuration object and iterates it to add each chain to a hash set that is returned to the caller.

- The getPermittedChainUsage method gets the usePermittedChains configuration object and returns a JsPermittedChainUsage enumeration set to ALL (the default), LISTED, or SSL_ENABLED, depending on the result, and returns the enumeration to the caller.

- The isBootstrapAllowed method checks the value of the bootstrapMemberPolicy configuration object, which has a default of SIBSERVICE_ENABLED and returns true if that default value is set or if the JsAdminService bus name is set. Otherwise, if the returned bootstrap member policy is set to MEMBERS_AND_NOMINATED, the nominatedBootstrapMembers configuration object is accessed and the values returned are iterated and compared with the Server Service configured cluster name, node name, and server name until a match between the node name and server name and bootstrap member name equivalents is found or there are no more values to iterate. The Boolean value as to whether the values are found or not is returned to the caller.

- The isBusAuditAllowed method returns the value of the busAuditAllowed member variable. This tells the caller whether or not an audit of the bus is acceptable.

- The loadAuditAllowed method accesses the Config Service from the WAS service registry to get access to the sib-security-audit.xml file contents to check if the allowAudit value is set; if it is, the busAuditAllowed member variable is set to true, and if it is not, it is set to false.

- There are two variations of the addConfigChangeListener method. In both the dynamic configuration manager is accessed to get at the bus's settings to check if SIB_AUDIT or SIB_AUTHORIZATIONS configuration values are set and, if so, the listener is registered with security; otherwise it is registered with the bus.

The MessageStore and MessageStoreImpl Classes

At the highest level, the message store classes act as a front end to underlying storage mechanisms. Updates to the storage mechanisms require transaction support to ensure consistency, so the message store makes use of its own transaction manager (XidManager), and messages must be expired and tidied up, so an expiry manager (Expirer) is used. Storage of individual items takes place by writing to the cache manager (CacheLoader), and from there the related file store or data base storage is written, although initialization is handled through the message store classes.

The abstract MessageStore class implements the following interfaces:

- JsEngineComponent

- JsMonitoredComponent

- JsHealthMonitor

- JsReloadableComponent

- MessageStoreInterface

Most of its methods do nothing or return member variables, apart from the xmlRequestWrite* methods that handle I/O of XML and the createInstance method that instantiates and returns a com.ibm.ws.sib.msgstore.impl.MessageStoreImpl object.

The MessageStoreImpl class extends the MessageStore abstract class and implements the MessageStoreConstants and XmlConstants interfaces. The constructor initializes member variables, and creates new XidManager and Expirer objects, which it stores in member variables for later use.

The XidManager manages transaction IDs and then implements the distributed transaction support (i.e., start, end, commit, prepare, etc.) for updates to the message store for the messaging engine. The Expirer handles the timing out (i.e., message expiry) of messages and tidying up of messages in the message store, with alarms set that cause periodic tidying up. Most of the methods implemented by the class merely return the values of member variables. We will just look at some key methods:

- On initialization, via the initialize method, the data source settings for the message store are obtained from the messaging engine configuration if a database configuration exists, or if a file store configuration exists the directory and the maximum and minimum temporary and permanent storage size settings are obtained. Instrumentation is started at this time.

- When the start method is called, exceptions are cleared and the state is tracked, and then the item maps and links that manage the relationship between in-flight messages and the message store are initialized. The ItemStorageManager is created and initialized and the persistent message store is started. The transaction factory for the message store persistence is then started along with the lock generator and cache loader.

- When the stop method is called, the expirer, cache loader, maps, and persistent message store are all stopped. When the destroy method is called, the instrumentation is terminated.

- The findById and _findById methods take an item ID, follow the link to the message in the cache, and return the item itself. The cache is accessed via the RootMembership class and the ItemStorageManager that handles the individual item links.

- The add method calls the addItemStream method of the RootMembership class reference to add an item stream for a given lock ID and transaction.

- The commitPreparedTransaction method takes a transaction ID string, creates a new persistent transaction ID for it, and calls commit on the XidManager reference, passing the ID to it as a parameter.

- The expirerStart and expirerStop methods call start and stop, respectively, on the Expirer class reference for the given expiry interval and messaging engine reference.

- The findFirstMatching method takes a Filter reference and returns an item by delegating to the RootMembership class reference findFirstMatchingItemStream call to access the item for the given filter.

- The newNonLockingCursor method takes a filter and delegates to the newNonLocking ItemStreamCursor method of the RootMembership class reference and passes in the filter, which returns a cursor allowing enumeration of the messages stored that meet the filter criteria.

- The `removeFirstMatching` method takes a filter and a transaction reference and delegates to the `removeFirstMatchingItemStream` method of the `RootMembership` class reference, with the filter and transaction references passed as parameters, which allows messages to be transactionally removed from the store that meet the filter criteria.

- The `getPreparedTransactions` method returns a list of in-doubt transactions it obtains from the `XidManager` reference.

- The `getUniqueLockId` method delegates to a different ID generator depending on the storage strategy for the messaging engine, but returns a lock ID.

- The `rollbackPreparedTransaction` method takes a transaction ID string and creates a new persistent transaction ID for it and calls `rollback` on the `XidManager` reference, passing the ID as a parameter.

The `RootMembership` class used by some of the preceding methods is like the underlying storage manager for a database in that it maintains a map of tuples (i.e., mathematical set theory name for a row in a database) in a stream that are mapped to an underlying persistent message store that is stored as a reference obtained from the message store itself. The mechanism works with either the database persistent message store or the file-based persistent message store, as it accesses both via the same interface methods. However, the `RootMembership` class is part of the caching mechanism in that it maintains a copy of the active items and their relationships (via links) in memory.

Many of the underlying searches to look up message items are delegated to the underlying persistent message store itself. It builds a hash map of items in the persistent message store and maintains that and the links between items in memory. Generally, new item links are appended. The persistent message store used by this class is passed via the `PersistentMessageStore` interface, which is actually implemented by the `PersistentMessageStoreImpl` class.

The `PerstistentMessageStoreImpl` class is the one that controls the JDBC and SQL access to a data source, but it delegates most of the work of forming the SQL to the lower-level `DatasourceController`, `TableManager`, `SpillDispatcher`, and `PersistentDispatcher` classes. The `DatasourceController` class manages the connection and access to the data source for persistence. The `TableManager` maintains a list of tables that it creates for the target data source and then handles inserts, updates, deletes, and selects from these along with transactions. The dispatchers handle the dispatching of persistence-related tasks.

The SIB includes several other classes whose names are misleading at first glance, such as `SIBRemoteMessageImpl` and `SIBTransmitMessageImpl`. The majority of these classes do not perform any action but are representational of the state related to some action. Most of the real work is done by the implementation classes at the Channel Framework Service or Bus and Messaging Engine level.

Web Services Gateway

The main subject of this chapter has been the JMS messaging functionality provided by the SIB messaging engine, but the SIB includes a number of other functions provided by some of its subsystems. The Web Services Gateway functionality, which is one such subsystem in the SIB, has existed in the WAS arena for a long time. It is essentially intended to hide the internal web services routes, formats, and functionality for an enterprise from external users and is essentially a façade or proxy for internally exposed WAS web services. In the past this existed as functionality in its own right, but now is implemented as part of the SIB. This makes sense because it is essentially performing the function of a mediation, and this, with its pre-SCA standard and WebSphere ESB implementation of mediations, is handled within the SIB itself.

The mediation functions the Web Services Gateway has to perform consists of

- Altering the destination of a message

- Handling custom headers

- Applying and removing message-level security

- Performing protocol transformation such as HTTP to JMS or HTTPS to HTTP

The core functionality of the Web Services Gateway is designed to work with SOAP messages.

The Web Services Gateway functionality is implemented by a number of classes within the `com.ibm.ws.wsgw.*` package structure within the `com.ibm.ws.sib.server.jar` plugin file. The implementation is controlled from the `com.ibm.ws.sib.webservices.component.SIBWSComponent`. The component installs listeners for the Config Service and Meta Data Service to watch for new deployments that contain any WAR or EJB-JAR files that might contain service components of relevance. If it finds them, it installs the necessary servlet listeners and JAX-RPC handler support to map them to something that can be mediated, and then it installs the appropriate endpoint listeners to front those services.

The functionality of the Web Services Gateway is more of an extension to the WAS JavaEE support that is based on the core implementation, so we will not consider it in more detail here. In the longer term, the functionality of the Web Services Gateway is likely to be taken over by one of the WebSphere or WebSphere DataPower appliances in most organizations.

Web Services Notification

The Web Services Notification standard from the OASIS (Organization for the Advancement of Structured Information Standards) standards body is simple. It is designed to allow a central publisher to send notifications or events to multiple subscribers using web services protocols and is essentially a web services publish and subscribe mechanism. Inside WAS, publish and subscribe functionality already existed in JMS and that is handled by the SIB.

Inside the SIB implementation in `com.ibm.ws.sib.server.jar`, the Web Services Notification support, as we can see from the `plugin.xml` entry for the Web Services Notification component, is handled by the `WSNComponentImpl` class. This and its related classes sit under the `com.ibm.ws.sib.wsn.*` or `com.ibm.ws.sib.wsnotification.*` package structure. Essentially, the class uses a number of other related classes to set up a registry of subscribers for WS-Notification services and endpoints and then delegates the work of handling the events to the underlying local bus engine.

As for the Web Services Gateway, this implementation will not be considered more fully here as it is more of a user of the core SIB facilities that extends its functionality. However, in the case of the WS-Notification support, the underlying JMS implementation to support a web services standard for event notifications seems a sensible one.

Summary

This chapter looked at the Service Integration Bus Messaging Engine implementation and how it supports JMS using its own underlying JFAP protocol or the MQFAP protocol that allows it to communicate with WebSphere MQ implementations as a peer. The implementation is essentially handled in two key subsystems, the channels and chains of the Channel Framework Service and the components that manage them, and the MessagingEngine, JsBus, and JsMessagingEngine classes and functions that handle the setup of the environment for persistent storage to a database or the file system and the semantics of handling the configuration of messaging. The MessageProcessor class acts as part of the underlying glue between the components.

The Web Services Gateway and Web Services Notification facilities were briefly examined and shown to be no more than thin wrappers around the functionality that already exists in the SIB to support the semantics of JMS messaging, mediation, and publish and subscribe handling. Many other IBM products and technologies build on the SIB this way, such as WebSphere Enterprise Service Bus and WebSphere Process Server, so this is a common pattern.

CHAPTER 9

∎∎∎

High Availability

To understand how high availability works in WebSphere Application Server 7 Network Deployment (WAS-ND), you first have to understand how to distinguish high availability from scalability. These concepts have a large overlap due to the horizontal "scale out" scalability features that also result in higher availability. This chapter concentrates on just those components that recover singleton functionality on another WAS instance when the original instance fails; i.e., the emphasis is on singletons and their state management. Both scalability and high-availability features are unique to WAS-ND and the products that build upon it.

With WAS-ND, horizontal scalability overlaps with high availability insofar as having instances in a cluster on more than one physical machine means that failure of one physical machine does not result in complete application failure, because other instances take on its workload in addition to that same type of work they were already doing. *High availability* relates to another instance taking on some unique new work that was previously being undertaken by another single instance in the cluster. Scalability is covered in Chapter 10, so for the purposes of explaining WAS as a whole without any overlap, this chapter concentrates on the WAS HAManager subsystem and how it implements high-availability functionality. This chapter also examines how transaction logging is performed and how these logs are used for recovery after failure, following up on the brief coverage in Chapter 4.

WAS-ND and High Availability

You first need to understand the context in which WAS scalability and high availability fit. As mentioned, for scalability and high availability, you need the enterprise deployment solution for WAS, WAS-ND. With this edition of WAS, multiple instances can be deployed into an enterprise to run the same applications and support failover and scalability for high volumes.

To control this environment, a centralized and specialized WAS instance is used that manages the configuration of the environment and the applications: the Deployment Manager. The Deployment Manager keeps track of all the nodes it is responsible for and the XML configuration files that set up each node. The *WAS cell* is the administration unit controlled by the Deployment Manager that consists of all the nodes (essentially the operating system images hosting the WAS instances), the clusters, the instances, and the deployed applications.

WAS Cells

Each WAS cell consists of one or more instances, which may be arranged into one or more clusters, running on one or more nodes. As just mentioned, a node is effectively an operating system (OS) image that hosts WAS instances, but, more specifically, it consists of a Node Agent, which is a specialized WAS instance for managing a group of instances running in a single OS image, and the WAS instances themselves. The Node Agent communicates with the Deployment Manager to get the configuration information, in terms of XML files, for the instances it runs and any additional instances in the same clusters on other nodes.

The WAS clusters consist of one or more WAS instances. If these instances are on the same node, the type of configuration is called *vertical clustering*, which is useful for scalability purposes to exploit the physical resources of the node to enhance throughput. Vertical clustering supports high availability only for the scenario in which a WAS instance on the same node fails. If the instances in the cluster are on different nodes, the type of configuration is called *horizontal clustering*, which supports scalability *and* high availability. The infrastructure and implementation for both vertical and horizontal clustering are not entirely the same, so I will wait until Chapter 10 to describe some components, but note here that whereas horizontal clustering fully supports high availability, vertical clustering has only limited high-availability support. Our focus for high availability is on singletons at the cluster level (i.e., those components that should only exist once in a cluster) and how resilience is maintained for these components.

Within the WAS cell, multiple clusters can be configured and, within these clusters, replication can be used to keep the cluster members in sync. I will cover this in Chapter 10 in the discussion of session management.

To control synchronization of the configuration and limit the amount of unnecessary traffic between nodes, WAS sets up core groups of instances. The default core group is the size of the cell, but multiple core groups can be configured within the cell.

Bridging between core groups is possible using the aptly named CoreGroupBridge facility. Core groups may need to share availability information, so the bridge service sets up a server to host the Core Group Bridge Service, which is handled by the code in com.ibm. ws.coregroupbridge.jar controlled by the CGBridgeService class in the CoreGroupBridge component. The collaborating core groups are known as an access point.

Core Groups and High Availability

A core group is effectively a high-availability domain in which failover and replication artifacts are contained and controlled. Each WAS instance must be a member of only one core group. A core group must contain at least one Node Agent or a Deployment Manager instance. All instances are added to the DefaultCoreGroup core group when created, but can be moved to other core groups. All members of a core group must be able to see and communicate bi-directionally with all other core group members. Topology changes within a core group that affect subscribing components are notified by the HAGroupCallback interface.

Singleton services that require high availability create high-availability groups, such as those required by the Service Integration Bus (SIB), and these groups are controlled by the Group Manager component of HAManager to ensure that one instance of the singleton is always available within and under the control of the core group. The HAGroup high-availability grouping has a name consisting of name-value pairs such as the component name and a policy to apply. The policy controls the rules to apply when a member joins or leaves the group, i.e., all active, m of n active, one of n active, and quorum required or no quorum, which refer to how many of the members in the group are active at one time and whether quorum is or is not required.

A cluster groups WAS instances within a cell for the purpose of high availability and scalability. It is the cluster that gives the ability to share running state. Clusters are effectively just a group of like WAS instances running the same applications. All instances in a cluster must be members of the same core group. The cluster members can share information between them, such as session objects, and can take ownership of each other's transactions when a failover occurs. Their configuration takes place within the WAS Deployment Manager environment, and the cluster description can be pushed out to web servers that then load balance requests across the cluster members.

For failover of web and web services sessions between cluster members, either a JSESSIONID cookie, query string, or header is used; or the SSL-related equivalent SSLJSESSION configuration, with the instance ID appended to identify the instance that last handled a session so that the web server can implement sticky sessions and only route to another cluster member when a failure occurs. Data Replication Services (DRS) replicates the session objects from one cluster member to another, or the session information can be persisted to a shared database environment. The synchronization between cluster members on which DRS builds is based on the Distribution and Consistency Services (DCS) communications framework within WAS and the Reliable Multicast Messaging (RMM) mechanism it uses under the covers.

For transaction management, WAS writes transaction log entries detailing the state of the transactional change, what resources are involved, and whether they have acknowledged that they have both received the request to prepare for the change (ready to commit) and then made the change (commit). This is known as *two-phase commit*. With WAS, entries are written to files that can be made highly available via some file management infrastructure (e.g., Network File System v4) such that another WAS instance can take over the work (i.e., in WAS recovery mode) to apply the requested changes by communicating back to the resource coordinators to recover in-doubt transactions to get to a consistent state.

To understand the requirements that the WAS high-availability solutions have to meet, you need to look at what fails over and why. With stateless applications, WAS runs active-active instances, so there is no failover exactly, only a failure of processing by the failed WAS instance in the cluster. The difficulty is with state, such as maintained in sessions, in distributed transactions, or in the SIB messaging engine default requirement to maintain a single instance within the cluster to ensure message ordering is maintained.

Transaction Log Management

Transactions behave differently depending on whether they act through a single resource (one-phase commit) or multiple resources (two-phase commit) for distributed transactions. The same conceptual infrastructure based on transaction logs is required for both, but the difference is who maintains those logs. With a distributed transaction where WAS is the transaction coordinator, it is WAS that must maintain the transaction logs. The Open Group XA standard for distributed transaction processing (DTP) defines the interactions between a transaction coordinator and the resource managers, and WAS adheres to this standard with the assistance of appropriate JDBC, JMS, and JCA driver support.

To maintain transaction integrity where WAS is the transaction coordinator for distributed transactions, WAS uses transaction logs. These are files into which the context for a change and the details of what resources are to be changed are written before notifying resource coordinators to ensure they are "ready to commit," after which the state of each is written when each has responded to the subsequent "commit" instruction. If a failure occurs somewhere in the environment between writing the data to the target database, the information in the transaction logs on either the transaction coordinator (WAS) or the resource (e.g., DBMS) can be used to recover the agreed position. If it is WAS that has failed, then on startup the transaction log is used as the recovery log to ensure the environment and all of the resources are in the agreed consistent state and that either every change in the transaction has been applied to all resources or every change has been rolled back.

Nothing to do with a transaction should be "in doubt," so the transactional state should appear to all outsiders to the system to be integral, i.e., all-or-nothing, with no interim steps to reach that integral state visible. The transaction should have ACID properties—i.e., be atomic (all or nothing), consistent (all dependent changes applied), integral (no interim steps visible to the outside world), and durable (once committed there should be no reversion to the previous state).

Each WAS instance has a transaction log that is used whenever an XA or two-phase commit transaction is initiated under the control of WAS. This transaction or recovery log can be registered for high-availability support for WAS to automatically have an instance apply any in-doubt transaction entries while running in recovery mode after a failure occurs in another node. This requires the recovery or transaction logs to be available in a network or file location that is visible from every other server instance that could potentially take over applying those log entries. In past WAS releases, logs had to be applied manually because there were issues with earlier network file systems, such as NFSv3, that did not release writer file locks on failure. However, with the advent of the secure NFSv4 protocol, which does release writer file locks, recovery can be automatic as long as a WAS instance can be nominated within the group to take over the work of the failed node.

Generally, the WAS transaction service is engaged as part of the normal Java EE standard transaction facilities whenever all-or-nothing changes must be made under the control of WAS rather than another resource manager. In normal use, the WAS transaction service just writes the entries to the transaction logs to say what changes are needed, where they are to be applied, whether all resource managers agreed to commit, and, afterward, whether the change was committed by each resource manager.

HAManager High-Availability Mechanism

The HAManager is essentially a Java implementation of a failover mechanism, like IBM's own HACMP, but one that runs inside the Java Virtual Machine process itself. It consists of three core components, as shown in Figure 9-1: the Group Manager, the Bulletin Board, and the Agent. These components all sit on top of DCS, particularly the RMM facilities. The main role of DCS is to manage the state of singleton components that register their own HAGroup with the Group Manager. This behavior is embodied in the WAS SIB Messaging Engine or Transaction Manager, which are both singletons that register an HAGroup and related policy; so it is state that is communicated between the different instances to maintain consistency that HAManager takes responsibility for.

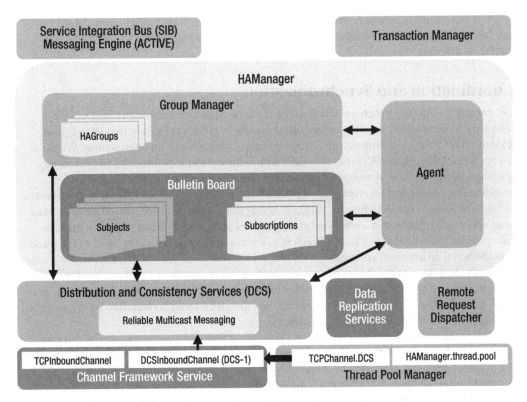

Figure 9-1. *HAManager architecture*

In WAS 7, the core group behavior is controlled via pluggable providers, so the description here applies to the default Discovery and Failure providers that are similar to those from WAS version 6.1.

High-Availability Communications

Members of the cluster/core group use RMM to send state messages, including serialized objects. These messages are sent to the Bulletin Board component inside the HAManager and to other interested parties; i.e., those that are potential targets for failover subscribe to these messages. Instances post messages to the bulletin board and other instances subscribe to the changes. Connection messages are sent consistently, providing an effective heartbeat. The discovery checks in WAS 7 take place every 60 seconds by default, but in mixed WAS 6.*x* and 7 environments, the checks to retry unavailable connections take place under the control of the IBM_CS_UNICAST_DISCOVERY_INTERVAL_SECS property, which defaults to 60 seconds.

Communications transport mechanisms can be of three types, with the DCS transport chain used as default or the DCS.Secure transport chain used if SSL is required. For multicast transport, standard UDP is used. Wherever the Channel Framework Service overhead would be excessive, a standard sockets-based network connection is used for unicast transport, although this option is deprecated for future use and remains only for backward compatibility.

Security is controlled within a core group using a combination of the WAS LTPA token being exchanged between instances and SSL.

It is important to be aware that the DCS communications transport chain is shared with the DRS and Dynacache, so buffers must be increased if these are in use, to avoid adverse effects on failover.

Coordination and Synchronization

On startup, a WAS JVM process starts the CoreStack HAManager component and subsystem, which immediately tries to contact other members of the core group that WAS JVM is a member of. This is the Core Group Discovery protocol that looks for connections. When the instance finds other WAS JVMs that exist within the core group, it initiates a process to join that core group and, if accepted, subscribes to the bulletin board services from other instances and sends and receives messages. This join process causes all HAManager instances to log a message to the WAS logs (DCSV1032I) saying that a new instance has joined the group, after which the HAManager View Synchrony protocol and process starts. This synchronization process exists so that the state of each of the group members is known by all other group members and all are synchronized.

With view synchrony, the set of communicating group members that form the view ensures that activities that were taking place for the old view complete, which pushes up network and CPU resource usage for a time. One core group member is elected to send its current configuration to all other core group members.

Detection of failures is handled by the Core Group Failure Detection protocol that triggers when inbound or outbound sockets used by HAManager are closed unexpectedly or when the active heartbeat is missed for a consecutive number of slots. Heartbeat periods are 30 seconds by default, and only after 180 seconds will a failure be detected in a pure WAS 7 environment. For mixed WAS 6.*x* and 7 environments, the heartbeat period is controlled by the IBM_CS_FD_PERIOD_SECS property, which is 30 seconds by default, and the number of slots that can be missed before a failure is assumed is controlled by the IBM_CS_FD_CONSECUTIVE_MISSED property. On failure of a WAS JVM, the Group Discovery protocol is executed and then the View Synchrony process is again run to ensure synchronization. In this case, the JVM ID of each instance is compared, and the one with the lowest JVM ID becomes the coordinator for the group, which is usually the Deployment Manager or the Node Agent.

The policy that is applied to control the behavior of the core group for HAManager is managed by the Group Manager component, which also controls the membership of the group, and is enforced and applied by the Agent component.

Every core group has a coordinator instance that manages the failover of the singletons that must be highly available and controls the distribution of state data to members registered to receive it. Election of new coordinators takes place whenever a core group member stops or starts, which is known as a *view change*.

The view synchrony negotiation and subscription management can generate a lot of network traffic and CPU overhead in handling the notifications, so it is wise to split large environments into a number of smaller core groups consisting of 20 instances or fewer. Multiple coordinators can be configured if necessary to avoid the excessive resource usage. Servers that are stable and have excess capacity should be the preferred target coordinators.

When a component or subsystem registers with HAManager, it creates an HAGroup and a policy for that HAGroup. This policy controls how many instances will have the subsystem active after a failover and whether a quorum is required.

HAManager Implementation

The HAManager implementation, unlike the scalability features of WAS that also support some high-availability features of WAS, is found in the `com.ibm.ws.runtime.jar` file. The Core Group Bridge implementation mentioned earlier is found in the `com.ibm.ws.coregroupbridge.jar` file. You can find the interfaces for each of the core components under the `com.ibm.wsspi.hamanager.*` package structure and find the implementations under the `com.ibm.ws.hamanager.*` package structure. This section examines each of the core components of the HAManager in turn.

Pay particular attention to the JMS-like use of `onMessage` throughout the subsystems as a result of the underlying communications behavior and mechanisms. A `WorkQueue` class implements queuing to schedule notifications in a manner similar to that of WebSphere MQ or the SIB Messaging Engine.

The Controller: HAManagerImpl

The `HAManagerImpl` class implements the `HAManager` and `HAManagerCordinatorCallback` interfaces and sits within the `com.ibm.ws.hamanager.impl` package. It embeds the `IsAliveBucket` and `IsAliveManager` inner classes. One key class that is used throughout the HAManager implementation is the `HAGroupImpl` class that handles the sending of messages to group members and some of the decisions as to the state of the group, including the identification of failures.

HAManagerImpl Inner Classes

The `IsAliveBucket` inner class includes methods to add and remove `HAGroups`, a method to get the length of time the group has been alive, a method to reassign an `HAGroup` to a different core group, and a method to send pings to each of the `HAGroups` to ensure they are alive.

The `IsAliveManager` inner class decorates the functionality of the `IsAliveBucket` class in that most calls delegate to it by looking up the bucket for the given "alive time." `IsAliveManager` implements the `AlarmListener` interface and, when the `alarm` method is called, uses the bucket to send pings. This effectively implements the heartbeat functionality. The class includes methods to add and remove `HAGroup` members, handle policy changes, and manage buckets for a given "alive time."

Handling Groups

The `HAManagerImpl` class maintains a `TreeMap` of local groups, a message cache, a heartbeat pinger using the `IsAliveManager` inner class for the given core group name, and a coordinator reference. It sets up a callback for the coordinator to call back into this `HAManagerImpl` object. There are a number of important methods, introduced next, that are used to implement the group synchronization and manage group membership.

The joinGroup Method

The `joinGroup` method takes a group name, a map of member properties, and an `HAGroupCallback` reference as parameters. It gets a reference to the `HAGroup` for the given group name and the Policy Manager reference from the coordinator. The Policy Manager reference is used to look up the HA policy rule for a given group name, and this is used to create a new HAGroupImpl object for the given group name, rule, properties, and group callback reference for this HAManager reference.

This HAGroupImpl reference is stored in the local core group TreeMap keyed by the given group name. The HAGroupImpl object is then added to the heartbeat pinger IsAliveManager underlying bucket using the addGroup method. The private localGroupMembershipChanged method is then called for the HAGroupImpl object reference before the object reference is returned to the caller.

The getStateForAllGroups Method

The getStateForAllGroups method iterates the local group TreeMap and for each iteration gets the HAGroupImpl reference from which it obtains the group state and the active coordinator. While doing this, it updates the cluster process state messages array for the group name and group state.

The hasActiveMembersInMinorityPartition Method

The hasActiveMembersInMinorityPartition method iterates the local group TreeMap and for each iteration gets the HAGroupImpl reference, from which it gets the IBM_hc group properties, and from this gets the group name. If it has the group name (i.e., it is not null) and the isQuorumSensitiveWithActiveMember method is called for the HAGroupImpl reference and returns true, and if the coordinator doesClusterHaveQuorum call returns false, the whole method returns true; otherwise it returns false.

The groupStateUpdate Method

The groupStateUpdate method takes a GroupMemberActivationCmdMsg reference as a parameter, from which a map of commands is extracted and iterated. For each command in the map, the group name and group member state are extracted by the method. If the state is ACTIVATING, activateLocalMember is called for the group name. If the state is DEACTIVATING, deactivateLocalMember is called for the group name. If the state is IDLE, enableLocalMember is called for the group name. If the state is DISABLED, disableLocalMember is called for the group name with a flag to set the state to DISABLED. If the state is GROUP_DISABLED, disableLocalMember is called for the group name with a flag to set the state to GROUP_DISABLED.

The groupMembershipUpdate Method

The groupMembershipUpdate method takes a GroupUpdateMsg reference as a parameter, from which the elements are extracted into a map that is then iterated. The group name and members are extracted for each iterated element by the method and the group member IDs are collected. The HAGroupImpl reference is then extracted from the local group TreeMap for the given group name and its membershipChanged method is called and the group member ID array is passed into it.

The onMessage Method

The onMessage method, just like that from JMS, takes a sender string and a GroupLocalMessage reference as a parameter. The message is extracted from the reference as an array of bytes along with the group name of the target group and the GroupMemberId of the source sender. The HAGroupImpl is extracted from the local group TreeMap for the given group name and its onMessage method is called and the source is passed along with the array of bytes from the original message.

The reloadPolicies Method

In the reloadPolicies method, the Policy Manager reference is obtained from the coordinator. Each of the local group TreeMap entries is iterated by the method and for each iterated entry the HAGroupImpl reference object has its updatePolicy method called to pass in a rule. The values of the HAGroupImpl object and the rule are extracted in each iteration, with the rule obtained by calling findHAPolicyRuleForGroup for the group name from the Policy Manager. The IsAliveManager pinger that handles the heartbeat is updated through a call to its policiesChanged method.

The shutdown Method

The shutdown method simply calls the stopAllHAGroups method.

The localGroupStateChanged Method

The localGroupStateChanged method takes an HAGroupImpl reference as a parameter, from which it extracts the group name and group state, and the message cache is updated with this information using the sendGroupStateUpdate method.

The localGroupMembershipChanged Method

The localGroupMembershipChanged method takes an HAGroupImpl reference and a Boolean indicator as to whether the change is to leave as parameters. If the leave indicator is set, a group state object is created by the method using the start time of the HAGroupImpl object, the group name is used to remove the entry from the local group TreeMap, and the removeGroup method is called on the IsAliveManager pinger object for the HAGroupImpl object reference before that object's doLeave method is called. If the leave indicator is not set, the group state is extracted from the HAGroupImpl object. The message cache is updated for the group name and group state through a call to its sendGroupStateUpdate method.

The isHardwareQuorumEnforced Method

The isHardwareQuorumEnforced method takes a group name as a parameter and delegates to the same call on the coordinator.

The activateLocalMember Method

The activateLocalMember method takes a group name as a parameter and calls the activate method on the HAGroupImpl object extracted from the local group TreeMap using the group name.

The deactivateLocalMember Method

The deactivateLocalMember method takes a group name as a parameter and calls the deactivate method on the HAGroupImpl object it extracts from the local group TreeMap using the group name.

The enableLocalMember Method

The enableLocalMember method takes a group name as a parameter and calls the adminEnable method on the HAGroupImpl object extracted from the local group TreeMap using the group name.

The disableLocalMember Method

The disableLocalMember method takes a group name and a GroupMemberState reference as parameters and calls the adminDisable method on the HAGroupImpl object extracted from the local group TreeMap using the group name and passing the GroupMemberState reference.

The stopAllHAGroups Method

The stopAllHAGroups method iterates each member of the local group TreeMap to extract the group name, and from this the HAGroupImpl reference, and the shutdown method is called on each of these references.

The getActiveCoordinatorIndex Method

The getActiveCoordinatorIndex method takes a group name and the number of coordinators as parameters and passes these on to an HAManager utility class and its calculateCoordinatorIndex method.

Bulletin Board

The Bulletin Board subsystem works on principles similar to JMS, JMS listeners, and the JMS publish-and-subscribe mechanisms. This is not surprising, because the Bulletin Board subsystem is implemented using the DCS RMM communications subsystem. Essentially, the system is built on the use of posts of messages to subjects, and subscribers watching for notification of new posts for that subject. Bulletin boards exist within a scope and have multiple subjects that can be subscribed to and posted to.

The Bulletin Board functionality is controlled by the BulletinBoardImpl implementation class, which implements the BulletinBoard interface.

The BulletinBoard Interface

The BulletinBoard interface contains a number of methods that will help your understanding of the intention of the Bulletin Board component:

- createSubject: Takes a BulletinBoardScope reference and a string describing the subject as parameters and returns a SubjectInfo reference

- close: Takes no parameters

- createPost: Takes a SubjectInfo reference as a parameter and returns a SubjectPost reference

- `subscribe`: Takes a `SubjectInfo` reference and a `SubjectSubscriptionEvents` reference as parameters and returns a `SubjectSubscription` reference

- `subscribeProxy`: Takes a `SubjectInfo` reference and a `SubjectSubscriptionProxyEvents` reference as parameters and returns a `SubjectSubscription` reference

If you take "subject" as a synonym for "topic" and "post" as a synonym for "message," the preceding should start to appear to be similar to JMS publish-and-subscribe mechanisms.

The BulletinBoardImpl Class

In the implementation class, the constructor takes a string containing the bulletin board name and a `LocalBulletinBoardStateManager` reference as parameters that are saved for later use and then the method creates an `ArrayList` of posts created for the bulletin board and an `ArrayList` of subscriptions created for the bulletin board. The `LocalBulletinBoardStateManager` object does much of the state management work for the bulletin board. Let's look at some key methods within this class. There are two `createPost` methods, taking one and two parameters respectively, that we must consider among the set of methods within this class.

The close Method

The `close` method enumerates all of the posts created for the bulletin board and closes the active subject posts in the list, then clears the `ArrayList` for the posts, enumerates the subscriptions created for the bulletin board and closes them, and then clears the `ArrayList` for the subscriptions. It finally marks the bulletin board as closed.

The subscribe Method

The `subscribe` method checks the parameters and that the bulletin board is not closed and then calls the `subscribe` method on the reference for the `LocalBulletinBoardStateManager`, passing the `SubjectInfo` key and the `SubjectSubscriptionEvents` reference to get a `Subject Subscription` reference returned. This `SubjectSubscription` reference is then added to the subscriptions `ArrayList` and its reference is returned to the caller.

The subscribeProxy Method

The `subscribeProxy` method checks the parameters and that the bulletin board is not closed and then calls the `subscribeProxy` method on the reference for the `LocalBulletinBoardStateManager`, passing the `SubjectInfo` key and the `SubjectSubscriptionProxyEvents` reference to get a `SubjectSubscription` reference returned. This `SubjectSubscription` reference is then added to the subscriptions `ArrayList` and its reference is returned to the caller.

The createSubject Method

The `createSubject` method checks its parameters and that the bulletin board is not closed, creates a new `SubjectInfoImpl` object for the given bulletin board name, scope, and subject, and returns this object to the caller.

The createPost Method

The createPost method that takes a single parameter checks that the SubjectInfo parameter is not null and that the bulletin board is not closed, and then calls the createPost method for the passed-in SubjectInfo reference on the reference for the LocalBulletinBoardStateManager. From the LocalBulletinBoardStateManager reference, the method gets a new SubjectPost reference returned that it adds to the posts created for the bulletin board ArrayList before returning that SubjectPost reference to the caller.

The createPost method that takes a SubjectInfo reference as a parameter and a SubjectValue proxy post parameter checks that the values aren't null and that the bulletin board is not closed and then creates a new SubjectInfoImpl object reference for the passed-in SubjectInfo reference. The method then extracts the server name, values, and version information from the SubjectValue proxy post parameter and passes these along with the new SubjectInfoImpl reference to the createProxyPost method of the reference for the LocalBulletinBoardStateManager to get a new SubjectPost reference. This SubjectPost reference is then added to the ArrayList of posts created for the bulletin board before also being returned to the caller.

The check Method

The check method simply checks that the bulletin board is open and, if it isn't, throws an exception. This method is used throughout the public interface of the bulletin board implementation.

Local Bulletin Board State Manager

The LocalBulletinBoardStateManager class handles most of the real implementation work for the bulletin board. It has callback methods that notify via the SubjectSubscriptionEvents and SubjectSubscriptionProxyEvents mechanisms and interfaces that a given subscription should be notified of updates. It also maintains queues that it uses to implement the bulletin board functionality, DCS interfaces to handle notification to other WAS instances, a cache of messages, and maps of subjects and subscribers.

The class keeps a reference to the coordinator for the core group so it can maintain its member list for notification purposes and can update it with PMI metrics. When handling proxy posts, it ensures that the given server posting is in the core group and then updates the subject list map with the new post and the message cache for the given subject. When handling normal posts, it adds the value into the map for the given subject.

The BulletinBoardPost class is used as a helper for creating the post and this class handles the DCS membership details. The message cache is used to send updates for a given subject when a post update occurs. Subscription for subject is again handled through array lists and the event mechanisms. The handling of core group changes, with the resulting notifications through the bulletin boards, and the bulletin board housekeeping are all handled through this class.

Bulletin Board Data Related Classes

The data being posted is handled by the BulletinBoardPost class, which basically maintains details of post versions and the server making the post along with a string of bytes representing the post.

The SubjectPost class ties the BulletinBoardPost data up with the local bulletin board state manager handling it and the subject it relates to.

The SubjectInfoImpl class relates the bulletin board name, the scope, the version of the subject, and the subject itself. The subject is just a string.

Agent

The Agent component is implemented in the AgentImpl class that implements the Agent and HAGroupCallback interfaces. It maintains the list of members, HAGroup names, and target servers. Each instance follows the pattern of ibm_agent.seq*XX* for its ID. It handles the resizing of the groups and the notification of changes via messages to all of the group members.

Messages have a quality of service associated with them. It is the Agent that handles the protocols associated with HAManager. Primary and secondary Agent instances are associated with a group, and these are created and destroyed as a result of operations in this class. Most control is delegated to an AgentClassImpl reference that was passed to the constructor, which actually joins the HAManager group and creates a data stack for it and then sends the messages to the members of that group, and it is this AgentClassImpl class that creates the AgentImpl object. The DataStack interface handles the sending of messages. The AgentImpl class mainly handles the protocols and validity checks.

The AgentImpl class follows the JMS style of handling message receipt through its onMessage method, which takes a sender ID that identifies which member sent the message and the message itself. The messages received here are used to destroy the given agent instance.

The various sendMessage implementations take a given quality of service indicator and message, and possibly one or more member destinations, and delegate to the AgentClassImpl reference sendMixedMessage method to handle the delivery.

In the membershipChanged method, which takes a group name and an array of group member IDs as parameters, the state of members in the membership is checked and the IDs of the highest and lowest sequence numbers identifying the agents in the membership are checked, which are all used to choose the new coordinator or primary agent for the group. When a primary agent has been chosen, a secondary agent is also chosen using the sequence numbers. The sequence numbers are associated with the ibm_agent.seq property that is associated with the group member details. This is the method that handles the protocols.

Group Manager

This is implemented in the GroupManagerImpl class. It maintains a reference to its controlling HAManager and core group name that are passed in as parameters. Some key methods are outlined next.

The joinGroup Method

The joinGroup method takes a group name, a map of member properties, and an HAGroupCallback reference as parameters and these are merely passed on in a delegated call to the joinGroup method of the HAManager object reference.

The createGroupName Method

The createGroupName method takes a map of group properties, which are immediately validated, as a parameter and the group name is extracted as a string from these and passed on with the properties and the core group name reference maintained by the Group Manager to the constructor when a new GroupNameImpl object is created. This newly created object is returned to the caller.

The createdPartitionedManagerGroup Method

The createdPartitionedManagerGroup method takes a group name, member properties map, and managed group data array as parameters and these are used along with a reference to the Group Manager itself to create a new PartitionedManagerGroupImpl object that is returned to the caller.

The createGroupNameInternal Method

The createGroupNameInternal method takes a map of group properties as a parameter from which the group name is extracted as a string. The group name, group properties, and the core group reference maintained by the Group Manager are passed to the constructor when a new GroupNameImpl object is created and returned to the caller. The difference between this method and the createGroupName method is that the group properties are not validated in this method.

DCS, RMM, Channels, and Chains

I will say more about the underlying communications that support load balancing, scalability, and high availability in the next chapter. I have already mentioned that there are specific messaging features used by the HAManager environment to communicate with other members, and at the highest level this appears like JMS with a similar API.

The actual transport mechanism is based on listening on the port identified by the DCS_UNICAST_ADDRESS configuration in the serverindex.xml file. For nonsecure communications, this DCS chain uses the TCPInboundChannel and DCSInboundChannel tied to the TCPChannel.DCS thread pool. For the DCS_SECURE chain setup, the DCSInboundChannel is preceded by an SSLInboundChannel between it and the TCPInboundChannel.

I have covered the transport but not the actual data transported. The data is handled in the form of messages, most of which consist of notifications to the bulletin boards. This mechanism is known as Reliable Multicast Messaging (RMM), and the JMS-like API is used to drive it. The key points to recognize in the name are that the protocol is reliable, with acknowledgments with TCP, and is multicast, with messages sent to a list of members.

Transactions and Recovery

The aim of transaction management and the recovery management mechanisms covered in this chapter is to ensure the integrity of state and data. The two mechanisms have to work hand in hand. I mentioned this briefly earlier in the chapter.

A transaction in its technical sense must have ACID properties:

Atomicity: All operations in the transaction happen or none of them happen. No interim states are persisted.

Consistency: Transactions convert from one consistent persisted state to another consistent persisted state without necessarily ensuring consistent state for all operations in between.

Isolation: The updates and interim changes performed by a transaction are transparent to those of any other transaction.

Durability: Once a transaction commits, its updates will survive even if one of the participating nodes fails.

These properties are all under the management, to some extent, of the Transaction Manager. The durability property is where the Recovery Manager comes into play.

WAS is not a database manager, where ACID properties are traditionally handled, but it may sit in front of multiple state management mechanisms such as JMS, JCA adapters, and DBMSs. In this way WAS, as covered by the Java EE specification, handles coordination of distributed transactions in accordance with the X/Open CAE Distributed Transaction Processing XA standards. XA covers two-phase commit, where a transaction coordinator notifies participating resource managers (i.e., DBMSs, JMS, JCA adapters, etc.) that they must be prepared to commit their changes and, when all have agreed, sends a commit notification to each. On a prepare-to-commit notification, each resource manager, and the transaction coordinator, will write the changes to a transaction log with this notification. When the commit notification is received, the changes are persisted to the main store of data, messages are sent, EIS system changes occur, etc. If a failure in the WAS instance acting as a transaction coordinator or resource manager occurs (i.e., for JCA or JMS) between the prepare-to-commit and the commit notifications, then the recovery facilities come into play; either on another WAS instance or when the WAS instance restarts.

Each resource manager has its own local transaction management mechanism, which is often referred to as the Resource Manager Local Transactions (RMLT) support, that is implemented according to the requirements of the APIs for that resource manager. For example, for JMS, when a session is created AUTO_ACKNOWLEDGE can be set and the commit and rollback methods can be used to handle the transactional behavior of a send call. For JDBC, the connection object can have setAutoCommit called, and again the commit and rollback methods can control the transactional behavior of the execute or executeUpdate method calls.

An XA transaction is a global transaction function into which the local resource manager has to be enlisted in order to participate. This enlisting happens under the control of a UserTransaction object or the container. The user transaction starts with a call to the begin method, followed by an operation on the first resource, which results in a call from the container to the resource manager via the getXAResource method, followed by the enlistResource method of the Java Transaction Service and the creation of a transaction ID (Xid). This is then followed by a call to the start method on the XAResource interface and the operation to be performed, such as a send or execute. This set of operations is repeated for the other XA resources until the transaction closes the connections, resulting in a call from the container to the transaction delistResource method. When commit is called, the transaction object calls prepare on the XAResource interface of each resource manager and then the commit method is called for each resource manager when the set of prepare notifications completes. At each stage, the transaction operations are logged by the transaction manager and the receipt of each notification is logged by each of the resource managers. The logging is used to recover a consistent state from an in-doubt state when a failure occurs. The flow is shown in Figure 9-2.

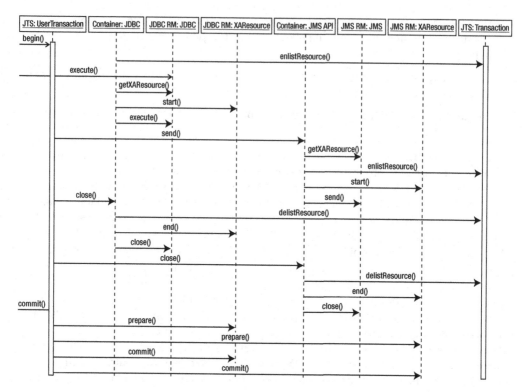

Figure 9-2. *Transaction management execution flow*

This mechanism underpins all Java EE transactional operations using the Java Transaction Service (JTS) and is the functionality that WAS must implement. The components we are considering handle the logging and management of the WAS distributed environment to support this transaction management operation.

In this section we won't consider the Java Transaction API (JTA) or its operation in the JTS, but we will look at the implementation that underpins it.

Transaction Manager Implementation

Transaction management consists of a number of components. You previously saw that the Transaction component that supports the application server transaction service is provided by the TxServiceImpl implementation class. This component has a number of dependencies, including dependencies on the Recovery Log, Local Transaction, and Transaction Recovery components, so we must look at each of these in turn.

The Transaction Component and the TxServiceImpl Implementation

The com.ibm.ws.runtime.component.TxServiceImpl component supports the registered com.ibm.ws.runtime.service.TxService interface, but doesn't implement it. It extends the WsComponentImpl class, to support controlled stopping and starting, and implements the

RecoveryAgent interface. We will look at the methods that make up these interfaces and provide the implementation of this transaction component implementation.

The RecoveryAgent Interface

The RecoveryAgent interface offers prepareForRecovery, initiateRecovery, terminateRecovery, logDirectories, and agentReportedFailure methods, which each take a FailureScope as a parameter, and disableFileLocking, isSnapshotSafe, and logFileWarning methods, among others. The TxServiceImpl class implements these methods to provide its functionality.

The lookupTranService Method

The private lookupTranService uses the Config Service to get access to the server.xml file for the instance that it uses to look up the Transaction Service. From the Config Service it gets the list of components that it iterates looking for the ApplicationServer component, and after having found this it iterates the services until it finds the TransactionService for which it then returns the service reference.

The isHAConfigurationValid Method

The private isHAConfigurationValid method uses the Repository Service to get access to the cluster and cell details, which it then validates using the gatherServerConfig private method.

The gatherServerConfig Method

The private gatherServerConfig method enumerates the nodes within the cell and accesses the serverindex.xml file for each, from which the serverEntries section is accessed and the recoveryLog details are extracted from the fully qualified HAManager-compatible server name. The recoveryLog configuration object reference is stored in a map keyed by the server name.

The validateClusterConfig Method

The validateClusterConfig method enumerates the clusters within the local cell and, for each, reads the cluster.xml file until it finds the local cluster name entry. For this it checks the enableHA setting to ensure HA is enabled and then it iterates the cluster members to get the member and node names. The transactionLogDirectory entry is read for the given server.

The initialize Method

In the initialize method, if the process is running as a Node Agent and the platform is zOS, the ControllerTransactionManagerSet instance is restarted with RRS. The lookupTranService method is called to get the transaction service reference and this is passed to the ConfigurationProviderImpl and TransactionServiceMetaData initialize methods. The registerRecoveryCollaborator method is then called, passing a reference to this component on the server process obtained from the WsRegistry.

A check is set to see if WAS is running in recovery mode and, if so, the recoveryOnlyMode flag is set on the RecoveryManager reference. A check is then made to see if the HA configuration is valid. Properties for the JTS and JTA are then set for the server, with different configuration for zOS and other platforms. Specific libraries are loaded on zOS to integrate with the core zOS subsystems. If the process is running as a control region JVM on zOS, the `ControllerTransactionManagerSet` instance is restarted with RRS. Timeouts are then set and the classloaders are configured. The Work Manager Service and Cluster Member Service are then configured.

The start Method

In the `start` method, the `startProcessing` method is called on the `TransactionServiceMetaData` object, the component registers with the Recovery Director and accesses the ORB Service, and then configures the failure scope for the `RecoveryDirector` reference. On zOS, platform-specific logging is initialized. A transaction service reference is obtained from the `TransactionManagerFactory`. The `XAFlowCallbackControl` class is then initialized. On non-zOS platforms, the transaction component registers with the workload manager and the user transaction reference is exported. A new `TransactionWorkloadRegulator` object is created and is registered with the workload controller before the transaction manager helper `start` method is called.

The stop Method

The `stop` method does nothing.

The destroy Method

The `destroy` method is different between zOS and non-zOS platforms. On non-zOS platforms, checks are made to see if replay is complete and if the transaction manager is quiesced before the failure scope is configured. On zOS platforms, the `ControllerTransactionManagerSet` reference `shutdown` method is called.

The getThreadPool Method

The `getThreadPool` method uses the Thread Pool Manager Service to get access to the default thread pool, which is returned to the caller.

The exportUserTx Method

The `exportUserTx` method gets access to and rebinds against the user transaction environment and performs a recursive rebind.

The registerWithRecoveryDirector Method

The `registerWithRecoveryDirector` method calls the `recoveryDirector` method on the `RecoveryDirectorFactory` object and uses the returned `recoveryDirector` reference to call its `registerService` method to register the component with it to get a `RecoveryLogManager` reference that is then set as the log manager reference in the configuration.

The activateMBeans Method

The `activateMBeans` method uses the `MBeanFactory` to activate MBeans for the transaction service and the transaction.

The registerWithWLM Method

The private registerWithWLM method accesses the WAS registry to get access to the WLM Service and register the TxService component with it.

The accessOrbService Method

The private accessOrbService method accesses the WAS registry to get access to the ORB Service and register the TxService component with it. The CORBAUtils helper class setORB method is used to register the ORB reference returned by the ORB Service.

The initializeZOSLogging Method

The initializeZOSLogging method gets the failure scope controller and the Recovery Director transaction log configuration for that failure scope. Properties and the partner recovery log are configured and synchronized with the Recovery Manager for zOS.

The prepareForRecovery Method

The prepareForRecovery method takes the FailureScope reference but does nothing.

The initiateRecovery Method

The initiateRecovery method takes the FailureScope reference and checks with the Recovery Manager to see if it is running in recovery-only mode. It then obtains the to-be-recovered server name and transaction log configuration and sets up the failure scope controller for that server. It then gets the RecoveryManager reference and configures the tranlog and partnerlog properties before getting the RecoveryLogManager reference for the configuration and getting access to the transaction log and partner log themselves.

The failure scope controller is then used to create the Recovery Manager using this TxService component and both logs and daemon threads are obtained from the thread pool to execute the Recovery Manager. More properties are set and then output. The TransactionHARecoveryAlarm startRecovery method is then called for the Recovery Manager and log properties. On zOS, the startServantRecovery method is called. Finally, the RecoveryDirector initialRecoveryComplete method is called for the TxService component and the failure scope. On non-zOS platforms, the Server Service is used to get access to a server reference and its recoveryCollaboratorComplete method is called for the TxService component reference.

The terminateRecovery Method

The terminateRecovery method takes a FailureScope reference as a parameter. The Recovery Director reference is obtained, the FailureScopeController shutdown method is called, and this is followed by a call to the terminationComplete method on the recoveryDirector instance passing in the FailureScope reference and the TxService component reference.

The logDirectories Method

The logDirectories method gets the transaction log configuration and extracts the directories into a String array for returning to the caller.

The agentReportedFailure Method

The agentReportedFailure method does nothing.

The disableFileLocking Method

The disableFileLocking method checks the configuration provider to see if file locking is enabled and returns a Boolean indicating whether it is.

The isSnapshotSafe Method

The isSnapshotSafe method delegates to a method of the same name on the TransactionServiceMetaData class and returns the result.

The recoveryComplete Method

The recoveryComplete method gets access to a server reference from the Server Service and calls its recoveryCollaboratorComplete method passing in the TxService reference.

The Recovery Log Component and the RecLogServiceImpl Implementation

This component implements the durability property of the transaction ACID requirements. When a WAS instance starts up it may be running in recovery mode with an aim of tidying up failed or in-doubt transactions rather than performing normal operations. This component handles the recovery operations before any other operations are performed.

On initialization, the cell and cluster configuration are accessed and a RecoveryLogAccessControllerImpl object is created along with an AlarmManagerImpl object. The recovery log configuration is scanned to get an understanding of resources available for recovery operations, and a property listener is installed for the application server to see state changes. The failure scope is then configured. zOS-specific initialization is performed that includes loading libraries that are specific to the platform and its features. Configuration for HA is performed as part of the general initialization, which includes checks to ensure HA is enabled, and the server Recovery Log Service registers with HAManager with its own HAGroup.

Deactivating and leaving the HAGroup is also handled within the Recovery Log component, along with checks for hardware quorum to support recovery.

The recovery log directors and alarms are configured in fine-grained methods, with the compression alarm interval properties accessed from the transaction service configuration outlined previously.

The Local Transaction Component and the LTCCallbacksComponentImpl Implementation

One of the key areas that causes issues within WAS stems from the undefined nature of the Java EE specification as to what should happen when transaction management is not declared. Essentially, when a request comes into the web container that results in accesses to multiple databases and a number of web services, the resources for each access in terms of connections and threads are held on to until the response is sent back to the caller in case the database or service is accessed again, to avoid the request deadlocking itself. This is called local transaction containment (LTC) and causes excess resource usage over what would be expected. This component handles some of that.

In the `start` method, the `LTCUOWCallback` class `createUserTransactionCallback` method is called to start a unit of work. If the `ActivitySessionService` is enabled, the `LTCUOWCallback` `createUserActivitySessionCallback` method is also called. This sets up the transactional behavior for the undefined state.

This is a dependent component for the `TxService` transaction service but is only loosely related.

The Local Transaction Containment mechanisms that are part of WAS are poorly understood and are often the cause of slow running, unexpectedly low performance or capacity, or excessive resource usage for applications running on WAS. It is important that developers understand the concept and its effects and segment application functionality accordingly. For example, calling a large number of web services on the same thread as an incoming web request will cause the available resources to go down, so the pattern adopted by IBM for WebSphere ESB should be used and a separate layer of WAS instances running SIB and the service clients should be separated from the web user interface and accessed via JMS.

The Transaction Recovery Component and the TxRecoveryServiceImpl Implementation

This simple component calls the `RecoveryManager` `classLoaderReady` method when started.

The RecoveryManager

This does a lot of the work of handling recovery. The implementation is part of the `com.ibm.ws.tx.jta` package within the `com.ibm.ws.runtime.jar` plugin.

The `handleXAResourceRecord` is important for recovery. This handles resynchronization and recovery of XA transactions between the recovery ID set's low and high watermarks. Each resource record is read and then applied. XA resource record entries are added to the partner log table.

The key to the `RecoveryManager` is the `handleTranRecord` method. New transactions are set up and reconstructed from the transaction log entries, and if a transaction resource adapter for the resource manager is available, the execution context handler for the transaction is used to add the transaction to those that must be applied. If reconstruction fails, the recoverable units are removed.

Summary

This chapter looked at how the HAManager subsystem works for ensuring high availability for singletons. It examined how it works through a JMS-like mechanism with an agent and a bulletin board handling subjects to which posts are made, with a group manager handling groups of registered subsystems requiring high-availability support.

This chapter also provided a high-level look at the components of the transaction service implementation from the aspect of high availability. Particular attention should be paid to the recovery log handling when WAS is running in recovery mode to process recovery logs of failed instances.

CHAPTER 10

■ ■ ■

Load Balancing and Scalability

As I mentioned in Chapter 9, there is a large overlap between the WebSphere Application Server high-availability features (covered in that chapter) and the scalability features, which also include load balancing. This overlap is apparent in the WAS implementation and in the way the infrastructure behaves. As I also covered in Chapter 9, there is a distinction between high availability and scalability despite the common infrastructure, so this chapter concentrates on the components that are primarily used for load balancing and scaling, even though they also support high availability. The subject of high availability on its own will be left as an examination of HAManager and the components that support failover. The components examined in this chapter are

- The WebSphere HTTP plugin, `plugin-cfg.xml`, and `JSESSIONID/SSLJSESSION` handling
- Data Replication Services (DRS)
- Distribution and Consistency Services (DCS)

A Brief Overview of WAS Load Balancing

There are three different types of load balancing to consider:

- Using the `JSESSIONID/SSLJSESSION` handling, which is primarily used for web traffic and essentially relies on the HTTP plugin in the external HTTP server to do its work when routing for web traffic and web services.
- Load balancing of EJB components and other subsystems when separated into a different deployment tier.
- The On Demand Router (ODR) functionality that the WebSphere Application Server XD/WAS Virtual Enterprise product uses; more specifically, how this ODR functionality gets its loading information from WAS-ND instances. This type of load balancing is touched on only briefly in this chapter.

Before getting into the details, I'll first describe what happens with a typical application in a standard infrastructure consisting of a pool of HTTP servers, probably running the IBM HTTP Server, with the HTTP plugin running inside it that is forwarding requests to a tier of clustered WAS instances on one or more physical machines. This pattern accommodates either vertical or horizontal clustering, or both.

Static WebSphere Infrastructure Configuration

Throughout this book I've assumed that you have some familiarity with typical WAS deployments. I'll describe load-balancing features and components in the context of an enterprise-scale WAS deployment consisting of a cell with multiple clusters overlaid on the physical infrastructure of HTTP servers and application servers. I'll give you a refresher on what these concepts mean in this context.

A cell is a unit of configuration and controls the configuration of a set of WAS resources via Node Agents on each node or operating system that runs one or more WAS instances, all administered from a central Deployment Manager. With WAS 7 it is possible to have a specialized Deployment Manager that deploys to other cells, called a Job Manager, but for the purposes of this chapter the configuration is not affected.

Within a cell, the unit of communication between nodes is the core group. There is a default core group, but as cells get bigger, groups of instances can be split into multiple core groups for administrative purposes, but all are still controlled by a central Deployment Manager.

Within the cell are one or more clusters of WAS instances that run the same applications with the same configurations, and these are used as units of scalability and high availability because they can all handle the same requests for load-balancing purposes and can take over each other's work where state is involved if the appropriate session replication or database handling is enabled. Vertical clustering has multiple WAS instances on the same node for scalability purposes, and horizontal clustering has WAS instances across nodes for both high availability and scalability.

The Deployment Manager is not clustered using WAS active-active technologies, so an external high-availability (HA) solution, such as PowerHA/HACMP, is required.

Load balancing of requests is typically handled externally from an external web server that forwards requests.

This is all shown in Figure 10-1 using a typical pair of pSeries/System P machines hosted in two different data centers as an example. There is a pair of clusters with an instance on each machine to support both vertical and horizontal clustering for maximum performance and availability. Both clusters are within the same cell so they have access to the same set of deployed applications and configuration. On each machine—or, to be more accurate, each operating system image—a Node Agent is deployed to manage the configuration for the cluster instances and to act as a single point of communication for the Deployment Manager to coordinate and control the configuration. The combination of instances managed by the Node Agent is known as a node. Deployment Managers do not support WAS clustering with the HAManager, so some external clustering software, in this case PowerHA/HACMP, is shown to provide resilience for administration.

Within our highly scalable and available hypothetical enterprise in Figure 10-1, each data center has a pair of web servers for resilience and scalability, fronted by a load-balancing router, probably run by an external Internet service provider (ISP). The web servers are all running a standard HTTP server, such as IBM HTTP Server (IHS), and hosting the proxy plugin that forwards requests to one of the WAS instances. The choice of instance to forward the request to is configured in the `plugin-cfg.xml` file that identifies instances in a cluster and the weightings to control which instances are preferred. Forwarding requests to local instances in the same data center is preferable for performance. The `JSESSIONID` cookie is used to say which instance last handled the request to maintain sticky sessions.

Clustering and Availability

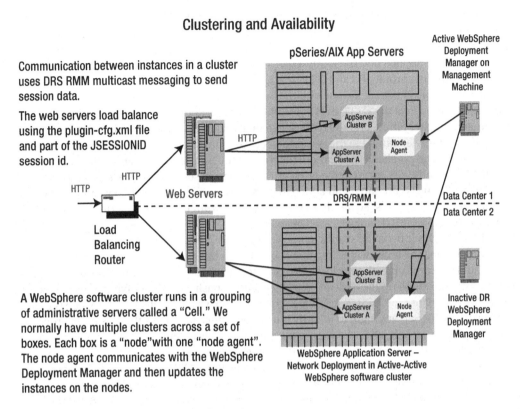

Communication between instances in a cluster uses DRS RMM multicast messaging to send session data.

The web servers load balance using the plugin-cfg.xml file and part of the JSESSIONID session id.

A WebSphere software cluster runs in a grouping of administrative servers called a "Cell." We normally have multiple clusters across a set of boxes. Each box is a "node"with one "node agent". The node agent communicates with the WebSphere Deployment Manager and then updates the instances on the nodes.

Figure 10-1. *WAS clustering static deployment*

An Application Is Deployed

When an EAR file is deployed to WAS, the Application Manager Service notifies registered listeners and the Meta Data Service notifies its listeners of the contents of the deployment descriptors. To do this the WSModel code in Eclipse is used to break the deployed archive into its constituent parts. The Admin Service has been involved in the deployment and has done its bit in ensuring the right configuration is in the right place. If the deployed application EAR file contains a WAR file or if a WAR file is deployed, the administrator who has taken on the deployer role has the option of generating an HTTP plugin XML configuration file for the application for use in an HTTP server such as the Apache 2.X–derived IBM HTTP Server 7.

This generation can be handled by clicking on the appropriate options in the Deployment Manager System Console or by running the GenPluginCfg.sh or GenPluginCfg.bat script and will result in a plugin-cfg.xml file being produced. This file contains the URL routing information for the target application within WAS, a weighting for the server instances hosting the application, and identification of a load-balancing algorithm.

Runtime Application Clustering

When the first request from a user comes into WAS for the application, there will not be a session, so the load-balancing algorithm (e.g., round-robin) will be used to forward the request to the target application server instance. The URL received by the HTTP server will be compared against the `plugin-cfg.xml` file contents using the code provided by the HTTP plugin DLL or shared object for the given HTTP server, and if the URL is listed in the file, the weighting and algorithm will be applied and the request will be forwarded.

The forwarding protocol is an HTTP or HTTPS derivative and results in commands passing across the pipe in textual format with the forwarded request. The receiving application takes the request in via the HTTP or HTTPS inbound chain and passes it up through the web container implementation, and the request eventually makes its way into the target servlet or JSP-derived servlet named in the `WebApp` object. Assuming a session is required, which makes sense for any realistic application, the rules of the Java EE specification dictate that an `HTTPSession` object is set up in the web container to represent the user session and that a `JSESSIONID` value is generated and added to a response cookie or via URL rewriting in the response-embedded URLs. So far, there is nothing extraordinary in this description. For SSL sessions, the `SSLJSESSION` cookie is used instead.

The really clever behavior comes in the way the `JSESSIONID` value is generated in the WAS implementation. The Java EE specification suggests that this should be a unique and random value, but IBM came up with the clever idea of it not being entirely random. The application server instance setting up the `HTTPSession` object adds a hash value identifying its own process to the `JSESSIONID` or `SSLJSESSION` response, which is known as the clone ID. This value is then used by the HTTP Server plugin to identify the WAS instance that owns the session in order to route requests back to it when the user sends the next request. Remember, the clone ID is an identifier for the JVM instance processing the request.

When the next request from the user is received by the HTTP Server, it again is passed to the HTTP Server plugin, which compares the requested URL against the XML configuration file. An attempt is then made by the plugin to forward the request to the WAS instance that handled the request last time. The instance, formerly called a clone, identifier in the `JSESSIONID` cookie or URL string, i.e., the clone ID, allows that WAS instance to be identified. If the plugin can't open an HTTP or HTTPS connection to the same instance that handled the request last time, the contents of the `plugin-cfg-xml` file are read to identify which other WAS instances are members of the same cluster, and one is chosen to receive this new request.

To ensure that all nodes in a cluster can handle a given request, the WAS instances that are members of the cluster must all either be stateless, store state in a common location (i.e., a session database), or replicate the sessions between them. This is all configured by entries in the `server.xml` file. Session replication between instances takes place using the JMS-like Distribution and Consistency Service (DCS) Reliable Multicast Messaging (RMM) support as part of the Data Replication Services (DRS) functionality within WAS, which is extremely fast for small session object collections but has an overhead, so for large loads the buffer size dedicated to this should be increased. Use of a session database removes the intracluster communications overhead at the cost of accesses to the database and possible database consistency message overhead. Use of a database may appear to be slower, but as most databases cache commonly or recently accessed data, the performance overhead is minimal. With in-memory replication using DRS, minimal session information should be stored, with stored keys and references rather than in-memory object copies being best practice.

In general, all requests that do not have a session ID are load balanced according to the routing algorithm chosen and the weighting, with the decision made using the plugin. WAS-ND does have additional functionality, however, that supports the On Demand Router (ODR) that WAS-XD/WAS Virtual Enterprise builds on. In this there are methods within the WAS-ND runtime that help more complex rules to be applied to make a decision on where a request is to be routed. Consider the `clusterIdent*` methods mentioned in previous chapters as an example.

The HTTP Plugin and PlugInCfg.xml

Assume that you are configuring an IBM HTTP Server or other Apache 2–derived web server for the purposes of this exercise, although the procedure is similar for other HTTP servers. Currently, IBM ships Apache 2.0.*X*–derived HTTP servers rather than the more current 2.2 version, and versions 6.1 and 7.0 are current for use with WAS 7 dependent on the target platform.

The IBM HTTP Server range is derived from Apache 2.0.*X* and differ in two fundamental ways. IBM tests and certifies a combination of modules for use with the IBM HTTP Server when used in combination with other IBM products such as WAS, and this configuration supports management via agents and tools such as the WAS Deployment Manager. IBM HTTP Server also differs in that IBM is able to license or use security and other features from its own proprietary solutions and from other vendors, which the open source community cannot do, and then can integrate this with the HTTP runtime. This is shown in Figure 10-2, where a typical deployment of WAS 7 is again shown on pSeries\System P machines. This infrastructure shows the WAS proxy plugin shared object (`mod_was_ap2_http.so`) hosted in the IBM HTTP Server and using the `plugin-cfg.xml` file to forward requests to WAS, but also shows the web server handling static web pages locally.

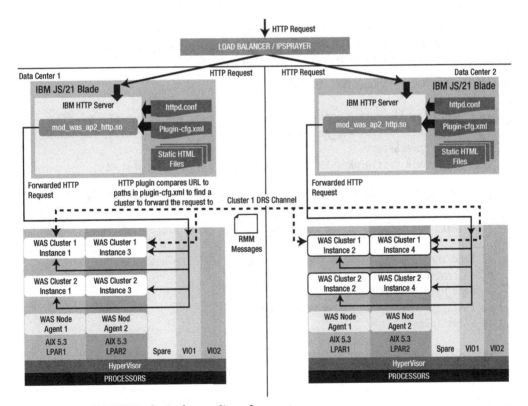

Figure 10-2. *WAS HTTP plugin forwarding of requests*

Extensions to the base functionality of the HTTP server are delivered in the form of modules. The detail of how these are written is beyond the scope of this book, but essentially a module exists in the form of a shared object or DLL that makes use of the Apache API to load itself into the Apache web server processes and to register handlers to monitor and manipulate various phases of the HTTP processing chain. The module offers a RegisterHooks function that then uses various ap_hook_* functions to add its functionality to the chain. Each function added to the chain must adhere to the appropriate signature for that part of the chain.

The most important part of the chain is handled via the function called through registration with the ap_hook_handler function. The code inside the WAS plugin for this function must read the given request, perform the lookup in the plugin-cfg.xml file, open or reuse a socket to the target WAS instance for that given URL and JSESSIONID, and forward the request for handling. When the response is returned from the WAS instance, it must call the Apache ap_send_http_header and either the ap_rwrite or ap_rputs functions to return the response from the WAS instance to the original caller. This behavior, although not specific to WAS, is covered in the Apache HTTP Server module documentation.

The registration inside the plugin of modules has the following form:

```
static void RegisterHooks(apr_pool_t *pPool)
{
    ap_hook_post_config(MyInit, NULL, NULL, APR_HOOK_MIDDLE);
    ap_hook_handler(MyHandler, NULL, NULL, APR_HOOK_MIDDLE);
    …
}
```

The handler for each request has the following form and takes a request record holding the request details and pointers to the configuration information:

```
static int MyHandler(request_rec *pReq)
{
    // Read the configuration information so we can find the plugin-cfg.xml file
    SPerDir *perDir *pPerDir=ap_get_module_config(pReq->per_dir_config, &my_module);
    SperServer *pPerServer=
      ap_get_module_config(pReq->server->module_config, &my_module);

    // Read plugin-cfg.xml and make routing decisions based on its contents

    // Forward the request to the target WAS instance for processing

    // Send the response back to the caller, first with the header
    pReq->content_type="text/html";
    ap_send_http_header(pReq);
    ap_rputs(..., pReq); // Response from WAS
    ap_rflush(pReq);

    return OK;
}
```

The module is loaded into the HTTP Server process using `LoadModule` entries in the `httpd.conf` file:

```
LoadModule
    was_ap20_module    /usr/IBM/IHS/Plugins/bin/mod_was_ap20.http.so
```

The configuration file used to control the plugin is handled via the `WebSpherePluginConfig` directive:

```
WebSpherePluginConfig
            /usr/IBM/IHS/Plugins/config/webserver1/plugin-cfg.xml
```

Throughout this discussion, I have referred to default names of items but these can be overridden. For example, the `JSESSIONID` referred to in the `plugin-cfg.xml` file is handled through the `<Uri AffinityCookie...>` setting for the given cluster:

```
<Uri AffinityCookie="JSESSIONID" AffinityUrlIdentifier="jsessionid"
    Name="/MyAppName/*" />
```

Similarly, the name of the `plugin-cfg.xml` file is controlled by the entries in the `httpd.conf` file. Load balancing affinity for session routing can be switched off through use of the `IgnoreAffinityRequests` element, but for the purpose of this chapter we will not go into any more detail on the handling of this.

Server-side configuration of responses to the HTTP Server plugin is handled by the `server.xml` `webserverPluginSettings` element, such as enabling of timeouts, configuration of connections, and enabling of extended handshaking.

So, take a look at the WAS plugin binary file to see how it is structured. You can use the Unix `strings` command for this to see the functions performed by the plugin so that you can get a better understanding of what the plugin does:

```
$ strings mod_was_ap20_http.so | grep websphere
websphereInit
websphereShouldHandleRequest
websphereHandleRequest
webspherePortNumberForMatching
websphereUpdateConfig
websphereGetConfigFilename
websphereGetConfig
websphereReleaseConfig
websphereCheckConfig
websphereBeginRequest
websphereCloseConnection
websphereEndRequest
websphereUriMatch
websphereVhostMatch
websphereFindServerGroup
websphereGetPortForAppServer
websphereAddSpecialHeaders
websphereCreateClient
```

```
websphereSocketIsClosed
websphereExtendedHandshake
websphereGetStream
websphereExecute
websphereGetDWLMTable
websphereReplyToBrowser
websphereFindTransport
websphereParseSessionID
websphereParseCloneIDs
websphereHandleSessionAffinity
websphereFindServer
websphereWriteRequestReadResponse
websphereGetChunkedResponse
websphereParsePartitionIDs
```

At startup the websphereInit function is called to initialize the module and get and apply its configuration. For each request, the websphereHandleRequest function is called from the HTTP Server, and this uses a number of lower-level functions as follows:

1. The websphereBeginRequest function reads the plugin-cfg.xml configuration file and initiates the request handling.

2. The websphereUriMatch function compares the target URI with each of those that must be handled by WAS configured in the plugin-cfg.xml file. This is called by the websphereShouldHandleRequest function that uses it to check if a URI matches, and if so returns a decision to route the request to an appropriate WAS instance to the calling function.

3. The websphereGetDLWMTable function gets the Distributed Workload Manager (DWLM) information for routing information. This information contains the cluster topology for given active applications and services.

4. The websphereHandleSessionAffinity function checks the JSESSIONID value to identify an instance to route to using the clone ID.

5. The websphereFindServer function targets the given clone instance for the clone ID.

6. The websphereExecute function forwards the request after using websphereExtendedHandshake to check whether the target instance is available. The websphereExecute function waits for a response from the WAS instance that it can return to the original requester.

7. The websphereReplyToBrowser function sends the response to the caller.

For the purposes of load balancing, the websphereHandleSessionAffinity function uses the JSESSIONID or other affinity value for routing, so this is important for your understanding.

You have now traced the flow of a request through the HTTP Server, as the request and response objects are passed on to the HTTP Server plugin for processing, and this has forwarded the request to an application server instance via the websphereExecute function with the routing performed using the websphereHandleSessionAffinity function. When the WAS instance responds, the contents are returned to the caller using the websphereReplyToBrowser function.

JSESSIONID Handling Within WAS

This section examines the key parts of WAS that handle the JSESSIONID value and what they do with it. The discussion also applies to SSLJSESSION handling. To do this you need to open the JAR files for the plugins and perform a grep to find the classes that contain the string JSESSIONID. I will restrict the discussion to the following JAR files:

- com.ibm.ws.runtime.jar
- com.ibm.ws.webcontainer.jar
- com.ibm.wsfp.main.jar

These are the main files of interest.

JSESSIONID and com.ibm.ws.runtime.jar

When you execute a grep on the directory created by unarchiving com.ibm.ws.jar, you get the following list of entries found for the JSESSIONID:

```
META-INF/ODCSchema.xml:     <property name="sessionAffinityCookie" type="String"
defaultValue="JSESSIONID"/>
Binary file com/ibm/websphere/plugincfg/generator/ConfigurationParser$ServerData.
class matches
Binary file com/ibm/websphere/plugincfg/generator/ConfigurationParser.class matches
Binary file com/ibm/websphere/plugincfg/generator/PluginDocumentGenerator.
class matches
Binary file com/ibm/websphere/validation/base/config/level51/ServerValidator_51.
class matches
Binary file com/ibm/websphere/validation/base/config/level60/ServerValidator_60_
Default.class matches
Binary file com/ibm/websphere/validation/base/config/level61/ServerValidator_61_
Default.class matches
Binary file com/ibm/websphere/validation/base/config/level70/ServerValidator_70_
Default.class matches
Binary file com/ibm/ws/dwlm/client/HttpSessionAffinityModule.class matches
Binary file com/ibm/ws/httptunnel/channel/WSHttpTunnelPluginConfigHelper.class
matches
Binary file com/ibm/ws/odc/cell/TreeBuilder.class matches
Binary file com/ibm/ws/webservices/engine/transport/http/HTTPConstants.class matches
Binary file com/ibm/ws/webservices/engine/transport/http/HTTPSender.class matches
```

The first entry refers to ODCSchema.xml. This entry is used to create the plugin-cfg.xml file sessionAffinityCookie entry. This is used by the GenPluginCfg.sh script that generates the HTTP Server plugin configuration file and also by the Administration System Console, both of which use the PluginDocumentGenerator class.

The PluginDocumentGenerator class creates the elements within the plugin-cfg.xml file. One of the elements is the GetDWLMTable element with PrimaryServers and BackupServers. The clusters, clone IDs, load balancing weightings, timeouts, and maximum connections are all configured from here. Special handling is required for portlet applications.

The ServerValidator_*XX* classes are used to validate the configuration of the environment.

To understand the HttpSessionAffinityModule class functionality, you need to understand the DWLMClient component, its DWLMClientImpl implementation class, and its use of the On Demand Configuration (ODC) TreeBuilder class:

- The DWLMClient component is part of the ODR functionality that is part of the WAS-XD/WAS Virtual Enterprise package and is essentially based on a customized portion of WAS functionality. The DWLMClient component is similar in its behavior to the HTTP Server plugin but is more dynamic.

- The DWLMClientImpl class is part of the ODR, which has the ODC representing the dynamic configuration of the cell as accessed via the ODCTree class, and the RequestMapper and Autonomic Request Flow Manager (ARFM) directing the flow of requests to the appropriate instance for handling. The ODC TreeBuilder class is a helper class that builds the information for use by the ODCTree class.

The ODC component has "transactions" that can change the cell configuration, possibly starting new instances, and automatic generation of a new plugin XML configuration can take place afterward. The HttpSessionAffinityModule class handles the routing of requests based on the session affinity as identified by the JSESSIONID value. While the JSESSIONID handling and the ODR functionality here applies to HTTP traffic, the ARFM and DWLMClient also handle other routing such as Internet Inter-Orb Protocol (IIOP) traffic. All such traffic routing is based on priorities within the cell for applications.

The controller for all of this is the DWLMClientImpl component, which implements the DWLMClient and ODCTransaction interfaces. Pay particular attention to the MapRequestToTarget method, which takes an HttpRequestMessage and a local port as parameters and uses a RequestMapper to map a request to an ODC node; this mapper uses the ODC tree and, in selecting the target, uses the HttpSessionAffinityModule.

The HttpSessionAffinity module gets the application affinity cookie from the ODC node, which can be used to handle the SSLJSESSION cookie that uses SSL IDs to perform the same function as the JSESSIONID and other custom cookies. The jsessionid or JSESSIONID value is obtained from the request and the partition and clone ID mapping functionality is performed to identify the target instance. The clone ID is the instance identifier that is part of the JSESSIONID string and is used to look up a server in the cluster. If the target server is no longer available, the affinity is broken and the cluster is evaluated to find a new server. If there are none available, the request fails. The ODCTree functionality is used to underpin this.

The preceding functionality is general web container functionality. The HttpSender class, and the static value holder HttpConstants class supporting it, is specific to web services. The JSESSIONID and SSLJSESSION handling is within the invoke call for outbound connections, where a cluster instance to target for an End Point Reference (EPR) is looked up to be the recipient of the request and any affinity requirement for the web service request is taken account of before the request is forwarded. Most web services are stateless, so this code should not be heavily exercised. The clusterIdenFromEPR is used against a set of endpoint criteria and the addressing is taken account of, and if the target is external to the application server and the EPR is for a WLM-owned instance, then the JSESSIONID and SSLJSESSION handling is used as part of the context map that is used for routing to the actual host, port, and URL. The handling is the same as for normal web requests, although the clusterIdenFromEPR and identityToCFEndPoint methods do hide some of the routing decisions. Much of this was covered in the web services chapter (Chapter 7). This class combination supports JAX-RPC web services.

In general, load balancing is performed in either round-robin form with weightings or based on loads, depending on the environment configuration, unless some sort of session affinity is required, in which case the JSESSIONID or SSLJSESSION identifier comes into play to handle the routing target.

JSESSIONID and com.ibm.ws.webcontainer.jar

This subsystem has three classes that handle JSESSIONID, which again you can see by executing the grep utility:

```
$ grep -R JSESSIONID *
Binary file com/ibm/ws/session/SessionManagerConfig.class matches
Binary file com/ibm/ws/session/WsSessionMgrComponentImpl.class matches
Binary file com/ibm/wsspi/session/ISessionAffinityManager.class matches
```

The SessionManagerConfig class is just a simple class that has accessors and mutators for multiple configuration items for web session management, including URL rewriting, cookies, session cookie names, session data replication service settings, session database data source, password, and ID, and invalidation settings.

The WsSessionMgrComponentImpl class has a number of functions, including acting as a controller for session management, interfacing to the WLM Service, and controlling DRS to replicate state between cluster instances. It uses the SessionManagerConfig class to determine whether MemtoMem mode is set (i.e., DRS) and, if so, sets up DRS appropriately. HAManager (CoreStack) is used to control failover of state and take over from another instance. The SessionManagerConfig class is initialized from this component. If a session database is configured, then the initialization of the database is handled as part of the session manager configuration initialization. Tuning of the session information is handled from here.

The ISessionAffinityManager interface class is part of a larger com.ibm.wsspi.session.* set of classes to handle session affinity and how it is affected by the session lifecycle dictated by the Java EE specification. The interface is implemented by the SessionAffinityManager class, which is part of the com.ibm.ws.* package hierarchy. The ISessionAffinityManager interface handles the return of cluster instance identifiers (clone IDs) for a given JSESSIONID to support routing. The key method in the interface is the analyzeRequest method that analyzes a servlet request to extract the session ID information, which is then passed to other methods to extract the constituents to allow a SessionAffinityContext reference to be returned to be used for the routing decision making.

The ISessionObserver interface, which is also part of the com.ibm.wsspi.session.* package hierarchy and is implemented by the SessionEventDispatcher class and others, handles lifecycle management for the session, and when the web container handles activation, passivation, creation, or destruction of a session, the interface and the methods supporting it are used. The sessionAffinityBroke method is of particular interest when an instance identified by JSESSIONID fails, as it is the notification mechanism used to update session affinity, at least in theory. The SessionEventDispatcher class implements this interface, and its implementation of the sessionAffinityBroke method enumerates observer objects supporting the ISessionObserver interface and calls their sessionAffinityBroke methods, most of which do nothing or just update statistics. The SessionEventAdapter class handles the life cycle of objects on a session and also implements the ISessionObserver interface.

The IStorer interface is used to store sessions. The WsManualSessionStorer, WsTBWSessionStorer, and EOSSessionStorer classes all implement this interface. These classes are used to store sessions under the control of the SessionManager class, with the SessionManagerConfig class providing the configuration that dictates which storer is used.

The architecture of how this fits together is shown in Figure 10-3.

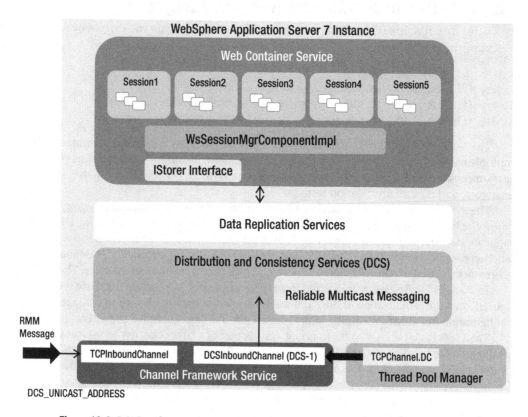

Figure 10-3. *WAS web container session replication and management*

JSESSIONID and com.ibm.wsfp.main.jar

If you look at the handling inside this JAR file, you see two classes only that contain references to JSESSIONID:

```
$ grep -R JSESSIONID *
Binary file com/ibm/ws/websvcs/transport/http/OutboundURLTargetResolver.class
matches
Binary file com/ibm/ws/websvcs/transport/http/WSHTTPConstants.class matches
```

The WSHTTPConstants class is a simple class that contains static strings for general use elsewhere. The COOKIEID_HTTP_SESSION value is JSESSIONID and the COOKIEID_SSL_SESSION value is SSLJSESSION. These constant values are meant for use elsewhere in WAS but are not actually used.

The OutboundURLTargetResolver class handling of session affinity and routing replicates the functionality of the HttpSender class previously described, although this is for JAX-WS Axis2-based services rather than the JAX-RPC services supported by the HttpSender class.

Clustering and com.ibm.ws.wlm.jar

This section covers the core plugin subsystem of the Distributed Workload Manager (DWLM) that handles the dynamic WAS clustering functionality that is external to the Admin Service and Config Service owned configuration, and that also provides the high-availability function-ality for the HAManager. This section concentrates on the load-balancing functionality and the state affinity.

In the component the cluster topology and set management are handled, with func-tions for identifying each cluster member. Adding and leaving the cluster is handled by this component. The ClusterObserver interface is used to notify users who register an interface of membership changes. IIOP failover for CORBA transactions is handled in the component. This is part of the Cluster Service.

Within the component, TransactionAffinityModule and AffinityManager classes handle the monitoring of affinity of CORBA components and the related transactions, and the AffinitySelector class handles routing to alternative instances. All of this makes use of the topography functionality within the component for cells, clusters, and instances.

A set of rules is used, based on the SelectionAdvisor and SelectionCriteriaImpl classes, for handling routing and cluster decisions. Random and weighted proportional algorithms are used for the decisions. An affinity key is used to handle state management for failover, with the AffinityModule and its AffinityIdKey affinity identifier and the AffinityId class.

In the server.xml file, the ORB, which handles the CORBA IIOP functionality and the failover of remote EJBs, registers the com.ibm.ws.wlm.client.WLMClient class as an ORB plugin and registers WLM interceptors. This shows how the EJB failover and the WLM functionality are related.

Session Replication, DRS, and DCS

Earlier in this chapter you saw that the WsSessionMgrComponentImpl class managed the setup of the interface to DRS that keeps session information between cluster instances in sync, a process known as session replication. An alternative is available through writing session information as binary large objects (blobs) to a session database. In either case, the IStorer interface is used and the WsSessionMgrComponentImpl class is the controller. Earlier in the book you saw that DRS was set up via the MultibrokerDomainImpl class, so we will now look a little more closely at this.

Communications for DRS are shared with DCS. The TCPInboundChannel for DCS_UNICAST _ADDRESS that has a maximum of 20,000 open connections and a timeout of 60 seconds as configured in server.xml is the starting point. There are two DCSInboundChannel channels set up by default in `server.xml` that are then combined with the `TCPInboundChannel` to set up the DCS chain and the `DCS-Secure` chain. The `server.xml` set up for the `ThreadPoolManager` set up a thread pool between 5 and 20 threads by default, called `TCPChannel.DCS`, for use by DCS. The `multibroker.xml` file handles the configuration of replication domains. On startup the DRS `MultibrokerDomainImpl` class creates its own distinct thread pool separately from that of DCS, and this operates at a higher level above the DCS communications facilities.

The Cluster Member Service that maintains the WLM support for the cluster is used to identify instances in the cluster, so the DCS multibroker domain functionality registers an interest with the service to look for changes in topology. It is the `ClusterObserver` interface support that enables it to watch for members being added to or removed from a cluster.

DRS has a role mode of client and server, and each side of a replication communication takes a role as client or server or both. DRS maintains a set of message listeners for the messages sent by the underlying DCS infrastructure. The messages used are the RMM JMS-like notifications that, for the benefit of session handling, transmit serialized objects. This allows synchronization between the nodes to occur.

Summary

In this brief chapter you looked at the functioning of load balancing within a typical clustered WAS environment, and how the HTTP Server and its plugin start the ball rolling for load balancing and session affinity using `JSESSIONID`. You then moved through the functionality on the WAS side of things, starting with the `DWLMClient` functionality that supports the WAS-XD/WAS Virtual Enterprise ODR, and then moving more generally into how session affinity is handled by the base WAS runtime, web services, and the web container. Finally, you saw how sessions interface to DRS to copy objects between instances in a cluster using DCS as an underlying transport infrastructure.

CHAPTER 11

■ ■ ■

Configuration

Throughout this book I have referred to a number of core services that underpin the WebSphere Application Server operation, one of which is the Config Service. Essentially the Config Service is a dynamic interface into the configuration of the cell, its clusters, and each individual WAS instance. The configuration itself just consists of a set of XML files, many of which also have been referenced throughout this book. This chapter examines some of these XML files and looks at the key sections in the most important file, server.xml.

Directory Structure

On most Unix systems, WAS installs under the opt or usr directory. For example, on AIX the runtime is installed under /usr/IBM/WebSphere/AppServer. Different configurations of the basic runtime are set up in custom profiles based on profile templates stored in the profiles directory that link back to the core binaries. For example, the AppSrv01 profile is based on a default or managed configuration for an application server, and the Dmgr profile is based on a management profile template.

The layout of the directories and the contents of the directories are briefly explained in Table 11-1. The top-level directory where WAS is installed is referred to as Main in the table.

Table 11-1. *WAS Installation Directory Structure*

Directory	Level	Description
bin	Main and profile	Either contains WAS binary executables (i.e., scripts or shared objects, etc.) or links to them. The links or scripts that wrap the links are in the profiles-based subdirectory rather than the binaries themselves.
config	Profile	Contains the directory structure for the XML files controlling the configuration of the environment.
configuration	Main	Contains the config.ini file used to control the Eclipse Equinox OSGi base configuration and startup. It may also contain directories, which may be hidden, in which OSGi-level log files may be stored for plugin/bundle components.

Continued

Table 11-1. *Continued*

Directory	Level	Description
deploytool	Main	Contains the itp directory holding an Eclipse-based tool for application deployment. This ships with its own complete Eclipse 3.4 runtime environment.
derby	Main	Contains the embedded and network server versions of the lightweight Java-based Apache Derby database management server.
dev	Main	Contains development support libraries, i.e., the j2ee.jar files for different J2EE and Java EE versions under a directory structure.
etc	Main and profile	Contains various additional support files, such as xforms/Web Services Feature Pack, VMM/WIM Virtual Member Manager support, some tmx4j JMX support files, and samples for the WS-Security web services setup. In the profile version, some security key and certificate files are stored.
features	Main	Contains some Eclipse feature files used to control, group, and update the WAS Eclipse plugins. The subdirectories each contain a feature.xml file that lists plugins and versions that have prerequisites and dependencies that should be configured, managed, and upgraded together.
firststeps	Main and profile	Contains either the profile template subdirectories containing the firststeps application HTML and script files, or the HTML and script files themselves at the profile level. The application assists initial configuration.
installableApps	Main and profile	Contains the deployment files (i.e., EAR, WAR, EJB-JAR, etc.) for applications that are available for deployment to the cell or profile application servers for this installation.
installedApps	Profile	Contains the application deployed code from installableApps that the profile instances are configured to run.
installedConnectors	Main and profile	Contains the JCA resource adapter archive (RAR) files containing connectors used by the application server to interface to external or legacy systems. Those available are at the top-level directory structure and those configured for a profile are at the profile level.
instutils	Main	Contains the installation utilities from the installation factory framework for customized installation support.
java	Main	Contains the IBM J9 JVM for Java 6, JRE, and lib files used by this installation of WAS.

Directory	Level	Description
lafiles	Main	Contains the license agreement files in multiple languages for the WAS installation.
lib	Main	Contains supporting Java JAR and RAR library files for the J2EE environment, including files for WebSphere MQ Java support, command-line utilities, mail and JACL support, Dynacache edge support, SIB resource adapter support, and other files. There is a hidden file on Unix that identifies the Eclipse installation in use: .eclipseproduct. For a WAS 7 installation, this contains: name=Eclipse Platform id=org.eclipse.platform version=3.2.0 This file is used along with the startup.jar file and bootstrap.jar files, which are also in the lib directory, for a very basic Eclipse environment.
links	Main	Contains links into the Eclipse plugins directory structure.
logs	Main and profile	Contains the log files for the main installation or, at the profile level, the server instances (startServer.log/stopServer.log, stdout, etc.) running for this installation.
optionalLibraries	Main	Contains directories for optional Java JAR files available for the environment, such as JWL JavaScript Widget Library, WebSphere JPA, Jython, Struts, and the JSF-Portlet bridge.
plugins	Main	Contains the Eclipse Equinox OSGi runtime bundles and plugins and the core WAS runtime environment.
profileTemplates	Main	Contains directories for each of the installation profile types and the XML configuration files and ant scripts used to set up the profiles, i.e., the installed configurations of WAS to fulfill a particular role.
profiles	Main	Contains the configured profile role-based installations of WAS for the platform based on profileTemplates. Common profiles will be the Dmgr01 profile created by the dmgr profile template and the AppSrv01 profile created by the managed profile template. Individual server instances configured for that role exist in a directory structure under this directory.
properties	Main and profile	Contains the DTD, XML configuration, and property files for the installation and profile.
runtimes	Main	Contains admin and thin client JAR files, and a resource adapter for client SIB usage.
samples	Main and profile	Contains sample applications that demonstrate either good application architecture or WAS extensions.

Continued

Table 11-1. *Continued*

Directory	Level	Description
sar2war_tool	Main	Contains a script and XML configuration to create a WAR file from a Session Initiation Protocol (SIP) SAR file to allow it to be deployed to WAS.
Scheduler	Main	Contains the database schema creation scripts and DDL DBMSs to create a database schema that supports the WAS Scheduler Service allowing application code to be executed to a schedule or diary.
scriptLibraries	Main	Contains supporting libraries to allow scripting of WAS deployment and management. The supplied files are Python (.py extension) files.
systemApps	Main	Contains the system-level application deployment EAR files. This includes the File Transfer, Scheduler Calendar, Event Service, and Virtual Member Manager support applications.
temp	Main and profile	Used for temporary storage for WAS general use, such as for storing serialized objects for a running instance or some property files.
tmsStorage	Profile	Contains a persisted copy of the tasks being run. Used by a Deployment Manager or Job Manager profile instance only.
tranlog	Profile	Contains the tranlog and partner log files used for recovery and XA distributed transaction support for the instances. These files are best stored on a shared storage medium, such as an NFSv4 cluster, to support takeover by another instance to resolve in-doubt transactions on failure.
UDDIReg	Main	Contains the client, database scripts, and creation scripts for implementation of the IBM UDDI registry. This standard supports lookup of web services within an enterprise. For modern installations, don't use this but instead get the WebSphere Service Registry and Repository product to run on WAS as this supports modern standards and a workflow for management of deployment.
uninstall	Main	Contains a Java application and XML configuration files to uninstall WAS.
universalDriver	Main	Contains a Java DB2J JDBC driver.
util	Main	Contains scripts written in Jacl or Unix shell scripts to set up a WAS cell core group, SIB web services, the Scheduler, and other WAS features.
web	Main	Contains web pages documenting some of the WAS architecture models.
wstemp	Profile	Contains temporary configuration changes from the Deployment Manager.

Under the profiles directory and the individual configured profile, in the config direc-tory, the core XML files for the instance are stored, with configurations for the cell, clusters, nodes, and servers all identified and stored separately in a directory structure named after the names of these configuration type instances.

The structure of the config directories is as shown in Listing 11-1, with named files that do not change their location in some directories and the directory structures only where this changes with installation.

Listing 11-1. *WAS Configuration Directory Structure*

```
backup/
cells/
    cell1/
        cell.xml
        applications/
            application1.ear/
            application2.ear/
        bindings/
            binding1/
            binding2/
            defaultBindings.xml
        blas/
            application1/
            application2/
        clusters/
            cluster1/
                cluster.xml
            cluster2/
                cluster.xml
        coregroups/
            DefaultCoreGroup/
                coregroup.xml
            coregroup1/
                coregroup.xml
        nodegroups/
            DefaultNodeGroup/
                nodegroup.xml
            nodegroup1/
                nodegroup.xml
        nodes/
            node1/
                ...
                node.xml
                servers/
                    server1/
                        ...
```

```
                            server.xml
                    server2/
                        ...
                            server.xml
            node2/
                ...
                node.xml
                servers/
                    server1/
                        ...
                    server2/
                        ...
            PolicySets/
                PolicySet1/
                    ...
                PolicySet2/
                    ...
            PolicyTypes/
                PolicyType1/
                    ...
                PolicyType2/
                    ...
temp/
    download/
        cells/
            ...
        templates/
            ....
        waspolicies/
            ....
templates/
    PolicySets/
        PolicySet1/
            ...
        PolicySet2/
            ...
    chains/
        hamanager-chains.xml
        sibservice-chains.xml
        webconatinr-chains.xml
        orb-chains.xml
        sipcontainer-chains.xml
    servertypes/
        APPLICATION_SERVER/
            ...
        GENERIC_SERVER/
            ...
```

```
    WEB_SERVER/
        ...
buses/
    default/
        sib-authorisations.xml
default/
    admin-authz.xml
    audit-authz.xml
    cluster-components.xml
    coregroup-template.xml
    resource-templates.xml
    server-component-templates.xml
    virtualhosts.xml
system/
    JMS-resource-provider-templates.xml
    jdbc-resource-provider-only-templates.xml
    jdbc-resource-provider-templates.xml
    multibroker.xml
    nodes/
        servers/
            nodeagent/
                ...
    pme-resource-provider-templates.xml
    sibjmsresources-ra.xml
    wmqjmsresources-ra.xml
waspolicies/
    default/
        policy.xml
```

XML Files

The WebSphere Application Server configuration is stored in XML files under the application server `profiles/PROFILE/config` directory. We will look at the WAS enterprise management and high-availability deployment structures (e.g., cell, cluster, node, etc.), but this time in the context of the XML files that control those structures.

The top-level WAS configuration item, called a cell, is the core unit of management. With WAS 7, the Job Manager can manage multiple cells with their own Deployment Manager, but the cell is traditionally managed with a Deployment Manager. The top-level cell topology is defined in `cell.xml`.

Within the cell there are nodes, with a Node Agent and multiple server instances. The nodes are organized into node groups and, for some management control, core groups (which are important for HAManager and SIB, for example). The node topology is controlled by `nodes.xml`.

Server instances are grouped into clusters for load-balancing and failover purposes. The cluster topology is controlled by `cluster.xml`.

The Deployment Manager controls the XML files for each of these top-level configuration items and pushes them out to the Node Agents that manage the configurations for the instances on their nodes.

At the core of the WAS installations for a server instance are the `server.xml` file and `serverindex.xml` files for the given instance, although other XML files also play a part. These XML files, however they are administered, ultimately control the environment and are dynamically accessed within WAS via the Config Manager Service. This file structure is shown in Table 11-2.

Table 11-2. *WAS Core Configuration XML Files*

File	Purpose
admin-authz.xml	Contains the mappings of users and groups of users to server roles.
cell.xml	Contains a small amount of information as to whether the cell is STANDALONE or DISTRIBUTED.
coregroupbridge.xml	Contains the configuration of the core group bridge for bridging between core groups for high availability.
cluster.xml	Contains the cluster topology configuration for high availability and scalability.
hamanagerservice.xml	Contains the timeout, thread pool configuration, and buffer management configuration for the HAManager subsystem.
installed-channels.xml	Contains some installed channel details.
libraries.xml	Contains the optional library configuration, i.e., Java Server Faces (JSF) configuration for the web container.
multibroker.xml	Contains the Data Replication Services reliable multicast messaging configuration that also underpins DynaCache.
namestore.xml	Contains the configuration for data persistence binding.
naming-authz.xml	Contains the mappings of users and groups of users to roles for naming operations.
nodes.xml	Contains the cell node topology information.
ODCSchema.xml	Contains the underpinning schema information controlling the production of plugin-cfg.xml.
perftuners.xml	Contains the application- and system-level monitoring advisors configuration.
persistence.xml	Contains the configured access paths for JPA.
pmi-config.xml	Contains the PMI performance metrics configuration.
plugin-cfg.xml	Contains the configuration file for the HTTP server proxy plugin used to route requests from a web server to an application server instance.
pmirm.xml	Contains the PMI performance metrics and filtering configuration for subsystems.
resources-cei.xml	Contains the Common Event Infrastructure (CEI) provider configuration.

File	Purpose
resources-pme502.xml	Contains the WAS 5.02 Programming Model Extensions (PME) configuration.
resources-pme.xml	Contains the PME configuration.
resources.xml	Contains the configuration information for the J2C/JCA resource adapter providers.
security.xml	Contains the security configuration in terms of WAS, J2EE, and JCA specifics. This covers single sign-on, trust association interceptors, and CSIv2 IIOP security.
server.xml	Contains the configuration of the WAS runtime in terms of transport chains and mappings, connection and buffer configuration, and thread pools. This is the most important configuration file for WAS.
serverindex.xml	Contains the configuration of port mapping for listeners for WAS. This needs to be changed for each instance on a node to avoid port clashes.
sib-bus.xml	Contains the configuration for each bus for the Service Integration Bus (SIB).
sib-destinations.xml	Contains the configured destinations for the SIB.
sib-engines.xml	Contains the configured messaging engines for the SIB.
sib-mediations.xml	Contains the mediations configured for the SIB.
sib-mqserverbusmembers.xml	Contains the configured MQ Servers that are members of a bus for the SIB.
sib-security-audit.xml	Contains the security configuration for the SIB.
sib-service.xml	Contains the configuration for the SIB services.
systemapps.xml	Contains the configuration for system-level applications such as the file transfer service.
variables.xml	Contains the environment variable type substitution mappings for internal configuration variables to their actual values for WAS.
virtualhosts.xml	Contains the configuration of virtual hosts. The minimum this will contain is the default_host configuration.
ws-security.xml	Contains the configuration for the numerous WS-Security settings such as the certificate and key store, login types, and encryption to support the web services engines.

Configuration may be handled at the cell, cluster, node, and instance levels so some of these XML configuration files may be found at more than one place in the administrative configuration and its directory tree, but the file for the instance takes precedence.

Some non-XML files are also used for configuration, particularly in the security area, where key stores and certificates must be managed in accord with industry standards. For example, LTPA (Lightweight Third Party Authentication) tokens and key stores are found in the ltpa.jceks, key.p12, and trust.p12 files.

The server.xml File Structure

The structure of the server.xml file often seems complex at first, but a closer look shows that it consists of a few important subsections that configure a number of instances of different subsystems. Every WAS server instance will have its own server.xml file. The subsections and the subsystems they are related to are briefly explained in this section.

The outermost element of the server.xml file that encloses the body is the process:Server tag. This identifies the XMI files that contain the schemas for the configuration and the name of the server instance being configured, often server1.

The stateManagement element says how the server should initialize, and usually contains the initialState of START.

The statisticsProvider element configures the statistics gathering for the ORB Service.

The next major subsections are the services subdocuments, with one block for each of the major services underpinning the WAS runtime. We will not look at each of these, but just some of the key service subsections with their own structure. These key services are identified in the plugin.xml file.

- The adminservice:AdminService services subsection includes a number of connectors elements that configure connectors, the configRepository service element, and the pluginConfigService element.

- The traceservice:TraceService services subsection configures the tracelog file.

- The logginservice.ras.RASLoggingService services subsection configures the activity log file.

- The orb.ObjectRequestBroker services subsection contains properties, plugins, and interceptor elements to configure its runtime behavior and contains a threadPool element to set up the thread pooling underpinning the ORB.

- The channelservice.TransportChannelService services subsection supports the Channel Framework Service and contains a number of transportChannels and chains elements to configure timeouts and mappings to ports in the serverindex.xml file for a channel and the combination of channels that forms a chain.

- The threadpoolmanager:ThreadPoolManager services subsection contains a number of threadPools elements that configure the maximum and minimum sizes and configuration for thread pools underpinning key subsystems.

- The loggingservice.http:HTTPAccessLoggingService services subsection includes the errorLog and accessLog elements that configure the http_error.log and http_access.log files, respectively.

The errorStreamRedirect and outputStreamRedirect elements are *not* services elements but map the error and output file handles for the JVM to named files.

The next major subsection is the set of components' subsections for individual subsystems within WAS, which may contain embedded services and components sections. This maps to the relationship between containers and components (i.e., containers are components that embed other components within the WAS code) and the configuration in the com.ibm.ws.runtime.jar plugin and its plugin.xml file.

- The first components section is for the `namingserver:NameServer` component. This is a simple subsection that only contains a `stateManagement` element telling the component to `START`.

- The `applicationserver:ApplicationServer` components section configures the main Application Server container and embeds the `applicationserver:TransactionService` and `applicationserver:DynamicCache` services, the `applicationserver.webcontainer:WebContainer` components element that configures the web container with its own services elements, the `applicationserver.ejbcontainer:EJBContainer` components element that configures the EJB container with its own services elements, and the `portletcontainer:PortletContainer` and `applicationserver.sipcontainer:SIPContainer` components elements.

- The final entry within the components section is for the `webserverPluginSettings` with its own element that configures the HTTP proxy plugin.

The last major subsection of `server.xml` is the `ProcessDefinitions` subdocument that contains `ioRedirect`, `execution`, `monitoringPolicy`, and `jvmEntries` elements and subsections with `systemProperties` elements, all of which contribute to the properties and configuration for the JVM itself. The garbage collection, JVM command-line entries, and process settings for the JVM are all configured in this subsection.

Summary

This brief chapter examined the configuration of WAS. You have looked at the directory structure of an installation and what is stored in the different locations, and then how the configuration of that environment is all represented by a set of XML files. These XML files can be found on the file system for static configuration of the cell, clusters, core groups, node groups, nodes, and instances, but are also dynamically accessed and used for configuration via calls into the Config Service and registration of listeners with it to watch for changes. The core of the WAS configuration is the `server.xml` file that sets up the main WAS runtime.

CHAPTER 12

■■■

Related Products

IBM produces and sells a number of related products designed to deploy to the WebSphere Application Server environment. Most of these are just standard Java Enterprise Edition (JavaEE) applications, but some of the more WAS-centric products hook and extend its functionality in addition to shipping JavaEE or Java 2 Platform, Enterprise Edition (J2EE) applications. This chapter looks briefly at these extension products: WebSphere Enterprise Service Bus (WESB), WebSphere Process Server, and WebSphere Portal Server. The examination will be brief since this book is about WAS and not about these products. Also, at the time of the writing of this book, the version 7 of these products had not been released; although we can see the architectural direction from the 6.1 versions.

WebSphere ESB

One of the current growth areas in enterprise IT is integration based on a service-oriented architecture (SOA), that is, the presentation of coarse-grained business-level services, in terms of their logical operations, using web services technologies. Under the covers, point integration uses a mix of technologies, and transformation with composition takes place to present the appropriate format before the web services technologies are added to the mix. One concept that builds on this is that of the Enterprise Service Bus (ESB). It adds mediation (e.g., transformation) of services to present new services while hiding the location of the real service provider. The key to distinguishing an ESB from earlier EAI (Enterprise Application Integration) technologies is that it is standards-based (i.e., web services standards) and provides location independence alongside mediation. Products have been built around this concept, and WESB is IBM's offering for the J2EE space. When process orchestration and support for long-running transactions are added, the result is WebSphere Process Server, which builds on the WESB product. With an ESB, a service consumer makes requests of the bus without knowing the details of the provider.

WESB is the smallest incremental extension to the base WAS product in the family of WebSphere Application Server–based integration products. Essentially, WESB is a standards-based ESB product that provides web services support using HTTP and JMS and J2EE Connector Architecture (JCA)–based integration and supports the Service Component Architecture (SCA) standard. In this product, mediation modules are produced, which are Java-based wirings of inbound and outbound services with transformations. There are similar competing products from other vendors that are also based on the SCA standard.

The database data sources, inbound and outbound web service descriptions, JCA adapters, messages, and so on and most any source of data are described using XML, compliant with the OASIS Service Data Objects (SDO) standard that is based on the JSR235 specification. Support for the SDO standard is built into WAS with an implementation generated from the Eclipse Modeling Framework.

The composite transformations from one SDO representation to another are defined using the composites in an SCA XML document, with bindings to particular underlying implementations and technologies. SCA is also an OASIS standard, but one that is designed to supplement the SDO standard. The SCA implementation technology in WESB is Java-based, although the SCA standard is not tied to the Java language; for example, there are Apache Tuscany SCA implementations for both Java and C++ bindings. WAS includes limited legacy (pre-standards) mediation support inside the Service Integration Bus (SIB), and WAS 7 extends this with the Tuscany Java implementation in the SCA Feature Pack. But the WESB implementation is designed for true enterprise-level capabilities.

When WESB is deployed onto WebSphere Application Server Network Deployment (WAS-ND), it requires a number of database tables and SIB queues to be set up. It keeps mediation configuration and status in the database, and the flow between the application-level mediation components is handled via Java Message Service (JMS) and SIB with Service Message Objects (SMO) messages. SMOs are a derivative of the SDO standard customized for internal WESB and WebSphere Process Server operations.

When examining a typical WESB deployment environment, you can see a number of JavaEE applications and other artifacts. However, if you look at the runtime for development for WESB that sits inside the WebSphere Integration Developer and examine the plugins directory, you can see the distinct way in which WESB extends WAS, as demonstrated in Listing 12-1.

Listing 12-1. *WebSphere Integration Developer: WESB Plugins*

```
...
com.ibm.sibx.migration_6.1.0.jar
com.ibm.sibx.runtime_6.1.0.jar
com.ibm.sibx.wccm_6.1.0.jar
com.ibm.soacore.runtime_6.1.0.jar
com.ibm.soacore.sca_6.1.0.jar
com.ibm.soacore.wccm_6.1.0.jar
...
com.ibm.wbicmn.infra_6.1.0.jar
com.ibm.wbicmn.runtime_6.1.0.jar
com.ibm.wbicmn.system_6.1.0.jar
com.ibm.wbicmn.wccm_6.1.0.jar
com.ibm.wbicore.migration_6.1.0.jar
...
```

As you can see in Listing 12-1, the SIB is extended in the com.ibm.sibx.runtime_6.1.0.jar file, and the extensions to support its reconfiguration are in the com.ibm.sibx.wccm_6.1.0.jar file. Remember that the wccm refers to the WebSphere Common Configuration Model.

The core of the WESB functionality is in the `com.ibm.soacore.runtime_6.1.0.jar` file, with the `com.ibm.soacore.sca_6.1.0.jar` file providing the SCA support and the `com.ibm.soacore.wccm_6.1.0.jar` file providing the configuration support for the soacore plugins. The IBM family of integration products, formerly branded as WebSphere Business Integration, such as WESB and WebSphere Process Server, has common core infrastructure functionality for management, scaling, resilience, and so forth. This can be seen in the `com.ibm.wbicmn.infra_6.1.0.jar`, `com.ibm.wbicmn.runtime_6.1.0.jar`, `com.ibm.wbicmn.system_6.1.0.jar`, `com.ibm.wbicmn.wccm_6.1.0.jar`, and `com.ibm.wbicore.migration_6.1.0.jar` files. These are all plugins that extend WAS to provide new functionality. In this case they extend WAS 6.1.

The com.ibm.sibx.runtime_6.1.0.jar Plugin

If you examine the `com.ibm.sibx.runtime_6.1.0.jar` file and look in its `plugin.xml` file, you can see how SIB is extended for WESB. Under the `com.ibmn.wsspi.extension.applicationserver-startup` extension point, you can see three component implementations declared:

- `com.ibm.ws.sibx.admin.runtime.SIBXAdminService`

- `com.ibm.ws.sibx.scax.mediation.component.SIBXMediationComponent`

- `com.ibm.wbi.debug.sib.mediation.init.WBIDebugComponentImpl`

The key component, the `SIBXMediationComponent` class, implements the `DeployedObjectListener` interface, and in its `stateChanged` method it looks for mediation modules that are not the `sca.default` module. It sets up internal mediation flow components to handle the routing in the EJB container and also sets up associated classloaders for its module types.

On initialization, the `SIBXMediationComponent` component registers itself with the WAS `WsServiceRegistry` as supporting the `SIBXMediationComponent` service with support for the SMO representation, mediation modules, and mediation flows. When started, the component registers the `DeployedObjectListener` with the Application Manager Service. This component checks for modules of type `com.ibm.ws.sca.scdl.moduletype.mediation`. Essentially, the SIBX modules don't really extend SIB; they sit alongside it and provide a full implementation because SIB has only limited and non-standards-compliant internal mediation support.

The com.ibm.soacore.sca_6.1.0.jar Plugin

If you examine the `com.ibm.soacore.sca_6.1.0.jar` file and its `plugin.xml` file, you see the `com.ibm.ws.bo.handler.BOInstanceValidatorHandlerBootStrap` and `com.ibm.ws.sca.internal.managed.ManagedServerComponentImpl` components declared under the `com.ibm.wsspi.extension.applicationserver-startup` extension point.

The `ManagedServerComponentImpl` class is an important component that provides supporting infrastructure for the SCA and SIB functionality. It registers itself as a service with the WAS service registry and adds support for additional metadata, transaction management, and SIB asynchronous handlers to support SCA alongside new WebSphere MQ message queueing and JMS package representations. It then installs a number of listeners, including another `DeployedObjectListener`.

The component also sets up its SCA support with its own SIB bus name, `SCA_BUS_ID`. When an application is deployed, the WAR and EJB JAR files are examined to see if there is anything the component needs to do. If so, it uses its own classloaders to provide the necessary support. The BO references throughout the WESB code refer to the Business Object module integration components within the IBM business integration stack.

The com.ibm.soacore.runtime_6.1.0.jar Plugin

If you examine the com.ibm.soacore.runtime_6.1.0.jar file and its plugin.xml, you see that a number of components are started at server startup and application server startup, with most being for configuration and monitoring. Of these, the following are most important:

- The com.ibm.ws.bo.BOBootStrap class installs a DeployedObjectListener registered with the Application Manager Service and uses the BOCore class to install support for BO modules via an Eclipse Modeling Framework Ecore package, as in the previous SCA mediation modules.

- coreserver.WBISessionService, implemented by the com.ibm.ws.session. WBISessionBootStrap class, builds WBI (WebSphere Business Integration) session support upon the Work Area functionality built into WAS. This class uses the Application Manager Service to register a property listener for state changes so it can manage the WBI Session wrapper when the underlying work area support changes.

- The com.ibm.ws.al.bootstrap.WASBootstrap class registers MBeans for the environment and ensures the necessary support artifacts are loaded. It once again uses the DeployedObjectListener and PropertyChangeListener interfaces registered with the Application Manager Service to monitor deployments and changes in state to ensure that changes to an application or application server as a whole are propagated to the modules and components within the control of the WESB extensions.

- eventservice.EventsService is implemented by the com.ibm.ws.cem.EventFactoryStartup class. One of the things that WESB and WebSphere Process Server provide is the Common Event Infrastructure (CEI) that captures and stores business events in support of Business Activity Monitoring. The EventFactoryStartup class initializes this support by setting up the necessary Java Naming and Directory Interface (JNDI) integration and the event factory emitters to log the business events.

The com.ibm.wbicmn.runtime_6.1.0.jar Plugin

Finally, if you examine the com.ibm.wbicmn.runtime_6.1.0.jar file and its plugin.xml file, you see that the com.ibm.wbiserver.commondb.admin.CommonDBComponentImpl implementation class and the wbiaservice.WebSphereBusinessIntegrationAdapterService component implemented in the com.ibm.ws.wbia.WBIAServiceImpl class are both started when the application server loading phase runs.

The CommonDBComponentImpl class again installs a DeployedObjectListener via the Application Manager Service and manages the schema and configuration for deployed WESB applications and their integration with the databases supporting the platform.

The WBIAServiceImpl starts the WebSphere Business Integration Adapter Service and manages the factory classes that support the adapters. This facilitates the use of the WebSphere Business Integration Adapter family of products to integrate third-party EIS

(Enterprise Information System) environments with WESB or WebSphere Process Server acting as an integration broker.

WebSphere Process Server

WebSphere Process Server is a strict superset of the WebSphere ESB product and includes all of its features and components, but support is added to it for process orchestration and choreography. Full SCA support is included, as for WebSphere ESB, but support is also added for the WS-BPEL (Business Process Execution Language web service) standard and its integration with SCA. As is expected with a process orchestration server, there is support for long-running transactions and enhanced compensation facilities. There is even some workflow support to integrate human orchestration components. To support long-running transactions, persistence is important because the state needs to be held in a searchable form, so additional databases are required.

Since WebSphere Process Server is a strict superset of WebSphere ESB, all of the same components can be found in each. The Business Process Choreographer (BPC), also included, provides the core WS-BPEL orchestration support and the WebSphere Process Server (WPS) runtime classes. See Listing 12-2 for more details.

Listing 12-2. *WebSphere Integration Developer: WebSphere Process Server Plugins*

```
com.ibm.bpc.client_6.1.0.jar
com.ibm.bpc.common.nl1_6.1.0.jar
com.ibm.bpc.common.nl2_6.1.0.jar
com.ibm.bpc.common.prereq_6.1.0.jar
com.ibm.bpc.common_6.1.0.jar
com.ibm.bpc.config_6.1.0.jar
com.ibm.bpc.core_6.1.0.jar
com.ibm.bpc.migration_6.1.0.jar
com.ibm.bpc.model_6.1.0.jar
com.ibm.bpc.runtime_6.1.0.jar
com.ibm.bpc.wccm_6.1.0.jar
...
com.ibm.wps.runtime_6.1.0.jar
com.ibm.wps.wccm_6.1.0.jar

...
```

The key plugins in this, besides those for WebSphere ESB, are the com.ibm.bpc. runtime_6.1.0.jar file, to support the Business Process Choreographer, and the com.ibm. wps.runtime_6.1.0.jar file, to support the core WebSphere Process Server runtime. As before, the model plugins provide the module definition support using the Eclipse Modeling Framework (EMF) Ecore, and wccm plugins integrate with the WebSphere Common Configuration Model (WCCM) infrastructure. The core plugin for the Business Process Choreographer is a resource bundle and provides utility classes for exception handling, logging, and tracing. The component architecture for WebSphere Process Server and its WebSphere ESB subset is shown in Figure 12-1.

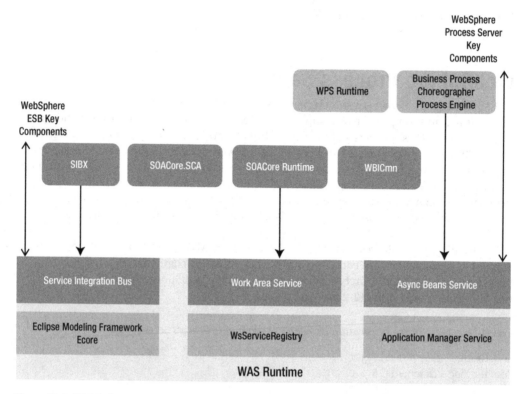

Figure 12-1. *WebSphere Process Server and WebSphere ESB architecture components*

The com.ibm.bpc.runtime_6.1.0.jar Plugin

If you examine the com.ibm.bpc.runtime_6.1.0.jar file and its plugin.xml file, you see a number of components started as part of the application server container startup:

- The bpelflowmanager.BPELFlowManager service is implemented by the com.ibm.bpe.framework.ProcessContainer class. The ProcessContainer class extends the BPCService class that provides the DeployedObjectHandler support to examine deployments. It also does the following:

  - Sets up the environment, MBeans, and integration with the Application Manager Service to examine deployed applications and then builds upon the WAS Async Beans

  - Installs the BPEL Flow Manager engine and a Process Container collaborator

  - Uses the Config Service to set itself up appropriately

  - Makes use of the databases set up for that purpose

  - Integrates with the EJB container that runs much of its code via message-driven beans (MDBs)

  - Is notified by and adds support for process components that may require execution at a particular date and time, when an application is started

- The `humantaskmanager.HumanTaskManager` service, implemented by the `com.ibm.task.mbean.HumanTaskManager` class, extends the `BPCService` class and initializes the `HumanTaskApplicationManager` infrastructure and MBeans. Again, it registers with the Application Manager Service to examine deployed applications to add support for Human Tasks with the Business Process Choreographer and integrates the EJB container with its code using MDBs.

- The `staffservice.StaffService` service, implemented by the `com.ibm.ws.staffsupport.StaffServiceImpl` class, sets up the staff support and integration with JNDI.

- The `bpcserver.BPCContainer` service, implemented by the `com.ibm.bpe.framework.BPCContainerRuntimeComponent`, initializes the `BPCContainer` and the `BPCDataStore` component that integrates with the database to add business process choreographer support, create the database schema, and create the database tables.

It is the `com.ibm.bpc.runtime_6.1.0.jar` file that provides the WS-BPEL and its related SCA support.

Immediately you can see that the components of the WebSphere Process Server runtime related to process orchestration are referred to as part of the Business Process Engine (BPE).

The com.ibm.wps.runtime_6.1.0.jar Plugin

If you examine the `com.ibm.wps.runtime_6.1.0.jar` file and open its `plugin.xml` file, you see a number of components that are started up as part of the application server container startup and one component that is started up as part of the EJB container startup to provide the Extended Messaging Service. The following are the key classes that start up as part of the application server startup:

- `com.ibm.wbiserver.sequencing.service.EsBootStrap` causes the `BaseEsService` to be started when the environment is started, and stopped when the environment is stopped. This provides the event sequencing support. Again, the Application Manager Service is used to register a `DeployedObjectListener` and a `PropertyChangeListener` to examine deployed application modules to see if any need the facilities of the event sequencing service. The `WorkManager` support in WAS is used under the covers to enable the sequencing of events coming into an SCA component.

- `com.ibm.wbiservers.brules.runtime.component.BusinessRulesComponentImpl` simply initializes the business rules runtime via the `BusinessRulesRuntimeImpl` class that starts the Business Rules Service and sets up the MBean for it. WebSphere Process Server supports the running of business rules as part of the decision-making process for WS-BPEL components for routing and execution purposes. IBM's purchase of the ILOG company and its JRules product will change this area because JRules will become the main rules engine for IBM BPM (Business Process Management) products such as WebSphere Process Server.

- `com.ibm.wbiserver.statementmachine.BusinessStateMachineServiceImpl` uses the Application Manager Service and its `DeployedObjectListener` callback support to examine modules that require `sacl` state machine support. The `StateMachineDefinition` class is used to provide that support.

- Extended Messaging Service support is provided by the `com.ibm.ws.ems.ExtendedMessagingServiceImpl` class.

WebSphere Portal Server

WebSphere Portal Server is an "integration on the glass" solution that offers improved presentation facilities over the base WAS web container. Like other portal servers, the user interface is split into a number of UI application components called *portlets* that each display their contents independently to a space allotted on a shared page.

The earlier WebSphere Portal Server 6.0 product supported JSR168-compliant portlets. These are essentially a special class of servlet that renders to given shared page response and supports the Web Services for Remote Portlets (WSRP) standard that allows a remote portal server to display content from a portlet. The JSR168 and WSRP standards supported by the earlier product were limited by a lack of data sharing, which essentially limited the abilities of the product and other similar standards-based portal servers like it. Interestingly, the WAS 6.1 product also supports the JSR168 and WSRP standards in its portlet container, although it only displays a single portlet at a time.

Portal servers traditionally also make use of LDAP directories and databases to support personalization of content for a particular user (i.e., the application and portal server decide what combination of portlets to target to a particular user or role) and customization (i.e., the user decides what combinations of portlets to use by selecting from a portlet catalog). WAS 7 builds on the WAS 6.1 support and provides JSR286 and WSRP v2 support for data sharing between portlets, although it still only supports a single portlet on a page at a time. WebSphere Portal Server 6.1 supports the same standards with multiple portlets for a rich user interface experience.

The WebSphere Portal Server 6.1.0.1 product implementation examined here is a little different than the WebSphere ESB 6.1 and WebSphere Process Server 6.1 products in a number of ways. The extension to the base WAS product is more limited, with almost all of the functionality being added in standard J2EE applications deployed to the base application server rather than via an extensive plugin infrastructure that hooks into the core WAS runtime infrastructure services. Also, WebSphere Portal Server 6.1.0.1 is WAS 7 "tolerant," meaning it runs on both WAS 6.1 and WAS 7.0 with the same functionality and is fully supported for being deployed to a WAS 7 base as well as a WAS 6.1 base.

WAS 7 includes a portlet container to allow JSR286 portlets to be handled for full-page portlet display. WebSphere Portal Server 6.1.0.1 also provides a JSR286 Portlet Container but displays multiple portlets to a page with full integration between them, so it must hook into the WAS web container and build upon the existing JSR286 support. The "hooking" mechanism simply works by deploying web applications that handle the multiple portlets displayed via the WebSphere Portal Server's own servlet functionality.

WebSphere Portal Server 6.1.0.1 mostly provides J2EE applications for Ajax support, UI frameworks, and database and LDAP support for personalization. However, it does deploy a plugin called `wp.ext.jar` to extend WAS.

The wp.ext.jar Plugin

If you examine the `plugin.xml` file for the `wp.ext.jar` plugin, you find that the plugin merely supplies tag libraries to support portal rendering and Web 2.0 tags. The expected integration with the WAS runtime is handled purely through deployed J2EE applications, apart from the tag libraries provision of a framework for handling multiple portlets with the portlet container.

Summary

Although none of the products we have examined (WebSphere ESB 6.1, WebSphere Process Server 6.1, and WebSphere Portal Server 6.1) is designed to be built on WebSphere Application Server 7, the application server component model is essentially the same between WAS 6.1 and WAS 7, so we can deduce future behavior. We took a look at the extensions in these products that target the earlier application server to see how they extend the base application server functionality rather than just deploy to it.

We used runtimes from WebSphere Integration Developer to provide a single centralized build to examine. In each case, the products deploy standard J2EE applications, but also provide plugins that make use of base application server functionality to supplement the existing functionality to support new workloads and module types. The use of the base Application Manager Service to deploy listeners to examine modules to see if they target the particular product extension, and the use of new Eclipse Modeling Framework core module definitions, is key to each of these products, as is the use of the WebSphere Common Configuration Model for configuration.

WebSphere ESB introduces a core runtime infrastructure that adds support for integrating the Common Event Infrastructure. WebSphere Process Server builds on WESB and on the Work Area support for long-running transactions in base WAS. The core runtime for both WebSphere ESB and WebSphere Process Server supports Business Objects and SCA mediation modules and WebSphere Business Integration Adapters. The SIBX and SOACore components add full SCA mediation support based on EJBs to the existing facilities provided by the Service Integration Bus mediation infrastructure.

WebSphere Process Server is a strict superset of the WebSphere ESB product, so includes all of the facilities and components of it, but adds the Business Process Choreographer and core Process Server runtime facilities. The Business Process Choreographer builds upon the Async Beans support inside WAS and provides support for WS-BPEL with a Flow Manager, staff and human task management services, and a process engine. Additional infrastructure facilities are also added to provide business rules support, event sequencing, and business state machine support.

The WebSphere Portal Server extends WAS in a different way. Although both WAS 7 and WebSphere Portal Server 6.1.0.1 provide JSR286 containers and can co-reside, the `wp.ext.jar` plugin that gets deployed to a WAS 7 environment merely includes tag libraries and relies on standard J2EE archives containing code to route portal page requests to portlets. The WebSphere Portal Server builds on WAS almost exclusively via documented J2EE interfaces to provide its functionality.

APPENDIX

■ ■ ■

Mapping of WAS Extension Points to the Extensions That Use Them

Table A-1 shows for the WAS7Monitor bundle that you created in Chapter 3 the mapping of extension points in the WAS 7 Eclipse Extension Registry to the extensions that use them.

Table A-1. *WAS 7 Extension Point to Extension Mapping*

Bundle/Plug-in Extension Point	Extensions
com.ibm.wsspi.extension.cache-resourcemgr-config	–
org.eclipse.jdt.core.classpathContainerInitializer	–
org.eclipse.emf.ecore.generated_package	–
org.eclipse.core.runtime.contentTypes	–
com.ibm.wsspi.extension.handler	–
com.ibm.wsspi.proxy.extension.filter	–
org.eclipse.core.filesystem.filesystems	org.eclipse.core.filesystem.local, org.eclipse.core.filesystem.null
com.ibm.wsfp.main.rm-persistence	–
com.ibm.ws.bootstrap.resource-file	–
com.ibm.wsspi.extension.job-manager-components	–
com.ibm.wsspi.rrd.rrd-extension-delegator	–
com.ibm.wsspi.extension.ws-resources-def	com.ibm.ws.admin.services.WebSphere Resources, com.ibm.ws.coregroupbridge.WebSphere Resources, com.ibm.wsfp.main.WebSphere Resources, com.ibm.ws.proxy.admin.WebSphere Resources
org.eclipse.emf.ecore.extension_parser	–
com.ibm.ws.wccmbase.anp-defs	–
com.ibm.wsspi.extension.message-bundle	–

Continued

Table A-1. *Continued*

Bundle/Plug-in Extension Point	Extensions
org.eclipse.core.resources.modelProviders	org.eclipse.core.resources.modelProvider
com.ibm.wsspi.extension.hamanager-startup	–
com.ibm.wsspi.rrd.generators	–
com.ibm.ws.portletcontainer.portlet-document-filter-config	–
org.eclipse.ant.core.antTasks	–
com.ibm.wsspi.extension.ejbcontainer-startup	–
org.eclipse.core.runtime.applications	com.ibm.ws.bootstrap.WSLauncher, com.ibm.ws.debug.osgi.StartConsole, com.ibm.ws.debug.osgi.Noop, org.eclipse.jdt.core.JavaCodeFormatter, com.ibm.ws.runtime.startWsServer, org.eclipse.ant.core.antRunner
org.eclipse.core.runtime.products	–
com.ibm.wsspi.extension.server-startup	–
com.ibm.wsspi.extension.resource-binders	–
org.eclipse.core.resources.markers	org.eclipse.emf.ecore.diagnostic, org.eclipse.jdt.core.problem, org.eclipse.jdt.core.buildpath_problem, org.eclipse.jdt.core.transient_problem, org.eclipse.jdt.core.task, org.eclipse.core.resources.marker, org.eclipse.core.resources.problemmarker, org.eclipse.core.resources.taskmarker, org.eclipse.core.resources.bookmark, org.eclipse.core.resources.textmarker
org.eclipse.jdt.core.compilationParticipant	–
com.ibm.wsspi.extension.taglibcacheconfig-xml	–
com.ibm.wsspi.proxy.extension.protocol-provider-factory	–
com.ibm.wsspi.extension.application-server-components-CR	–
com.ibm.wsfp.main.ibmaxis2-app-ctx-migrator-client	com.ibm.wsfp.main.Addr-Client, com.ibm.wsfp.main.Transport-Client
com.ibm.wsspi.extension.mbean-provider	–
com.ibm.wsspi.extension.channel-framework-channel-factory-type	–
com.ibm.wsspi.extension.admin-endpoint-extension	–
com.ibm.wsspi.extension.server-recovery-mode-control-region-startup	–
com.ibm.wsspi.extension.admin-job-handler-extension	–

Bundle/Plug-in Extension Point	Extensions
com.ibm.wsspi.extension.configservice-metadata	com.ibm.ws.admin.core.admin_jmx_configservice-metadata, com.ibm.ws.admin.services.admin_jmx_configservice-metadata, com.ibm.events.client.cei_configservice-metadata, com.ibm.ws.sib.server.SIB config service metadata
com.ibm.wsspi.extension.applicationserver-startup	–
com.ibm.wsspi.extension.impl-factory	–
com.ibm.wsfp.main.ibmaxis2-unknown-epr-config-ctxt-loader-plugin	com.ibm.wsfp.main.RMUnknownEPRCfgCtxLoader
com.ibm.wsspi.extension.config-schemadiff	com.ibm.ws.admin.core.admin_jmx-config-schemadiff, com.ibm.ws.sib.server.sib-config-schemadiff
com.ibm.wsfp.main.ibmaxis2-qos-policytypeloader	com.ibm.wsfp.main.RMPolicyTypeLoader, com.ibm.wsfp.main.HttpPolicyTypeLoader, com.ibm.wsfp.main.SSLPolicyTypeLoader, com.ibm.wsfp.main.JMSPolicyTypeLoader
com.ibm.wsspi.extension.was-migration-ddconversiontool	–
com.ibm.wsspi.extension.content-depl-providers	com.ibm.ws.admin.services.DefaultContentHandler, com.ibm.ws.proxy.ProxyFilterContentHandler, com.ibm.ws.proxy.CustomAdvisorContentHandler
com.ibm.wsspi.sib.extension.MessagingEngineControlListener	–
com.ibm.wsspi.extension.jmsMessageListenerSetters	com.ibm.ws.runtime.messageListenerSettersForWrappers, com.ibm.ws.sib.server.messageListenerSettersForWrappers, com.ibm.ws.sib.server.messageListenerSettersForWMQJCARA
com.ibm.wsspi.proxy.extension.filter-context	–
org.eclipse.core.expressions.propertyTesters	–
com.ibm.ws.bootstrap.invocationHandlers	–
com.ibm.wsspi.extension.channel-framework-channel-type	–
com.ibm.wsspi.extension.servlet-context-facade-registry-xml	–
com.ibm.wsspi.extension.logger-properties	–
com.ibm.wsspi.extension.operation-depl-providers	com.ibm.ws.admin.services.DefaultOperationFactory, com.ibm.ws.proxy.ProxyFilterOperationFactory, com.ibm.ws.proxy.CustomAdvisorOperationFactory
com.ibm.wsspi.extension.server-control-region-startup	–
com.ibm.wsfp.main.ibmaxis2-qos-bindingloader	com.ibm.wsfp.main.RMBindingLoader, com.ibm.wsfp.main.HttpDefaultBindingLoader, com.ibm.wsfp.main.SSLDefaultBindingLoader, com.ibm.wsfp.main.JMSDefaultBindingLoader

Continued

Table A-1. *Continued*

Bundle/Plug-in Extension Point	Extensions
com.ibm.wsfp.main.ibmaxis2-service-config-plugin	com.ibm.wsfp.main.WSAConfigPlugin, com.ibm.wsfp.main.RMConfigPlugin, com.ibm.wsfp.main.HttpConfigPlugin, com.ibm.wsfp.main.SSLConfigPlugin, com.ibm.wspolicy.main.WSPolicyConfigPlugin
com.ibm.wsspi.extension.admin-command-def	com.ibm.ws.admin.core.AdminServices, com.ibm.ws.admin.services.AdminServices, com.ibm.ws.admin.services.BLA commands, com.ibm.ws.runtime.Runtime, com.ibm.ws.admin.system.AdminSystem, com.tivoli.pd.amwas.core.amwas-admin-command-def, com.ibm.ws.sib.server.SIB Admin Commands, com.ibm.ws.dpmanager.AdminServices, com.ibm.ws.sib.webservices.wsgw.SIB Admin Commands, com.ibm.ws.cimgr.CentralizedInstall
com.ibm.wsfp.main.ibmaxis2-thread-ctx-migrator-client	com.ibm.wsfp.main.WSPolicy-Client, com.ibm.wsfp.main.WSRM-Client-TCM, com.ibm.wsfp.main.SecurityCtxMigrator-Client-TCM, com.ibm.wsfp.main.WSSecurityCtxMigrator-Client-TCM, com.ibm.wsfp.main.WSTX-Client-TCM
com.ibm.wsfp.main.ibmaxis2-qos-module-server	com.ibm.wsfp.main.WSSecurity-Server, com.ibm.wsfp.main.WSTX-Server, com.ibm.wsfp.main.WSReliableMessaging-Server, com.ibm.wsfp.main.WASAxis2PMIRM-Server, com.ibm.wsfp.main.WASAxis2PMI-Server, com.ibm.wsfp.main.Addressing-Server, com.ibm.wsfp.main.WSDM-Server com.ibm.wspolicy.main.WSPolicyServerMex
com.ibm.wsfp.main.ibmaxis2-unknown-epr-resolver-plugin	com.ibm.wsfp.main.RMUnknownEPRResolver
com.ibm.wsspi.extension.admin-job-extension	com.ibm.ws.admin.system.admin-jobs-built-in, com.ibm.ws.admin.system.MySensor-Jobs
com.ibm.wsspi.extension.extension-checker	–
com.ibm.wsspi.extension.admin-authz-def	com.ibm.ws.admin.core.AdminSecurity, com.ibm.ws.admin.services.AdminSecurity
com.ibm.ws.portletcontainer.collaborator-config	–
com.ibm.wsspi.extension.folder-sync-filter	com.ibm.ws.admin.services.J2eeAppFolderFilter, com.ibm.ws.admin.services.BLASyncFolderFilter, com.ibm.ws.admin.services.SecurityDomainFolderFilter
com.ibm.wsspi.extension.client-components	–
com.ibm.wsspi.extension.pmiCustomExtension	–
com.ibm.wsspi.extension.scheduler-startup	–
com.ibm.wsfp.main.custom-handler-server	–

Bundle/Plug-in Extension Point	Extensions
`org.eclipse.ant.core.extraClasspathEntries`	–
`org.eclipse.core.variables.valueVariables`	–
`org.eclipse.core.resources.teamHook`	–
`com.ibm.wsfp.main.ibmaxis2-qos-admin-policytypeloader`	–
`com.ibm.wsspi.proxy.extension.applyProtocolVersionRangeSelector`	–
`com.ibm.wsspi.extension.server-control-region-components`	–
`com.ibm.wspolicy.main.ibmwspolicy-qos-wspolicyassertionprocessor`	–
`com.ibm.wsspi.extension.dmz-admin-agent-components`	–
`com.ibm.wsspi.extension.protectedclasses-policy`	–
`org.eclipse.core.resources.builders`	`org.eclipse.jdt.core.javabuilder`

`com.ibm.wsspi.extension.server-model-init`	`com.ibm.ws.wccmbase.base_model_read_only_init,`
	`com.ibm.ws.wccmbase.base_model_read_write_init,`
	`com.ibm.events.client.cei_model_init,`
	`com.ibm.ws.sib.wccm.sib_model_init,`
	`com.ibm.ws.sib.wccm.sib_resource_model_init,`
	`com.ibm.ws.sib.wccm.wsn_model_init,`
	`com.ibm.ws.wccm.cimgr.cimgr_model_init`

`com.ibm.wsspi.extension.dmgr-side-extension-checker`	–
`com.ibm.wsspi.extension.security-scanner-config`	–
`com.ibm.wsspi.rrd.rrd-emf-packages`	–
`com.ibm.wsspi.extension.service-provider`	`com.ibm.ws.runtime.webservices-service-provider,` `com.ibm.ws.sib.server.sib-service-provider`
`com.ibm.wsspi.extension.server-recovery-mode-components`	–
`com.ibm.wsfp.main.ibmaxis2-transport-shutdown-plugin`	–
`org.eclipse.core.resources.fileModificationValidator`	–
`com.ibm.wsspi.extension.sysapp`	`com.ibm.ws.runtime.transaction-sysapp`
`com.ibm.wsspi.extension.managed-object-metadata-collector`	`com.ibm.ws.admin.core.admin_jmx_managed-object-metadata-collector,` `com.ibm.ws.cimgr.CIMMetadataCollectorImpl`
`com.ibm.wsspi.extension.admin-managed-resource-extension`	–
`com.ibm.wsspi.extension.admin-subsystem-extension`	–
`com.ibm.wsspi.extension.syswebservices`	`com.ibm.ws.runtime.wsaddressing_impl-syswebservices,` `com.ibm.ws.runtime.webservices-syswebservices`

Continued

Table A-1. *Continued*

Bundle/Plug-in Extension Point	Extensions
com.ibm.ws.bootstrap.applications	com.ibm.ws.admin.core.CollectManagedObjectMetadata, com.ibm.ws.admin.services.WsAdmin, com.ibm.ws.admin.services.WsServerLauncher, com.ibm.ws.admin.services.WsServerStop, com.ibm.ws.admin.services.ServerStatus, com.ibm.ws.admin.services.BackupConfigUtility, com.ibm.ws.admin.services.RestoreConfigUtility, com.ibm.ws.admin.services.FindEJBTimersCommand, com.ibm.ws.admin.services.CancelEJBTimersCommand, com.ibm.ws.admin.services.NodeFederationUtility, com.ibm.ws.admin.services.NodeUninstallPrep, com.ibm.ws.admin.services.NodeCleanupUtility, com.ibm.ws.admin.services.NodeRemovalUtility, com.ibm.ws.admin.services.NodeSyncUtility, com.ibm.ws.admin.services.NodeRenameUtility, com.ibm.ws.admin.services.DisplayWASInstance, com.ibm.ws.admin.services.ChangeWASServer, com.ibm.ws.admin.services.ProfileRegistrationUtility, com.ibm.ws.admin.services.ProfileDeregistrationUtility, com.ibm.ws.debug.osgi.StartOsgiConsole, com.ibm.ws.debug.osgi.OsgiCfgInit, com.ibm.ws.migration.WASPreUpgrade, com.ibm.ws.migration.WASPostUpgrade, com.ibm.ws.migration.ConvertScriptCompatibility, com.ibm.ws.migration.ConversionTool, com.ibm.ws.migration.ClientUpgrade, com.ibm.ws.runtime.RetrieveSigners, com.ibm.ws.runtime.CertificateAuthorityAction, com.ibm.ws.runtime.CollectManagedObjectMetadata, com.ibm.ws.runtime.InstallActionInvoker, com.ibm.ws.runtime.WsServer, com.ibm.ws.runtime.LaunchBatchCompiler, com.ibm.ws.runtime.LaunchWSAnt, com.ibm.ws.runtime.CreateEJBStubsCommand, com.ibm.ws.runtime.LaunchClient, com.ibm.ws.runtime.LaunchClientApi, com.ibm.ws.runtime.DumpExtensionRegistry, com.ibm.ws.runtime.WsProfile, com.ibm.ws.runtime.WsProfileAdminListener, com.ibm.ws.admin.system.JobManager Restore, com.ibm.jaxb.tools.Driver, com.ibm.jaxb.tools.SchemaGenerator, com.ibm.wsfp.main.EndpointEnabler, com.ibm.uddi.UDDIValueSet, com.ibm.jaxws.tools.WsGen com.ibm.jaxws.tools.WsImport, com.ibm.ws.vm.WsVMAutomount
com.ibm.wsspi.extension.pmiJmxMapperExtension	—
com.ibm.wsspi.extension.soap-request-monitor	com.ibm.ws.runtime.transaction_impl-soap-request-monitor
com.ibm.wsspi.extension.dmgr-components-CR	—

Bundle/Plug-in Extension Point	Extensions
com.ibm.wsfp.main.ibmaxis2-qos-module-client	com.ibm.wsfp.main.WSSecurity-Client, com.ibm.wsfp.main.WSReliableMessaging-Client, com.ibm.wsfp.main.WASAxis2PMIRM-Client, com.ibm.wsfp.main.Addressing-Client
com.ibm.wsspi.rrd.handlers	—
com.ibm.wsspi.extension.webservices	com.ibm.ws.runtime.wsaddressing_impl-webservices, com.ibm.ws.runtime.dynacache-webservices, com.ibm.ws.runtime.pmi_rm-webservices, com.ibm.ws.runtime.security_wssecurity-webservices, com.ibm.ws.runtime.webservices-webservices, com.ibm.ws.runtime.i18n-webservices, com.ibm.ws.runtime.transaction_impl-webservices
com.ibm.wsfp.main.webservice-admin-serviceindex-manager	—
com.ibm.wsspi.extension.server-config	—
com.ibm.wsspi.extension.server-activation	—
com.ibm.wsspi.extension.amm-defs	—
com.ibm.wsspi.extension.app-depl-providers	com.ibm.ws.admin.services.BLATaskProvider, com.ibm.ws.migration.Migration-app-depl-provider, com.ibm.ws.runtime.transaction-app-depl-provider, com.ibm.ws.runtime.appprofile_impl-app-depl-providers, com.ibm.ws.runtime.security_impl-app-depl-providers, com.ibm.ws.runtime.security_wssecurity-app-depl-providers, com.ibm.wsfp.main.WebServicesIndex-app-depl-provider, com.ibm.wsfp.main.appprofile_impl-app-depl-providers, com.ibm.ws.sip.container.WARToSARListener-app-depl-providers, com.ibm.ws.sip.container.SARToEARWrapperProvider-app-depl-providers, com.ibm.wsspi.rrd.RRDInstallTask-app-depl-provider, com.tivoli.pd.amwas.core.amwas-app-depl-provider
com.ibm.wsspi.extension.proxy-server-components	—
com.ibm.wsspi.extension.node-side-extension-checker	—
org.eclipse.core.contenttype.contentTypes	—
org.eclipse.ant.core.antTypes	—
com.ibm.wsspi.extension.content-depl-data-change-listeners	com.ibm.ws.admin.services.ContentListener
com.ibm.wsspi.extension.server-components	—
com.ibm.wsspi.extension.serializable	—
com.ibm.wsfp.main.custom-handler-client	—
org.eclipse.core.resources.moveDeleteHook	—
com.ibm.wsspi.extension.resourcemgr-config	—
com.ibm.wsfp.main.ibmaxis2-wsdl-post-processor-plugin	com.ibm.wsfp.main.UpdateWsdlEndpointUrlsPlugin, com.ibm.wspolicy.main.WSPolicy WSDL Post Procecssor Plugin

Continued

Table A-1. *Continued*

Bundle/Plug-in Extension Point	Extensions
`com.ibm.wsspi.extension.common-deployment-framework-exensionprovider`	–
`com.ibm.wsspi.extension.webcontainer-extension-factory`	–
`com.ibm.wsspi.extension.webcontainer-startup`	–
`org.eclipse.emf.ecore.factory_override`	–
`com.ibm.wsspi.extension.node-agent-components-CR`	–
`org.eclipse.core.variables.dynamicVariables`	–
`com.ibm.wsspi.extension.node-agent-components`	–
`org.eclipse.emf.ecore.protocol_parser`	–
`com.ibm.wsspi.proxy.extension.secureActionVersionRangeSelector`	–
`com.ibm.wsspi.extension.job-manager-components-CR`	–
`com.ibm.wsfp.main.ibmaxis2-app-ctx-migrator-server`	–
`com.ibm.wsspi.extension.client-startup`	–
`com.ibm.ws.bootstrap.manual-bundle-start`	–
`com.ibm.wsspi.extension.was-migration`	–
`org.eclipse.ant.core.antProperties`	–
`org.eclipse.equinox.preferences.preferences`	–
`org.eclipse.jdt.core.codeFormatter`	–
`org.eclipse.core.resources.refreshProviders`	–
`org.eclipse.core.runtime.adapters`	`org.eclipse.core.resources.resourceMappingAdapters`
`com.ibm.ws.portletcontainer.portlet-filter-config`	–
`org.eclipse.emf.ecore.package_registry_implementation`	–
`com.ibm.wsspi.extension.handlerlist`	–
`org.eclipse.emf.ecore.uri_mapping`	–
`com.ibm.wsspi.extension.admin-startup`	–
`com.ibm.wsspi.extension.admin-content-distribution-provider-extension`	`com.ibm.ws.admin.system.MySensorDistribution,` `com.ibm.ws.admin.system.DefaultDistribution`
`com.ibm.wsspi.extension.scripting-extension`	`com.ibm.ws.runtime.hamanagerimpl_scripting-extension`
`com.ibm.wsspi.extension.customBindingProvider`	`com.ibm.ws.runtime.wsaddressing-customBindingProvider,` `com.ibm.ws.runtime.transaction-customBindingProvider,` `com.ibm.ws.sib.server.wsnotification-customBindingProvider`
`com.ibm.wsspi.extension.annotation-helpers`	–
`com.ibm.wsspi.extension.admin-agent-components-CR`	–
`com.ibm.wsspi.extension.admin-content-execution-provider-extension`	–
`org.eclipse.jdt.core.classpathVariableInitializer`	–

Bundle/Plug-in Extension Point	Extensions
org.eclipse.core.resources.natures	org.eclipse.jdt.core.javanature
com.ibm.wsspi.extension.dmgr-components	–
org.eclipse.core.runtime.preferences	org.eclipse.core.resources.preferences
com.ibm.wsspi.extension.cache-provider	–
com.ibm.wsfp.main.ibmaxis2-thread-ctx-migrator-server	com.ibm.wsfp.main.WSIntegration-Server, com.ibm.wsfp.main.WSRM-Server-TCM, com.ibm.wsfp.main.SecurityCtxMigrator-Server-TCM, com.ibm.wsfp.main.WSSecurityCtxMigrator-Server-TCM, com.ibm.wsfp.main.Addr-JAXWS21-TCM, com.ibm.wsfp.main.WSTX-Server-TCM
com.ibm.wsspi.extension.server-recovery-mode-startup	–
com.ibm.wsspi.extension.asset-repository-providers	com.ibm.ws.admin.services.DefaultAssetHandler
com.ibm.wsspi.extension.document-sync-filter	com.ibm.ws.admin.services.J2eeAppBinaryFilter
com.ibm.wsspi.extension.application-server-components	–
com.ibm.wsspi.extension.security-domain-validation	com.ibm.ws.sib.server.SIBSecurityDomainResourceValidator
com.ibm.wsspi.extension.admin-agent-components	–
com.ibm.wsspi.extension.security-collaborator	–

Index

You Need the Companion eBook

Your purchase of this book entitles you to buy the companion PDF-version eBook for only $10. Take the weightless companion with you anywhere.

We believe this Apress title will prove so indispensable that you'll want to carry it with you everywhere, which is why we are offering the companion eBook (in PDF format) for $10 to customers who purchase this book now. Convenient and fully searchable, the PDF version of any content-rich, page-heavy Apress book makes a valuable addition to your programming library. You can easily find and copy code—or perform examples by quickly toggling between instructions and the application. Even simultaneously tackling a donut, diet soda, and complex code becomes simplified with hands-free eBooks!

Once you purchase your book, getting the $10 companion eBook is simple:

❶ Visit **www.apress.com/promo/tendollars/**.

❷ Complete a basic registration form to receive a randomly generated question about this title.

❸ Answer the question correctly in 60 seconds, and you will receive a promotional code to redeem for the $10.00 eBook.

Apress®
THE EXPERT'S VOICE™

2855 TELEGRAPH AVENUE | SUITE 600 | BERKELEY, CA 94705

Offer valid through 12/2009.